DE GAULLE

AND THE

UNITED STATES

DE GAULLE
AND THE
UNITED STATES

A Centennial Reappraisal

edited by

ROBERT O. PAXTON
AND
NICHOLAS WAHL

BERG
Oxford / Providence, USA

First published in 1994 by
Berg Publishers Limited
Editorial offices:
150 Cowley Road, Oxford, OX4 1JJ, UK
221 Waterman Road, Providence, RI 02906, USA

Library of Congress Cataloging-in-Publication Data
A catalogue record for this book is available from the Library of Congress.

British Library Cataloguing in Publication Data
A catalogue record for this book is available from the British Library.

ISBN 0 85496 998 5 (Cloth)
1 85973 066 3 (Paper)

Printed in the United Kingdom by WBC Bookbinders, Bridgend, Mid Glamorgan.

Table of Contents

PART III: OPINIONS, PERCEPTIONS, AND MISPERCEPTIONS

Acknowledgement

Berg Publishers and the editors wish to acknowledge the generous support of the Fondation Charles de Gaulle who, with students in mind, have enabled us to make this book available in a paperback edition.

FOREWORD

De Gaulle and the Americans Since 1940

Nicholas Wahl

Charles de Gaulle entered history with a famous radio speech from London on 18 June 1940, in which he called upon his compatriots to continue the struggle against Germany. Few heard the speech then, and even fewer remember that the United States was one of the three countries cited by name at the beginning of the Appel du 18 Juin: "For France is not alone . . . she can, as England, draw without limit upon the immense industrial potential of the United States." America was, in fact, a key element in the strategic reasoning that led de Gaulle to London in June 1940. Moreover, it was a rather isolated reasoning, for no other French military or civilian leader of the day thought, as de Gaulle did, that "this war is a world war."[1] In a radio speech on 24 June 1940, de Gaulle predicted, a bit prematurely, that France would soon "see in the New World a thousand immense material and moral forces which, perhaps, will rise one day to crush the enemies of liberty." He would have to wait almost two years for the realization of this prophecy. De Gaulle's strategic insight about America actually dated from the early 1930s, as did his opinion of the American society's strengths and weaknesses. During his six crucial years (1931–1937) in the veritable "think tank" that was the Ministry of War's Secrétariat général de la Défense Nationale, de Gaulle had the opportunity to reflect upon

1. The French commander-in-chief, Maxime Weygand, had said that England would have its neck wrung like a chicken in six weeks (to which Churchill is supposed to have replied: "Some chicken, some neck!"); Pierre Laval recalled at his treason trial in 1945 that no one in his right mind in June 1940 could have thought that the Allies would win the war; and Marshal Pétain had often said since the end of May that the war was over and that the Americans, whom-he claimed to "know well," would never come to the rescue of the British.

American economic power and its military potential.[2] "The gigantic possibilities of American industry" that he evoked in a radio speech on 22 June 1940 were, in fact, those he had studied in his article six years before.

But the hidden and more negative face of American power would appear to de Gaulle as soon as the United States entered the war. His 1934 article on America's economy had noted that the "profit motive alone inspires all activity and underlies all hierarchies." These were views strongly marked by the traditional social catholicism of his family milieu. Among traditionalist French families who visited the United States before World War II, the accounts of their visits to the United States by Georges Duhamel, Paul Morand, and the conservative journalist Lucien Romier confirmed fears of an "American menace" to European bourgeois values and, on the eve of the Great Depression, of an American will to world domination.[3] While de Gaulle's reflections from the early 1930s do not include mention of this will to dominate, they do refer critically to the materialist values of American industrial society. This part of his 1932 analysis would eventually inspire in de Gaulle a reinterpretation of those "thousand immense material and moral forces" once he came into conflict with President Roosevelt's pro-Vichy policy and, later, with his own will to dominate the allies of the country he so fervently called upon in June 1940 to intervene in Europe.

If de Gaulle had set views on the United States before the war, one cannot say that official America had simultaneously discovered the existence of the future leader of the Free French. According to a recent study on de Gaulle and American opinion before 1941, American military journals gave little coverage to the rather copious writings of the general.[4] To be sure, the American military attaché in Paris had sent de Gaulle's book on motorized warfare (*Vers l'Armée de Métier*, translated as *The Army of the Future*) to Washington when it appeared in 1934. Unlike military journals of other countries, however, no American military journal reviewed it. Significantly, only one American officer, des-

2. Cf. Charles de Gaulle, *La mobilisation économique à l'étranger*, in: "La Revue Militaire Française," 1 January 1934. This was the only one of his many articles and books dedicated to an analysis of economic policy.

3. Cf. Georges Duhamel, *Scènes de la vie future* (1930); Paul Morand, *New York* (1929); Lucien Romier, *Who Will be Master: Europe or America?* (1928).

4. Christopher S. Thompson, *Prologue to Conflict: De Gaulle and the United States from First Impressions through 1940*, pages 13–32 below.

tined for a notable career during World War II, has admitted to having read the book in the 1930s: General George C. Patton, the man of the motorized break-throughs after the 1944 cross-channel invasion. As for the State Department, the first mention of de Gaulle is found in a diplomatic dispatch sent by Ambassador Bullitt on the occasion of the general's nomination to the Reynaud government on 5 June 1940. His name does not appear anywhere in the Roosevelt papers before 1941: not in the president's correspondence with Churchill, in his speeches, or in his private letters.[5]

Such disregard for a maverick French military writer is understandable in an America that, until France's defeat in 1940, had maintained an enormous respect for the French military high command, with its so-called scientific strategies and supposedly invincible forces and fortifications. The American military establishment had a particular sense of debt to the French army, dating from World War I and the subsequent years during which French officers continued to train their American counterparts. This establishment had little interest in the views of a marginal French military theorist who, moreover, had been formally condemned by his superiors for his unconventional ideas about tank warfare. Neither the American ambassador nor the modest American military intelligence services of the time had prepared either Roosevelt or the country's political elite for the German army's lightning victory. The unexpected French collapse and the parlous situation of the British in 1940 had deprived the United States of its first line of defense. Against the wisdom of Marshal Pétain, the apparent legal head of the French government and the well-known military hero of the last war, a totally unknown general was pretending to maintain the country war. At best, de Gaulle appeared to Washington in 1940 as a marginal diversion inspired by Churchill, and at worst, as a joke. But out of the trauma caused by the defeat of French arms there emerged America's pro-Vichy policy, which, in Washington's view, was essential in preventing Germany from gaining a foothold in the New World through use of the French Caribbean islands. Therefore, neutralizing the French fleet, which was still under Vichy control, was of the highest priority.

Later, in part to appease anti-Vichy opinion in the United States, Roosevelt attempted to give credibility to his French poli-

5. Cf. Christopher S. Thompson, ibid.

cy by stating that immutable French national interests were now being defended by an American "stewardship," not by either Vichy or Free France.[6] In support of this thesis, many of the French political refugees who had recently arrived in America and, according to the State Department, were supported by 85% of the French residents in the United States, publicly disavowed General de Gaulle's initiative and praised Roosevelt's expedient policy toward Vichy.[7] Then, from overly respecting French power before the collapse, Washington veered to the other extreme: the defeat was due to the decadence of French society and the weakness of her political system. This change was, in a sense, profoundly deserved since France was no longer the great moral and military force it had pretended to be for American eyes. As a result of this analysis, Roosevelt's intention to begin the forced dissolution of European colonial empires with that of the French: all the more reason to withholding American recognition from the Free French and its leader's mad claim to defend the continuity of French national interests.

De Gaulle's prejudices about the Americans were to persist after the war. In his view, the domination of American "material power" and the relative lack of such power among major European states would make it difficult for France to regain its "rank" in the world. As he explained to interviewers during his postwar years in the wilderness, international politics were like communicating jars in the physics laboratory: for the level of European and French power to rise, it was necessary for the level of American power to fall.[8] This was neither a matter of sentiment nor doctrine for the general, but simply a natural law of geopolitical

6. Interestingly, public opinion polls showed that Americans, even Roosevelt's strongest supporters, remained steadfastly pro-de Gaulle and anti-Vichy during the entire war. It was not until de Gaulle's return to power in 1958 that American opinion swung sharply against him and remained that way until his death.

7. Most active among them were the former diplomat Alexis Léger (the poet Saint-Jean Perse) and the former high counselor of the president. Sharing their views were the two best-known politician-refugees, Camille Chautemps and Pierre Cot, both prewar Radical ministers. It was Jean Monnet who invented the thesis of an American "stewardship" of French interests until the end of the war.

8. In an interview with the author in February 1958. Beginning in September 1953, first in connection with research for a doctoral dissertation, de Gaulle granted the author a number of interviews over the following fifteen years. Some of the interview material on the years before his return to power is cited in the dissertation: *De Gaulle and the Resistance: The Rise of Reform Politics in France* (Harvard Ph.D., 1956); other material, mainly on the general's constitutional ideas, is to be found in the author's "The French Constitution of 1958: The Initial Draft and its Origins," in *The American Political Science Review* (March 1959).

strategy that could not be ignored. It should be remembered that de Gaulle's education had been largely completed by 1914; for both good and ill, he remained a man of his times.

It was also this realpolitik outlook that allowed de Gaulle to be one of the first to foresee the postwar rivalry between the Soviet Union and the United States, and to seek, in a "third force" position within this rivalry, both a leadership role for France and a new balance of power between Europe and the United States.[9] During the postwar years, de Gaulle often explained in private that France would disagree with American leadership of the alliance as long as the United States dominated Europe with its "material hegemony"; this was the only way in which "space" could be found for France to exercise some independence and hence some semblance of "rank." After de Gaulle's return to power in 1958, this analysis persisted, but with some nuances. France would show solidarity with the United States during the great moments of Soviet challenge, such as Berlin and Cuba, but would resist NATO and the American policy toward the Third World, the Middle East, and even Canada – thus, his famous *Vive le Québec libre*, uttered practically on the doorstep of the United States!

To be sure, the disagreements were essentially strategic, for everything that temporarily weakened American hegemony gave France – and an aging de Gaulle – time to rebuild the "material (i.e., military) and moral power" needed to create an independent Europe, "from the Atlantic to the Urals" (to cite one of the general's favorite dimensions). It was precisely such an independent Europe that especially irritated the Americans, obsessed as they were during the cold war with the hegemonic American leadership of the alliance and with having the lone finger on the nuclear trigger. Curiously, the Americans never understood the extent to which de Gaulle always doubted that a nuclear exchange would ever take place. "Nuclear arms are like poison gas during the Second World War," he used to say.[10] Once back in power, he refused to believe that the Americans would take

9. Cf. Colonel Passy [André Dewavrin], *Souvenirs* (2 vols.), Monaco 1947. Passy was chief of Free French intelligence, and he recounts in his memoirs de Gaulle's comments on the Japanese attack on Pearl Harbor, 7 December 1941: "Now the war is definitely won! And the future will unfold for us in two phases: the first will be the Allied salvage of Germany; the second, I fear, might be a war between the Russians and the Americans and that war the Americans may well lose unless they are able to take the necessary measures in time." (As quoted in: Jean Lacouture, *De Gaulle: 1. Le rebelle 1890–1944*, 1990 ed., p. 522, translation by the author.)

10. In interviews with the author in November 1963 and March 1967.

the initiative to decide things by war: "they don't have the warrior spirit," said the old French officer, thus recalling his 1934 reflections on a society dominated by materialism and the profit motive.[11] The Soviet invasion of Czechoslovakia in 1968 ended de Gaulle's hopes for an eventual dissolution of the Eastern Bloc and, hence, an opening for a "European Europe," from the Atlantic to the Urals. Such a Europe then ceased to be a credible card to play, and when de Gaulle retired from power the following year, France remained under American hegemony – by "the very nature of things," as de Gaulle had been wont to say. Twenty years were to pass before the "nature of things" suddenly changed with the collapse of the Soviet Bloc and the unification of Germany, and a version of de Gaulle's dream for Europe actually appeared on the horizon. One of the interesting themes of the papers and debates that follow is this belated triumph of Gaullian ideas for Europe, which are incomplete for, among other reasons, the absence of someone with de Gaulle's stature and credible leadership abilities.

The Gaullian idea of Europe, although never styled as *l'Europe des patries* by the general, was firmly rooted in what, for him, was the immutable fact of the nation-state. This idea not only represented the highest loyalty for a conservative Frenchman of his generation, but above all, was evoked when he called France to resist both ideology and foreign occupation in June 1940. De Gaulle believed that nationality would "prevail" in Eastern Europe once the Soviet army ended what was tantamount to a military occupation. It is for this reason that, during the war, he preferred the Serb nationalist Mihailovic to the Croat communist Broz-Tito. It is also for this reason that he almost never failed to refer to the Soviet Union as *"la Russie"* and to the French communists as *"les séparatistes"* – that is, a party that worked to "separate" France from the West for the benefit of Russia in peacetime and that could be the collaborationist party of the Russian occupation in wartime. For de Gaulle, the communists' revolutionary ideology was incidental to their essential quality as domestic supporters of a foreign power.

But de Gaulle's respect for the national "fact" also motivated more modernist positions. Thus, his relatively early endorsement of Algerian independence, as well as his condemnation of American involvement in Vietnam, were due in large part to his belief

11. In an interview with the author in February 1958.

that wars in the mid-twentieth century against movements of national liberation could no longer be won. His attitudes toward both the Algerian revolution and the Vietnamese revolution were also guided by the cold war geostrategic considerations that served French national interest. If France did not end its war with Algerian nationalism, the United States and the United Nations would do so at France's expense in prestige and status vis-à-vis the Third World. And if the United States won its war in Vietnam, it could then turn on China, thus obliging France to align itself with the Americans at further cost to its independence.[12]

For de Gaulle, any intensification of the cold war meant polarization, and hence the need for France to mark its loyalty to the American alliance, thereby limiting its independence and contribute to American hegemony in Europe. Conversely, détente and any American retreat would allow the French room to maneuver and imply a decline of American hegemony. It was, of course, this Gaullian calculation that enraged succeeding generations of American policymakers, for whom American hegemony was essential for the Free World's resistance to the Soviet threat, not to mention for the logic of nuclear war. For this reason, many American officials in the 1960s and 1970s saw de Gaulle as a vainglorious anachronism of prewar Europe; for some, he was even an "objective" – if not an actual – ally of the Soviet Union.

In a narrow sense, de Gaulle was indeed an "objective" ally of the Russians; like the Russians, de Gaulle also hoped that the American troops would depart from Europe. But in his mind, this was necessary for a Russian departure from its external empire of eastern and central Europe. In a new Europe, without the Russian and American presence, the formerly occupied eastern nations could rejoin their western counterparts in a new confederal relationship that would allow safe coexistence for socialist and non-socialist states, including the two different Germanies. Perhaps in this new neutral Europe there could emerge one day a united Germany, well contained, of course, within a French-dominated "European Europe" that stretched "from the Atlantic to the Urals" – or almost.

But this Gaullian dream was not to be. After the Soviet invasion of Czechoslovakia in 1968, neither the general nor any other

12. De Gaulle's views on Algeria and Vietnam were expressed in interviews with the author in July 1961 and September 1968. They are well documented by his memoirs and by those of his associates.

leader of his time or of the two decades succeeding his death in 1970 believed that the Soviets would voluntarily leave Eastern Europe, which would then allow for an American departure from Western Europe. When, almost twenty years later, the Eastern Bloc dissolved and non-socialist regimes took power in almost all of the former communist states (and Germany was suddenly reunited), surprise was total. De Gaulle's prediction had come to pass only partially: the national "fact" had indeed prevailed in eastern and central Europe, but that "fact" also included Germany in the form of a rapid and premature reunification. The collapse of the Eastern Bloc also meant the collapse of the economies of the former communist states, thus making them inapt for immediate inclusion in existing European institutions, but all the more ripe for economic domination by a united Germany. Neither they nor Britain or the European community could provide a credible counter-weight to a likely German hegemony on the continent.

It is this new balance of power during the immediate post-cold war years that might have suggested to de Gaulle a radical change in French policy. Was a continental Europe in which France might need to confront a powerful united Germany a Europe that was really ready for an American pull-out? Indeed, was not this Europe one in which NATO had a new role to play and one that France could once again support, providing the "corset" that credibly contained the new Germany by a continued American military presence on the continent? Since European circumstances had radically changed, why should French strategic doctrine also not change? A version of this question was the theoretical issue underlying de Gaulle's earliest military writings, themselves based on his ruminations in German POW camps over the evolution of strategy and tactics during the Great War.[13] As a result of his battle experiences and his observations of the closing phases of the war, he had become a supreme pragmatist: firepower had made the offensive doctrine of 1914 out of date, and the new defensive doctrine based on increased firepower valid only until tanks and armored vehicles brought back the offensive war of movement. It is within a parallel logic that de Gaulle's post-cold war volte-face with regard to NATO and the United States is conceivable.

13. Cf. Charles de Gaulle, "Doctrine à priori où doctrtine des circonstances," in: *La Revue Militaire Française*, Paris, 15 March 1925.

Thus, one might now ask if, with a powerful united Germany in the heart of his "Europe from the Atlantic to the Urals," the Atlantic border of Europe might not have become for de Gaulle, as it may yet become for his successors, a border situated at New York rather than at Brest or Liverpool? In 1992, a Europe that stretched from "America to the Urals" would appear to present the safest course for a France once again faced with a "German problem" and, indeed, for a Europe that is in general facing similar nineteenth-century nightmares.

One is further tempted to say, moreover, that with the decline of the bipolar cold war world and with a new European "architecture" in gestation, the old tensions between France and the United States make little sense fifty years after their birth in de Gaulle's London and Roosevelt's Washington. One would be wrong, of course, for those tensions reflect a clash of interests that will remain a part of French-American relations for as long as the two nations pursue foreign policies that they believe have been thrust upon them by the circumstances of the mid-twentieth century: the American need to exert western leadership, the French need to regain "rank" in world affairs. Soon, however, the circumstances of the mid-nineteen-hundreds will be more than half a century behind us. It is likely that de Gaulle, the grand pragmatist, would have been especially sensitive to the changed circumstances of this century's last decade, circumstances that may have made his earlier analysis of Europe's future now seem correct, and yet may have made his policies to achieve French leadership in that Europe now seem increasingly out of date. Nothing would have more concentrated the mind of a French professional soldier born in 1890 than the rise of a powerful reunited Germany in the midst of a new and dizzying chaos of national rivalries to the east and south of western Europe. At the very least, the general surely would have asked himself – if not others – whether the task of recovering French "rank" in the world was still dependent on maintaining a distance from the American alliance. At any rate, a post-cold war reassessment of de Gaulle's relations with the United States reveals, at the very least, a far-sighted realism instead of the anachronistic vainglory and crude anti-Americanism that American officials have traditionally seen as motivating the general's policies toward the United States.

INTRODUCTION

De Gaulle and the United States

Robert O. Paxton

In April 1990, in the centennial year of the birth of Charles de Gaulle, a group of American and French scholars and public officials spent three days in New York, on the campuses of Columbia University and New York University, exploring the tempestuous and sometimes bitter relationship between de Gaulle's France and the United States. This book contains some of the papers presented in that conference and some selections from the debates they provoked.

This conference, planned and directed locally, was a major link in an international cycle of commemoration, which was coordinated by the Institut Charles de Gaulle in Paris and culminated in a great international conference in Paris in November 1990.

The format of the New York conference was one pioneered at the Institut d'Etudes Politiques in Paris in the 1960s, and applied many times since then in Europe and the United States to understanding the recent past. This format brings together both scholars and witnesses, such as retired government officials, well-connected journalists of the period, and former political leaders. In this format, each participant applies his or her own particular expertise to the question at hand. The scholars, some of them too young to have experienced the events under discussion, have enjoyed access to government archives and private papers. The witnesses, having been present at the drafting of those papers, then point out what they consider to be the historians' misreadings. They may even suggest that a document on which a historian bases major conclusions was a smokescreen. The scholars may then reply – or think in their inmost hearts – that the witnesses' memories have been clouded by years of second thoughts. Out of such collisions between research and memory begins to emerge a viable reconstruction of the past.

The New York conference on de Gaulle and the United States followed this format as fully as possible, given the lapse of time. Archives were opening up. Yet many witnesses were still alive, even though de Gaulle's *Appel du 18 Juin* went back fifty years and his return to power thirty-two years. The French witnesses were all close associates of de Gaulle, and their lucidity and passion were impressive testimony to de Gaulle's capacity to attract and retain forceful associates. Some surviving American witnesses declined to attend. One wrote that he did not wish to be "the skunk at your garden party." Although this conference clearly reflected some mellowing of American feelings toward de Gaulle, particularly among scholars, there were echoes of the hostile emotions aroused in the United States by de Gaulle's astute maneuvering to enjoy American nuclear protection while demolishing American designs for NATO, for European unification, for nuclear strategy, and for East-West relations, not to mention tiffs over Vietnam, foreign investment, and Quebec. Though time had softened their sharpest edges, these passions were not dead in 1990.

From the moment of his lonely stand in London on 18 June 1940, to his death in 1970, and even after, Charles de Gaulle rarely left indifferent the people and the government of the United States. Some Americans, some of the time, were his fervent admirers. His popularity as head of Free France won him a joyous ticker tape parade in Manhattan in August 1945. Other Americans – and even some of the same Americans – execrated him at other times. Americans angry at de Gaulle's expulsion of NATO headquarters from France poured good French wine into Manhattan gutters in 1966 to express their outrage. One of the editors of this volume has in his possession a dart board that permits the Gaullophobe player to aim projectiles at the general's face, which is portrayed in a particularly bombastic posture. The board was given to him by his students at Berkeley in that same year, the moment of maximum American anti-Gaullist irritation.

Charles de Gaulle's own attitudes toward the United States were complex, even contradictory, at least on the surface. He grew up steeped in the condescension for vulgar, brash America that was taken for granted in an upper-class, conservative, intellectual French family like the de Gaulles. It was Charles de

Gaulle's capacity to transcend his milieu, however, that made him a great man. De Gaulle deeply admired the United States in some ways, more so than many French people from a similar background. In June 1940, he bet his career and life on what he foresaw would be the United States' predominant role in the coalition that would defeat Hitler. But American culture was profoundly alien to the sensibility of this moody aristocrat, who was pessimistic about the course of history, attuned to social Catholic doctrines about work and the family, and passionately committed to the greatness of France.

In the worldview of Charles de Gaulle, what mattered was the eternal competition for self-fulfillment among the Great Nations, among whom France must retain a leading place or perish. De Gaulle, from 1940 on, saw the United States as an increasingly weighty player in that game, one whose embrace France simultaneously needed and feared. That tension between the need for the ally and the fear of being smothered by it defined the general's policy toward the United States. His serene confidence that he could remain an ally while saying "non" to the alliance's concrete institutions baffled and enraged most Americans, except for a few reared in the traditions of European realpolitik. The remarks below by Henry Kissinger are a particularly eloquent statement of that latter point of view.

Overlaying these world-political calculations in de Gaulle's perceptions of the United States was a lifetime of experience, much of it unhappy, with the United States government. American recognition of the "other" France of Marshal Pétain in 1940 (to be sure, shared by most of the rest of the world), followed by Roosevelt's maneuvers to replace de Gaulle as head of those French actively fighting the Germans with a more tractable figure, such as General Giraud, and climaxed by Roosevelt's stubborn refusal to recognize de Gaulle as the leader of France until 23 October 1944 (the last major government in the world to do so) could hardly have failed to leave bitter traces. The reader will note the vigor with which Bernard Tricot denies, in the debates published below, that President de Gaulle's policy in the 1960s bore any trace of revenge for the humiliations suffered by General de Gaulle during 1940–44.

It is true that de Gaulle was not governed mainly by emotion in his life-long calculation of French national interest, though he was a man of intense feelings. Thus, to ask whether de Gaulle "liked" the United States or not is an absurd question. Only an

American who believes that foreign policy is like dating would raise such a question. But it would be equally wrong to deny that de Gaulle could occasionally appear to enjoy turning the knife in the wound.

By an accident of history, de Gaulle held his country's destiny in his hands at the moment the United States emerged as the predominant political, economic, and cultural force in what its publicists liked to call the "Free World," i.e., the years between 1940 and 1970. Inevitably, the United States was at the center of Gaullian thought and practice about world strategy. For the Americans, however, France was but one "ally," or client state, among many others. That asymmetry sharpened the tension. It pained de Gaulle to recognize that the United States mattered more to France than France mattered to the United States.

That very asymmetry made it harder for de Gaulle to compromise. Head of a "fundamentally symbolic undertaking,"[1] the leader of Free France could not afford to appear to be the servant of those whose recognition and subsidies he required. Even, as head of the French State twenty years later, he was keenly aware that the therapeutic dose of self-confidence he wanted to administer to his country depended less on veritable independence than on the appearance of independence.[2] De Gaulle's gift for political theater had few equals, but Roosevelt, Churchill, Johnson, Kennedy, and Nixon came close. The stage was set for clashes that were personal as well as national. So FDR in public made light of "the bride" and "Joan of Arc." So de Gaulle declined to meet the crippled president aboard his warship at Algiers in February 1945. But had Roosevelt not been clumsy to claim to play host to the French president in a French city? In a positive key, however, there was the triumphal visit of the Kennedys to Paris, and the vast impression made by the somber French president, in uniform, towering over the other heads of state at the funerals of Kennedy and Eisenhower.

In more official dealings with the United States, too, de Gaulle could appear to blow hot and cold, though always within the general parameters we have laid out above. His defiant refusal of his own country's armistice with Hitler in June 1940 was the

1. Jean Lacouture, *De Gaulle: The Ruler, 1945–1970* (New York: Norton, 1992), p. 14.

2. Thus he never alluded to the dependence of the supersonic bombers of the first generation of his "force de frappe" on aerial refueling by KC-128 tanker aircraft bought in the United States.

most "pro-American" act of his career. It rested upon an astonishing leap of faith in an eventual United States entry into the war, and ultimate victory, 18 months before Pearl Harbor. Even in his so-called anti-American years, in the mid 1960s, de Gaulle's strategy of maneuvering between the blocs depended on those blocs' endurance. Witness the dismay with which even today Gaullists confront any weakening of the United States' commitment to Europe. Even in the 1960s, de Gaulle took for granted the United States' nuclear umbrella. The existence of a powerful United States served de Gaulle as a fixed pole around which he could cantilever French political and military power upward a few notches by seeming to assert his independence of it, thus conspicuously demonstrating national independence without real risk for his country. A mighty America was even a useful *repoussoir* for his revival of French self-confidence.

De Gaulle backed the United States more vigorously than other European leaders whenever the Soviet Union turned recklessly aggressive. He was even firmer than the United States against Khrushchev's threats to change the status of Berlin in 1961; and he was Kennedy's firmest supporter in Europe during the Cuban missile crisis in 1962. In contrast, he played an "anti-American" card during the calmer mid-1960s (while stoutly maintaining that he remained within the alliance) because he believed that his country could never recover from the humiliation of Sedan in 1940, of Dien-Bien-Phu in 1952, and in the djebels of Algeria in 1961 unless he resoundingly demonstrated France's capacity to act for herself on the world stage. When the Soviet Union invaded Czechoslovakia in August 1968, he drew close to the United States again. He was a consummate player of balance-of-power politics, faced with an America that tended to consider foreign policy a matter of friendships and moral stances.

Many of the papers below examine the varied responses of American presidents and the American public to de Gaulle's stings. Roosevelt's animosity to de Gaulle has been thoroughly aired. It has even been carried too far: Roosevelt did not "like" de Gaulle's Vichy rivals in 1940–42; he only assumed (correctly) that they had de facto power over France. Roosevelt practiced realpolitik, too, at least at the beginning; the trouble was that personal dislike made him persist in his unwillingness to recognize de Gaulle long after reality should have suggested another course. Thus, it was over de Gaulle that the undisputed wartime leader of the United States, that master of consensus, fell most out of step with his people. Antipathy to de Gaulle was the most unpopular element of Roosevelt's wartime foreign policy.

In the 1960s, the American people and government were in step, and both reacted emotionally against de Gaulle. Nixon is the most interesting case because he was exempt from that emotional antagonism. He regarded de Gaulle as a model exemplar of balance-of-power diplomacy, whose self-confident France was an asset to the United States national interest. Shaken both by the Soviet invasion of Czechoslovakia and by the student-worker uprising of May 1968, de Gaulle also needed to mend relations with the United States. In early 1969, therefore, Nixon and de Gaulle found a mutual interest in flattering each other. That was the moment when Nixon's staff quietly let French officials understand that the United States no longer opposed the "force de frappe," although the secret American working-level cooperation with French nuclear armament research, recently revealed by Richard Ullman, did not actually begin until after de Gaulle's death.[3] The US government was again out of step with its people about de Gaulle, but this time on the favorable side. It also helped that Alain Clément, whose scholarly but critical reporting from Washington for the *Le Monde* had been colored by a visceral distaste for Lyndon Johnson, was replaced on Nixon's accession by the more neutral Jacques Amalric.

This conference made genuinely new findings on two levels. There was new factual information. For example, the paper by Christopher Thompson on de Gaulle's attitudes toward the United States in the 1930s and the early American responses to him breaks entirely new ground. Raoul Aglion adds new precisions about how deeply influenced Roosevelt was in his anti-Gaullist attitudes by French exiles in the United States, such as Alexis Léger. There is new information from de Gaulle's former defense minister, Pierre Messmer, about NATO and nuclear weapons. Kim Munhollond offers a new perspective on how middle-level American officials in London in 1942–43, better aware than Roo-

3. Richard H. Ullman, "The Covert French Connection," *Foreign Policy*, #75, Summer 1989, pp. 3–33. The leading French authority on these matters, while not denying Ullman's revelations, rejects any intimation that the French nuclear armaments program was not independent. Maurice Vaïsse, "Avant–propos," *Relations Internationales*, #59, autumn 1989, pp. 297–300.

sevelt of the significance of Free France, gradually undermined the president's attempted boycott of de Gaulle. There are pungent new details from the papers of John Foster Dulles, John F. Kennedy, Lyndon Johnson, and others.

The conference was also innovative in more general terms. It was based on the premise that the troubled relationship between the United States and de Gaulle's France tells us about broader things than just the history of a specific moment. It tells us a lot about how Americans form their images of friends and enemies, and how foreign policy is conceived, executed, and perceived in the two countries.

This conference deliberately tried to escape from the raw emotional reactions of both Americans and French in the 1960s. A basic premise of the conference was that to explain American attitudes toward de Gaulle, or de Gaulle's attitudes toward the United States, in terms of simple "likes" and "dislikes" is a gross oversimplification. De Gaulle was never "anti-American" in a purely emotional way, and most Americans were never universally or permanently hostile to him. The two were joined in a complex minuet of values and interests. Their moments of warmth and coolness tell us a great deal about Americans and their vision of the world, and a lot about how de Gaulle saw the world, as well as how he governed.

The conference also provided an occasion to look at the relationship in a longer perspective. By 1990, twenty years after his death, de Gaulle's views of the world in the 1960s, so heretical in the United States, seemed astonishingly prescient. Skeptical of ideological interpretations of world affairs, de Gaulle generally spoke of "Russia" rather than as of the Soviet Union, and regarded "Russian" policies as reflections of calculated national interest rather than as a blind application of ideology. As the Soviet Union disintegrated, de Gaulle's conception of the Russians, not as an "evil empire," but as another Great Nation in the power game to be courted (as in 1944 and 1965) or combatted (as in the 1950s and in 1961–62), seems far more realistic than the more ideological and static American view. In the conflict between the United States and de Gaulle over approaches to the Soviet Union (though by 1969 both were practicing competitive détente), it was de Gaulle's approach that has been vindicated by time. The world has become the multipolar arena de Gaulle claimed to prefer.

Could the same be said of de Gaulle's positions on other issues around which he and the United States quarreled: NATO, European integration, nuclear policy? Was it de Gaulle's visions of Europe, of NATO, of the role of Germany, rather than the Americans', that have been realized? Has de Gaulle made a lasting difference? Here the answer must be much more nuanced. The New York conference did not arrive at ultimate judgments of de Gaulle's lasting impact on the world, but some attempt must be made to establish a balance sheet.

De Gaulle's influence on European integration was lasting in one respect: decision-making power within the European Community shifted permanently away from the Commission and to the Council, following the "empty chair" crisis de Gaulle provoked in 1965 and the Luxemburg Compromise that embodied de Gaulle's preference for a "Europe of States." Today the political weight of Europe resides where de Gaulle wanted it to be, in the Council, and not in a supranational Commission. That decision, ironically, made it possible for Britain to join later and for the widening of the Community to progress more rapidly than its deepening. Even as the veto power is nibbled away and common European law and institutions spread, the member states are not about to disappear into "a United States of Europe." Nor does the United States of America any longer try to make it so.

German preponderance in this Europe was not what de Gaulle had worked for, of course. He wanted a Europe whose natural center was Paris. Today, that seems decreasingly likely, as the elements upon which French preponderance in Europe once rested have weakened (the French nuclear monopoly in continental western Europe counting for less, for example) or vanished (Germany being no longer divided) in post-cold war Europe. We know that de Gaulle would have faced these problems resourcefully, for his startling conversion from the obsessive anti-Germanism of his young officer days and of the Liberation to the warm friendship with Adenauer offers another demonstration of his agility. The balance of power within the Europe of 1993, however, does not demonstrate de Gaulle's lasting impact.

Nor would de Gaulle have been happy with the increasing hegemony of a worldwide popular culture in which American entertainers and promotors play a leading part (though not the exclusive role claimed by some in France). What he would-have seen as the "Americanization" of European culture would have filled him with despair.

On the deepest level, was de Gaulle right about the nation-state as the irreplaceable foundation of noble human action? No one has discovered a substitute. The "World of States" is an insecure place, however, and the spread of nuclear weapons, which President de Gaulle's France encouraged, has made it more so. If all the ambitious leaders of all the proud nation-states were guided by de Gaulle's restraint and judgment and sense of the common good, the "World of States" would work adequately. But de Gaulle's "World of States" run by lesser statesmen is a dangerous place.

De Gaulle's most lasting achievement, finally, was a confident France. Even though what passes for Gaullism in the France of the 1990s is not necessarily what the general would have done today, no one in the United States thinks of suggesting that the strong and independent Fifth Republic is not more favorable to the interests of the United States than the superficially more compliant, but weaker (and, down deep, more resentful), Fourth Republic.

We wish to thank all those who made this conference possible. We built upon three indispensable foundations. First, a substantial grant from the Sterling Currier Fund of Columbia University made the conference possible financially. Second, New York University provided the Conference Headquarters and the essential administrative efforts of Jair Pruitt, Max Berley, and the staff of the Institute of French Studies. Third, the Maison Française of Columbia University, under the direction of Jacqueline Desrez, organized efficaciously the uptown segment of the conference. The Institut Charles de Gaulle in Paris, the French Cultural Services in New York, and Air France all made important contributions. Aurora Wolfgang and Michel Dassule made transcriptions and translations from the French, and members of the staff of the Institute on Western Europe of Columbia University assisted in preparing this volume for publication.

PART I
THE AMERICANS AND DE GAULLE, 1940–58

CHAPTER ONE

FROM FREE FRANCE TO THE LIBERATION, 1940–44

❖1❖

Prologue to Conflict: De Gaulle and the United States, From First Impressions Through 1940

Christopher S. Thompson

Historians who have studied the relationship between Charles de Gaulle and the United States have quite rightly chosen World War II as its starting point. It was then that de Gaulle, as the leader of Free France, first emerged as a force and a personality with whom America would have to reckon. Although still a novice in international relations, the fifty-year-old de Gaulle was a well-read and well-traveled man of strong convictions and the author of four books and a number of articles. With this in mind, de Gaulle's relations with the United States before 1941, from his perceptions of America in the interwar period through his first months as the leader of Free France, appear worthy of examination. In focusing on this earlier period, I propose to address the following four questions: First, what were de Gaulle's thoughts concerning America before World War II? Second, to what extent were Americans at that time aware of his military writings? Third, what role did the United States play in de Gaulle's thinking during the summer and fall of 1940? And finally, what were the reactions of the United States government and the American press to de Gaulle from the moment he joined Paul Reynaud's cabinet in June 1940 through the end of that year?

❖

On New Year's Day, 1934, an article entitled "La Mobilisation Economique à l'Etranger" by Lieutenant-Colonel Charles de Gaulle appeared in the *Revue Militaire Française*. In the article, de Gaulle examines the measures taken by the governments of Belgium, Italy, and the United States to prepare for the smoothest possible transition from a peacetime to a wartime economy.[1] The section devoted to the American model – i.e., the National Defense Act of 1920 – constitutes de Gaulle's only thoroughly researched and rigorously analytical treatment of the United States between the wars. As such, it deserves particular attention.

The National Defense Act of 1920 encompassed a wide range of military reforms as well as a significant innovation in the peacetime tactical and administrative organization of the nation.[2] The latter included a series of unprecedented measures designed to facilitate the transition from peacetime to wartime industrial production. De Gaulle was impressed with several features of the American approach: the ability of the government and military hierarchy to recognize and learn from their errors in World War I, the innovativeness and energy that went into the elaboration and implementation of the new program, and the role played by businessmen and industrialists in this process.

De Gaulle found this third feature particularly intriguing. Both on a regional level and within seven distinct branches of the armed services, prominent civilians working in key industries were taking part in study committees and acting as expert advisors to the military specialists. Such close collaboration was proving beneficial to both the government and private sector, and by engendering a spirit of cooperation and mutual understanding, it significantly enhanced the coordination and the overall efficiency of the mobilization program. In describing these initiatives, de Gaulle hoped the political, military, and economic elites in his own country would take note of their positive features as a similar program was developed and implemented in France.

De Gaulle's study of the American model led him to examine

1. De Gaulle had been interested in economic mobilization for wartime since World War I. At the time he wrote this article, he was the head of the Third Section of the "Secrétariat Général de la Défense Nationale," where he had been charged – amongst other responsibilities – with drafting the text of a law on the Organization of the Nation for Wartime. For his interest in this question see de Gaulle's *Lettres Notes et Carnets* (Paris: Librairie Plon, 1980), vol. II, pp. 460–97, and vol. III, pp. 229–40, 363–65, 370–72, 415–38.

the underlying reasons for its success. In the process, what began as a favorable evaluation of American preparedness for industrial mobilization becomes a critique of American society and its fundamental values:

> But the most logical and complete preparatory measures would be worth little if the businessmen who executed them did not bring to bear the same pursuit of efficiency which they apply to their business affairs in peacetime. In order to encourage them to do so the state creates a profit motive. Even in wartime, no American could ever imagine acting without this potent motivation.[3]

For de Gaulle, American society is above all characterized by the uncontested rule of the almighty dollar, and Americans by their pursuit of it. With this in mind, and given the inadequacy of the relevant legislation, de Gaulle fears an economic free-for-all in which the financial bottom-line will outweigh all other considerations – whether legal, moral, or social. Furthermore, he doubts whether the contracts (setting profit limits) passed between the Ministry of War and the business community can withstand the latter's determination to maximize their gains:

> In a country whose rules of administrative law are far from being as clear and as rigorous as ours, their implementation of contracts [setting profit limits] would be open to a variety of interpretations. One must add, moreover, that such imprecision does not trouble Americans for they are more preoccupied with obtaining results than guarantees.[4]

According to de Gaulle, Americans must restrain their ruthless pursuit of the almighty dollar and strike an equitable balance between profits, national defense needs, and social justice. He recommends that the State play a more active role in the distribution of the country's vast resources lest speculation and competition disrupt the carefully prepared process of industrial mobilization.

De Gaulle's image of American society remains somewhat caricatured:

2. Weigley, Russell F.: *History of the United States Army* (enlarged edition) (Bloomington, Indiana: Indiana University Press, 1984), pp. 395–420. For a first-hand account by one of the men involved in the drafting of the National Defense Act of 1920, see Palmer, John McAuley: *America in Arms: The Experience of the United States with Military Organization* (New Haven: Yale University Press, 1941), pp. 165–90.

3. De Gaulle, Charles: *Trois Etudes* (Paris: Editions Berger-Levrault, 1945), p. 131.

4. Ibid, pp. 132–33.

> Their social system, in which material profit is the motivation of all activity and the basis of all hierarchy, allows for the powerful motive of private interest to be widely brought into play.[5]

As for the article's stated purpose – what France might learn from the United States – it is nowhere to be found in de Gaulle's conclusion:

> And it is not unreasonable to think that private initiative, heavy expenditures, and big dividends, which constitute the basis of the American system, will sooner or later be replaced by the more rigorous conceptions of thrift, duty, and equality.[6]

The implicit suggestion is that it is Americans who would do well to model themselves on the more responsible, equitable, and humanitarian societies found elsewhere.

In the final analysis, de Gaulle remains divided between genuine admiration for the energy, creativity, resourcefulness, and achievements of the American people and profound disapproval of their unrestrained materialism. But apart from advocating increased State intervention to limit excesses, de Gaulle does not resolve the larger question: Does American economic achievement require – as well as spawn – the value system he deplores? Whatever the answer, one has the distinct impression that de Gaulle feels that America's vast material resources and economic potential are being wasted on a people with such abject values.

De Gaulle's antipathy to American values resulted, at least in part, from personal experience. While serving in Poland in 1919, he wrote: "Americans, Englishmen, and even Italians are rushing to Warsaw. As insolent as they are useless, they are motivated by the obvious if unspoken desire to develop business ties."[7] But in order to fully appreciate de Gaulle's attitude, it is necessary to consider it in the context of the rapid deterioration of the American image in interwar France.

Initially greeted with enthusiasm by the French for their contributions to the victorious war effort, American soldiers – and by extension, all Americans – soon came to be seen as rowdy drunks who were fond of jazz and easy women, and whose relatively high pay was driving up prices in France's devastated postwar

5. Ibid, p. 135.
6. Ibid, p. 136.
7. De Gaulle, *Lettres Notes et Carnets*, vol. III, p. 30: Letter to his father from Poland, dated 7 June 1919.

economy.[8] When the U.S. Senate refused to ratify the Treaty of Versailles,[9] de Gaulle shared his countrymen's sense of betrayal: "Who can guarantee us the eternal alliance and, more to the point, the immediate and effective alliance of England and America?"[10] This was not the last time de Gaulle was to question the reliability of France's Anglo-Saxon allies.

When the U.S. government refused to link French war debts to German reparations the American image sank to new depths. Far from recognizing the immense human and material losses suffered by the French in the war, greedy Americans seemed determined to suck France dry of its remaining wealth.[11] This distressing vision was exacerbated by the fear that foreigners were buying up national riches, thus morally, physically, and culturally contaminating France.[12] In such a climate, American arrogance and confidence in the superiority of their capitalist system was poorly received. Most Frenchmen thoroughly disapproved of speculative practices and deeply resented the arrival in the mid-1920s of Americans intent on taking advantage of an exchange rate rendered favorable by the anemic state of the French franc.[13] De Gaulle must have been aware of this negative image, as it received great play in the French press and public opinion.[14] Furthermore, a number of very critical books on American capitalism were published in France between the wars and enjoyed immense success.[15] While de Gaulle may not have read them, it would seem unlikely that he was not familiar with their theses.

On a more positive note, the interwar period also saw the publication in France of a significant number of scholarly works on the United States Constitution.[16] They focused particularly on the role of the Supreme Court and its right to decide a law's unconstitutionality,[17] the evolution of federalism, and the relationship

8. Duroselle, Jean-Baptiste: La *France et les Etats-Unis des origines à nos jours* (Paris: Editions du Seuil, 1976), pp. 116–17; Schor, Ralph: *L'Opinion française et les étrangers en France 1919–1939* (Paris: Publication de la Sorbonne, 1985), p. 161.

9. Duroselle, p. 126.

10. De Gaulle, *Lettres Notes et Carnets*, vol. III, p. 67: Lecture on the Franco-Polish Alliance, dated December 1919.

11. Duroselle, pp. 133–36.

12. Schor, pp. 77, 120.

13. Ibid, pp. 161–62, 467–68.

14. Duroselle, p. 136.

15. Ibid, p. 153.

16. Lacorne, Denis; Rupnik, Jacques; Toinet, Marie-France, et al. (eds): *L'Amérique dans les têtes* (Paris: Hachette, 1986), p. 231.

17. Ibid, p. 237.

between the executive and legislative branches.[18] De Gaulle was not immune to an occasional interest in American constitutional practices: during World War I, he noted that State Supreme Courts, like the federal Supreme Court, could declare a law unconstitutional.[19] Years later, in conversations in London with René Cassin, de Gaulle expressed particular interest in the manner in which the American president was elected and was astonished when he learned that the president could not dissolve the Congress.[20] De Gaulle's interest in these questions notwithstanding, one must be very cautious when evaluating the influence of the U.S. Constitution on his own constitutional ideas. If today – but only since 1974 – the Constitutional Council, like the Supreme Court, can declare a law unconstitutional, such was not de Gaulle's intention in 1958 when the constitution of the Fifth Republic was drafted.[21] As for the election of the French president by universal suffrage, its adoption in 1962 had far more to do with the current internal French political climate than with a desire to follow the American example, of which de Gaulle remained wary.[22]

On 12 January 1940, Charles de Gaulle noted the capital importance of American aid in providing France with the material means to wage war against Germany.[23] Six months later, almost to the day, in a letter to Paul Reynaud that was never sent, de Gaulle warned his friend that negotiating with the Germans would result in forfeiting future aid from the United States.[24] His familiarity with American measures for economic mobilization had convinced him that the industrial potential for wartime production in the United States would prove crucial in the war against the Axis powers.

In eight of his radio broadcasts to France during the summer and fall of 1940, the leader of Free France referred either explicitly or implicitly to the support soon to come from the United States for those who continued to oppose Hitler. The terms he used were undoubtedly intended to convince his compatriots

18. Ibid, p. 245.

19. De Gaulle, *Letters Notes et Carnets*, vol. II, p. 329.

20. Cassin, René: *Les Hommes Partis de Rien* (Paris: Plon, 1974), p. 133.

21. Duverger, Maurice: *Le Système Politique Français: Droit Constitutionnel et systèmes politiques* (Paris: Presses Universitaires de France, 1985), pp. 439–51.

22. Debré, Jean-Louis: *Les Idées Constitutionelles de Général de Gaulle* (Paris: Librairie Generale de Droit et de Jurisprudence, 1974), p. 273.

23. De Gaulle, *Lettres Notes et Carnets*, vol. III, p. 464: Notes on the creation of a Ministry for the Conduct of the War, dated 12 January 1940.

that continued resistance was not futile: "the immense industry of the United States,"[25] "the gigantic capacities of American industry,"[26] "a thousand immense material and moral forces,"[27] "immense weapons manufactures,"[28] "the immense American power."[29]

These vast American resources also provided de Gaulle with an important argument against the capitulation of France, which Marshal Pétain had justified in a speech on 25 June 1940. The next day, de Gaulle responded from London: "You have forgone the resources to be offered in the future by immense America."[30] Two months later, de Gaulle again criticized the "treason" of the Vichy government and military hierarchy for being both absurd and dishonorable: "an irresistible current is drawing the New World to the defense of liberty."[31]

To reinforce and complement his many radio broadcasts, de Gaulle posted a proclamation in London. It stated briefly but eloquently his view of how the war would ultimately unfold and of the role France must play in this evolution:

> In the free world, immense powers have not yet made their contributions. One day, these powers will crush the enemy. On that day France must be on the side of victory. If she is, she will become what she was before, a great and independent nation. That, and that alone, is my goal.[32]

Behind yet another bold reference to American power lurked the nagging question of why the United States still failed to contribute to the war effort against Hitler.

If he remained generally hopeful that the Allies would soon receive American aid, de Gaulle soon became concerned that the United States harbored designs on the French Empire.[33] He was convinced that most Americans viewed France's eclipse as final, and he feared that they would take unilateral steps, particularly

24. Ibid, pp. 477–78: letter to Paul Reynaud, dated 14 June 1940, never sent.
25. De Gaulle, Charles: *Discours et Messages*, vol. I (Paris: Librairie Plon, 1970), p. 3: radio broadcast, 18 June 1940.
26. Ibid, p. 6: radio broadcast, 22 June 1940.
27. Ibid, p. 8: radio broadcast, 24 June 1940.
28. Ibid, p. 25: radio broadcast, 12 August 1940.
29. Ibid, p. 146: radio broadcast, 21 October 1940.
30. Ibid, p. 9: radio broadcast, 26 June 1940.
31. Ibid, p. 29: radio broadcast, 22 August 1940.
32. Ibid, p. 19: proclamation, dated July 1940.
33. Newhouse, John: *De Gaulle and the Anglo-Saxons* (London: Andre Deutsch Ltd, 1970), p. 36.

with respect to French possessions in North America and the Carribean,[34] which could ultimately result in the disorderly disintegration of France's empire, whose territorial integrity he had pledged to defend. The specter of the American eagle – or should one say vulture? – preying on helpless French colonies would haunt him throughout the war. As early as the fall of 1940, de Gaulle began taking whatever initiatives his weak position permitted him to prevent this intolerable scenario from becoming a reality.

De Gaulle sent a telegram from Freetown on September 18 to Vice-Admiral Muselier and Colonel Fontaine at Free French headquarters in London, in which he discussed taking control of French colonies in the Western Hemisphere.[35] In late October, he met with the American consul in Leopoldville, now Kinshasa, and presented him with a note for Roosevelt and U.S. Secretary of State Cordell Hull. In the note, he made clear his stand on French possessions in the Western Hemisphere: the Havana Pact[36] notwithstanding, the unilateral occupation of French colonies by American troops would constitute an additional affront at a time of grave national distress. It would also be an unnecessary humiliation, as Free French forces were quite capable of preventing these colonies from falling into Axis hands. De Gaulle also announced the formation of the Council for the Defense of the French Empire, which would be responsible for administering and defending all French territories that had rejected the Armistice. In concluding, de Gaulle suggested that an agreement could be reached permitting American use of air and naval bases on these colonies.[37] There is no official U.S. reply on record, but there can be little doubt that Hull was not pleased by this initiative from a man whose credibility with the State Department, following events at Dakar in September, was nonexistent.[38]

This lack of response did not deter de Gaulle as he continued to attend to the plight of French possessions in the Western Hemisphere. On November 9, he wired Colonel Fontaine in Lon-

34. Deporte, Anton W.: *De Gaulle's Foreign Policy 1944–1946* (Cambridge, MA: Harvard University Press, 1968), p. 30.

35. De Gaulle, *Lettres Notes et Carnets*, vol. III, pp. 115–16.

36. The Havana Pact, signed in July 1940 by the United States and the countries of Latin America, stated that these nations agreed to oppose, by force if necessary, any transfer of sovereignty involving territories belonging to the warring nations.

37. De Gaulle, *Lettres Notes et Carnets*, vol. III, pp. 150–52.

38. Cook, Don: *Charles de Gaulle* (New York: G.P. Putnam's Sons, 1983), pp. 121–22; White, Dorothy Shipley: *Seeds of Discord: De Gaulle, Free France and the Allies* (Syracuse, NY: Syracuse University Press, 1964), p. 209.

don, outlining the situation in the North American islands of Saint Pierre and Miquelon; given that the local population favored Free France, an immediate naval action was in order to ensure the adherence of the islands to his movement.[39] This action was ultimately deferred 13 months. When it finally took place, it further poisoned de Gaulle's relations with the U.S. State Department.

Apart from the perceived threat to the French Empire, there were other factors that contributed to the unfavorable impression of the United States de Gaulle developed during his first months as the head of Free France.

No doubt Roosevelt's negative response to Reynaud's plea for help in June was a source of disappointment to de Gaulle and the first indication that the United States might be slow to intervene on behalf of the Allies.[40] De Gaulle also felt, as did a number of ranking State Department officials, including Hull,[41] that the decision of U.S. Ambassador William Bullitt to remain in Paris rather than follow the Reynaud government south was fundamentally ill-conceived. The presence of a diplomat of Bullitt's stature would have been proof of American confidence in, and support of, Reynaud's determination to continue fighting.[42] Instead, Bullitt, like his predecessors in France's two previous wars with Germany, stayed in Paris in an attempt to preserve the city from destruction.

De Gaulle, however, did distinguish between those responsible for American non-intervention and those favorable to American involvement in the war. In his *Memoirs*, de Gaulle recognizes Roosevelt's desire to act in the fall of 1940 and that it was the U.S. Congress and the press who, by systematically criticizing any initiative that even indirectly violated the Neutrality Act, prevented American aid to the Allies.[43]

Roosevelt's good intentions aside, de Gaulle obviously deplored and profoundly disagreed with American recognition of the Vichy regime. He grew increasingly bewildered by this policy as his movement grew in strength,[44] noting that the continued

39. De Gaulle, *Lettres Notes et Carnets*, vol. III, pp. 178–79.

40. Viorst, Milton: *Hostile Allies: FDR and Charles De Gaulle* (New York: The MacMillan Company, 1965), p. 25.

41. Davis, Forrest and Lindley, Ernest K.: *How War Came to America* (London: George Allen and Unwin Ltd, 1943), pp. 62–63.

42. De Gaulle, Charles: *Mémoires de Guerre: L'Appel 1940–1942* (Paris: Librairie Plon, 1954), p. 50.

43. Ibid, p. 122.

44. Viorst, p. 40.

presence of high-ranking diplomats in Vichy provided the regime with a degree of legitimacy that discouraged Frenchmen from joining the Free French.[45] When Pétain's October meeting with Hitler officially issued in the era of collaboration with the Nazis, and the U.S. still refused to deviate from their Vichy line, de Gaulle was bitterly disappointed.[46] Admiral Leahy's arrival in Vichy in December as the U.S. ambassador was another affront to Free France, coming as it did after Laval's appointment in the Vichy government had confirmed the regime's collaborationist bent. To make matters even worse, the admiral was particularly unsuited for his new post, having virtually no political or diplomatic experience and little understanding or knowledge of the French people.[47] The apparent incoherence of American policy could only have confirmed the conclusion at which de Gaulle had arrived in a conversation with Churchill in August: "in the final analysis, England is an island; France, the cape of a continent; America, another world."[48]

The extent to which American military circles were aware of de Gaulle's military writings before June 1940 requires a thorough examination of American military journals and U.S. military attaché reports from Paris.

Reference to de Gaulle first appeared in the July 1924 issue of *The Cavalry Journal*. An article he wrote for the 15 December 1923 issue of the *Revue Militaire Générale* is given brief mention in the section devoted to the foreign military press. Entitled "L'Envers d'un décor," the article discusses the difficulties encountered by the Central Powers in obtaining unity of command during World War I.[49] This subject was to be the focus of de Gaulle's first book, *La Discorde chez l'Ennemi*, published in 1924.

It was not until the mid-1930s that de Gaulle again attracted the attention of the U.S. military. In May 1934, the American military attaché in Paris mailed a copy of de Gaulle's recently published work, *Vers l'armée de métier*,[50] to the chief of the Military Intelligence Division in Washington. Noting that "this book has

45. De Gaulle, *Mémoires de Guerre: L'Appel 1940–1942*, p. 73.
46. Ibid, p. 118.
47. Schoenbrun, David: *The Three Lives of Charles De Gaulle* (New York: Atheneum, 1966), pp. 123–24.
48. De Gaulle, *Mémoires de Guerre: L'Appel 1940–1942*, p. 88.
49. *The Cavalry Journal*, July 1924, p. 348.
50. Military Intelligence Division 2015–1179/1.

attracted considerable attention in France," the attaché also sent his superiors a two-page summary of the book and a translation of André Pironneau's very favorable review from the *Echo de Paris* 7 May 1934.[51] A second report, received in early October 1934, notes that "this book continues to receive lengthy comment in the Press" and includes an article in *Le Temps* by General Baratier (French Army, retired). In this article, Baratier, who subscribes to de Gaulle's thesis, examines specific measures required to implement a motorized and mechanized professional army in France.[52] In early 1935, another article by Baratier was sent to MID. It includes a passing reference to "one of those heavy divisions whose structure was mentioned by Colonel de Gaulle."[53] Finally, in March 1937, the question of France's tank doctrine was once again raised, and a third article by Baratier mentions de Gaulle several times, as well as an earlier tank expert, Colonel Estienne, and the British specialist, General J. F. C. Fuller. By 1937, Baratier has reconsidered his support for the de Gaulle/Fuller line, which argued that tank units be independently used to outflank the enemy and penetrate deep into his territory. He concludes that, given the development of anti-tank weapons, the limited use of tanks advocated by the French General Staff is now to be recommended.[54] It should be noted that if de Gaulle's name did occasionally surface in reports on tanks, it was entirely absent from the numerous reports filed in the late 1930s dealing with French industrial mobilization.

Oddly enough, considering the attention paid it by the military attaché in Paris, *Vers l'armée de métier* does not seem to have been reviewed by a single military journal in the United States. This is significant, as reviews of a number of other French books and articles on the subject of tanks and motorized divisions appeared in *The Cavalry Journal* throughout the thirties. These works include a full range of opinions, from arguing for the use of tanks in war movement (along the de Gaulle line) to rejecting tanks as unsuitable for use in a sudden invasion and advocating the retention of horses for military purposes.[55]

51. MID 2015–1179/1.
52. MID 2015–1179/2.
53. MID 2015–1179/3.
54. MID 2015–1179/4.
55. See the *Cavalry Journal*: Nov-Dec 1931, pp. 53–54; May-June 1933, pp. 53–54; Nov-Dec 1933, p. 37; Sept-Oct 1934, p. 73; March-April 1936, pp. 151-52; July-Aug 1936, p. 346; Nov-Dec 1936, pp. 531–32; Jan-Feb 1937, pp. 79–80; May-June 1937, p. 290.

The American military had been debating this issue since the late 1920s. The central question was formulated much as de Gaulle would frame it in the 1930s: Should the tank be developed as a "new arm, capable of striking with the speed and shock power of cavalry, but with some of the staying force of infantry," or should it be left up to each arm of the military to develop its own possibilities for mechanization? When the latter option prevailed, the development of the tank and its use within an armored force of combined branches languished.[56] The 1930s continued to see the publication of dozens of articles on this question in *The Cavalry Journal*. While there were many references to, and occasional contributions by, British tank experts B. H. Liddell Hart and J. F. C. Fuller, de Gaulle was never mentioned.

The only book by de Gaulle to be reviewed in an American military journal was *La France et son armée*, published in 1938. *The American Military History Journal*'s Summer 1940 issue briefly mentions it. In the same issue, there are reviews of other French books on military subjects, including one on tank warfare by Lieutenant-Colonel Perré.[57] This would seem to confirm the overall impression that the U.S. military did not consider de Gaulle to be the leading French expert on tanks, but, at best, one of several French writers worthy of attention. Indeed, apart from the chief of MID, it is doubtful that many members of the U.S. military were aware of de Gaulle's writings, let alone had read them. It was not until 1941 that *Vers l'armée de métier* was translated into English,[58] which no doubt severely restricted de Gaulle's potential American readership before the war. One American officer interested in tanks did read *Vers l'armée de métier* in the mid-1930s, but it is clear that George Patton was the exception, perhaps even unique, in this regard.[59]

Finally, there is the case of James Marlow's *De Gaulle and the Coming Invasion of Germany*. Favorably reviewed in both *The Cavalry Journal* and *The Infantry Journal*, this short work seems to have been the first book about de Gaulle in any language – and the only one to appear in 1940. The title reflects Marlow's questionable thesis that de Gaulle's writings and public statements

56. Weigley, pp. 410–11.

57. *The American Military History Journal*, Summer 1940, p. 116.

58. It was originally published in 1941 as *The Army of the Future* by J.B. Lippencott Company, Philadelphia.

59. Farago, Ladislas: *Patton: Ordeal and Triumph* (New York: Ivan Obolensky, Inc., 1963), pp. 120–22.

point clearly and consciously to the manner in which victory over Hitler shall be achieved. The book contains a brief biographical sketch of de Gaulle, quotes liberally from his published writings, and paints an unabashedly hyperbolic and frequently inaccurate picture of de Gaulle's reputation as a military genius:

> Among the military thinkers of the present age, General De Gaulle has rightly come to be regarded as one of the greatest, if not the greatest, of exponents of modern warfare with highly technical and mechanized forces.[60]

> General de Gaulle was an acknowledged expert on military science, not only in France, but in military circles throughout the world.[61]

> It is not only in military literature that General de Gaulle has impressed his personality on the modern world that knows him, and has influenced all the military powers of Europe with his advanced views. During the present war he had an opportunity, limited by the means at is disposal, to put his theories into practice, and with striking success.[62]

Marlow sees de Gaulle as a savior, "the Man of Destiny," whose sincere modesty prevents him from claiming such a role for himself.[63] In point of fact, de Gaulle was thoroughly convinced of his mission to save France and rarely coy about conveying that conviction to others. Nevertheless, the book's inaccuracies and pro-de Gaulle bias should not obscure its significance as the first relatively in-depth look that some Americans got of the already controversial Frenchman. Whether it was, as one review enthusiastically claimed, "a fighting book for all Americans who want no false Maginot line of defense between democracy and dictatorship,"[64] is open to question.

If de Gaulle was known to at least a few members of the American military before June 1940, there is every indication that the U.S. embassy in Paris and the State Department were completely unaware of his existence before he joined Reynaud's cabinet early that month.[65] The very day de Gaulle entered the government, Ambassador Bullitt wired Cordell Hull a brief but favor-

60. Marlow, James: *De Gaulle and the Coming Invasion of Germany* (New York: E.P. Dutton and Co., Inc., 1940), p. 19.
61. Ibid, p. 28.
62. Ibid, p. 49.
63. Ibid, p. 22.
64. *The Cavalry Journal*, Nov-Dec 1940, p. 562. The review in *The Infantry Journal* is on page 636 of the Nov-Dec 1940 issue.
65. Cook, p. 92.

able evaluation of the new undersecretary for war: "Two weeks ago this General was a colonel in the tank corps. He showed great initiative and courage in stemming the German advance on Paris . . . . He is a young man who appears to be vigorous and intelligent."[66] A second telegram four days later confirmed that de Gaulle was "in reality . . . now directing the Ministry of War."[67] From London, on June 12, came Winston Churchill's assessment: "Reynaud . . . is for fighting on and he has a young general de Gaulle who believes much can be done."[68] In spite of these references to de Gaulle, it seems unlikely that Roosevelt took note of the Frenchman in June.[69] Nor, for that matter, did he show much interest in de Gaulle during the rest of the year; de Gaulle is not once mentioned in the president's correspondence with Churchill in 1940,[70] and the same holds true for his public papers, addresses,[71] and personal correspondence of that year.[72] At the time, there were more important matters for Roosevelt to discuss than the barely perceptible emergence of a quantitatively insignificant resistance movement and its upstart leader.[73]

By the end of June, as the U.S. pursued its Vichy policy, the initially favorable reaction to de Gaulle was giving way to a growing realization that he might prove to be a nuisance. The State Department was well informed of Pétain's bitterness towards his former protégé and the anger and indignation with which Laval, members of the French military, and officials of the Bank of France greeted Churchill's recognition of de Gaulle's French National Committee.[74] If the U.S. was to play its Vichy card to the fullest, formal relations with de Gaulle seemed out of the question.

In August, as sub-Saharan French Africa began to declare for de Gaulle, American officials reported this evolution without taking sides. American consuls general in Casablanca and

66. *Foreign Relations of the United States*, 1940, vol. I, pp. 240–41.

67. Bullitt, Orville H. (ed): *For the President: Personal and Secret Correspondence between Franklin D. Roosevelt and William C. Bullitt* (Boston: Houghton Mifflin Company, 1972), p. 457.

68. *FRUS*, vol. I, pp. 246–47 (1940).

69. Viorst, p. 1; Aglion, Raoul: *Roosevelt and De Gaulle* (New York: The Free Press, 1988), p. 12.

70. Kimball, Warren F. (ed): *Churchill and Roosevelt: The Complete Correspondence*, vol. I (Princeton, N.J.: Princeton University Press, 1984).

71. Roosevelt, Franklin D.: *The Public Papers and Addresses of Franklin D. Roosevelt* vol. IX (New York: Russell and Russell, 1969).

72. Roosevelt, Franklin D.: *F.D.R.: His Personal Letters*, vol. IV (New York: Duell, Sloan and Pearce, 1950).

73. Aglion, p. 55.

74. *FRUS*, vol. I, pp. 266–67 (1940); FRUS, 1940, vol. II, p. 465.

Algiers downplayed the impact of these events on Morocco (where there was "no fight left in the local French population"[75]) and on Algeria (where the "de Gaulle movement [was] not strong enough to declare itself for Free France"[76]). This no doubt confirmed Hull's sense that de Gaulle could not ultimately "deliver the goods" and that the policy towards Vichy remained the United States' best option. In early September, in a cable to the American consul at Léopoldville, Hull made the official American position clear: "The Department desires to avoid as far as possible raising any question of principle in the matter of relations between this Government and the de Gaulle Committee."[77] Any remaining chance for an understanding with de Gaulle – if indeed it ever existed – evaporated three weeks later over Dakar.

It is doubtful whether, from the American point of view, de Gaulle could have chosen a more sensitive target to attack unsuccessfully than Dakar; since its port, airstrips, facilities, and relative impregnability made it one of the best harbors between Europe and Capetown. Furthermore, its proximity to Brazil made a German invasion of the Western Hemisphere a frightening possibility should Dakar fall into Axis hands.[78] The last thing the United States wanted was for German attention to be unnecessarily and prematurely focused on a spot of such immense strategic value. Not surprisingly, once informed by Churchill of the planned attack, Roosevelt responded with a curt, unambiguous cable: "All right – but succeed!"[79]

When the jointly led Free French and British operation was rebuffed by a governor and troops loyal to Pétain, de Gaulle quickly came to be seen as the incompetent leader of a dangerously amateurish movement that was incapable of preventing security leaks, like the ones that had allegedly contributed to this fiasco.[80] The State Department received cables from American diplomats in Africa, the Middle East, and London indicating the de Gaulle had been discredited and support for him destroyed following the events at Dakar.[81] Undersecretary of State Sumner

75. *FRUS*, 1940, vol. II, p. 580.
76. *FRUS*, 1940, vol. II, p. 605.
77. *FRUS*, 1940, vol. II, p. 641.
78. White, p. 178; Davis and Lindley, p. 50.
79. White, p. 202.
80. Cook, pp. 112–13. There is considerable agreement on the carelessness and indiscretions of the Free French prior to Dakar, including stories of members of the Free French forces toasting their future success at Dakar in public. René Cassin disputes these stories and maintains there were no such leaks.
81. 75. *FRUS*, 1940, vol. II, p. 591–92, 911–12; *FRUS*, vol. III, 1940, pp. 48–49.

Welles summed up the official American reaction when he described the operation as a "total failure, not only because several French warships under Vichy's orders helped to repel the attack, but more particularly because of de Gaulle's mistaken belief that the local garrison and officials would support him if he appeared on the scene."[82] Roosevelt was not amused and concluded that de Gaulle had been guilty of "putting his ambitions above French and allied interests."[83] According to Robert Murphy, a high-ranking diplomat close to the president, "Roosevelt never lost the distrust of de Gaulle's judgment and discretion which he formed then."[84]

The publication in late October of the Brazzaville Manifesto, in which, among other things, de Gaulle announced his intention to exercise his powers in the name of France, rendered any understanding with the United States virtually impossible. His announcement, for all intents and purposes, forced an all-or-nothing choice on Washington a scant four weeks after Dakar had cruelly exposed his limitations, thereby confirming the apparent soundness of the State Department's Vichy policy.[85]

Given the limited exposure de Gaulle received in specialized journals, it is not surprising that he was absolutely unknown to the American press before June 1940. Rare articles on Paul Reynaud in the 1930s, even when they noted his interest in military questions,[86] made no reference to the man whose ideas on tank warfare had inspired his own book, *Le problème militaire Français*.[87] It was only when de Gaulle joined Reynaud's government after a cabinet shake-up in early June that the press began to take note of this "lanky, pale, mustached military innovator."[88] *Newsweek* saw the addition of the "Caterpillar Prophet" as "Reynaud's most important appointment."[89] *The New York Times* agreed: "[The Cabinet changes] are significant, but one case illustrates all. As his collaborator in the Ministry of War M. Reynaud

82. Welles, Sumner: *Seven Decisions that Shaped History* (New York: Harper and Brothers, Publishers, 1950, 1951), p. 36.

83. Murphy, Robert Daniel: *Diplomat Among Warriors* (Garden City, NY: Doubleday and Company, 1964), p. 76.

84. Ibid, p. 76.

85. Funk, Arthur Layton: *Charles de Gaulle: The Crucial Years, 1943–1944* (Norman, OK: The University of Oklahoma Press, 1959), pp. 11–12.

86. *Christian Science Monitor Weekly Magazine*, October 28, 1939, p. 7.

87. Reynaud was a vocal advocate of de Gaulle's ideas on tank warfare in the 1930s. See vol. II, p. 147 of his *Mémoires* (Paris: Flammarion, 1963).

88. *Time*, 17 June 1940, p. 31.

89. *Newsweek*, 17 June 1940, p. 20.

has picked Brigadier General Charles de Gaulle who for years has been advocating that France must have an offensive force of tanks and motorized divisions."[90] Initial biographical sketches of de Gaulle stressed his recently vindicated ideas on tank warfare and often noted his recent promotion.

De Gaulle's famous radio broadcast on 18 June 1940 received far less exposure than had his appointment to Reynaud's cabinet. If *The New York Times* did quote from his text, neither *Time* nor *Newsweek* mentioned it in their June 24 issues. By then, important events in France, most notably the signing of the Franco-German Armistice on June 22, had drawn attention away from de Gaulle's efforts in London. The Frenchman soon appeared to be no more than a "dud shell that had fallen without exploding."[91]

In July, the press reported on de Gaulle infrequently and with growing skepticism. A caption under one of his pictures read somewhat mockingly "Charles de Gaulle, General or Monsieur?"[92] On July 8, both *Time* and *Newsweek* cast serious doubt on the value of Britain's formal recognition of "long-nosed"[93] General Charles de Gaulle's French National Committee, which seemed "doomed to restricted usefulness at most."[94] Another caption, "Britain's man,"[95] raised the thorny question of de Gaulle's autonomy vis-à-vis his hosts. An article in *Time* later in the month epitomized de Gaulle's flagging image in the United States:

> The Man on Horseback who will try to make France strong again had not appeared last week . . . some people thought that if the British should win, General Charles de Gaulle would be such a man. More likely it would be someone as obscure as Adolf Hitler in 1918.[96]

One can hardly fault this journalist for betting against de Gaulle in July 1940, but behind his incongruous comparison his logic seems questionable; for if past obscurity was to be used as a criterion for future prominence, would not the de Gaulle of 1925 compete with the Hitler of 1918? American perceptions of de Gaulle were no doubt further confused when Pierre Lazareff, the ex-editor of *Paris-Soir*, described him in an article for *Life* as an "ambi-

90. *New York Times*, 7 June 1940, p. 6.
91. White, p. 114.
92. *Time*, 1 July 1940, p. 25.
93. *Time*, 8 July 1940, p. 32.
94. *Newsweek*, 8 July 1940, p. 24.
95. *Newsweek*, 8 July 1940, p. 23.
96. *Time*, 22 July 1940, p. 24.

tious royalist."[97] By the time a number of African colonies joined de Gaulle's movement in late August, his image and credibility were such that *The New York Times* attributed these developments to the achievements of the RAF rather than to de Gaulle's growing prestige.[98]

During the month of September, the press began to give de Gaulle credit[99] as "the colonial parade to [his] defiant standard . . . was in full swing."[100] The "new heights of Gallic oratory" to which de Gaulle had been "stirred" appeared to be bearing fruit, and his image improved correspondingly.[101] Unfortunately for de Gaulle, it was at this juncture that the fiasco at Dakar occurred.

The reaction of the American press was equal parts scorn and sarcasm. *The New York Times* described the operation as "a sad mistake" made by de Gaulle, who had clearly been misled about the attitude of the local population. The British communique that attempted to absolve him of responsibility for the failure was uncharitably dismissed as a "masterpiece of naïveté."[102] *Newsweek* dubbed the operation an "inglorious failure,"[103] while *Time* spoke of a "serious defeat" and mocked the British for their historical "weakness for lost causes." *Time* documented this charge with a curious exposition of a similar failure in 1795 at Quiberon Bay, only this time it was the hapless de Gaulle who played the part of the "leader of the emigrés"! *Time* concluded its coverage of Dakar by pointing out that city's importance as an air- and seaport and its relative proximity to the tip of Brazil.[104]

Before the year was out, however, there was a noticeable change in the press' attitude towards de Gaulle. This was due, to a large degree, to a supportive speech by Churchill,[105] but also to more Free French gains in Africa. By late November and early December, *Time* was acknowledging that "in Africa the situation was more disturbing for the Germans [in part because] General Charles de Gaulle continue[d] his consolidation of Free Frenchmen there."[106] A successful coup in Gabon provided a timely

97. *Life*, 26 August 1940, p. 75.
98. *New York Times*, 30 August 1940, p. 6.
99. *Newsweek*, 9 September 1940, pp. 35–36.
100. *Time*, 23 September 1940, p. 29.
101. *Time*, 9 September 1940, p. 29.
102. *New York Times*, 26 September 1940, p. 1.
103. *Newsweek*, 7 October 1940, pp. 24–25, 27.
104. *Time*, 7 October 1940, pp. 32, 24.
105. White, p. 201.
106. *Time*, 25 November 1940, p. 26.

counterbalance to the painful memory of Dakar. More importantly, de Gaulle's stature in metropolitan France seemed to be growing, as indicated by the story of French university students parading around with two fishing poles ("deux gaules").[107] The rapid rehabilitation of de Gaulle's public image in the United States indicates that Americans identified with his cause, particularly once his movement began to enjoy some success.

De Gaulle's article in 1934 and remarks in his letters and notebooks indicate that he had given the United States some thought before 1940. His research and personal experience confirmed the generally negative impression he must have received from most of the press and public opinion in interwar France. Certainly the picture of a profoundly individualistic and materialistic society, in which excess and social irresponsibility seemed to be encouraged, would have repulsed a man of his upbringing and personal convictions. In 1940, his new role as the leader of Free France required that he consider the United States not only as a future ally but also as a potential aggressor. American reluctance to enter the conflict economically – let alone militarily – and the threat of territorial encroachments by the U.S. were consistent with his image of a nation primarily concerned with the economic bottom-line. Americans had been quick to take advantage of French economic and monetary fragility in the 1920s; could they not be expected to behave similarly in 1940 with France even more vulnerable? Such base opportunism might also explain the apparent sympathy of the U.S. government for the defeatists and collaborators in Vichy.

American reactions to de Gaulle before June 1940 were rare. Other than George Patton and a zealous military attaché in Paris, de Gaulle's ideas concerning a motorized and mechanized army apparently attracted little or no attention from the U.S. military. His relative anonymity cannot be explained by a lack of interest in tank warfare. On the contrary, the subject was keenly debated in the 1930s within the U.S. Cavalry, and contributions to this debate by the foreign military press were regularly reviewed in *The Cavalry Journal*. But before the success of the German Blitzkrieg vindicated his ideas, de Gaulle was simply an author whose thesis had yet to be proved.

107. *Time*, 9 December 1940, p. 27.

The reactions of the American press and the U.S. State Department followed similar paths in 1940. Initial impressions in June were favorable, only to be followed by increasing skepticism and decreasing coverage in July and August. In late August, both the press and the State Department minimized the importance and impact of recent Free French gains in Africa. Then, just as the press was beginning to acknowledge de Gaulle's contribution to this success, Dakar confirmed earlier American doubts about de Gaulle, who was held responsible for the fiasco. Late in the year, however, the press and the State Department diverged in their assessments. While the latter, now committed to its Vichy policy, continued to see de Gaulle as a potentially dangerous bungler, the former kept an open mind and applauded when Free French initiatives met with success in November and December.

There can be no question that events *after* 1940, as well as the personalities involved, remain the key to understanding the relations between Charles de Gaulle and the United States. By then, unfortunately, and for reasons we have seen, the seeds of mutual suspicion and distrust had been planted, and each was watching the other with less than friendly eyes.

❖2❖

The Free French and the United States, From 1940 to 1944

Raoul Aglion

The threat of Hitler's designs on Europe in 1939 – i.e., the rapid conquest of his armies in Czechoslovakia and Poland – affected neither the French nor the Americans. France was protected, they thought, by the impregnable Maginot Line, and was defended by the first army in Europe, whose illustrious generals had been the victors of World War I.

The news became alarming in 1940, however, when the German panzer divisions entered Holland and Belgium and then destroyed the French army in six weeks. President Paul Reynaud made a desperate appeal to President Roosevelt, but because the Congress and American public opinion were staunchly isolationist, the latter wouldn't commit to any military aid and offered only words of encouragement. Lacking American aid, the French leaders capitulated.

How did the roughly 150,000 French men and women living in the United States react? First, the situation was met with complete stupor. The unthinkable had occurred, and quite rapidly the orders to the consulate from the provisional government in Bordeaux, and then from Vichy, would weigh heavily on the behavior of the French in America.

Mr. Doynel de Saint-Quentin, the French ambassador in Washington, withdrew on the orders of Vichy, leaving his position to Henri Haye, former mayor of Versailles, who subsequently proved to be the most aggressive and devoted agent of Vichy's pro-German policy. He succeeded in maintaining all of the consulates and the large majority of the French colonies under the aegis of Vichy. Nevertheless, from the moment de Gaulle made his appeal on 18 June 1940, a group of French patriots decided to organize in support of him. This is how, on 26 August 1940, Dr. Simard and Mr. Eugène Houdry brought together Frenchmen and Americans in Philadelphia to create an association called France For Ever, dedicated to spreading the ideal of the Free French in the United States and to influencing public opinion. Mr. Eugène Houdry, a French industrialist and naturalized American, was elected president in 1940 and re-elected in 1942.

This association played an important role in American public relations. It created chapters in 44 American towns and, by 1942, had about 9,000 members. It was responsible for spreading the image of de Gaulle and of France's fighting spirit everywhere. Several eminent Americans were members of this committee: Robert Sherwood, Charles P. Taft, Herbert Bayard Swope, William Allen Nelson, and Richard de Rochemond, who later became its president.

Although the vast majority of its members were American, its political committee was made up mostly of French war refugees, who manifested extraordinary enthusiasm for General de Gaulle and were generally intolerant of any dissension among the Frenchmen. Despite its successes with American public opinion, however, France For Ever was never able to obtain the adhesion of a large number of the French people living in the United States.

Very early on, General de Gaulle named Jacques de Sieyès, a former classmate at Saint-Cyr, personal delegate to the United States. In a speech made upon arriving from London, de Sieyès declared:

> The General was quite struck that of the 150,000 French residents in the United States, only a very small number joined France For Ever. He quoted a passage from a letter that the General had sent him:
>
> "I am asking you to travel the American continent and instigate the establishment of a Committee of the Free French in every great city or at least in every State.
>
> This committee will seek to assemble in an apolitical fashion all the French residents who believe that the cause of Free France cannot be separated from that of Great Britain and the United States, and that as Maritain says, France cannot be absent from a battle that her existence depends upon.
>
> For each of these Committees, I am asking you to find a Frenchman with public esteem to be its president. The different Committees, as they are being constituted, should join in a Federation of the Free

> French in the United States which, on the national level, will continually expose the efforts of the Free French to American public opinion.
>
> It will be necessary to find a President who can gather all the votes, and I will be glad to know whom the principal committees, once they are constituted, will nominate for this position."[1]

Unfortunately, the general's appeals, transmitted by Sieyès, were unsuccessful. It was at this time, August 1940, that Mr. Garreau-Dombasle, the commercial consultant to the French embassy, resigned and joined the Free French. No one followed him.

In a circular of the Free French in London, No. 4 of 13 July 1941, Mr. Garreau-Dombasle noted that only 602 out of the several thousand members were French. He commented:

> The proportion of our members to the totality of the French population remains tiny because of, on the one hand, the unbelievable apathy of most Frenchmen in the United States, and on the other hand, the campaigns of disparagement led by Vichy agents. This apathy is nothing new: before the war, the Federation of French Veterans had recruited only 327 members, while over 3000 veterans drew pensions at the Consulate.

Nevertheless, France For Ever succeeded in its intense propaganda effort directed towards Americans, aided by the fact that it was an American corporation legally registered in Philadelphia. The important collected funds were used to publish a monthly bulletin, an annual magazine, and different propaganda pamphlets; produce radio shows; and organize demonstrations throughout the United States.

De Gaulle was represented by three independent entities: De Sieyès, de Gaulle's personal representative; Garreau-Dombasle, the representative of the Free French; and France For Ever, which represented everybody. This confusion couldn't last for long, and on May 16, General de Gaulle decided to send René Pleven, one of his most effective associates, to the United States with the following instructions:

> 1. to establish permanent and direct relations with the State Department, to be maintained after his departure by a fully qualified political representative of the Free French;
>
> 2. to organize economic and financial relations between African Free France, Free French Oceania and the United States;

1. Personal letter from General de Gaulle to Jacques de Sieyès.

3. to organize, if possible, "direct" purchases of war material, following the Belgium system;

4. to create or recreate our committees;

5. to establish a center of information and propaganda in the United States; and

6. to organize the cooperation and the aid of private sources in the United States.

The general added that this mission was urgent and should be done discreetly, especially with regard to the British. He nonetheless informed Anthony Eden, secretary of state to the Foreign Office, and assured him that nothing would be done without the agreement of Lord Halifax, the British ambassador to the United States.

Pleven tried to organize the official representation of the Free French. Following the general's desire, Pleven looked for someone whose prestige would give his movement some public appeal.

Naturally, he asked Alexis Léger, the famous poet (under the name Saint John Perse) and former secretary general of the Ministry of Foreign Affairs. Léger refused because he thought that although the general was right in organizing a military force to fight alongside the British, he had no right to organize the National Committee or take political action. Pleven then consulted Jean Monnet, later to become the father of the Common Market, who refused because he considered his position at the British Supply Council in Washington to be more important. There remained Jacques Maritain, the illustrious philosopher who, while he rejected Pétain for having "no national mandate," didn't believe that de Gaulle had one either. As a matter of fact, Maritain added, his position as a philosopher compelled him not to take sides, to remain totally independent.

Jacques Maritain refused not only to be the general's delegate, but also to participate in the consultative council of the Free French. He thought that, in these tragic days, one had to respect Pétain's government even though he judged it quite severely. Obedience to Pétain's orders, he remarked, "cannot go further than what our conscience allows."

Having failed to find a single prestigious delegate to represent Free France, Pleven then thought of a delegation of five members. First, he chose Raoul Roussy de Sales, a known bilingual writer, who was at ease with both Americans and Frenchmen and had made some inroads in Washington circles.[2]

In Washington, Pleven met Etienne Boegner, a young French industrialist recommended by the British ambassador to Washington, who had fled France on 16 June 1940 and had gone to the United States via Lisbon. Boegner was the son of pastor Marc Boegner, president of the Protestant Churches of France, who would later heroically resist the Nazis in France, where he preferred to remain in order to share the suffering of his followers. Etienne Boegner was solicited and he accepted.

Pleven then asked me if I would accept a position as a delegate, with specific responsibility for the delegation in New York. At this time, I had been attaché to the cabinets of the Ministers of Trade and Finances in Paris. At the beginning of the war, I had been attaché to the French embassy in Cairo. Though nothing had prepared me for these heavy responsibilities, I accepted them nonetheless.

For the fourth delegate, Pleven thought of Jacques de Sieyès, who was de Gaulle's personal representative.

Finally, for the fifth delegate, Pleven recommended Adrien Tixier, representative of the International Labor Office in Washington and a militant trade unionist, who would make the delegation look less bourgeois, conservative, and intellectual. He had to counter the accusation made in certain American circles that de Gaulle was a "military dictator." Adrien Tixier was a rough and ambitious person, who in fact did not follow the general's instructions and came into conflict with de Sieyès, who was later relieved of his functions and sent to Syria. Etienne Boegner resigned after a quarrel with the general in London, and Roussy de Sales died in 1942 of a pulmonary infection. Of the five delegates, only Tixier in Washington and I in New York remained to represent Free France during the war. On 26 March 1942, Tixier made a spontaneous statement to Mr. Mathews, chargé d'affaires of the United States, that would considerably reduce the influence of the general and of the London National Committee: "General de Gaulle and his entourage in Carlton Gardens have no sense of the realities . . . and have no contact with the people. . . ."

He added:

> France is again going to become the battlefield before the end of the war. The beginnings of resistance in France must be carefully helped

2. Raoul Roussy de Sales. *l'Amérique entre en querre*. Paris: La Jeune Parque, 1948.

> but they can exist only through the people. But de Gaulle and his partisans have no contact with the people.

Tixier added that he would like the British clandestinely to:

> help men of confidence escape from France who would later organize the day of liberation. It so happens that the leaders of the Free French in London are so involved in their internal quarrels that they are incapable of creating the disinterested actions which are necessary for our movement.[3]

These criticisms of General de Gaulle and his committee curiously converged with those being made by Alexis Léger in the capital. They were perhaps more important since they emanated from the head of the Delegation of the Free French, who had just been named in Washington. Curiously, Tixier continued to criticize General de Gaulle on his visits to the State Department, as is unfortunately recorded in the American archives.

Moreover, Pleven was unable to organize the National Federation because very few wanted to belong to a support organization. The general had wanted such an organization and was very disappointed over its failure. Pleven, therefore, had to be content that France For Ever would inform the public of the action of de Gaulle and the Free French forces and spread the image of a courageous, suffering, and resistant France. Ultimately, however, the delegation de Gaulle had named did not exert much influence on the French population, which by and large, was not Gaullist.

What position did President Roosevelt and the American administration have on Free France and its delegation? Roosevelt's position would inevitably influence the residents of the United States, and they in turn would influence him. Although President Roosevelt was a friend of France, whose culture he admired, he had to contend with the isolationist mood of the American people at the time. "Your sons will not be sent to fight foreign wars, no matter where they are taking place," he declared in 1940. Hitler's rapid conquests would make Roosevelt change his mind, but American public opinion didn't follow. He answered Paul Reynaud's desperate plea in June 1940:

> We are doing our best in the United States to supply all the necessary material . . . but we cannot promise a military participation. According to our Constitution, only the Congress has the right to declare war. . . .[4]

3. *Foreign Relations of the United States* 1942, vol. 2, p. 59.
4. Kimball, Warren, *Churchill and Roosevelt: The Complete Correspondence*. Princeton: Princeton University Press, 1984, pp. 1–47.

The French disaster certainly upset the president and destroyed his illusions. From then on, he thought of France as a second-class country that would have to come under his tutelage in the future. Finally, he was greatly concerned by the possibility that the French fleet might cooperate with, or be turned over to, the Germans. He thus adopted a policy of appeasement vis-à-vis the Vichy government, which had an impact on the French community in the United States.

Pleven's mission, as I have stated, was to organize the French community, to create an official delegation of the Free French approved by the State Department, and to normalize relations between the United States and the Free French. For the most part, he succeeded, doing everything that was possible in this period. The Free French delegation, composed of Tixier, Boegner, Roussy de Sales, de Sieyès, and me, was approved by the State Department, given a semi-diplomatic statute, and obtained the use of a secret code and diplomatic pouch. The delegation was authorized to deliver passports in the name of Free France. In exchange, Pleven had proposed putting the air bases in French Equatorial Africa and the Pacific islands at the disposal of the Americans. Following this, an American mission went to Chad. Secretary of State Cordell Hull declared in September that there was a "community of interests" between Free France and the United States. Finally, on 11 November 1941, President Roosevelt authorized lend-lease for Free France with a British transfer.

In spite of Vichy and its still functioning embassy, relations between Free France and the United States improved. On December 6, Japan attacked Pearl Harbor, destroying most of the American fleet. America then entered the war, alongside Great Britain and Free France. The Free French now expected the United States to break off diplomatic relations with Vichy, but Roosevelt didn't do this because he was still afraid that the Vichy fleet would join his enemies. From then on, for the United States, there were two Frances: that of London and Brazzaville, which fought for liberty with the British Empire, and another France, subjected to German pressure. But an event suddenly upset the newly established relations between the United States and the Free French.

General de Gaulle, who hadn't been able to land at and occupy Dakar, thought there were French territories to liberate on the American continent: Guyana, Martinique and Guadeloupe, and the Saint Pierre and Miquelon islands. He sent Admiral Muselier with a flotilla of three corvettes to liberate these latter islands. The British, the Canadians and President Roosevelt were hostile to the idea, but de Gaulle decided that, since the territories were French, he did not need authorization for this operation. Muselier landed on December 24 and was triumphantly welcomed by the population which overwhelmingly voted by 98 percent for its incorporation into Free France.

Roosevelt was furious. Cordell Hull, who had just signed an agreement with Admiral Robert, the Vichy naval commander in the Caribbean, was afraid that his appeasement policy towards Vichy would be jeopardized, since he had promised to respect the status quo of French possessions in America. Returning from vacation, Cordell Hull made a famous statement, which he probably regretted later, saying that three "so-called Free French ships" had carried through an arbitrary operation, in contradiction with the signed agreements and without informing the State Department beforehand.[5]

This serious incident could have been avoided if Tixier hadn't prevented Admiral Muselier from going to Washington before the landing and if he had transmitted telegram No. 306 of 20 December 1941 from London, informing the State Department of the operation. The French people in America were terrified, and de Gaulle's five delegates feared the deterioration of their relations with the State Department. The American press, on the other hand, took the side of Free France and attacked the "so-called Secretary of State." Cordell Hull then tried to explain that he hadn't meant to call them the "so-called Free French," but that the epithet was addressed only to "the ships." The press, however, continued to criticize him.

In London, de Gaulle refused to withdraw his men from Saint Pierre, and he resisted the pressures to do so from Churchill and the Canadians. During one of Anthony Eden's interventions, he threatened to fire on the American warships if they tried to take the islands by force. But from then on, Roosevelt's relations with de Gaulle deteriorated. Cordell Hull held a grudge and led an incessantly hostile policy against the general. When the Declaration of the United Nations was signed by 26 countries on 1 January 1942, Free France was not invited.

Under the influence of the Vichy ambassador in Washington and of the consul general in New York, a large majority of the

5. Hull, Cordell *Memoirs*. London: Hodder and Stoughton, 1948, p. 1130.

French remained faithful to Marshal Pétain. A State Department investigation found that 85 percent of the French residents did not approve of the Free French and their leader. One must add that the embassy and general consulates of Vichy were also able to keep the majority of French activities under the aegis of Pétain: The Alliance Française, the Society of the Legion of Honor, the Chamber of Commerce, and the Veterans' Association, etc.

However, a large number of French refugees were arriving in New York, and this French emigration continued until the end of 1941. Day after day, New York's shores welcomed statesmen such as Camille Chautemps, Jacques Stern, Pierre Cot, and Guy La Chambre; parliamentarians such as Henri de Kerillis, Henry Torrès, and Edouard Jonas; writers such as André Maurois, Jules Romains, Antoine de Saint Exupéry, and Gontran de Poncins; men of the theater such as Henri Bernstein, Jacques Deval, and Louis Verneuil; journalists such as Geneviève Tabouis, André Géraud, Philippe Barrès, Emile Buré, Pierre Lazareff, and Eve Curie; diplomats and military men such as Alexis Léger and General Robert Odic; musicians such as Robert Casadesus and Nadia Boulanger; academics such as Gustave Cohen, Henri Laugier, Cyrille Arnavon, Jean and Francis Perrin, and Professor Hadamard; film directors and actors such as Julien Duvivier, René Clair, Jean Renoir, Jean Gabin, Victor Francen, and Ludmilla Pitoeff; businessmen and industrialists such as Mathis and Elsa Shiaparelli; and finally, painters and engravers such as Fernand Léger, Jean Pages, Floch, and Marc Chagall.

This list is not exhaustive. Indeed, about 40,000 Frenchmen were received in the United States between 1940 and 1942. Some, such as Henri Torrès, Henry Bernstein, Eve Curie, and Philippe Barrès, declared themselves for de Gaulle, but curiously, the vast majority refused to take sides. Few of them chose Vichy, as did André Maurois. Others, like Henri de Kerillis, Antoine de Saint Exupéry, and especially Alexis Léger, while hostile to Vichy, were also relentless enemies of de Gaulle.

❖

At that point, I thought it would be possible to bring French professors and writers together to sign a manifesto against the capitulation and the subjection to Germany. Professor Faucillon and Henry Barrès were enthusiastic, but a great majority refused to sign anything that might appear to approve of General de Gaulle.

The intellectuals were all anti-Nazi and anti-Vichy, but they had many qualms about General de Gaulle and the National Committee, which they considered unconstitutional, though they knew very little about it. Feeling the precariousness of living in a foreign country, others didn't want to approve of a foreign body that wasn't recognized by the government of the United States. In the end, the manifesto was abandoned. I then had a simpler and less politically charged idea: couldn't one create a Free France University in New York?

The professors approved this idea on the condition that we find a location and some funding. The negotiations began. Alvin Johnson, president of the New School for Social Research, said he would put some offices, free of cost, at the disposal of the new university. A number of generous Frenchmen also made small donations – in reality, very small – to the new institution. The name Université de la France Libre was rejected by a majority of the professors because they didn't want to be associated with the Gaullist "movement." The word "université" worried others who thought that we didn't have the moral right to create a real university outside of France. Finally, after endless negotiations and tergiversations, they voted unanimously on the name: Ecole Libre des Hautes Etudes (The Free School of Higher Education).

The French National Committee in London then decided to give its support and a subsidy that, although it was not very large, was very useful, and some of the Belgian professors obtained stipends from the Belgian government. Although there was an extraordinary concentration of European minds at that time in New York, in some specialized areas, there was a real dearth of professors.

The statutes were first written in December 1941, as was the curriculum. Of course, creating a university of French language and civilization in New York was a considerable task. We decided that the curriculum would be shaped by the professors themselves, roughly like the classes at the College de France. Because we were at war, finding students was also a problem. In reality, there were a few French students who were preparing their *Licenses* (i.e., B.A.s) before joining in the Free France forces. Other French and foreign students found classes that didn't exist elsewhere. In the end, the French refugees and an important number of Americans of all ages registered at the school.

The school was approved by the American authorities, who thought it was important to have a union of professors who were hostile to Nazism. Nevertheless, the memories of Saint Pierre and Miquelon remained, and the American officials did not mention de Gaulle in the congratulatory addresses they gave at the opening of the school.

The relations with the State Department, the secretary of defense, and the navy continued to improve. In New York, Mayor La Guardia never missed an opportunity to express his sympathy. Nevertheless, two new problems arose that complicated relations between the Delegation of the Free French and the American administration.

The American landing of troops in North Africa on 8 November 1942 was ordered without prior warning to General de Gaulle. After having excluded General de Gaulle from the landing, the American government had counted on the popularity of General Giraud to rally the French armies in North Africa. But the officers, influenced by Vichy propaganda, opposed the American landing by force and refused to follow Giraud's orders. Mr. Murphy, one of Roosevelt's diplomatic agents, convinced General Eisenhower to appoint Admiral Darlan to the post of high commissioner of France in North Africa, which he did on November 13. One must admit that the orders given by Darlan "in the name of Marshal Pétain" were often obeyed, and the opposition to the landing generally ceased.

From London, however, General de Gaulle protested Darlan's nomination. Churchill did the same, and the American and British press took sides for de Gaulle and against Darlan, who had been an ally of Hitler and had followed an anti-Allied policy at Vichy. The vehement opposition of the New York and Washington press irritated the State Department, which accused the Delegation of the Free French of agitating public opinion. In the flood of criticism, Roosevelt was obliged to declare to American journalists that this was only a temporary arrangement, and that he would get rid of Darlan as soon as he was no longer needed. To justify this move, Roosevelt repeated an altered version of a Bulgarian, Serb, Rumanian, or Greek Orthodox proverb: "In times of great danger, one is allowed to accompany the devil to the river, until the river is crossed." The State Department, however, maintained its position, fearing that if Darlan left, the ensuing void would be filled by a de Gaulle "takeover."

Elements of Vichy's former fleet now rallied to de Gaulle and came to American ports to be repaired and re-equipped. This led to a second incident that created even more tension with the

American administration. Before Darlan rallied to the Allies, these units of the French navy had been plied with pro-Nazi and anti-Allied propaganda. To what extent did they sincerely rally to de Gaulle? Pétain's portrait was conspicuously displayed in the cabins of several officers and crewmen. Soon after the American landing in North Africa, General Giraud's delegation opened its own military bureau in a sumptuous Fifth Avenue building, not far from Free France's military bureau. The proximity of these two offices, which both solicited and recruited volunteers for the liberation of France, created numerous confusions. Some sailors were misled by the French flag and signed up by mistake with General Giraud. Some then realized their mistake, but it was impossible for the Delegation of the Free French to renegotiate for them. We advised the recruits to stay put, to continue to fight for the same liberation of one France. Giraud`s military delegation vehemently protested when a significant number of sailors left their contingent for the naval forces of the Free French. One of his ships lost 60 percent of its crew. The battleship *Richelieu*, which arrived in New York on 15 February 1943 for urgent repair and a complete refitting, lost 350 men.

The navy energetically protested and then accused the delegation of spreading propaganda among the sailors to convince them to leave their ships. Our office, however, did not do this, and as a matter of fact, the salaries were lower in the Free France naval forces. We gave neither bonuses nor special advances. Subsequently, I heard that some sailors didn't trust their officers, who had been pro-German, anti-British, anti-American, and in all cases anti-Gaullist for more than two years. The violent protests by General Giraud's representatives were widely supported by all of the French colonies that hadn't rallied to de Gaulle. Henri de Kerillis and those who had previously supported Pétain called incessantly on the American authorities to stop the scandal that was proving Free France's popularity among the sailors.

One must admit that Admiral Fénard, who was representing General Giraud, refused to make any untimely statement and tried his best not to increase the tensions between both recruitment bureaus. Nevertheless, General Giraud's delegation thought that this problem not only endangered the future of its fleet, but was taking on the appearance of a plebiscite. On 3 March 1943, he obtained the following decision from the secretary of the navy:

> The American government is of the opinion that the friction that exists between French factions imperils the war effort. [The American government] will do all that is necessary to suppress it. It should be pointed out that the United States will help with the repair of the French ships to enable them to put out to sea as soon as possible and take part in the liberation of their country. The French ships now in the ports, once rearmed, will be very useful in operations to come, and the desertions impair the usefulness of these ships.
>
> These quarrels between Frenchmen only serve to hinder the military projects of the Allies, and the United States government wants them to come to an end.
>
> The arrest of the sailors who deserted has been coordinated by the Departments of Justice and of the Navy and as of today, twelve French sailors are being detained on Ellis Island. The deserters will be considered as undesirables and will be exposed to the sanctions of the Immigration Authorities.

The Secretary of the Navy's decision was motivated by political more than by military considerations. It violated the 2 August 1941 agreement between the National Committee and the Americans, which considered the crews of the Free French naval forces docked in the United States as Allied crews with automatic residency.

The conflict over the *Richelieu* reached all the way to President Roosevelt, to whom it was falsely reported that agents from the delegation, as well as women from one of our committees went into bars to offer sailors money for rallying to de Gaulle. The president was furious about the political consequences of the sailors' change in allegiance, and bitterly accused Churchill of complicity, insofar as de Gaulle's budget came from British advances.

Admiral Stark protested to General de Gaulle in London. The latter answered that these changes of allegiance were entirely spontaneous and had profound moral causes. To avoid the immobilization of the ships, de Gaulle offered to replace some of the crews and to lend the services of others who were unemployed while their ships were being repaired.

The American press, always critical of freedom of choice violations, very rapidly took the side of the sailors.

❖

Tixier was summoned to the State Department, where he was directed to obtain a decision from London officially condemning what it called "the deserters" and ordering the bureau of recruitment to refuse the further hiring of sailors. Tixier answered that the orders from London were categorical, that one could not refuse volunteers. He asked me to guarantee the defense of the twelve sailors detained by the American courts. I then contacted a famous lawyer, Arthur Garfield Hayes, who had been president of the ACLU and who specialized in human rights cases. He considered it his duty to defend them, and refused all honorarium.

The same day, *The New York Post* sympathetically recounted how immigration agents had arrested the sailors who had left the *Richelieu*:

> At least twelve have already been sent to Ellis Island to be deported or interned. All carried papers which proved that they had joined General de Gaulle's forces.

And he repeated:

> These sailors did not trust their officers. . . . They are not deserting but want to fight under the orders of officers that they trust.

By 2 February 1943, the rest of the press, including *The New York Times* and *The New York Herald Tribune*, had printed many stories about this sensational event. On March 11, in the *Herald Tribune*, Walter Lipmann concluded in his long article that it was imprudent to give arms and war material to armed forces "whose leaders may not have the same ideology as the Americans." On March 18, in a widely noted editorial called "Why," the *Herald Tribune* sympathetically analyzed the situation of the sailors, saying that it was an issue of principle. The editorial stressed that it was important to reject the ideology of Vichy's National Revolution. The article concluded: "But it seems that, in certain milieux in Washington, General de Gaulle deserves to be punished for having been right and stubborn about it." Radio commentaries intervened quite rapidly in the debate (Johannes Steel, WMCA; Lisa Sergio, WQXR; Hans Jacob, WOR).

After Arthur Garfield Hayes' first legal steps, Francis Biddle, the attorney general, decided that no more sailors would be arrested for illegal entrance in the United States, pending the judgement of those already on Ellis Island. In essence, he was announcing that a test case would be made with those already interned.

What was the administration really looking for? The press did not fail to discover and publish it:

> If the sailors were free to leave their ship, massive resignations would ensue. Half or maybe two thirds of *Richelieu's* 1,500 men would leave. The battleship, once repaired, would not be able to sail.

The naval authorities thought that the arrest of the twelve sailors would create a sufficiently strong impression on the rest of crew to prevent them from leaving.

Finally, on 22 April 1943, an agreement was reached between General Giraud and the Delegation of the Free French that called for a commission of officers from both sides to decide which sailors would be allowed to leave their ships legally and rally to de Gaulle.

❖

The delegation's activities were impeded by the multiple conflicts and disagreements between President Roosevelt and General de Gaulle: Saint Pierre and Miquelon, the bases of Pointe Noir in Africa, New Caledonia in the Pacific, the problems that followed the American landing in North Africa and later in Normandy, and finally, the tardy recognition of the provisional government of the French Republic. Only the conflicts that directly affected the Delegation of the Free French are recounted here.

One could divide the history of those times into two periods: the first preceded the American landing in North Africa on 8 November 1942, and the second followed the rupture of diplomatic relations with Vichy. Until then, Free France had been unofficially recognized. After November 8, the duality of the French representation should have ceased, and the delegation alone recognized as representing French interests. During this second period, however, the State Department created another French authority: General Giraud and his "mission." This "mission" lasted only until General Giraud was supplanted by de Gaulle in Algiers. When Giraud resigned, the disappearance of the "Giraud mission" left the Delegation of the Free French to represent the Committee for the National Liberation of Algiers, which had succeeded the National Committee of London.

Although this committee, veritably a provisional government now solely presided over by General de Gaulle, represented all of the French residing outside of France and commanded all the armies, it still wasn't recognized by the American administration as a legitimate government. By 1943, after the scuttling of the Vichy fleet in Toulon, the United States no longer had to fear that it was being used by the Germans. Roosevelt's policy of appeasement vis-à-vis Vichy no longer had a purpose.

Under these conditions, one might have thought that the

Algiers committee would have been recognized but this was not the case. De Gaulle's triumphal welcome at Bayeux on 14 June 1944 was not enough to give him diplomatic recognition, which he received only several months later.

How could this extraordinary attitude towards de Gaulle, an ally, be explained? One can attribute it to the bad personal relations between Franklin Roosevelt and General de Gaulle, which I have dealt with at length in *Roosevelt et de Gaulle*.[6] The conflicts between the two men were nourished by the persistent hostility of the majority of the French residents in the United States towards de Gaulle and the strong influence of eminent refugees, such as Henri de Kerillis, Saint-Exupéry, and especially Alexis Léger. The latter – former ambassador and secretary of the Ministry of Foreign Affairs and a close friend of Archibald MacLeish, the President's confidant; Francis Biddle, the attorney general and a member of the presidential cabinet; Secretary of State Cordell Hull; and Deputy Secretary of State Sumner Welles – had a definite influence on Roosevelt.

On 8 November 1943, several months before the Normandy landing, Alexis Léger addressed a personal letter with abundant documentation to the president, warning him against General de Gaulle's "dictatorial" ambitions. The National Archives and those of the OSS are unfortunately quite eloquent regarding Leger's action and influence.

It was only under the pressure and the constraints of the international situation that on 23 October 1944, President Roosevelt finally recognized the provisional government of the French Republic and its president, General de Gaulle.

From then on, the Delegation of the Free French, which had lived through the diplomatic catastrophes of the war, ceased to exist. It was, naturally, transformed into the official representation of liberated France with its embassies and its consulates. One should add that the personal relations between the Free French and the American government officials were confidant and often cordial, despite the political tension and the non-recognition of Free France between 1941 and 1944. Public opinion, expressed by the press, often displayed much sympathy for Free France during the most tragic hours of her history.

6. Plon: Paris, 1984 and New York, 1987.

❖3❖

Roosevelt and De Gaulle

Robert Dallek

The only thing worse than having allies is not having them, Churchill once said. When it came to each other, Franklin Roosevelt and Charles de Gaulle were not so sure. The two greatest leaders of the United States and France in the twentieth century held clashing national and international goals that made them more antagonists than allies.

To Roosevelt, the history of French political instability during the Third Republic, military collapse under the weight of the German attack in 1940, and collaboration with Hitler signified the eclipse of French power and future influence in postwar international affairs. To de Gaulle, who became the leading spokesman for continued resistance to Germany after French defeat, Roosevelt and Secretary of State Cordell Hull were enemies of legitimate French aspirations to great-power status.

Roosevelt's antagonism to de Gaulle rested on three major considerations. First, recognition of de Gaulle as France's principal spokesman in 1940–43 would have destroyed all possibility of influencing the Vichy government. FDR believed that relations with the regime could prevent French military collaboration with Berlin. He was especially eager to keep the French fleet neutral in the fighting and French troops in North Africa from resisting the November 1942 invasion by U.S. forces. Second, a formal relationship with de Gaulle would have given legitimacy to someone many Frenchmen saw as a potential military dictator.[1] Roosevelt took the complaints of de Gaulle's French critics at face value and set him down as someone with little genuine regard for representative government. Third, support for de Gaulle

1. For tensions between French supporters and opponents of Vichy and particularly opposition to de Gaulle, see Raoul Aglion, *Roosevelt & De Gaulle: Allies in Conflict* (New York, 1988).

would have meant the restoration of France's oversea's empire. FDR saw an end to the French Empire as not only eliminating potential postwar upheaval by oppressed colonies, but also as an opportunity to project American air and sea power into Dakar and Indochina, bases he considered essential to America's postwar role as a world policeman.

Tensions between Roosevelt and de Gaulle first erupted over the occupation on 25 December 1941 of Saint Pierre and Miquelon, tiny islands off the coast of Newfoundland. By ordering Free French forces to seize the islands, de Gaulle called into question FDR's promise to Vichy of eleven days before to maintain the status quo in France's overseas possessions. Roosevelt and Hull worried – needlessly, as it turned out – that de Gaulle's action would provoke Vichy into sending its fleet to recapture the islands or join the German fleet against England. The successful Free French attack embarrassed Roosevelt and Hull by winning general approval in the American press and providing an occasion for criticism of the administration's pro-Vichy policy.[2]

The invasion of North Africa generated additional conflict between the two leaders. Roosevelt, who now saw de Gaulle as an unreliable ally, excluded him from any part in the attack. Convinced that it would defeat American efforts "to attach a large part of the French African forces to our expedition," Roosevelt assured that de Gaulle was not even informed of the invasion in advance. When American collaboration with Admiral Francois Darlan, the commander-in-chief of all Vichy forces, followed the invasion, de Gaulle and his representatives attacked American policy. At a White House meeting in which two of de Gaulle's aides insistently protested the arrangements with Darlan, Roosevelt lost his temper: "Of course I'm dealing with Darlan," he shouted, "since Darlan's giving me Algiers! Tomorrow I'd deal with Laval, if Laval were to offer me Paris![3]

The imperfect results of this policy may partly explain Roosevelt's testiness toward his critics. Although the arrangement with Darlan brought a quick halt to French resistance, saved

2. Ibid, chapter viii.

3. See William L. Langer, *Our Vichy Gamble* (New York, 1947), pp. 289–90, 295, 297–98; Forrest C. Pogue, *George C. Marshall: Ordeal and Hope, 1939–1942* (London, 1968), pp. 413–14; Francis L. Loewenheim, et al., eds., *Roosevelt and Churchill: Their Secret Wartime Correspondence* (New York, 1975), p. 252; Winston S. Churchill, *The Second World War: The Hinge of Fate* (New York, 1962), pp. 525–26; *Foreign Relations of the United States, 1942,* II (Washington, D.C., 1961), pp. 546–47; *The War Memoirs of Charles De Gaulle: Unity, 1942–1944* (New York, 1959), p. 53.

lives, and put Dakar under Allied control, it had no effect on the French fleet at Toulon, which was scuttled, and small impact on the fight for Tunisia, where the Germans quickly sent substantial forces and the French were unable to provide significant help. In addition, it left pro-Nazi Frenchmen in positions of power. Because of these developments, Churchill told Roosevelt on 9 December 1942: "not only have our enemies been thus encouraged, but our friends have been correspondingly confused and cast down." Roosevelt tried to dilute some of the effects of the Darlan deal by inviting de Gaulle to visit him in Washington at the end of December. But when Darlan was assassinated in Algiers by a young French monarchist on December 24, FDR suggested that de Gaulle postpone the meeting until there was a new arrangement in North Africa.[4]

This was one of the tasks Roosevelt and Churchill faced at their Casablanca conference in January 1943. Before he left for the meeting, Roosevelt complained to his military chiefs that the British Foreign Office was trying to organize a French government under de Gaulle, but he would continue to resist the attempt as an undemocratic imposition of a political authority on the French people. To find a way out of this "French quagmire," Roosevelt accepted Churchill's suggestion that de Gaulle be offered joint political control of French North Africa with General Henri Giraud, a man FDR described as "a rather simple-minded soldier" who had gained some notoriety by escaping from Nazi imprisonment. Since such an agreement would largely silence British and American critics of his French policy and still leave a decision on political power for the future, Roosevelt agreed.

But de Gaulle resisted. When Churchill invited him to come to Casablanca, he refused. He was reluctant to meet under Allied auspices, where he might come under pressure to compromise with Vichyites, and he was also insulted that the invitation had not come from FDR. Assurances from Churchill that he would be free of Allied pressure, and injunctions not to miss an opportunity to advance his own and Allied causes, still failed to persuade de Gaulle. Roosevelt took a certain amount of pleasure in these British difficulties with their handpicked man. "I have got the bridegroom, where is the bride?" Roosevelt cabled British For-

4. Langer, *Our Vichy Gamble*, pp. 374–81; Churchill, *Hinge of Fate*, pp. 554–60; *Foreign Relations of the U.S., 1942*, II, pp. 546, 548, 555.

eign Minister Anthony Eden in London. "The temperamental lady de Gaulle . . . is showing no intention of getting into bed with Giraud," FDR wired Hull. After Roosevelt added his name to the invitation and Churchill threatened to abandon him, de Gaulle reluctantly agreed to come.[5]

But de Gaulle was no easier to deal with in Casablanca than he had been in London. Arriving at the conference on January 22, he met in succession with Giraud, Churchill, and Roosevelt. He upbraided Giraud for agreeing "to meet in a barbed-wire encampment among foreign powers." He complained to Churchill of being surrounded by American bayonets on French territory, and responded to his description of the Anglo-American proposal for governing the French Empire as "adequate at the quite respectable level of an American sergeant." He dismissed the plan as a violation of French sovereignty that he would not support. He arrived "cold and austere" for his first meeting with the president, who complained afterward that he "found the General rigid and unresponsive to his urgent desire to get on with the war." De Gaulle saw the president as charming but imperious. "Behind his patrician mask of courtesy," he later wrote, "Roosevelt regarded me without benevolence." He "meant the peace to be an American peace, convinced that he must be the one to dictate its structure, that the states which had been overrun should be subject to his judgment, and that France in particular should recognize him as its savior and its arbiter." De Gaulle again rejected the Anglo-American plan, which Roosevelt also put before him. But "we took care not to meet head on," de Gaulle later recorded, "realizing that the clash would lead to nothing and that, for the sake of the future, we each had much to gain by getting along together."

Roosevelt was never as dictatorial and unbending as de Gaulle believed. But he was correct in thinking that Roosevelt envisaged a role for France well short of de Gaulle's ideas. In a discussion with Soviet Foreign Minister Molotov eight months before, Roosevelt had included France as one of the nations that should

5. *Foreign Relations of the United States, 1943*, II (Washington, D.C., 1962), pp. 23ff.; *Foreign Relations of the United States: Conferences at Washington, 1941–1942, and Casablanca, 1943* (Washington, D.C., 1968), pp. 513–14, 609–12, 809ff.; Robert Murphy, *Diplomat Among Warriors* (New York, 1964), pp. 169–72; Harold Macmillan, *The Blast of War, 1939–1945* (London, 1967), pp. 239–49; Anthony Eden, *The Memoirs of Anthony Eden, Earl of Avon: The Reckoning* (Boston, 1965), pp. 416–21; Churchill, *Hinge of Fate*, pp. 591–92; *War Memoirs of de Gaulle, 1942–1944*, pp. 78–84.

be disarmed after the war. When Molotov specifically asked about the re-establishment of France as a Great Power, he replied, "that might perhaps be possible within ten or twenty years." Further, he reproached Ambassador Robert Murphy at Casablanca for having given Giraud a guarantee about the return of every part of the empire to France. He also discussed with Murphy and General Dwight D. Eisenhower, the commander of American forces in North Africa, his plan to encourage extensive reductions in the French Empire. In front of Churchill and French Resident General Auguste Noguès during a dinner with the Sultan of Morocco, he pointedly sympathized with colonial aspirations for independence and discussed the possibility of postwar economic cooperation between the United States and Morocco.[6]

During the last day and a half of the conference, furious efforts by Roosevelt, Churchill, and their aides to impose an agreement on de Gaulle failed. In a meeting later described by de Gaulle as "the most ungracious" he had had with Churchill during the war, the prime minister showered him "with bitter reproaches." When Roosevelt heard that de Gaulle proposed to Giraud that he, de Gaulle, would be Clemenceau and Giraud Foch (French military chief of staff in World War I), the president exclaimed, "Yesterday he wanted to be Joan of Arc – and now he wants to be the somewhat more worldly Clemenceau." At a final meeting between the president, Churchill, and de Gaulle on the 24th, despite an "urgent plea" by Roosevelt expressed "in pretty powerful terms," de Gaulle would not agree to a communique with Giraud drawn up by Murphy and British Ambassador Harold Macmillan.

When Roosevelt, however, coupled further pressure by him and Churchill with the argument that even a show of unity would serve the needs of Allied morale, de Gaulle promised that he and Giraud would put out a communique of their own. "In human affairs," FDR said, "the public must be offered a drama. The news of your meeting with Giraud in the midst of a conference in which Churchill and I were taking part, if this news were to be accompanied by a joint declaration of the French leaders – even if it concerned only a theoretical agreement– would produce the dramatic effect we need." With that same end in view,

6. Ibid, pp. 84–89; *Foreign Relations of the U.S.: Conferences at Washington and Casablanca*, pp. 692–96; *Foreign Relations of the United States, 1942*, III, (Washington, D.C., 1962), pp. 568–69; Robert Sherwood, *Roosevelt and Hopkins* (New York, 1950), p. 685; Murphy, *Diplomat Among Warriors*, pp. 168, 172–73.

de Gaulle also agreed to shake hands with Giraud before press photographers. For all their differences, de Gaulle shared Roosevelt's belief in the need for at least a show of unity against the common enemy.[7]

On his return to the United States, Roosevelt left little doubt among his intimates about his feelings. During his first week back in Washington, he asked Hull to convey his "annoyance" to Eden "at the continued propaganda emanating from de Gaulle headquarters in London." He labeled the Free French attitude "a continuing irritant," and asked that steps be taken "to allay the irritation." At the same time, Roosevelt also began telling the apocryphal story that de Gaulle compared himself to Joan of Arc and Clemenceau, and that he had urged de Gaulle to choose one or the other, since he could not be like both of them. At a meeting with the American Society of Newspaper Editors, he further vented his annoyance by describing how he had tricked de Gaulle into shaking hands with Giraud. "If you run into a copy of the picture," he said with obvious amusement, "look at the expression on de Gaulle's face!" He had no intention, he also said, of satisfying de Gaulle's desire to be recognized as the "spirit" or "soul" of France. Decisions about French rule, he firmly declared, must wait until the people of France can have their say. Clearly, after Casablanca, Roosevelt saw the French political problem as still very much alive.[8]

The aftermath of Casablanca was continuing conflict between Churchill, Roosevelt, and de Gaulle over who should control French forces and speak for France during the war. De Gaulle's efforts to assume both roles, subordinate Giraud to a secondary position, and remove the Vichyite governor general of West Africa moved Roosevelt to tell Churchill that he was "fed up" with de Gaulle and "absolutely convinced that he has been and is injuring our war effort . . . that he is a very dangerous threat to us

7. *War Memoirs of de Gaulle, 1942–1944*, pp. 89–95; Murphy, *Diplomat Among Warriors*, pp. 173–75; Macmillan, *Blast of War, 1939–1945*, pp. 249–54; *Foreign Relations of the U.S.: Conferences at Washington and Casablanca*, pp. 705–7, 722–25, 822–23; Sherwood, *Roosevelt and Hopkins*, pp. 691–93.

8. *Foreign Relations of the U.S.: Conferences at Washington and Casablanca*, pp. 823–28; *Foreign Relations of the U.S., 1943*, II, pp. 47–51; Sherwood, *Roosevelt and Hopkins*, p. 868; Cordell Hull, *The Memoirs of Cordell Hull*, II (New York, 1948), pp. 1207–10; Samuel I. Rosenmen, ed., *The Public Papers and Addresses of Franklin D. Roosevelt: 1943*, (New York, 1950), pp. 83–86; for a different view of Roosevelt's understanding of French affairs after Casablanca, see Murphy, *Diplomat Among Warriors*, pp. 175–76; and Macmillan, *Blast of War, 1939–1945*, pp. 254–55.

. . . and that he would double-cross both of us at the first opportunity." Churchill rejected Roosevelt's suggestion that they "break" with de Gaulle, and de Gaulle himself avoided a showdown with the president by agreeing to have Giraud command French forces in North and West Africa while he controlled all forces in the rest of the empire.[9]

A debate over whether to recognize de Gaulle's French Committee of National Liberation succeeded the argument over who should control French forces. At the Quebec conference in August 1943, when neither Churchill nor Roosevelt could agree on a common formula for dealing with the committee, they issued separate statements. While both welcomed the establishment of the committee as a vehicle for fighting the war, which both also described as of "paramount" concern, they diverged sharply on the measure of recognition each would accord. The American declaration explicitly ruled out recognition "of a government of France or the French Empire," and limited its acceptance of the committee to the administration of "those French overseas territories which acknowledge its authority" and to functions "within specific limitations during the war." By contrast, the British said nothing about the committee as a government of France or the empire, and specifically acknowledged it "as the body qualified to ensure the conduct of the French effort in the war within the framework of inter-allied cooperation." Other differences in wording suggested that the British were more confident of the committee's determination to cooperate in the fighting and more receptive to having it become a full-blown ally. For Roosevelt and the State Department, full recognition would have meant encouraging the possibility of a postwar dictatorship in France and undermining prospects for postwar American influence in Dakar and Indochina, which Roosevelt continued to see as essential to future security in the Americas and Asia. For the British, who appreciated that de Gaulle had wider French support than Roosevelt believed and saw de Gaulle as an indispensable symbol of French resistance and a potential ally against postwar Soviet expansion in Europe, acceptance of

9. *Foreign Relations of the U.S., 1943*, II, pp. 110ff.; FDR to Eisenhower, 17 June 1943, Map Room Papers, Franklin D. Roosevelt Library, Hyde Park, New York; *Foreign Relations of the United States: Conferences at Washington and Quebec, 1943* (Washington, D.C., 1970), p. 324; Arthur L. Funk, *Charles De Gaulle: The Crucial Years, 1943–1944* (Norman, OK, 1959), pp. 116–45; *Roosevelt and Churchill: Secret Wartime Correspondence*, pp. 344–47.

the committee conformed with their immediate and long-term national interests.[10]

Events in the year following the Quebec meeting deepened the antagonism between Roosevelt and de Gaulle. In the fall of 1943, de Gaulle forced Giraud out of the National Committee and responded to Lebanese demands for independence by suspending their constitution, dismissing their parliament, and imprisoning their ministers. "The general attitude of the Committee and especially de Gaulle," Roosevelt told Hull, "is shown in the Lebanon affair. De Gaulle is now claiming the right to speak for all of France and is talking openly about how he intends to set up his government in France as soon as the Allies get in there." In December, the arrest of three prominent Vichyites, who had aided the Allied attack in North Africa, further convinced Roosevelt that de Gaulle's committee intended to impose itself upon France without regard for the popular will or the risk of civil war.[11]

During the first half of 1944, arguments that de Gaulle spoke for most of France and that recognition of his committee as the provisional government would serve the cross-Channel attack left FDR unmoved. He refused to believe that "there are only two major groups in France today – the Vichy gang, and the other characterized by unreasoning admiration for de Gaulle." Nor did FDR believe that the OVERLORD attack depended on accepting de Gaulle as the provisional ruler of France. "I am in complete agreement with you that the French National Spirit should be working with us in OVERLORD to prevent unnecessary loss of American and British lives," he cabled Churchill ten days before the attack. But "at the present time I am unable to see how an Allied establishment of the Committee as a Government of France would save the lives of any of our men." After all, he told Churchill in a follow-up message, "we do not know definitely

10. *Ibid.*; *Foreign Relations of the U.S., 1943*, II, pp. 160–62, 171–77, 181–84; FDR to Churchill, 8 July 1943; FDR to Eisenhower and Murphy, 8 July 1943, Map Room Papers, FDRL; *Foreign Relations of the U.S.: Conferences at Washington and Quebec, 1943*, pp. 661–71, 916–17, 919–20, 934, 953, 1101–11, 1169–71; Eden, *The Reckoning*, pp. 466–68; Hull, *Memoirs*, II, pp. 1232–33, 1241–42; Winston S. Churchill, *The Second World War: Closing the Ring* (New York, 1962), pp. 77, 80.

11. Funk, *De Gaulle: Crucial Years, 1943–1944*, pp. 191–98; Milton Viorst, *Hostile Allies: FDR and De Gaulle* (New York, 1965), pp. 181–82, 186–87; *Foreign Relations of the United States: Conferences at Cairo and Tehran, 1943* (Washington, D.C., 1961), pp. 189–90; *Foreign Relations of the U.S., 1943*, II, pp. 193–200; Elliott Roosevelt, ed., *F.D.R.: His Personal Letters, 1928–1945* (New York, 1947–1950), II, pp. 1473–74.

what the state of that French spirit is and we will not know until we get to France." Also, "as a matter of practical fact," they would not be calling on "French military strength" to help OVERLORD until well after D-Day or the invasion of southern France. As for the argument that they needed de Gaulle's full cooperation to assure easy control of occupied France, Roosevelt dismissed it as an effort to "stampede us into according full recognition of the *Comité*." Specifically, de Gaulle's refusal to endorse Allied military francs as a legitimate currency unless they agreed to issue them in the name of his provisional government impressed Roosevelt as an empty threat. "I would certainly not importune de Gaulle to make any supporting statement whatever regarding the currency," he advised Churchill. "Provided it is clear that he acts entirely on his own responsibility . . . he can sign any statement on currency in whatever capacity he likes, even that of the King of Siam."[12]

Although Roosevelt insisted that it was "utter nonsense" to describe his behavior toward de Gaulle as animated by personal dislike, it is difficult to discount this as a contributing factor. "I am perfectly willing to have de Gaulle made President, or Emperor, or King or anything else," he told General Marshall, "so long as the action comes in an untrammeled and unforced way from the French people themselves." Yet other FDR comments on de Gaulle belie these words. "The only thing I am interested in," he told Under Secretary of State Edward R. Stettinius, Jr. in May, "is not having de Gaulle and the National Committee named as the government of France." He expected no cooperation from de Gaulle, he advised Churchill in June. "It seems clear that prima donnas do not change their spots." He would not now permit that "'jackenape' to seize the government," he told Secretary of War Henry Stimson ten days after the Allies landed in France.

Animus toward de Gaulle was not limited to FDR. The general provoked other Americans as well. Stimson said that Hull "hated de Gaulle so fiercely that he was almost incoherent on the

12. FDR to Marshall, 2 June 1944, President's Secretary's File: Safe: Marshall; FDR to Elmer Davis, June 1, 1944, PSF:OWI, FDRL; *Foreign Relations of the United States, 1944,* III (Washington, D.C., 1965), pp. 683, 692–94, 707–708; FDR to Eisenhower, 12 May 1944; Churchill to FDR, May 12, 26, 27, 28, June 7, 9, 1944; FDR to Churchill, June 9, 12, 1944, all in MRP, FDRL; Funk, *De Gaulle: Crucial Years, 1943–1944,* pp. 217–26, 237ff.; Viorst, *Hostile Allies,* pp. 189–201; John M. Blum, *From the Morgenthau Diaries: Years of War, 1941–1945* (Boston, 1967), pp. 165–77.

subject." De Gaulle's refusal to broadcast his support of the invasion as it began, to endorse the supplemental currency, or to send more than a handful of French liaison officers with the invading forces put Marshall in a "white fury." If the American public learned what de Gaulle had been doing to hamper the invasion, Marshall declared, it would demand a break with the French National Committee.[13]

Roosevelt's desire to assure popular control in France and his personal antagonism only partly explain his opposition to de Gaulle in 1944. More than ever at that time, there were postwar considerations. Civil strife in France, which FDR believed a likely consequence of de Gaulle's assumption of power, would create not only instability in Europe but also American reluctance to take a meaningful part in European affairs. As important, de Gaulle's control of France would block Roosevelt's plan to abolish the French colonial empire and place some of its strategically located colonies under United Nations control. More specifically, it would play havoc with FDR's plans for Dakar in West Africa and French Indochina. "Dakar is of such vital importance to the protection of the South Atlantic and South America," FDR had advised Eisenhower in June 1943, "that I should be compelled to send American troops there if any problematical changes were sought by de Gaulle." Likewise, Roosevelt wished to convert Indochina into a strategic base that the United Nations, and the United States in particular, would use to keep the postwar peace.[14]

In July 1944, despite his antagonism to de Gaulle, Roosevelt felt compelled to invite him to the United States. Fearful that his continued refusal to accord de Gaulle a fuller measure of recognition might deprive Anglo-American forces of help from the Resistance and jeopardize the use of French divisions in the assault on southern France, Roosevelt agreed to have him visit Washington. In three lengthy conversations with de Gaulle during four days, Roosevelt avoided all references to immediate issues, talking instead about long-term political goals. He sketched his plans in "light touches . . . and so skillfully," de

13. FDR to Marshall, 2 June 1944, PSF: Safe: Marshall, FDRL; Edward R. Stettinius, Jr., MS. Diary, 8 May 1944, University of Virginia Library, Charlottesville, VA; *Foreign Relations of the U.S., 1944*, III, pp. 707–8; Blum, *From the Morgenthau Diaries, 1941–1945*, pp. 173–74.

14. See Robert Dallek, *Franklin D. Roosevelt and American Foreign Policy, 1932–1945* (New York, 1979), pp. 459–61.

Gaulle recorded in his memoirs, "that it was difficult to contradict this artist, this seducer, in any categorical way."

Nevertheless, Roosevelt made it clear to de Gaulle that France was not to share in the postwar responsibilities assigned to the Big Four (Britain, China, Russia, and the United States), that she was to lose her overseas empire, and that some French territory would have to serve as United Nations bases under American military control. Though de Gaulle argued against the president's conception of France's postwar role, he appreciated that he had no impact on FDR. "To regain her place," he told FDR at the close of their talks, "France must count only on herself. 'It is true,'" the president replied, "'that to serve France no one can replace the French people.'" Roosevelt's only concession to de Gaulle during this visit was to recognize de Gaulle's National Committee as the "temporary *de facto* authority for civil administration in France."[15]

By February 1945, however, Roosevelt concluded that he had no choice but to give de Gaulle and France a larger say in postwar affairs. By the time of the Yalta conference, Roosevelt was convinced that the United States Congress and public would support "reasonable measures to safeguard the future peace but . . . this would [not] extend to the maintenance of an appreciable American force in Europe" for more than two years. To help fill the power vacuum an American withdrawal would leave in controlling Germany, Roosevelt now agreed to arm eight more French divisions and to create a German occupation zone for France. Although he had rejected de Gaulle's request to share in the discussions at Yalta, he felt compelled to make France a member of the Control Council for Germany.[16]

The full extent of Roosevelt's shift in attitude toward de Gaulle and France showed itself in his changing policy toward Indochina in March, a month before his death. Now convinced that de Gaulle had a legitimate hold on the French people, that antagonism to an open-ended involvement in European affairs would

15. Henry L. Stimson and McGeorge Bundy, *On Active Service in Peace and War* (New York, 1948), pp. 550–51; de Gaulle, *Memoirs, 1942–1944*, pp. 265–72; *Foreign Relations of the U.S., 1944*, III, pp. 693–94, 713, 718–19, 723–24; Viorst, *Hostile Allies*, pp. 207–9.

16. *Foreign Relations of the United States: Conferences at Malta and Yalta, 1945* (Washington, D.C., 1955), pp. 572–73, 611–19, 283ff., 899–900; *Foreign Relations of the U.S., 1944*, III, pp. 739–48; W. Averell Harriman and Elie Abel, *Special Envoy to Churchill and Stalin, 1941–1946* (New York, 1975), pp. 401–2.

force a greater reliance on French power to keep the peace, and that Chinese internal instability would make it impossible for Chiang Kai-shek's government to help the United States administer Indochina, Roosevelt agreed to the restoration of French control in Southeast Asia. In mid-March 1945, when de Gaulle asked for American help for French resistance to a full-scale Japanese takeover in Indochina, Roosevelt told an aide that he would agree to a French trusteeship there if ultimate independence were promised. On March 16, the American ambassador to France told FDR that de Gaulle had coupled a plea for American help to French forces in Indochina with a warning that a failure to help restore French power would force her to become "one of the federated states under the Russian aegis. . . . When Germany falls," de Gaulle said, "they will be on us. . . . We do not want to become Communists; we do not want to fall into the Russian orbit but we hope you do not push us into it." Two days later, Roosevelt ordered American air forces to aid the French in Indochina on the condition that such action not interfere with operations against Japan.[17]

Although Roosevelt's realism in the closing days of his life and the European war led him to alter his policy toward France, the tensions between the president and de Gaulle continued to have echoes in postwar French policy toward the United States long after FDR had passed from the scene. The political contest of wills between the two men grew out of circumstances, clashing conceptions of national and international needs, and personal rancor. Yet in spite of their difficulties, they both made compromises that allowed the larger common purposes of Nazi defeat and postwar cooperation against Communist advance to hold first priority in what they did. If Roosevelt and de Gaulle were allies in spite of themselves, it was nevertheless their alliance of a kind, to paraphrase the British historian Christopher Thorne, rather than their antagonism that was most important in shaping great historical events.

17. See Dallek, *FDR and American Foreign Policy, 1932–1945*, pp. 511–13.

❖4❖

The United States and the Free French

Kim Munholland

Although a definitive history of the Free French movement remains to be written, there is an extensive literature on relations between the United States and General de Gaulle's movement. A great deal of effort has gone into determining why the Americans and the Free French, both committed to the defeat of Nazi Germany and the liberation of France and the rest of Europe, should have experienced such a difficult and frequently acrimonious relationship during World War II. Explanations often focus on Roosevelt's personal dislike and distrust of de Gaulle, an attitude that was reinforced by officials in the State Department and by French exiles in the United States, such as Alexis Léger, who considered the Free French movement to be an instrument for de Gaulle's personal power. On the other hand, de Gaulle from the outset feared American intentions to impose its own peace terms at the end of the conflict without regard for French interests. Behind Roosevelt's lofty phrases, de Gaulle detected the sound of American hegemony. The result was a profound distrust and mutual suspicion that led to repeated misunderstandings. These personal differences appear in the many biographies of both leaders and in the general accounts of wartime diplomacy. One author has aptly described the relationship as one of "hostile allies."[1]

American differences with the Free French also stemmed from policy issues. The American persistence in its "Vichy gamble" and subsequent search for an alternative to de Gaulle in dealing with wartime France has elicited a literature that is also marked by a great deal of vehemence, either in defense or in criticism of

1. Milton Viorst, *Hostile Allies: FDR and Charles de Gaulle* (NY: Macmillan, 1965).

American policy.[2] More recent studies have focused on the misconceptions that Americans held of France, particularly in public opinion, or have described the relationship as marked by as much illusion as reality.[3]

This paper does not intend to revisit these animosities and disputes of high politics, but rather will look at the way in which Americans at a somewhat lower, or "intermediate," level, those who had direct and frequent opportunities to deal with the Free French on a regular basis, responded to the Free French movement and came to argue for an accommodation to it. These contacts reflected some of the broader issues and differences that marked U.S.-Free French relations during the war, but they also showed the way in which American official opinion progressed from early skepticism about de Gaulle and the Free French to an eventual acknowledgment of de Gaulle as the representative of French interests and spokesman for a revived France. It was not only the "liberal press" or "Republican isolationist" opponents of the New Deal who provided criticisms of American policies toward the Free French; pressure for a better understanding of the Free French came from Americans at a secondary, or what might be described as an operational, level of this connection. Relations were never easy, but American officials, particularly American military representatives who had to deal with the Free French on a regular basis, developed a pragmatic attitude toward General de Gaulle and his movement that tried to overcome the deep, official hostility that persisted at the higher levels of government. The evolution of these views of the Free French movement revealed certain perceptions of France on the part of the Americans that differed from General de Gaulle's "certain idea of

2. The first shot in this "historians' dispute" was the publication of William L. Langer's *Our Vichy Gamble* [New York: Knopf, 1947], a study that was undertaken at the request of Cordell Hull. See, Langer to Hull, 17/4/44, U.S. National Archives and Records Administration [NARA], State Department Decimal File [State Dec File], 851.00/3187. Langer had access to still unclassified documents, and he claimed that there were no pressures for him to reach a prescribed judgment. Generally, Langer's analysis is accurate and fair until the conclusion, where he denounces the soft-headed "idealism" of those who had the temerity to question America's realistic policy toward Vichy. The reply came in a review of Langer's book by another historian who specialized in French history, Louis Gottschalk, "Our Vichy Fumble," *Journal of Modern History*, vol. 20, no. 1 [March 1948]: 47–56.

3. Julian Hurstfield, *America and the French Nation 1939–1945* [Chapel Hill: UNC Press, 1986], and Henry Blumenthal, *Illusion and Reality in Franco-American Diplomacy 1914–1945* [Baton Rouge: Louisiana State University Press, 1986].

France," but they came to see in de Gaulle the only realistic alternative to upheaval in France at the time of liberation.

When France suffered military defeat in 1940, the event came as a shock to informed opinion in the United States, which assumed that the French army was strong enough to hold German panzers in the north and could count on the impregnability of the Maginot Line. The sudden defeat brought the reality of the European war across the Atlantic. If the French Empire fell into German hands, the security of America's isolation in the Western Hemisphere was no longer assured. Dakar lay only 1500 miles from South America, where it was believed German agents were active. The collapse of France increased the exposure of the Western Hemisphere to fascist penetration. The State Department asked its consuls in French colonial territories to report any tendency of French troops to continue the war. The reports from Africa noted an initial confusion and uncertainty; the Belgian governor of the Congo sent an appeal to all French governors, urging them to join in an African bloc of colonial territories to carry on the war, whatever the actions taken by the Bordeaux government, but this appeal had no immediate sequel.[4] The Australian minister in Washington reported news from the other end of the globe in which the Administrative Council in New Caledonia had passed a resolution giving its support to the French National Committee in London, and he asked if the U.S. Government would consider including French possessions in a declaration favoring maintenance of the status quo in the Pacific.[5] In the meantime, as all French colonies and overseas possessions initially seemed to accept the authority of Vichy during the summer of 1940, the American government showed little further interest in signs of resistance and recognized Pétain as the successor to the now fallen Third Republic. France had fallen from republican grace, and the American "Vichy gamble" to keep the French fleet and empire from German hands had begun. No notice was given to de Gaulle's appeal of 18 June 1940.

While the French defeat had come as a shock, it also seemed to confirm certain American opinions about French "decadence" and internal weaknesses of the political system as fundamental

4. State to consuls, 24 June 1940 and replies of 25 June 1940, NARA, State Dec File, 740.0011EW1939/4174,5,6, and *Foreign Relations of the United States*, [FRUS], 1940, vol. 11: 636–38.

5. Memorandum, 27 June 1940, NARA, State Dec. File 851.01/73.

explanations for the collapse.[6] Although studies of France published in the United States before the war expressed admiration for democratic values and a strong sense of individual rights, other studies, such as John Gunther's popular *Inside Europe*, described French politics as the "reducto ad absurdum" of democracy.[7] For some, the French appeared unable to adapt to a modern, industrial order with the same organizational skills and discipline that marked the achievements of the British or the Germans or the Americans. Somehow, the French people, while still capable of impressive cultural achievements, had not kept pace with the economic or technological developments of the modern industrial order.[8] Such views were reinforced by the comparative character studies of André Siegfried, a frequent visitor to the United States, who praised a France that remained loyal to pre-industrial ideals and values and whose workers refused to become blind servants of machines. The Third Republic was the France of the artisan, of the peasant still in touch with the land, and of the good, republican citizen of Alain, rightly suspicious of authority or any tendency toward Bonapartism and dictatorship.[9] It was this democratic, republican, individualistic, but internally divided France that had gone down to defeat; yet it was presumed that this same democratic France would be restored whenever Hitler was defeated and France liberated. In the meantime, American policy turned to preventing the French fleet from being taken over by the Nazi government.

American interest in the Free French movement revived with the rallies of French colonies in Africa and the Pacific. From Leopoldville and Lagos, the American consuls provided details of the way in which Chad and the other territories of French Equatorial Africa joined the Free French cause.[10] The consul in Leopoldville was positive in his reporting of these events, noting that "the change of Government and declaration for de Gaulle were greeted with great enthusiasm on both sides of the Congo

6. The "causes" of France's 1940 defeat have been extensively debated. The American reaction at the time has been recently analyzed by Julian G. Hurstfield, *America and the French Nation*, ch. 2, "American Attitudes toward France in 1940," *passim*.

7. John Gunther, *Inside Europe* [New York: Harper & Brothers, 1940 ed.]: 182, 187.

8. John B. Wold, *France, 1815 to the Present* [New York: Prentice-Hall, 1940]: 547.

9. See André Siegfried, *France: A Study in Nationality* [New Haven: Yale University Press, 1930], *passim*.

10. FRUS 1940, vol. 11: 636–45.

River."[11] For events in the Pacific, the American minister to Australia, C. E. Gauss, kept the State Department informed of the rally and referendum in Tahiti on 3 September 1940 that committed that colony to a continuation of the war effort alongside the British Commonwealth, and he provided accurate and detailed accounts of the dramatic events that brought New Caledonia into the Free French camp on September 10.[12]

At the same time, the failure of the Anglo-French effort to rally French West Africa at Dakar had a negative impact on American views of the Free French movement, which now appeared to be no more than an inept tool of British strategy. Indeed, the Americans feared that the Dakar failure and the successful resistance of Vichy forces to the Anglo-French attack had simply increased the possibility of German penetration into French West Africa. Even more, British and American newspapers ridiculed the folly of the Dakar attempt and blamed de Gaulle for its conception and its failure. De Gaulle bitterly commented upon the "tempest of anger" in London and "a hurricane of sarcasms" in Washington that were unleashed against him.[13] As part of the postmortem on the Dakar fiasco, reports of sloppy security, in which Free French officers had toasted the success of the Dakar mission at a London restaurant before departing Great Britain, reached the United States. The legacy of Dakar was to be a long one in Allied wartime relations, since the Americans were now convinced that the Free French could not be trusted, particularly if there should ever be an attempt to bring the French territories in West and North Africa back into the war.

Anglo-American doubts about the Free French only strengthened de Gaulle's resolve to continue, and he was further heartened by his reception in Equatorial Africa, where a cheering crowd gave him a heroic welcome. He arrived in the colonial town of Duala to be overwhelmed, as he later put it, by the sight of French civil servants, colonists, Black African leaders, and officers and troops of the colonial forces, "swimming in a full tide of patriotic euphoria." The reception at Duala strengthened his sense of pride and his conviction that he embodied the basic interests of France; henceforth, in his behavior, actions, and com-

11. Leopoldville to State, 25 September 1940, State Dec File 740.0011EW/6273.

12. Gauss to State, 21 and 28 August 1940, 3, 9, 14 and 19 September 1940, NARA State Dec Files, 851L.00/02, 05, and 740.0011EW 1939/5586, 5819.

13. Charles de Gaulle, *Mémoires de Guerre*, vol. 1: *L'Appel, 1940–1942* [Paris: Plon, 1954]: 108.

portment, he had constantly to project an image of eternal France and his image as the bearer of a sacred trust. "The fact of embodying for my comrades the destiny of our cause, for the French masses the symbol of their hope, for foreigners the image of an indomitable France amidst its ordeals," he wrote, "was to dictate my bearing and impose upon my personality an attitude that I could never again change."[14] This African experience stiffened de Gaulle in both his determination to continue the struggle and in a pattern of behavior that would lead to further frictions with his Allies. His determination to never relax and to be constantly aware and vigilant toward the interests of France became a source of bewilderment, particularly for Americans, who had difficulty understanding how an individual could embody a nation.[15] In the American political tradition, the fundamental source of nationhood was not an individual, but a document, the constitution, and American presidents were sworn to uphold a legal instrument that had almost as much symbolic, even mystical, importance and resonance as the concept "France" did for de Gaulle.

Greatly bolstered by his experience in Free French Africa, de Gaulle prepared for further action, notably plans to bring Gabon into the Free French ranks, which was accomplished in early November. He also initiated preparations for a military operation against Italian forces in Libya, and he organized military units that would fight alongside British forces in Ethiopia and Egypt in the spring of 1941. But a decisive step toward the formation of the Free French into a political organization that could represent national interests came with his Brazzaville manifesto on 27 October 1940.

De Gaulle had returned to Brazzaville from an inspection tour of Free French territories on 24 October 1940, the day Pétain had met with Hitler at Montoire to discuss terms of Franco-German relations. At the same time, he received reports of contacts between British diplomats and Vichy representatives in Madrid. Out of a fear that the British might deal with Vichy to obtain further guarantees of the neutrality of the French Empire, de Gaulle decided that the moment had come to claim formal legitimacy

14. Ibid: 111.

15. This attitude was later expressed by A. A. Berle, the assistant secretary of state, who paid hommage to the "individual heroism" of de Gaulle, but then noted, "we have always recognized that France was bigger than any one man." Memorandum, 1 July 1943, NARA State Dec File 851.01/2352/

for Free France in representing French interests, particularly in the parts of the empire that had rallied. With Montoire in mind and with fears that British support might waver, de Gaulle made his Brazzaville manifesto, which "would deny legitimacy to Vichy, would constitute myself the trustee of French interests, [and] would exercise in the liberated territories the attributes of a government."[16] The instrument for Free French administration was to be the Empire Defense Council, which became the first governing body for the Free French movement and undertook to exercise "provisional power" in the name of the French Republic. Various leaders who were in London or were serving as governors of territories that had rallied composed the council.[17] The establishment of the Empire Defense Council was the first official, political action [ordinance one] of the Free French.

To further escape the shadow of British sponsorship, which Vichy propaganda used to try to discredit his movement, de Gaulle initiated a first contact with the United States. On October 26, he informed the American consul in Brazzaville that a Council for the Defense of the French empire was being created as of the next day, and that this organization would assume the powers "that belonged to the last Free French government" and undertake the administration of all territories that had refused the armistice. In this message, de Gaulle offered to administer French territories in the Western Hemisphere that might have to be occupied by the United States; the council would provide Free French forces for their defense and would make bases available to the Americans on French soil without, he noted, asking for destroyers as compensation. He warned that any occupation of French territory unilaterally "would cause profound grief to all Frenchmen."[18] The American consul forwarded the message, but there was no response from Washington. Throughout the rallies, Washington had warned the consuls abroad to avoid raising any questions of principle with the de Gaulle committee. The American attitude toward the rally of French African and Pacific terri-

16. De Gaulle, *Mémoires*, vol. 1: 119.

17. Members of the council were General Catroux, de Gaulle's emissary to the Middle East in Cairo; René Cassin, Captain Thierry d'Argenlieu, and Admiral Muselier in London; Félix Eboué, governor of Chad; General de Larminat, governor general of French Equatorial Africa, and General Medical Officer Adolphe Sicé in Brazzaville; General Leclerc, governor of the Cameroons; and, finally, high commissioner for the Pacific, Governor Sautot in Noumea.

18. Leopoldville to State, 27 October 1940, FRUS 1940, vol. II, pp. 504–5.

tories to the Free French movement, and now the formation of the Empire Defense Council, was officially "non-committal."

Although there was no official American response to de Gaulle's offer to provide administration of French territories in the Western Hemisphere, the presence in Martinique of a French naval force, including an aircraft carrier and 26 American aircraft that had been purchased and were on the way to France at the time of the armistice, focused American interest on the status of these possessions. A great deal of diplomatic activity took place in the summer and fall of 1940 over the issue of Martinique and its potential threat to the security of the United States. This culminated in a conversation and informal agreement between Admiral Greenslade of the U.S. Navy and Admiral Robert, the French governor for Martinique and Guadeloupe, which provided for a neutralization of the aircraft and required notification of any movement of French naval forces.

Negotiations between the local Vichy French authority, Admiral Robert, and an American naval representative were considered harmful to Free France. From the perspective of the Free French, these negotiations meant connivance with Vichy, and they also meant a neutralization of the French Empire, which eroded the spirit of resistance embodied in the Free French movement. The American tendency to deal with local officials and not Free France came to be seen as a more or less deliberate attempt to exploit French weakness and deny the Free French claim to represent a continuation of the wartime alliance with Great Britain and therefore be entitled to a place at the peace table. The issue of local arrangements in Martinique and elsewhere provided an ongoing source of difference and friction between Americans and the Free French.

Little notice was taken of de Gaulle or the Free French movement during the winter of 1940–41, as American representatives continued to deal with Vichy in matters relating to French overseas territories that had not rallied to Free France. Then in the spring of 1941, interest in the Free French movement again revived over concern about the status of Free French territories in Equatorial Africa and the Pacific. American representatives overseas, notably Anthony Drexel Biddle, now American ambassador to the European governments-in-exile in London, suggested that serious attention be given to the Free French and what they might offer. In March, Biddle reported that he had been approached "discreetly" by members of the de Gaulle movement.[19] He described these individuals, whom he had encountered in Tours and Bordeaux in 1940, as "serious, loyal Frenchmen." Shortly afterward, Biddle received a report from an American journalist, Ben Lucien Burman, whom he had met on board a transatlantic flight and had asked to provide some information on the de Gaulle movement in Equatorial Africa. Burman's report was enthusiastic. The Free French in Africa were endowed with a magnificent spirit, like early American patriots. "They represent every quality cherished by Americans." They had refused to accept defeat and at great personal sacrifice had made their way to Africa to continue the struggle. Burman urged that they be given assistance in all forms, including arms and aircraft, and that some formula be found to establish an official contact so that they would be assured that the United States supported them. He noted the strategic importance of the African territories controlled by the Free French, but the most important consideration was that support for the de Gaulle movement would help in "re-building the morale of defeated French people throughout the world."[20] In this early American image, the Free French appeared to be patriotic republicans who had spontaneously chosen to defend their freedom against the forces of tyranny. In his covering letter to FDR, Biddle endorsed Burman's views of the Free French.[21]

A few days later, Biddle had a conversation with René Pleven, who was soon to depart for Washington. Pleven gave Biddle two memoranda, one on "The German Threat to French Africa" and the other from de Gaulle that restated his willingness to cooperate with the United States should an American occupation of portions of the French Empire be contemplated, with proviso that French sovereignty and integrity be assured through a Free French administration of those territories.[22] In his covering letters

19. René Pleven assumed responsibility for making such contacts. In a telegram to de Gaulle in Brazzaville, he stated that the Free French committee was making "great propaganda efforts" with the two ambassadors, Winant and Biddle, and with American correspondents in London. See Pleven to de Gaulle, 16 May 1941, Archives Nationales [AN], Papiers Cassin, 382 AP52.

20. Burman to Biddle, 10 May 1941, British Public Record Office, Kew [PRO], F.O. 371/28320. Several years later, Burman published an account of his tour through Free French Africa. Ben Lucien Burman, *The Generals Wear Cork Hats* [New York: Taplinger, 1963].

21. Biddle to FDR, 9 May 1941, FDR Library and Archive, Hyde Park, N.Y., President's Secretary's File [PSF], Diplomatic, Box 34.

22. De Gaulle gave a fuller version of this memo to the American minister in Cairo, Alexander Kirk. Kirk to Secretary of State, 8 June 1941, FRUS 1941, vol. 2, pp. 570–72.

to Washington, Biddle summarized Pleven's argument for de Gaulle. The American ambassador noted the strategic value of those French territories under Free French control, the importance of bringing them back into the war, the significance of an independent Free French administration to offset Vichy propaganda that claimed de Gaulle was opening the way for a British seizure of the French Empire, and de Gaulle's determination to act as "trustee" of all rallied territories until such time as the French people could express their wishes freely.

Biddle placed great hopes in the Pleven mission. In his letter to Roosevelt, Biddle stated that Pleven sought "some gesture of sympathy and understanding" in Washington. Citing his early acquaintance with Pleven, Biddle praised him as "a serious, sincere, courageous and intelligent patriot." The British Foreign Office hoped that Pleven might overcome the State Department's reservations about de Gaulle and gain recognition. A memorandum that supported Pleven's efforts argued, "it should be possible to persuade the State Department that it is now time to come out wholeheartedly for de Gaulle, and cut the painter with Vichy."[23]

These assurances fell on deaf ears. Roosevelt responded laconically to Biddle, "Frankly, I think it probably would be difficult for me to see Mr. Pleven" during his stay in Washington. All that was conceded was that Sumner Welles would have a representative of the State Department meet with Pleven.[24] The State Department and Roosevelt stuck to the Vichy gamble, unable to contemplate a "two track" diplomacy. Although de Gaulle's representative was able to sort out quarrels among Free French supporters in the United States, Pleven failed to move the American government any closer toward a measure of recognition or even acceptance of the Free French movement. When Welles received Pleven, the reception was reserved, and Welles explicitly rejected a proposal to provide lend-lease assistance to the Free French. Thus, attempts by Biddle to create a favorable image and win some understanding or acceptance for the Free French were no more successful than the Pleven mission itself.

American interests in the Free French also extended to the Pacific as tension with Japan increased during the winter of 1940-

23. "U.S. Relations with Free French Colonies," 22 May 1941, PRO, FO371/28320.

24. Biddle to FDR with enclosures, 12, 15, 26 May 1941, FDR Library, PSF, Diplomatic Box 34.

41. In April, the Americans arranged with the Free French to establish a consulate in New Caledonia to offset the influence of the Japanese consul, who was showing an extraordinary interest in New Caledonia's mineral resources. Henri Sautot, who was high commissioner for the Pacific, governor of New Caledonia, and a member of the Empire Defense Council, requested that an American representative be sent to the island. After some negotiations in which one of de Gaulle's representatives in the United States complained of the way in which French interests in the Pacific were being ignored, agreement was reached and Karl de Giers MacVitty took up his post in Noumea in early April 1941.[25]

While offering some support against Japanese pressures, the American presence in New Caledonia raised Free French anxiety that the Americans might be tempted to exploit local conditions and make arrangements on the spot that would prove detrimental to French interests, as de Gaulle saw them. Time had come to send a representative of Free French authority to the Pacific to bolster Sautot. As negotiations for the appointment of an American consul in Noumea were under way, de Gaulle informed Sautot that "the growing complexity of the region" required that a special mission be sent to Free French territories in the Pacific.[26] These "complexities" consisted both of a growing threat of Japanese expansion and an American interest in the Free French colonies. When the first Free French mission to the Pacific, headed by the former governor general of Cameroon, Richard Brunot, proved to be something of a fiasco, de Gaulle decided to send his personal emissary, Captain Thierry d'Argenlieu, promoted to the rank of rear admiral, and made him high commissioner for the Pacific, replacing Sautot in this position.[27]

De Gaulle's decision to replace Sautot with d'Argenlieu reflected the advice he had received in London from a former colonial administrator, who claimed that Sautot, for all of his courage, was not up to the task of defending French interests in the Pacific and was influenced by local, autonomist opinion on the island.

25. Garreau-Dombasle [NY] to Gen. Fontaine [London], 14 February 1941 and same to de Gaulle, 18 February 1941, Archives, Ministère des Affaires Étrangères [MAE] Guerre 1939–45, vol. 309.

26. De Gaulle to Sautot, 11 February 1941, MAE Guerre 1939–45, CNF vol. 79, and Charles de Gaulle, *Lettres, Notes et Carnets: Juin 1940–Juillet 1941* [Paris: Plon, 1981]: 253.

27. Details of the Brunot mission and d'Argenlieu's appointment may be found in my article, "The Trials of the Free French in New Caledonia, 1940–1942," *French Historical Studies*, vol. XIV, no. 4, Fall 1986: 555–57.

This assessment was false and misleading, but with various powers showing a lively interest in the South Pacific, de Gaulle wished to reinforce and centralize Free French control over this distant possession. Furthermore, a new administrative body, the French National Committee, was formed in London in September, which effectively replaced the Empire Defense Council as the governing authority of the Free French movement, and de Gaulle was determined that the Allies would henceforth conduct all negotiations with regard to Free French territories through the FNC.

When d'Argenlieu arrived in the Free French colony, he found an Allied presence already on the island. By previous agreement with London, the Australians had sent a military team to strengthen New Caledonia's coastal defenses and to extend the local runway to accommodate heavy bombers. The Americans also were interested in military facilities in New Caledonia, and in September, de Gaulle offered to allow American air forces to use Free French bases in Africa and the Pacific. An American military delegation arrived unannounced in New Caledonia shortly after d'Argenlieu appeared on the scene. The Americans, much to the annoyance of d'Argenlieu, proceeded to carry out an inspection of facilities without bothering to inform or consult with the Free French leader, and at one point he halted all military construction until London sent authorization for Allied activities on the island. The behavior of the American military representatives did not alleviate Gaullist suspicions of American disregard for the Free French. As the war in the Pacific approached, d'Argenlieu realized that he would have to work with the Australians and the Americans to assure the defense of the island, but in this process he assured de Gaulle that "the rights and sovereignty of France will be protected in all such encounters."[28]

After Pearl Harbor and with the Japanese overrunning one outpost after another in the Western Pacific, the Americans hastily assembled a military expedition and requested Adrien Tixier, the Free French representative in Washington, to obtain de Gaulle's permission to allow New Caledonia to be used as an Allied base of operations in the South Pacific. An agreement was signed on 15 January 1942, in which the Americans could use facilities in New Caledonia as long as French sovereignty was respected. In exchange for permission to use New Caledonia, the

28. D'Argenlieu to CNF, 17 November 1941, AN, Cassin papers 382 AP 59.

Americans promised to send lend-lease assistance and provide a military force to defend the island. However, de Gaulle feared that the Americans would ignore the authority of the FNC, and he hoped to extract some measure of recognition from the United States for his cooperation. He instructed d'Argenlieu to have all matters negotiated through London, since any American attempt to deal with local authorities on the spot was a calculated "meddling" in French internal affairs and amounted to a "plot" to break up the French Empire.[29] This fear of predatory American ambitions toward France set the stage for a much more serious confrontation between d'Argenlieu and the Americans a few weeks later. In an effort to reassure Free French authorities, the State Department promised to recognize Free French control over those territories that had rallied, and promised "the maintenance of the integrity of France and the French Empire and the eventual restoration of the independence of all French territories."[30]

D'Argenlieu had been informed of the American intention to send a force to defend the island from the Japanese, but he had no indication of the size of the American force or when it would arrive. In January, he cabled for more information, but was given no further details beyond assurance that the Americans were coming.[31] Much to the astonishment of d'Argenlieu and everyone else on New Caledonia, an American convoy, bearing the troops of Task Force 6814, appeared in Noumea harbor on the morning of 12 March 1942. Soon the island was literally inundated with over 15,000 American troops, and many more arrived within a few weeks. The size of this force meant that d'Argenlieu's hopes to command the Allied forces on the island were not realistic, and the American commander, Lieutenant General Alexander Patch, assumed responsibility for the island's defense.

The American forces were generally welcomed by the people of New Caledonia. Facilities were placed at the disposal of the Americans, receptions were held, and initial contacts were cordial. Soon, however, relations began to sour. Admiral d'Argenlieu accused Governor Sautot of yielding too readily to American demands, and at one point declared that Sautot had connived in

29. De Gaulle to d'Argenlieu 24 December 1941, MAE Guerre 1939–45, CNF vol. 28, and in *Lettres, Notes et Carnets, Juillet 41–Mai 43*,: 148–49.

30. Atherton to Tixier, 23 February 1942 [publicly announced at the end of the month], NARA State Dec Files 851L.01/11.

31. D'Argenlieu to de Gaulle, 20 January 1942, De Gaulle, *Memoires*, vol. 1: 515–17.

an American take-over of the island. Already relations between the two Free French officials had become strained, largely as the result of the haughty behavior of d'Argenlieu and his staff, which greatly offended the Caledonians. Sautot, on the other hand, enjoyed great popularity as the brave and heroic figure who had led the island's rally to the Free French cause in September 1940. Annoyed at Sautot's popularity, his easy-going manner, and his willingness to accept American demands, d'Argenlieu asked de Gaulle to recall Sautot to London for reassignment. When Sautot hesitated and asked de Gaulle to reconsider this order, d'Argenlieu had Sautot abducted, an action that provoked a massive demonstration against d'Argenlieu at the beginning of May.

The details of this riot on New Caledonia have been related elsewhere. What concerns us here is the impact that d'Argenlieu's actions and behavior had on American-Free French relations. D'Argenlieu claimed that the riot had been provoked by American meddling in internal French affairs, and he held Patch responsible for his difficulties. The Gaullist thesis of an American plot to take over New Caledonia revealed an extreme level of anxiety, amounting almost to a paranoia, over American intentions. From the American perspective, the riot had roots in d'Argenlieu's behavior and attitudes, but the problem was among the Free French and not the consequence of an ulterior motive. The problem was straightforward, not devious. The island had to be defended, and Patch insisted that he remain neutral in this squabble, although he had to consider the need for support among the islanders and the militia at a time when New Caledonia was threatened with a Japanese invasion. He could not alienate public opinion, which was 90 percent opposed to d'Argenlieu. Eventually, after a week of rioting and demonstrations, calm was restored on the island. De Gaulle appointed a new governor to replace Sautot, and after an interlude, d'Argenlieu left New Caledonia for Tahiti. By the end of the year, Admiral d'Argenlieu was back in London.

The episode on New Caledonia produced a minor crisis in American relations with Free France. In his reports to de Gaulle, d'Argenlieu created a version of events that placed the Americans and, particularly, General Patch, whom he persistently blamed for his troubles, in an unfavorable light. The thesis that the riot was part of a deliberate American plot to take over New

Caledonia was not an accurate account either of events or of American intentions, at least in 1942. Nevertheless, d'Argenlieu's version of what happened was readily accepted in London, since it confirmed Free French fears about American intentions toward the French Empire. Sautot's willingness to work with the Americans was interpreted as "playing the game of foreigners" who had designs on French possessions.[32] While American ambitions for New Caledonia were later revealed, at this point there was no evidence of such intention, and Patch repeatedly proclaimed that the Americans had come to defend New Caledonia and for no other purpose.[33] Patch tried to give his officers some understanding of the Free French position. "The Free French," he wrote, "should command our respect and admiration and we should treat them as allies who have been willing to sacrifice everything for our own common cause."[34]

American officials reacted to events on New Caledonia with a combination of an effort to comprehend Free French feelings and a great deal of bewilderment. Admiral d'Argenlieu's behavior was difficult to understand, since his own actions, particularly his ill-concealed disdain for the Caledonian settlers, rather than any American action, seemed to have provoked a riot at the very moment when the threat of a Japanese invasion was imminent. At the State Department, A. A. Berle's judgment on d'Argenlieu was that while others reported him to be a decent soul, "he appears to have gone to pieces in New Caledonia."[35] American officers deeply resented the accusations of d'Argenlieu and his

32. De Gaulle to Tixier (Washington), 9 May 1942, *Memoires*, vol. 1: 538–39. Gaullist condemnation of Patch continues to be presented in such works as Lacouture, *De Gaulle*, vol. 1, *Le Rebelle* [Paris, 1984]: 519.

33. In the latter stages of the war, American politicians proposed that New Caledonia might be given to the United States as compensation for wartime lend-lease, and Roosevelt suggested that an Allied military base be maintained in Noumea under the international trusteeship of Australia and New Zealand. The development of American designs upon New Caledonia before and during the war, expressed at different times by Roosevelt, the Navy, and Congress has been analyzed by Charles J. Weeks, Jr., "An Hour of Temptation: American Interests in New Caledonia, 1935–1945," *Australian Journal of Politics and History*, vol. 35, no. 2 (1989): 185–200.

34 "Memorandum to all officers," 10 September 1942, MAE Guerre 1939–45, CNF vol. 80. Indications of the Gaullist attitude toward the Americans in general and Patch in particular can be seen in d'Argenlieu's response to this order of the day, in which the Free French admiral interpreted this communication not as an attempt to find some basis for understanding and cooperation, but as a sign that Patch had been "called to order" by Washington.

35. Memorandum: Berle conversation with Tixier, 28 October 1942, NARA State Dec File 851.01/720 1/2.

staff that they had deliberately fomented trouble. This response revealed that the Americans did not fully appreciate the sensitivity of Free French representatives on the issue of Gaullist authority or Gaullist resentment at the State Department's Vichy policy. As Admiral Ghormley observed to Patch, "The Free French resent very much that our government . . . plays both ends against the middle. . . . [T]hey do deal with Vichy and they do deal with the Free French."[36] Any apparent challenge to Free French authority in whatever form became a threat to the integrity of the movement and its role as the defender of French interests. From this perspective, the Americans and their overwhelming material presence in New Caledonia seemed to be as serious a threat to Gaullist control of the French Empire as the external, military danger. The Americans, on the other hand, thought that the Free French were both the islanders, who had spontaneously rallied to de Gaulle, and the Free French representative, Admiral d'Argenlieu. The riot in New Caledonia and Admiral d'Argenlieu's actions strengthened an American impression that the Free French were more interested in their own political matters than in ways of cooperating to win the war.

Repercussions from New Caledonia reached Washington and London. General Patch asked instructions on how to deal with d'Argenlieu, whose behavior appeared obstructionist and uncooperative. After some discussion, it was decided to ask if General de Gaulle could not find another assignment for d'Argenlieu as soon as a new governor of New Caledonia could be found to replace Sautot. In London, negotiations with de Gaulle were conducted by Admiral Harold Stark, commander of U.S. Naval Forces in Europe, who was to become the major American representative to General de Gaulle and the Free French. Stark also tried to understand the Free French position on the New Caledonia question. He noted Free French resentments in the State Department's continued relations with Vichy officials in France, North Africa, and Martinique, which he felt had produced an extreme reaction against the Americans. He noted that d'Argenlieu believed that local separatists in New Caledonia might be tempted to return to Vichy control if this would save them from an invasion, or at least that was one interpretation that d'Argenlieu had forwarded to Free French headquarters in London. Yet

36. Ghormley to Patch, 2 August 1942, Appendix to "Report on Franco-American Relations," Op Arch Ad Hist Append 34[19][C].

Stark, who also had received Patch's reports, as well as reports from British and Australians in New Caledonia, concluded that the Gaullists in London were not fully informed of events on that distant island and that their perspective might have been distorted.[37]

Although the New Caledonia conflict was eventually settled, it left a legacy of resentment among the Americans in London, confirming a belief that General de Gaulle was deliberately uncooperative. The news from New Caledonia, combined with reports and rumors circulating in Washington at this time, gave the impression, which was quickly seized upon by Sumner Welles, that the Free French movement was about to fall apart, reinforcing Welles' belief that the movement was hopelessly divided.[38] Relations improved on 9 July 1942, however, with the recognition of the Free French as a military partner in the war against the Axis powers and the formal appointment, which de Gaulle saw as an important step toward full recognition, of Admiral Stark and General Bolte as American military representatives to the French National Committee. Despite this gesture, the tempest over New Caledonia and a continuing series of frictions led to a long analysis of the de Gaulle movement and its relationship to the United States by Commander Tracy Kittredge, Admiral Stark's chief-of-staff and liaison officer.

Kittredge was a reserve naval officer who had worked with Stark under Admiral W.S. Sims in London during World War I and had been recalled to active duty. During the 1930s, he had lived in France as representative of the Rockefeller Foundation. He was fluent in French, and he was as well versed as any American on French affairs and, particularly, recent events. At this point, however, he was unsympathetic to de Gaulle personally and shared some of the State Department's view, reinforced by Alexis Léger, of de Gaulle as a dictator in the making. His early antipathy toward de Gaulle and some of the Free French leaders became

37. Admiral Stark to Admiral King, and Memorandum, "Free French interpretation of the New Caledonia Situation," 27 June 1942, in Lt. Cr. Tracy B. Kittredge, "U.S.-Free French Relations 1942–44," Appendix B, Part I [Correspondence May-October 1942], Op Arch, NHC, Washington.

38. Reports of internal rifts within the Free French movement abounded in late May and June 1942. See, for example, William Donovan to Wallace Murray, Department of State, 8 June 1942, NARA State Dec File 851.01/504; OSS Report, "Discord within the Free French Movement," 19 June 1942, NARA, State Dec File 851.01/524 1/2; views fed by Alexis Léger, Memorandum: "Endeavor to Persuade Léger to Join Free French Committee," 18 June 1942, 851.01/506; and a report prepared by Raoul Angliou [sic], transmitted to the State Department by John Franklin Carter, 2 June 1942, NARA State Dec File 851.01/559.

known and led to bitter comments about Kittredge among the Gaullists and also among British officials in the Foreign Office. Nevertheless, Kittredge exemplified the way in which a segment of official American opinion in London moved from hostility toward grudging acceptance of de Gaulle as not only the leader and symbol of French resistance, but as the one individual capable of restoring France to a leading role in European politics. His reports, at least to an American reader, offered an attempt to discuss the Free French as objectively as possible in order to fathom its meaning and significance.

Kittredge's analysis of U.S.-Free French relations as of August 1942 opened with a discussion of the events that had led to the French defeat in 1940, and his report reflected certain prewar views held by the academic community in the United States. In particular, he noted that when the U.S. Senate failed to ratify the Treaty of Versailles, France was left with the full burden of maintaining the status quo on the continent, yet France lacked the resources to fulfill that role without international support. In Kittredge's assessment, France faced the dilemma between the wars of serving either as the continental ally and base of a British world system, or of becoming junior partner to a Germany dominating the whole of Europe and large parts of Asia and Africa. Debates over this problem filled French journals of opinion between the wars, he observed, and by the late 1930s, a number of French leaders, convinced that France had become a second-rate power, argued that appeasement with Germany on German terms was necessary. For them, the defeat of 1940 was no more than a reversal of alliances. On the other hand, advocates of the former view, such as Daladier, Blum, and Reynaud, had looked to the league and the support of Great Britain as the means for maintaining an enduring peace. In the crisis of 1940, Reynaud wanted to continue the struggle and sent de Gaulle to London to arrange for a transfer of troops and government to the empire. With Reynaud's resignation and the armistice, de Gaulle took up the banner of resistance and adherence to the British alliance. He established himself as the head of the Free French and created the Council of Empire to provide for the administration of those parts of the empire that also had chosen the path of resistance and fidelity to the British alliance.[39]

39. Tracy B. Kittredge, "The Present Situation, Organization and Program of the Free French Movement," August 1942, Kittredge Papers, carton 28, Hoover Institution Archives, Stanford, California.

While Kittredge's analysis was a perceptive statement of French prewar difficulties, it failed to see that de Gaulle's movement rejected either subordination to Germany, which was the path taken by Vichy, or the dependence upon Great Britain, which had been the fate of France before the war. At this point, Kittredge shared the State Department's view of de Gaulle as a creature of the British, which was also a charge that Vichy leveled against the Free French movement. Kittredge was aware of de Gaulle's sensitivities on this score, and pointed out that much of his bitterness toward the United States stemmed from a conviction that the United States policy toward Vichy produced a neutralization of the traditional French position in the World.

In this early analysis, Kittredge echoed the opinion of the State Department's Sumner Welles that the Free French movement was about to split into warring factions. Kittredge's associations with disenchanted anti-Gaullist French exiles residing in London, particularly Admiral Muselier and André Labarthe, greatly influenced his opinions and reports on the Free French at this time. Kittredge argued that de Gaulle's authoritarian manner and rigid insistence upon "unity" on his own terms had driven away many who might have been willing to join the Free French movement. He concluded his report with a confirmation of the American, or Roosevelt/Hull position, by claiming that an overwhelming majority of the French people would resent any British or American attempt to oppose de Gaulle and his clique on postwar France.

No sooner had this report been prepared and forwarded to Washington, than American views from London began to change in response to evidence of support for the Free French among resistance elements in France. Kittredge, for example, interviewed André Philip shortly after his arrival in London, and he reported Philip's insistence that many resistance organizations, including a number of labor groups, looked to de Gaulle as the leader of French resistance.[40] This information greatly impressed Admiral Stark, who subsequently argued that in any invasion of North Africa the Free French should be involved in planning and preparations.[41] Stark's advice, of course, was not followed, but it

40. Stark to Admiral King, 17 August 1942, covering letter to Kittredge's report on interview and analysis of André Philip, Kittredge, "U.S.-Free French Relations 1942–44,: appendix B, selected documents from the correspondence of Admiral Stark, Operational Archives, Naval History Center, U.S. Navy Yard, Washington, D.C.

41. Stark to Secretary Knox (Navy), 22 August 1942, ibid.

marked the beginning of an evolution toward an advocacy for de Gaulle that was to become stronger in the following year, despite some sharp and at times bitter disagreements between the Americans and the Gaullists in London.

The arrival of André Philip in London coincided with an important shift in the direction and source of support for the Free French movement. Initially, the movement had depended upon the spontaneous support of individuals who had agreed to continue resistance from abroad, including those who were in England at the time of the armistice, and the colonies that had rallied during the summer and fall of 1940. This colonial and "external" resistance gave the Free French a claim to legitimacy, but in the summer of 1942, the Free French movement turned increasingly toward the internal resistance to strengthen its claim to represent French interests. In May 1942, de Gaulle sent an appeal to labor groups in France that was designed to assure them that he wished a fully democratic France after the war.[42] Subsequently, an OSS report observed that de Gaulle had gained French labor's recognition "as the one French figure who represents the cause of liberation."[43] This evidence of de Gaulle's support inside France led American military representatives in London to urge that a high level Free French official go to Washington to convince the government of de Gaulle's growing support in France. A small propaganda offensive began in the hope that Washington could be persuaded. Earlier that summer, de Gaulle sent Emmanuel d'Astier de la Vigerie, who recently had escaped from France, to Washington in an attempt to inform American opinion of the true state of affairs inside France.[44] In the fall, as rumors of an Allied action in North Africa developed, a second emissary was sent to explain the Free French position to the American government. The agent chosen to attempt an improvement in Free French relations with the United States was André Philip. Philip took with him a letter from de Gaulle that again explained de Gaulle's position as head of the movement and trustee of French interests. The letter has been widely cited as an effort to persuade Roosevelt that de Gaulle had no dictatorial ambitions for post-

42. Mathews (London) to State, 9 May 1942, NARA State Dec File 851.01/437.

43. OSS Foreign Nationalities Branch, rept. 48, "de Gaulle, the Free French, and the French Underground," NARA, State Dec File 851.01/578.

44. De Gaulle to Free French Delegation, 10 June 1942, *Mémoirs*, vol. 1: 671. Arthur Layton Funk, *Charles de Gaulle: The Crucial Years 1943–1944* (Norman: University of Oklahoma Press, 1959), 27.

war France, but it also indicated why Free France could not be simply a military organization if France were to recover its position in world affairs.[45]

Both Stark and Kittredge hoped that Philip would make a favorable impression. Stark expressed his hopes to Ambassador Winant in London when he informed the ambassador that he had met Philip before his departure to North America and that he "had been much impressed."[46] He was convinced that Philip might even overcome Hull's almost pathological dislike of de Gaulle, stemming from the Saint Pierre and Miquelon affair. In any event, he thought that a conversation with Roosevelt would ease the way toward some reconciliation and unity among the various French factions and, if all went well, improve relations between the Free French and the United States government.

This interview proved to be a catastrophe. Philip, after missing his first appointment, arrived late and proceeded to lecture Roosevelt in a harsh, didactic manner on the moral improprieties of the Darlan deal.[47] Philip engaged in a lecture that pleased neither the president nor Welles, who was present. Roosevelt was astonished at the arrogance and ingratitude of Philip, who offered not one word of support or sympathy for American actions. When Roosevelt defended his deal with Darlan as an expedient but necessary step to end the French resistance to the Allied landings, Philip echoed de Gaulle's denunciation of this action as a deal with a traitor that sullied the honor of France for cynical American interests. Philip scarcely hid his contempt for the "realism" expressed by Roosevelt, and he compared the American president to Laval in his official report back to the French National Committee.[48] He particularly objected to Roosevelt's suggestion that he would make a deal with any "Quisling" who would sur-

45. There is some confusion over the date of this letter, which is indicated as October 26 in de Gaulle's memoirs but is indicated as having been written on the 6th in the copy in the State Department archives and in the example published in *Espoir*, no. 6 (1974), 38–40.

46. Stark to Winant, 18 November 1942, in Kittredge, "U.S.-Free French Relations,: NHC, Washington, D.C.

47. A good, brief account of this interview may be found in Funk, *De Gaulle*, 46.

48. Philip and Tixier, Libfrance to CNF, 22 November 1942, Archives Nationales, Section d'Outre-mer, CNF carton 8; Philip's sarcasms about Roosevelt are in the margin of this report; his contempt for Roosevelt has been confirmed by Jean Lacouture in *De Gaulle*, vol. 1: *Le rebelle* (Paris: Seuil, 1984), 545, and in an interview that he gave to Henri Michel, 13 June 1947, Archives Nationales, section contemporaine, AN72 AJ220.

render to him. He also raised the issue of American plans to impose a military government in France at the time of liberation, and informed Roosevelt that if France were treated like a colony under an army of occupation, the prestige of the United States would be damaged. Roosevelt was upset at this questioning of his motives, particularly his stated intention to liberate France and enable the French people to choose their regime. Exasperated with this encounter with de Gaulle's direct representative, Roosevelt asked his representatives in London, "Why did you send this man, Philip, to me?" Nevertheless, at the end of the interview, Roosevelt indicated that he would be pleased to see de Gaulle if the Free French leader should decide to come to Washington.

Philip came away from the interview convinced that Roosevelt was an imperial dictator, disguised as a "democratic" president, who wished to impose the American system on the rest of the world. In his report to the French National Committee, Philip concluded that American and Free French views on the future role of France were "diametrically opposed." He was convinced that American economic interests would insist on repayment for the sacrifices made during the war, and these "payments" might be at the expense of France.[49] Philip's attitude and manner confirmed the reports that the Americans were receiving from London on the growing anti-American views of the Free French. Etienne Boegner, who had just quarreled bitterly with de Gaulle, reported that "the whole atmosphere" at Carlton Gardens was hostile, the Free French were convinced that the Americans wanted "to set up a world octupus" and intended to appropriate portions of the French Empire for themselves.[50]

Despite the antagonistic atmosphere of the Philip interview, Stark and Kittredge still hoped that de Gaulle and General Catroux, a man they held in high esteem, would make favorable impressions and persuade the president of the value that could be gained from closer cooperation with the Free French. Despite de Gaulle's anger at the way in which the North African situation had been handled and the recognition of Darlan, he expressed his desire to go to Washington. Various dates and times were proposed. However, the trip was repeatedly postponed, await-

49. "Le Président Roosevelt et la politique américaine à l'égard de la France," 27 November 1942, ANSOM, CNF carton 8.

50. Memorandum: Attitude of the Free French in London, 1 October 1942, NARA State Dec File 851.01/672.

ing transportation, and then Roosevelt indicated that he could not be available in November. Then in a note to Sumner Welles, Roosevelt proposed meeting de Gaulle on 10 or 11 January, or else after 1 February 1943.[51] De Gaulle agreed, and arrangements were made for his departure for Washington at the end of December. Catroux would join him en route.

Before departure, Stark and Kittredge met with de Gaulle, who outlined his views of why difficulties had developed in relations between the Free French and the Americans. He stated that the Allies had made a mistake in dealing with local authorities in the French Empire. This policy ignored what he saw as the "essential unity of France," and he insisted that all French people look to one central, symbolic authority. Since 1940, that authority was either Pétain or de Gaulle. He argued that all local authorities derived from a central source and that this sense was essential for the fundamental unity of France. He acknowledged that Americans with a historical experience of federalism and local autonomy might "make the mistake of applying their own traditions to the French." During times of crisis in the past, some leader, whether Joan of Arc, Henry IV, the Jacobins, or Clemenceau, had always risen from the people to assume leadership and preserve the flame of "eternal France." The defeat of 1940 had thrust that responsibility upon him.[52] In making these observations, de Gaulle expressed a fundamental issue of misunderstanding between the Free French and the United States over the way in which a single individual might speak for a people and represent a centralized authority without having received the legitimation of a popular vote.

The planned meeting between the two leaders at the beginning of 1943, which might have dispelled some of the mutual mistrust, never occurred. Churchill intervened to prevent de Gaulle's plane from leaving at the last moment. The assassination of Admiral Darlan occurred on Christmas Eve, and shortly afterward a message arrived from Cordell Hull that advised against de Gaulle's trip under the circumstances. The meeting that did occur came at Anfa in conditions that did not augur well for improved relations between de Gaulle and the Americans. Perhaps an opportunity to resolve American differences with the

51. Roosevelt to Welles, 18 December 1942, NARA State Dec File 851.01/917 1/3.

52. "Record of Conversation of Admiral Stark with General," 17/12/42, Kittredge, "U.S. - Free French Relations," Append. B, part II, 66–71.

Free French had been lost. However, without an American willingness to accept de Gaulle's claim to represent not just Free [Fighting] France but "France," as de Gaulle had insisted in 1940, prospects for dispelling any misunderstandings through a meeting between de Gaulle and Roosevelt were unlikely.

The State Department and Roosevelt remained fixed in their opposition to de Gaulle and the Free French, but the military leadership showed a degree of pragmatism that eventually was to lead to an acceptance of de Gaulle as leader of the Free French movement. While the State Department continued to promote the cause of General Giraud in North Africa, some American officials in the War Department, notably John McCloy, began to favor a more sympathetic hearing for the Fighting French. At least in military matters, McCloy argued that the American position should not be so "standoffish." "After all," he observed, "the Fighting French have been fighting for us and with us for some time now, in fact we hold some very valuable bases made available to us by them." Even more, de Gaulle's military representative in Washington, General de Chevigné, had given a more accurate picture of the situation in North Africa before the landing, according to Eisenhower, than the information he had received from other sources.[53] Even General Marshall, who had strongly opposed informing the Free French of plans for North Africa on security grounds, began to argue in favor of closer dealings with Free French military representatives. "In the past we have always been fearful of their looseness in talk . . . in addition to the diplomatic involvements. It seems to me that we should now change our tune, our courtesies, and so forth."[54] But the American Vichy gamble had given way to the Giraudist gamble, and this became another source of antagonism.

Negotiations between de Gaulle and Giraud preoccupied the Americans in London throughout the spring of 1943. The complex and painful negotiations between Algiers and London during these months revived the American view that the Free French were hopelessly divided. De Gaulle's behavior, his frequent tirades, his unbending refusal to compromise in the interests of Allied unity, bewildered the Americans. The Americans believed that a "compromise," particularly any arrangement that would

53. J. J. McCloy, Memorandum for the Chief of Staff, 25 November 1942, NARA RG165, Records of the War Department, OPD 336 France.

54. Memorandum for General Strong, 17 November 1942, Ibid.

weaken a single, central authority or voice to represent France, was an abandonment of a principle or, worse yet, a "sell out" to American wishes.

At one point, relying on information provided by Kittredge, Stark predicted that key leaders in the Free French movement, notably Massigli and Catroux, were on the verge of abandoning de Gaulle out of disgust over de Gaulle's behavior during the negotiations with General Giraud.[55] This opinion reflected some of the critical views of de Gaulle and his political tendencies that the American military representatives received from within the Free French movement, including Maurice Dejean, whom de Gaulle had dismissed in October 1942 as foreign affairs commissioner for showing a disposition to compromise with the British over the Syrian business.[56] The British Foreign Office, by now strongly supporting de Gaulle and convinced that the Americans were pursuing a losing policy, argued that Kittredge was the source of much anti-Gaullist sentiment among the Americans.[57] On the other hand, the American embassy in London complained with some justification that the British Foreign Office deliberately exaggerated American hostility toward the Gaullists in an effort to gain favor with the Free French.[58] Such distortions did little to improve American relations with the Free French, since they fed Gaullist apprehensions about American policy. They also reflected a profound bitterness that was seriously straining American relations with Great Britain over the issue of the Free French at this time. Although he had personal reservations about de Gaulle and his authoritarian manner, Kittredge's reports to Washington reveal a conscientious attempt to judge the situation fairly and objectively. He and Admiral Stark were, as they put it, ready "to give the devil his due."[59]

Despite exasperation over the interminable disputes, which they often attributed to de Gaulle's rigidity, Kittredge and Stark

55. Stark to King, 4 April 1943, Kittredge, "U.S.-Free French Relations," NHC, Washington, D.C.

56. Mathews (London) to State, 26 February 1943, State Dep Dec File 851.01/1025 1/2PS/SS.

57. Memorandum: Free French-United States Relations, 10 April 1943, FO371/35993 (Z4549/2/17) and Campbell (Washington) to F.O., 13 April 1943, FO371/36194 and 36199.

58. Mathews to State, 15 and 31 March 1943, State Dec File 851.01/1054 and 1094.

59. Stark to Forrestal, 10 July 1944, Kittredge, "U.S.-Free French Relations," NHC, Washington, D.C.

recognized that de Gaulle's popularity was steadily increasing, according to reports from inside France, and that time was on his side. In March, they met with four representatives of the resistance in the presence of General Billotte. After this interview, they reported that not only did de Gaulle have wide support inside France, but that his following in North Africa was growing as well.[60] A decisive event in Kittredge's acceptance of de Gaulle as the most likely leader of a restored French nation came in late May with the arrival of a number of messages, including a letter from Eduard Herriot, whom the Americans had at times proposed as a more acceptable leader for Free France. Herriot pledged support for de Gaulle and expressed astonishment at both the American deal with Darlan and the ineptness of Giraud in not removing officials compromised with Vichy. A conversation with Pierre Viénot further convinced Kittredge that support for de Gaulle had spread in France and that Herriot's position reflected a broad consensus of the French people.[61]

When agreement between Giraud and de Gaulle was reached at the end of May, Stark sent Kittredge to Algiers to brief Eisenhower on relations with the Free French as seen from London. They hoped that true unity had been achieved at last and that the two generals would work together to strengthen French military contributions to the war effort. When Kittredge arrived in Algiers, he quickly sized up the situation, reporting back to Stark that, from the moment of the May agreement, it had become apparent that de Gaulle would soon gain control of the unified movement. Giraud's support came predominantly from former Vichy supporters, while de Gaulle could rely on a much wider spectrum of political opinion, ranging from moderate democrats through labor, the socialists, and communists in both North Africa and occupied France. "In North Africa as in France the Gaullist program seems to represent the majority of French opinion."[62] Moreover, he warned that other continental peoples looked to the way in which the French situation was being handled as an indication of policies that would be followed at the

60. Kittredge Memo, 5 March 1993, in "U.S.-Free French Relations," NHC, Washington, D.C.

61. Kittredge, "Letters and Reports of Conversations in London, 1942–43," 20 May 1943, Kittredge Papers, Carton 46, Hoover Institute Archives.

62. Kittredge to Stark, "Political Developments in the Giraud-de Gaulle Negotiations" 14 June 1993, in Kittredge, "U.S.-Free French Relations," NHC, Washington, D.C.

time of liberation. Thus, by mid-1943, Stark and Kittredge had become convinced that de Gaulle commanded a broad base of support and was the only realistic choice as head of the Algiers government or of any provisional government in liberated France, although the American military delegation still feared his "dictatorial" tendencies.

After Algiers, Kittredge traveled to Washington to present his views on de Gaulle and the new French Committee for National Liberation. He met with Secretary of the Navy Knox, to whom he had sent several reports, and with Cordell Hull. Kittredge provided a candid account of the difficulties that he and Stark had encountered in their dealings with the Gaullists in London, but he also expressed his view that de Gaulle was the leader whom the great majority of French now accepted as a symbol of both resistance and recovery. All of this did not please Hull, who still fervently hoped that de Gaulle would eventually be dropped, and Hull again threatened to halt American aid to the National Committee. In this interview, Kittredge was astonished and dismayed at Hull's persistent hostility toward de Gaulle and his ignorance of what was taking place within the Free French movement. The British Foreign Office, which had looked askance at American policy toward the Free French and deeply distrusted Kittredge, reported the Kittredge returned to London "appalled at Mr. Hull's attitude, at his preconceived notions and his failure to understand the essential nature of the French problem."[63] The British were delighted that Hull had converted Kittredge "into a vehement apologist, if not an admirer of, General de Gaulle."

Kittredge's advocacy of the Gaullist cause had little immediate impact on American policy, since his arguments seemed only to strengthen Hull's stubborn opposition to the Gaullists. For the moment, the FCNL had been accepted by the Americans as the organization responsible for administration of French territory, and an American representative of ambassadorial rank was appointed to Algiers, but formal recognition of de Gaulle as head of the provisional government remained more than a year away. The British Foreign Office nevertheless detected a gradual "evolution" in the attitude of the State Department by the end of 1943.[64]

With the establishment of the FCNL in Algiers, the American military delegation in London ceased to be the main point of con-

63. Peake to Mack 7 August 1943 FO371/35994.
64. Halifax (Washington) to Foreign Office, 6 November 1943, FO371/35994.

tact between the Gaullists and American officials in Washington. This task was now in the hands of the American representative in Algiers, Edwin Wilson, and the diplomatic business in London passed into the hands of the American embassy there. Still, both Stark and Kittredge, while relieved that a difficult task had been removed, maintained their interest in French relations and continued to have contacts with the French delegation on military matters. These contacts enabled them to gather further information about de Gaulle from various military leaders who came to London. One of these contacts was General de Lattre de Tassigny, who further confirmed the support for de Gaulle among the resistance elements, now including several military groups inside France. Stark and Kittredge were greatly impressed with de Lattre, and after a three hour conversation, arranged for a second interview with Ambassador Winant, who was equally taken by the French general.[65] Their views were communicated to Washington and found favorable reception among several American officials, such as John McCloy, the assistant secretary for war, and his superior, Henry Stimson.

Throughout the winter of 1943–44, American intelligence sources continually provided evidence of support for de Gaulle and the FCNL among resistance groups inside France and within the French population of North Africa. However, de Gaulle's support from the resistance raised fears among State Department officials that he would become the dupe of communist interests. At the time of his refusal to join the Free French movement a year earlier, Alexis Léger had raised the specter of de Gaulle seeking communist support in pursuit of his own political ambitions, and he claimed that de Gaulle intended to use ties with the Soviet Union as a way to escape being dependent on an alliance with the Anglo-Saxon powers. He regarded this as dangerous, for Léger saw the only hope of stability in the postwar world in a France tied to an Atlantic, Anglo-Saxon leadership, not in playing the continental alliance game of power politics.[66] A year later, General Odic, a long-time opponent of General de Gaulle among

65. "Memorandum for Winant," 11 November 1943, Kittredge, "U.S.-Free French Relations," NHC, Washington, D.C.; Kittredge supplied a full and accurate account of this interview to the Free French representatives in London, "Record of Conversation of General de Lattre de Tassigny with Ambassador Winant, 10 November 1943, AN, Section contemporaine, F1a3735.

66. Memorandum of conversation between Welles and Léger, 13 August 1942, NARA State Dec File 851.01/627A.

the exile French community, warned that de Gaulle intended to play the Russian and continental cards against the Western democracies, particularly the United States.[67]

The bogey of a Gaullist-communist combination against the Anglo-Saxon powers raised an alarm in Washington. At the request of the State Department, J. Edgar Hoover had the FBI investigate the Fighting French delegation to determine any communist connection.[68] From a fear of de Gaulle's "fascist" tendencies, the panic now turned in a quite different direction. Fortunately, a more balanced assessment also appeared. Military intelligence reports from abroad argued that de Gaulle was neither a fascist nor a communist fellow traveler, but a French leader who was determined not to return to the political habits of the Third Republic and who spoke frequently of a "revolution," in the sense of a national renewal, that represented something of a compromise between these two extremes. This report rejected the idea that de Gaulle would become a "man on horseback" at the time of liberation.[69]

As the invasion of Normandy approached, the question of provisional administration and government for liberated France became acute. The American plan was to establish a military administration for France along the lines of the military administration of civilian affairs in Italy, known as AMGOT, or American Military Government for Overseas Territories. Schools to train officers for these roles had been established in Virginia and at other campus locations. When the Free French found out about these plans, they were understandably upset that France would be treated as an occupied and defeated country.[70]

An opposition to AMGOT quickly appeared within the War Department. The strongest opponent was John McCloy, the assistant secretary for war, who pointed out the practical and political objections to the proposal. In a memorandum to Stimson, he urged a quick understanding and improvement in relations with the FCNL. There were several reasons for doing so: the

67. Summary of General Odic's Memorandum of 30 September 1943, State Dec File, 851.01/3067.

68. Hoover to Berle, 25 June 1943, NARA State Dec File 851.01/2798.

69. "Political ideas of Charles de Gaulle," Intelligence report #1262, 17 September 1943, NARA microfilm series M1221.

70. Free French alarm at plans for a military government for liberated France may be found in a detailed report of AMGOT preparations provided by Henri Seyrig, French cultural attaché in New York: Seyrig (NY) to Hoppenot (Washington), 26 July 1943, MAE Guerre 1939–45, Alger CFLN-GPRF, vol. 727.

military need not be burdened with the additional responsibility of administering civilian affairs; the committee had declared its intentions to restore democratic institutions; the committee offered effective contacts with resistance elements that would be of use in support of military operations; dealing with one authority would greatly simplify matters, both militarily and politically; the committee, according to intelligence reports (G-2), enjoyed widespread support; and AMGOT would provoke an angry backlash in France. "It would be 'dynamite' to intervene in the internal affairs of France as we used to do in small Central American states," he warned. He noted that the American government was officially opposed to AMGOT in France and that any attempt to have such an administration "would be obnoxious to the French people, whatever their political views." General Bedell Smith, Eisenhower's chief of staff, also urged working with the FCNL for the administration of France, and McCloy observed a bit tartly that to do so "would be consistent with the realistic approach to these matters which the War Department and the military commanders have always had."[71] During a trip to the United States, the American ambassador to the FCNL, Edwin Wilson, registered his opposition both to AMGOT and to any breakup of the French Empire in a meeting with Roosevelt.[72] As to the communist threat, Ambassador Biddle forwarded an intelligence report from London that there would be no mass rally to the Communist banner unless the Allies tried to impose their will upon France.[73]

Advocacy for acceptance of the FCNL and de Gaulle as the provisional government for France came also from the London delegation headed by Admiral Stark. Fearing the Allied landings would become the occasion for a revolutionary insurrection in France, the London military delegation urged that de Gaulle be given a part in the preparations for the invasion and be allowed to assume leadership of the French resistance. In a memorandum two weeks after the landings and on the eve of de Gaulle's visit to the United States, Kittredge argued that, despite de Gaulle's often abrasive manner and suspicions of the United States and Great Britain, "he is about the only figure who can save France

71. McCloy, Memoranda to Secretary of War, 13 and 20 January and 29 February 1944, NARA, RG 107 Records of the Office of the Secretary of War, ASW 370.8, France.

72. Memorandum of Conversation, NARA State Dec File 851.01/3185 1/2.

73. Biddle to State, 22 November 1943, NARA State Dec File 851.01/3226.

from a civil war, who can canalise and control the revolutionary excesses of the Communists and resisters, and who can provide a bridge between Right and Left." He noted that de Gaulle remained highly suspicious of strangers who might be tempted to exploit French weakness, and he warned that de Gaulle was ready to play off Britain, the United States, and the Soviet Union if it would advance the French cause. He acknowledged de Gaulle's popularity among the French, which was warmly demonstrated when de Gaulle went to Bayeux, and he expressed an admiration for de Gaulle's willingness to take a risk: "De Gaulle has always played for the highest stakes . . . and he has shown the most considerable diplomatic skill for one who is apparently so rigid." Above all, the long-standing American fear of a de Gaulle dictatorship was laid to rest. "My tentative and intuitive guess is that the worst danger of a xenophobe de Gaulle dictatorship has passed."[74]

Within the State Department, an inter-divisional committee on France made a series of policy recommendations that included a call for an early understanding with the FCNL on the administration of civilian affairs in France as soon as possible after liberation. The committee urged that France be given a major role in any postwar international organizations on an equal basis with the United States, Great Britain, the Soviet Union, and China. As for the form of government likely to emerge, the study group noted that the resistance, inclined toward a moderate and reformist socialism, preferred a stronger and more stable executive, a goal that also conformed to Gaullist preferences. The study also recommended that American policy support these objectives.[75] Thus, by the time of the Normandy landings, the Gaullist objectives of restoring France to a major role in international affairs and establishing a government with a strong central authority had gained advocates within the State Department itself.

At the time of the Normandy landings, a further, high-level effort to overcome Roosevelt's opposition to dealing with de Gaulle and the FCNL in the administration of liberated territory came from the War Department. Within a week of the landings,

74. Memorandum: "General de Gaulle," 20 June 1944, and letter Stark to Forrestal, 10 July 1944, in Kittredge, "U.S.-Free French Relations," NHC, Washington, D.C.

75. Memorandum: "The Treatment of France, Policy Recommendations," 30 May 1944, NARA, State Department RD 59, microfilm T1221.]

General Marshall, who was in England, cabled Secretary Stimson with a plea from Eisenhower to settle differences with de Gaulle and the FCNL over French civilian affairs. On June 15, they exchanged a long-distance telephone conversation in which Stimson stated that he had been "hard at work" trying to persuade the president and the secretary of state to take a "more realistic view" of the situation and "accept the policy of recognizing provisionally" the de Gaulle government. He found that Roosevelt remained fixed in his determination to carry out his own policy, regarding it as "a moral issue."[76]

A final episode in this story of the evolution of the American view of de Gaulle came with a visit of Admiral Stark to de Gaulle in Paris on the eve of the United States' full recognition of him as provisional head of the French government. At the request of the American embassy in Paris, Stark reported on his visit directly to both Secretary of State Hull and Admiral King. He stressed de Gaulle's cordiality and general friendliness. He also emphasized de Gaulle's popularity with the French people. Stark had no illusions about the problems de Gaulle faced in trying to reconcile the various political positions in the country, but de Gaulle seemed to stand above the political controversy as a truly national figure.[77] The purpose of the memorandum was to convince Washington that de Gaulle was the man of the hour, particularly as a hero who had restored French sovereignty and pride. The view was best expressed in a memorandum prepared by Stark's aide-de-camp:

> I believe the French are convinced that de Gaulle shares their desire to get free of both British and American supervision as quickly as possible, so that Frenchmen can try to settle French problems their own way. De Gaulle's strong nationalism and independence, which have often made him stiff-necked and difficult in the past, seem right in line with the current mood of the French people.[78]

Whether de Gaulle would succeed in uniting France remained to be seen, as Stark noted in his letter to Hull. The message, though, was clear. For the moment and the foreseeable future, de Gaulle would continue to hold the destiny of France. Ironically,

76. Telephone conversation between Mr. Stimson and Gen. Marshall, 15 June 1944, NARA RG 107, Box 5.

77. Letter Stark to Hull, 6 October 1944 and Stark to King, 7 October 1944, in Kittredge, "U.S.-Free French Relations," NHC, Washington, D.C.

78. Memorandum 9 October 1944 [Lt. Col. Bingham] in Kittredge, "U.S.-Free French Relations," NHC, Washington, D.C.

what de Gaulle's antagonist, Roosevelt, had claimed he wanted for France had taken place: the French people had chosen freely, and de Gaulle was the choice. The new France, at least it was hoped at the time, would be neither the easy-going Third Republic that many Americans had associated with the prewar regime, nor the subservient regime, dominated by Germany, that Vichy had installed. A Gaullist France would be a France on its own terms. This was the message that Admiral Stark tried to impart, and it represented a long and at times tortuous evolution in a certain American opinion that had passed from a suspicious view of de Gaulle as an upstart, authoritarian military commander to the one individual who seemed to embody French hopes for recovery and independence, while at the same time offering some guarantee against a revolutionary insurgency. The Americans were uncertain of de Gaulle's future and equally uncertain what a Gaullist France might be, but they were no longer confident that this would be a return to the old ways of the Third Republic.

Even the American threat to the French Empire, which had raised deep fears and suspicions within the Gaullist Free French movement from the very beginning, eventually yielded to an American realization that its dismantling was impractical. Roosevelt had made clear his desire to place certain parts of French overseas territory, notably Dakar and Indochina, under international mandate. As for New Caledonia, by 1943–44, Congress, the U.S. Navy, and Roosevelt himself indicated that the United States might at least claim a base at Noumea or economic concessions, if not outright control, as compensation for lend-lease given to Free France during the war. These goals yielded to the growing preoccupation with the Soviet Union and a desire not to alienate France from the Western camp.

U.S. relations with the Free French, then, were characterized by almost continuous confrontation from the very beginning. Gradually, Americans who had contact with the Free French and de Gaulle came to realize that his movement was more than a way of continuing the battle: it was vital to the struggle to restore France as a nation and a culture with a major place in the world. Any compromise might lead to a shattering of that hope. While frequently upset by the deliberately confrontational style of Gaullist dealings with foreigners, and resentful of Gaullist suspicions of American tendencies toward hegemony, an important segment of American official opinion came to the practical conclusion that there was no real alternative to a France restored on Gaullist terms. De Gaulle's actions in his dealings with the United States offered a clear lesson in the limits of power, even in an asymmetrical relationship. The example of the U.S.-Free French relationship during World War II also offered a sobering lesson on the difficulties in changing official attitudes in Washington, once those attitudes had become fixed into policy – a problem that would arise again at the time of the American war in Vietnam. But this is another topic.

Comment

Nicholas Wahl

I HAVE QUESTIONS, rather than long comments, though some of my questions do imply comments. Having available all this concentration of knowledge about this period really prompts me to pose questions that I've never been able to ask before. Concerning the establishment of the Free French in the United States in 1940–41, I've long wanted to know to what extent the early Free French were, at least partly, put in place by the British, who had an interest, after all, in having some kind of a French auxiliary movement. De Gaulle, in London in 1940, had a problem of setting himself apart from the British because of the immediate assumption that there would be a French military force based in England, which would be associated with the British when eventually there would be a cross-channel invasion or action elsewhere in the French territories. Why not, therefore, British help to the Free French in establishing themselves in the United States? After all, you yourself, Monsieur Aglion, came to America on a British passport. And one of your first visits was to the British consul general. The British consulate in New York in 1940 was a headquarters for British intelligence in the Western Hemisphere, with practically unlimited resources. William Stevenson, the Consul General, and his associates were undoubtedly people of great influence back in London,, with all the resources they needed to support British national interests in the United States. Why not some help for the Free French? I'm surprised the British Consul general didn't say to M. Aglion right away, "It's Garreau-Dombasle or X or Y," who is the leader of Free France in the United States. Perhaps there was a problem with de Gaulle, who may have preferred his old classmate, Jacques de Sieyès, and may have said that he wouldn't have anybody except Sieyès as Free French leader in the U.S. British intelligence may have said that, given de Gaulle's preference, there was nothing they could do about it, but "entre nous" it is Garreau-Dombasle, the career diplomat in Washington, whom we really like. At any rate, I wonder if M. Aglion could say a word about that?

Second, as far as Professor Dallek and the whole Roosevelt/de Gaulle hostility is concerned, I'm interested in Arthur Funk's view – or the implication of what he says – that, in fact, Alexis Léger wasn't very effective as an anti-de Gaulle influence. My own view is that, while he didn't get to see Roosevelt personally, he did see Sumner Welles, and Sumner Welles was the single most important counselor for Roosevelt in foreign policy at the time. Roosevelt, for various reasons, had confidence in Sumner Welles. Cordell Hull was a political appointee; Roosevelt knew his intellectual limitations and that he was there for internal political balance. But Sumner Welles was of his class, of his background, and a man in whose foreign policy judgement he had great confidence. But frankly, was not Alexis Léger – and this is a question I have again for M. Aglion and also Prof. Funk – among the French in America who really had an interest, a serious political interest, in turning Roosevelt against de Gaulle and, indeed, ultimately against the French Resistance? That is, turning Roosevelt against anybody who would produce a substitute for the Third Republic after the war? The Third Republic was well represented in Washington. I have in mind especially the most important of them, Camille Chautemps, who was in Washington from July 1940 on, and who was, we know, supported by State Department funds. And how about Pierre Cot, who was at Yale University, but spent a lot of time in Washington from 1941 on? How about the group of Radicals and freemasons who were important in the political and cultural life of France in the 1930s, and who were stranded here in New York? And people like Henri Laugier, who was well connected with the Radical Socialist Party and Freemasonry? How about all those French League of Nations people in the United States, whose future in postwar France depended on there being not too much of a change from the prewar political structure? In other words, I'm wondering whether one couldn't make a good case for the career interests of Camille Chautemps and Pierre Cot, pressing them to increase the natural hostility between Roosevelt and de Gaulle.

Finally, a comment and a question for Prof. Munholland on this matter of official hostility between Free France and Roosevelt. The change in American attitude Munholland dates from around the spring of 1943 is connected, I think, with an important new element that moves into American policy-making in 1943, that is, the influence of the OSS. The OSS was organized in the spring of 1942. Strategic intelligence in America was organized in great haste after Pearl Harbor. Now, what's interesting is that the OSS (which ironically was the forerunner of the CIA, which was very anti-de Gaulle during most of his postwar activities) was, during the war, the first to discover that de Gaulle represented something important in occupied France. Curiously enough, it was the scholars who were the desk officers and were in Washington, reading the reports of their agents who said, "This de Gaulle has put down roots, he has made contact with the internal resistance, which now in 1943 is led by de Gaulle because he has organized the liaison from London." And when the OSS became influential enough vis-à-vis the State Department, its position had to be answered, and the State Department defense and the White House were no longer alone in making an assessment of both de Gaulle and the Fighting French, the successor to Free France which included the Resistance within France.

Witness

Raoul Aglion

I WILL NOW ANSWER the questions regarding Lemaigre-Dubreuil, Léger, and the British authorities.

I had hardly spoken to Lemaigre-Dubreuil, who was in Washington at the time of the North American invasion of Algeria. He was a very important industrialist, who had actively collaborated with the Nazis until he foresaw the defeat of Hitler. He then turned to the Americans. He wanted to see France maintain a "Nazi form" of government after the Liberation, and he was very hostile to General de Gaulle.

Camille Chautemps, former prime minister of France, who first arrived as Pétain's envoy, attempted various intrigues in Washington without success. I refused to see him, despite his many requests.

Alexis Léger, former secretary general of the French Foreign Office, a great diplomat, and a Nobel Prize Poet, was exiled in Washington. He used his influence with Cordell Hull and Sumner Welles to oppose de Gaulle, whom he accused of being an apprentice dictator. He hated the general because, during the fall of France, Prime Minister Paul Reynaud had dismissed him from the Foreign Office, at the same time appointing de Gaulle as under secretary for defense. Léger's resentment of Paul Reynaud spilled over onto de Gaulle. I had long conversations with Léger on several occasions, and was unable to mollify a hostility that was seriously detrimental to the Free French movement and to the liberation of France itself.

I now turn to the second question regarding the British influence with the French movement. When General de Gaulle appointed me to the Free French Delegation in the United States, I had resigned as attaché to the French embassy in Cairo, which had submitted to Vichy. By order of Vichy, my French diplomatic passport was canceled and I could not, therefore, travel. Given these circumstances, the British embassy in Cairo issued me a passport, stating that "Raoul Aglion, a French citizen by birth, was under the protection of his British Majesty's Embassies and consular authorities." I was thus able to accomplish various missions for de Gaulle and also to be admitted to the United States. As I explained in my book, *Roosevelt and de Gaulle*, upon my arrival in New York, I contacted the British consul general, Sir Geoffrey Haggard, and asked him where the Free French Office was located. He gave me all the information I required. At that time, in January 1941, the Free French were not recognized in any way by the United States, which recognized only the Vichy embassy in Washington. I had no alternative than to send my confidential reports and cables through the code of the British consul. I also used his diplomatic pouch. De Gaulle answered through the same channel. The Free French were, at that time, entirely dependent on the British for all of their communications, and, of course, for the equipment of their forces. Nevertheless, our policy was independent of the British and their officials, who treated us as allies of an independent country. Their help was essential, at least until June 1941, when René Pleven, an emissary of de Gaulle, made an informal agreement with the State Department, which allowed the Free French to use their own code and diplomatic pouch. We were also authorized to deliver Free French passports and visas. As head of the Free French Delegation, I could then act as a de facto consul general for an independent, but unrecognized government.

Witness

Etienne Burin des Roziers

IT SEEMS INTERESTING TO ME to point out that at that time and even much later, de Gaulle was unaware of most of Roosevelt's personal feelings. And to support this, I can bring to you my personal testimony. I was in London during the very first days of 1943, right after de Gaulle's trip for the Anfa conference. For General de Gaulle, this conference was an ordeal. The decision to go to Anfa was made, by the way, by the National Committee. At first, de Gaulle refused to go, and when he returned, he was obviously very affected by the conditions in which this conference had taken place. Nevertheless, and this is what is interesting, he told us: "There is something positive. My interview with President Roosevelt was very satisfactory." And not only that but at that time, a telegram was sent from London to all our Free French outposts in which de Gaulle basically said that the conversation with Roosevelt had been positive, adding: "I have reasons to believe that President Roosevelt discovered Free France, and this can be of great consequence for the future."

This is the feeling which persisted in General de Gaulle's mind until he left power. He often said he was convinced that a "man to man" conversation with Roosevelt would be enough to resolve any misunderstandings. This leads me to disagree a little bit with what Mr. Dulles thought (according to one of the earlier papers), which is that Franco-American relations suffered for a long time as a result of this initial quarrel. This idea is quite common in France and was notably taken up by Jean Monnet, in his book, and by Prof. Grosser. I do not have the same impression. I was serving under General de Gaulle when he returned to power, and I can say that his personal relationship with Eisenhower and Kennedy (I really mean personal relations, whatever difficulties existed between our countries at that time), were very good, and even quite warm. Therefore, in my opinion, it is a mistake to think that this initial difficulty had any lasting consequences.

Now, if you will allow me, I will make a last comment concerning the fundamental reasons why, at that time, de Gaulle and

Roosevelt could not establish a good relationship. I believe the major difficulty (everybody knows it) appeared in Algiers. I first followed this development from London and then in Algiers. It was the time when the U.S. government was attributing a certain role to Darlan. I think it is then that the expression "expédient provisoire" (temporary solution) was first used. But this term seems to me to have characterized President Roosevelt's constant attitude, as far back as the events in St. Pierre et Miquelon, Martinique and New Caledonia. What exactly was this policy of "temporary solution"? It was in fact a policy that attempted to secure strategic positions (in the interest of the war effort), by dealing with the effective authorities in place, whether it be Vichy's administration (in Giraud's case it was a little less clear), or other people who could be controlled or counted on.

It was always a question of dealing with the most accommodating person. But this policy was in direct contradiction to General de Gaulle's main preoccupation which he expressed after the landing at Algiers: "Un seul combat pour une seule patrie" (one fight for one homeland)." This meant that his policy consisted of setting up a central power which would lead the French war effort inside and outside the country. In essence, the issue between de Gaulle and Giraud was quite similar to that between Jean Moulin (sent to France at that time by the General de Gaulle to unify the "résistance"), and people like Fresnay, who claimed to preserve the autonomy of sections of the resistance and who turned for that purpose to Mr. Donovan in Geneva. There was here a very real incompatibility.

One last word. I was the only witness other than Ambassador Caffery at the interview between de Gaulle and Mr. Hopkins, on the eve of the Yalta conference. I was a modest interpreter, and the ambassador didn't intervene at all.

The interview was really astonishing. It began badly because it was taking place at a very difficult period. De Gaulle was dissatisfied because he had not been invited to the Yalta conference. It was also in his character to distrust "éminences grises." He liked to deal with people who had an official function within the state, who had been given responsibilities. De Gaulle was willing to believe that Mr. Hopkins was playing a decisive role but he was ill-at-ease with him nonetheless. So the conversation started. Mr. Hopkins arrived with Mr. Caffery, General de Gaulle welcomed him and asked him to have a seat. A long silence followed.

Nobody said anything. For de Gaulle, since Mr. Hopkins had wanted to see him, it was he who had something to say. After a long moment which was very tense (especially for me, having nothing to translate), the conversation finally began and it was very interesting because it had the pretention, justified I believe, of dealing with the essential questions. Mr. Hopkins said to de Gaulle: "I would like to talk about what seems to me the fundamental reason for the "malaise" (this is the word he used), that has existed for so long between our two countries." And he went on: "The truth is that in June 40, the defeat of the French army, the institution of the Vichy government under German control, was for America and for President Roosevelt in particular, a painful surprise. And we have never gotten over it. It is at that time that we decided to deal with Vichy, and many things followed from this." Then General de Gaulle spoke. Without contradicting this way of seeing things, he added: "There is also something else. You have a choice to make. Either you believe that France still has a great role to play in the world, or you consider that after what my country went through, France is on the decline and can no longer be one of the leaders. If it is the second case, you are right. I believe, however, that France will come back stronger, and that France has an important role to play. And if that is the case, your behavior is regrettable and ill-inspired." In brief, this was the content of this meeting, and that is what I wanted to add as a witness.

CHAPTER TWO

FROM THE COLD WAR TO THE FIFTH REPUBLIC, 1944–58

❖5❖

Germany, the United States, and De Gaulle's Strategy for Economic Reconstruction, 1944–1946

John S. Hill

American policy explicitly set out to make France a chief pillar of a revived postwar Europe. French policy explicitly sought to recapture France's lost status as a great power. How did two such compatible policies lead to such a conflicted relationship? Different concepts of international security meant that the two countries talked past each other, seeming to make progress most easily on economic issues while coming into conflict on military security. An examination of the policies pursued toward Germany and the reconstruction of the French economy bring this problem into sharp focus. American ideas about the origins of international conflict compelled the French to adapt their more traditional concepts of military security.

Initially, de Gaulle had sought to gain the recognition of the great powers for the provisional government as the legitimate government of France. Beyond this basic goal, he sought to restore France to the ranks of the great powers themselves and guarantee France adequate military security against a revival of German power. He achieved the first of these goals in October 1944. This began a period of illusory success: additional forces were mobilized to give France a larger part in the assault on Germany; an alliance treaty signed with Russia in December, and a lend-lease agreement with the United States in February 1945, were much trumpeted.

Like Dead Sea fruit, these triumphs soon turned to ashes.

Excluded from Yalta and Potsdam in February and July 1945 (where basic decisions were made regarding the future of Germany), surprised by the atomic bombing of Japan, deprived of lend-lease almost before it had begun, unable to force the Council of Foreign Ministers to deal with its demands for revision of the Potsdam agreements in September 1945, and excluded once more from the consultations of the foreign ministers of the big three in Moscow in December 1945, France suffered a painful series of humiliations. Each reminded de Gaulle that France lacked the real strength for great power status.

Seeking new sources of power, de Gaulle favored particular policy options that turned out to have important long-term consequences. Economic reconstruction gained increasing importance as the means to, first, rebuild national strength by drawing in American aid and, second, tighten French claims on Germany, where the Americans raised a host of economic objections to French plans. Thus, de Gaulle began to engage France in several of the basic policies with which the Fourth Republic came to be identified.

I. Franco-American economic relations in European perspective.

A. American Reconstruction Strategy in 1945.

Already in January 1945, the State Department had argued in favor of supporting France in hopes of patching the rent fabric of the Franco-American relationship. France would be treated on the basis of its "potential" power once recovery had been achieved. Truman later acceded to this policy. Efforts to conciliate the French soon became trapped between France's own demands and the U.S. Army's insistence that the French were obstructing other essential American policies in Germany. Despite these difficulties, on 29 November 1945, the State Department still believed that a revived France could contribute to European stability and hoped to make France a "bulwark of democracy."[1]

A concern to root out the economic causes of domestic and international conflict formed the keystone of the State Department's diplomatic strategy. In the American analysis, the modern international industrial economy had suffered from the autarkical policies adopted by so many countries in response to the Great Depression. The collapse of the international monetary system in 1931 had disrupted world trade and set off a new

1. John Gimbel, *The Origins of the Marshall Plan* (Stanford, 1976), pp. 35–36, 38.

deflationary spiral. Tariff walls went up as each country sought to displace the costs of depression onto other countries. The fractured system resulting from protection amounted to less than the sum of its parts. No country could be entirely self-sufficient, given the complexity of modern production, so nations naturally cast a covetous eye on the possessions of foreign states that might complement their own resources. In a similar fashion at home, the shrinking "pie" of goods to be distributed among the members of a community set class against class. Democracies became deadlocked, people took to the streets in search of a savior, and dictators came to power, turning outward in an attempt to conquer what their economies did not produce. The institutions of the Bretton Woods system – i.e., the International Bank for Reconstruction and Development and the International Monetary Fund – were intended to achieve an open world economy conducive to peace and prosperity.[2]

During the war, both the State Department and the British sought to promote long-term political stability in liberated areas by providing economic aid intended to revive production, forestall unrest, and consolidate the positions of democratic governments. In the summer of 1944, discussion began among American officials of an interim program of aid to bridge the gap between military relief and the inauguration of the Bretton Woods programs. During the first half of 1945, the State Department formulated a comprehensive strategy for funding international reconstruction. State Department economists estimated world financial reconstruction needs at $25–30 billion through 1955. In expectation that the war in the Pacific would continue well into 1946, liberated countries were allowed to use their Lend-Lease Master Agreements to acquire civilian supply and industrial reconstruction goods during this so-called Stage II. The mass of new facilitating legislation passed through Congress in the summer of 1945.[3] However, the postwar period still seemed a long way off in July 1945.

2. Robert Pollard, *Economic Security and the Origins of the Cold War, 1945–1950*, (New York, 1985), pp. 10–17. Richard Gardner, *Sterling-Dollar Diplomacy in Current Perspective*, (New York, 1980), pp. 1–23, offers a similar evaluation of what he labels American "economism."

3. For an elegant statement of this line of thinking, see Dean Acheson's memorandum to the secretary of war in defense of the European civil-supply programs at Christmas 1944; FRUS, 1945, II, pp. 1059–61. On the preparation of the financial program, see: "Preliminary Estimates of Financial Requirements for Reconstruction and Development," 11 May 1945, FRUS, 1946, I, p. 1393, note 7. The preliminary estimate suggested these needs might be funded by $5–10 billion from the Export-Import Bank, $10 billion from the World Bank, and $10 billion from pri-

The sudden end of the war threw domestic and international economic policies into disarray. Truman immediately canceled lend-lease. Fearing that demobilization would lead to a renewed depression at home, Truman sought to stimulate the economy and maintain high employment, in part through extending credits to foreign countries to purchase American goods needed for reconstruction.[4]

Rapid conversion from a wartime to a peacetime economy wreaked havoc with international economic policy as well. Over a third of the additional lending authority granted to the Export-Import Bank to fund well-planned, long-term reconstruction strategies by European states immediately got soaked up by "lend-lease termination credits" as European countries borrowed to keep essential goods flowing. Rapid American inflation then reduced the value of the remainder. Truman told the State Department to begin working up the studies and legislation to complete the expansion of Export-Import Bank lending authority to the ceiling originally contemplated, a task that occupied the State Department until the end of November 1945.[5]

B. France's International Economic Strategy in Formation.

One aspect of France's effort to rebuild its strength drew much of its form and inspiration from this American effort to provide aid. Intimately informed of the thrust of American international economic policy, Jean Monnet elaborated a series of plans to draw in American resources in the service of French economic recovery. The anticipation of abundant American aid nudged the evolution of the postwar French political economy down certain paths.

Monnet had negotiated a whole series of aid programs, culminating in the Lend-Lease Master Agreement in February 1945.[6]

---

vate investment. On "Stage II," see: FRUS, 1946, I, p. 1395, note 10. On the lack of adequate planning for the end of the Lend-Lease Agreement, see: Robert J. Donovan, *Conflict and Crisis: The Presidency of Harry S. Truman, 1945–1948* (New York, 1977), pp. 53–54.

4. Donovan, *Conflict and Crisis*, pp. 108–9, 110–11, 113–14, 162; Statement of Honorable Leo T. Crowley, Chairman Board of Trustees, Export-Import Bank of Washington Before Senate Banking and Currency Committee, 17 July 1945, FRUS, 1946, I, pp. 1396–99.

5. See the account of the work of the National Advisory Council on International Monetary and Financial Problems, 21 August to 27 September 1945, FRUS, 1946, I, pp. 1399–1411.

6. Jean Monnet, *Memoirs* (New York, 1978), pp. 181, 209–10, 215–16, 218, 226; James J. Dougherty, *The Politics of Wartime Aid: American Economic Assistance to France and French Northwest Africa, 1940–1946* (Westport, 1978), pp. 167–70. The negotiations are documented in FRUS, 1944, III, pp. 757–61.

The latter program granted France lend-lease aid, which Monnet calculated at $2.5 billion worth of consumer and industrial goods through July 1946. Although France drew very heavily on these credits, it had received only $400 million of the anticipated $2.5 billion in goods when the Lend-Lease Agreement ended in August 1945.[7]

Before August 1945, however, American lend-lease aid had seemed to offer France this opportunity to rebuild the material base of national power at an accelerated rate while resolving a difficult problem in domestic politics. The whole issue of planning and reconstruction had become entangled in other bitter political conflicts since the Liberation. France's depleted economic resources could not be restored without heavy investment. At the same time, the extended penury of the Depression, war, and occupation had left all groups of Frenchmen deeply entrenched in defense of their own claims on the withered national income. Farmers, middle classes, and industrial workers were all equally determined that if someone had to sacrifice consumption to increase investment, it would not be they.

The draft program presented to the Interministerial Economic Committee by Pierre Mendès-France on 17 November 1944 had linked severe restrictions on consumption, accompanied by strict wage-price controls and a confiscation of surplus savings, to a planned development of the heavy industrial base.[8] The confiscation of accumulated savings that he advocated threatened to halt all deliveries of food from the countryside. Cruel shortages of essential goods and the political strength of the peasantry and middle classes militated against radical reforms and in favor of a vigorous effort to increase production. Industrial workers insisted on substantial wage increases as well. Finally, in the mind of the other members of the government, the Lend-Lease Agreement worked out in February 1945 promised to deluge France in essential goods, which would render the measures proposed by Mendès-France unnecessary. The rejection of his plans after much debate and delay led to Mendès-France's resignation. It also left important decisions about the nature of the postwar economy in suspense.[9]

7. Dougherty, *The Politics of Wartime Aid*, pp. 178–83, 191–92, 201–3.

8. Michel Margairaz, "La mise en place de l'Appareil de direction économique (1944–1947): des objectifs lointains aux choix du moment," Colloque: "La France en voie de modernisation," pp. 6–8.

9. Archives Nationales, F60/893, "Rapport de M. Picard," pp. 14–15, F60/898: "Note du Secrétariat Général du Comité Economique," 12 February 1945, and economic revival. F60/898: "Compte-rendu de la séance du 19 février 1945 du

Mendès-France's rival, Finance Minister René Pleven, swung to the other extreme when he relegated economic planning to a back burner for most of 1945, then slacked up on rationing and accepted large budget deficits. The cancellation of the Lend-Lease Agreement falsified the expectations upon which these policies had been adopted. Growing deficits and uncontrolled demand for goods were finding no counterpart in the form of expanded imports; price controls broke down, and the distributive conflicts born of a rapid inflation began to polarize French society once more. By October 1945, Pleven found himself driven to adopt Mendès-France's positions on the concentration of authority and the need for a plan.[10] Monnet's apparent ability to generate external resources, which all recognized to be one condition of survival, attracted a wide range of support for his suggestion of a new approach to economic modernization. This consensus helped root the mild "indicative" form of planning in the French political economy where other forms had been rejected.

Undeterred by his earlier reverse, Monnet still looked to America for help in reviving France's economy. Monnet proposed a sweeping renovation of the French industrial base through heavy investment as a means to draw in American resources. Monnet suggested that French agreement to the Bretton Woods system could be conditioned on America first supplying France with the means to modernize its economy to the point where France could compete on open world markets.[11] It is not surprising that the quick work done by Monnet's team in November 1945 revealed that France's basic problems sprang from prolonged disinvestment. Official reports in this sense already abounded.[12]

F60/898: "Note," 8 February 1945 (by Ramadier) analyze the food crisis. F60bis/386/2/1: "Note au Ministre [de l'Economie Nationale]. Programme d'Importations de 1946," 31 October 1945, stresses the importance of a plan for economic revival. F60/898: "Compte-rendu de la séance du 19 février 1945 du Comité Economique Interministériel" and F60/898: "Note du Secrériel" reveal the extent of French hopes from American aid. The emergence of the Monnet plan is skillfully displayed and penetratingly analyzed by Richard F. Kuisel, *Capitalism and the State in Modern France*, (Cambridge, 1981), pp. 196–202, 217–18. Margairaz, "La mise en place," pp. 10–11 offers an interesting interpretation of the same evidence.

10. Margairaz, "La mise en place," p. 14.

11. AN, AMF (Monnet Papers) 1/6/3: "Note sur les impressions préliminaires retirées des consultations que le Commissaire Général au Plan a été amené à avoir avec les représentants de l'administration et de la production," 23 January 1946.

12. Philippe Mioche, "Le démarrage du Plan Monnet," *Revue d'histoire moderne et contemporaine*, v. 31, #3 (1984), pp. 399–400; AN, AMF 1/6: "Notes de Jean Monnet sur le premier rapport de remise en marche de l'économie française en 1945, sur les objectifs pour 1946 et sur le bùt final d'atteindre," 11 November 1945. See

As had been the case in February, Monnet hoped to obtain American aid sufficient to support the modernization of France. This time, however, he hoped to obtain a one-time grant covering three years of the program.[13] Foreign Ministry estimates suggested that France needed $4.5 billion for three years, combining $1–1.5 billion for a stabilization fund with $1.5–2 billion in credits for machinery imports.[14] Given the concurrent planning in the State Department to provide France with $1–2 billion of financial aid, Monnet's proposed plan stood an excellent chance of building a constructive partnership between the two states.

II. The Franco-American quarrel over Germany.

While the American views on promoting international and domestic political stability were congruent with French domestic political and economic exigencies, the two countries fell out over Germany, where the French and American approaches to security could not be reconciled. The French refused to be bound by decisions regarding Germany made at Potsdam when they had not attended the conference. Instead, they used their veto on the Allied Control Council (ACC) to attempt to force an accommodation of French wishes.[15] In a memorandum submitted to the London Council of Foreign Ministers (CFM) on 11 September 1945, France argued that the Ruhr and Rhineland had to be severed from any new German state in order to deny Germany the military means and the geographical opportunity to wage aggressive war against France. The French representative on the ACC would be instructed to block any measures prejudicing such an

also Michel Margairaz, "Autour des Accords Blum-Byrnes: Jean Monnet entre le consensus national et le consensus atlantique," *Histoire, Economie, et Société*, 1982, #3, pp. 439–41.

13. Ambassador in France to secretary of state, 15 January 1946, FRUS, 1946, V, pp. 399–400; secretary of state to Caffery, 4 February 1946, FRUS, 1946, V, pp. 409–11; AN AMF/1/6/7: "Note remise avec note manuscrite de J.M. à M. André Philip, Ministre des Finances," 3 February 1946.

14. Ambassador in France to secretary of state, 14 November 1945, FRUS, 1945, IV, pp. 771–73: Lacroix-Riz, "Négociation et signature des accords Blum-Byrnes," *Revue d'histoire moderne et contemporaine*, v. 31, #3 (1984), p. 428–30. Just as importantly – perhaps more so – France had to gain access to adequate supplies of German coal if its economy was to revive. The secretary general of the Interministerial Economic Committee had argued in January 1946 that the striking French recovery made during 1945 could only be sustained with the aid of external credits, large-scale imports, and German coal. AN F60/925/6: "Note du Secrétaire Général sur la situation et la conjoncture économique en janvier 1946."

15. A. W. DePorte, *De Gaulle's Foreign Policy, 1944–1946*, (Cambridge, MA 1968), pp. 178–79, 181–82.

outcome until the question had finally been resolved.[16] France immediately obstructed the work of the Control Council and continued to block all agreement on central administrative agencies through the end of October 1945.[17]

As John Gimbel has pointed out, these French initiatives met a mixed response from the American government and, it might be added, from the British as well. Faced with the tightly defined and unsought responsibilities of making the Potsdam agreement work and maintaining order in occupied Germany, and unable to make the State Department assume responsibility for this mammoth task, the United States Army did not much care about the larger perspectives of either the French or the State Department. After the first weeks of French obstruction, General Lucius Clay, the deputy military governor, hit upon the strategem of concluding interzonal agreements with his Russian and British colleagues, thus bypassing the French. He submitted this plan to Washington and won its approval.[18]

However, the British and Russians refused to join in such arrangements, and Clay returned to demanding diplomatic pressure be applied to the French. Clay insisted that he had to know the geographical limits of the postwar German economy to determine reparations and when negotiating agreements with the other interested powers. French obstruction of four-power control in Germany threatened to disrupt the treatment of Germany as an economic unit and the implementation of the Potsdam agreements. Secretary of War Patterson pressed Byrnes hard again in late November 1945 to get the French in line and give the army some definite answers.[19]

The State Department and the British had a different set of priorities and were at least willing to hear what the French had to

16. "Control and Administration of Germany," Memorandum by the French Delegation to the Council of Foreign Ministers, 13 September 1945, *FRUS*, 1945, v. 3, pp. 869–71.

17. Murphy to secretary of state, 23 September 1945, *FRUS*, 1945, v. 3, pp. 871–73; "Note by the French Delegation of the Directorate of Transport. Creation of a Central German Transport Department," 19 September 1945, *FRUS*, 1945, v. 3, p. 877; Caffery to secretary of state, 27 September 1945, *FRUS*, 1945, v. 3, p. 878; Murphy to secretary of state, 12, 13, 18, 20, 28 October 1945, *FRUS*, 1945, v. 3, pp. 881–85, 887–88.

18. Murphy to secretary of state, 28 September 1945, *FRUS*, 1945, v. 3, pp. 878–79; Murphy to secretary of state, 29 September 1945, *FRUS*, 1945, v. 3, p. 879; Hilldring, director of civil affairs, War Department, to Clay, 20 October 1945, *FRUS*, 1945, v. 3, pp. 885–86.

19. Secretary of war to secretary of state, 21 November 1945, *FRUS*, 1945, v. 3, pp. 908–9.

say. Both were somewhat flexible on the future of Germany in August and September 1945. Consideration of the French proposals made a major contribution to fixing their ideas.

British Foreign Minister Ernest Bevin, hoping for a close relationship with France, did not initially reject the French plans for western Germany. During the London CFM, Bevin and Bidault agreed to carry out expert-level talks on the French proposals. Similarly, State Department officials still had some flexibility in their thinking about Germany. American diplomats agreed to the series of bilateral talks on the French proposals for the Ruhr and Rhineland suggested by Bevin and Bidault.[20]

Britain and France held the first set of bilateral talks on the French proposals from 12 to 26 October 1945. The French set out essentially the same program they had advanced at London. The French failed to persuade the British that the plan for separating the Ruhr from the rest of Germany could work in economic terms. The French argued that security concerns should predominate in deciding the fate of the Ruhr; the British felt that the loss of the Ruhr from their own occupation zone would impose an even more crushing economic burden upon them. Bevin also suspected that the French would allow the Russians some hand in running the internationalized Ruhr, while he preferred to give the Ruhr a strictly western orientation. The French appear to have understood that the British refusal to commit themselves amounted to rejection.[21] From this point on, the Foreign Ministry began to support Monnet's suggestions for planned economic development, since the plan's ambitious targets would require large suppliers of coke and coal. These could only come from western Germany, so French economic need would support their own primary concern with military security.[22] At this point, the two French strategies began to converge. Monnet's American approach would gain France the dollar credits it needed to

20. Sean Greenwood, "Bevin, the Ruhr, and the Division of Germany: August 1945-December 1946," *Historical Journal*, v. 29, #1 (1986), pp. 203–4; John W. Young, *Britain, France , and the Unity of Europe*, (1984), p. 28; Gallman, London, (from Dunn) to secretary of state, 11 October 1945, *FRUS*, 1945, v. 3, pp. 880–81.

21. Gallman, London, to secretary of state, 22 October 1945, *FRUS*, 1945, v. 3, p. 886 and n. 41; Young, *Britain, France, and the Unity of Europe*, p. 28; Greenwood, "Bevin," pp. 204–5; Alan Bullock, *Ernest Bevin, Foreign Secretary*, (New York, 1983), pp. 148–49; Winant, London, to secretary of state, 16 November 1945, *FRUS*, 1945, v. 3, pp. 894–95.

22. Frances M. B. Lynch, "Resolving the Paradox of the Monnet Plan: National and International Planning in French Reconstruction: *Economic History Review*, v. 37, #2 (May 1984), p. 236.

import capital goods for industrial modernization. The Foreign Ministry's German approach had a more ambiguous quality. While the Monnet plan could bolster French military security claims on the Ruhr and Rhineland by adding an economic justification, the Foreign Ministry's approach promised to supply France with the abundant raw materials required by the plan.

Pushed by an extraordinary French diplomatic blitz and by the exasperated Clay's demands for help, Secretary of State Byrnes agreed to informal talks between experts.[23] These discussions, held in Paris from 15 to 20 November 1945, merely replicated the Anglo-French talks. The French wanted the Ruhr, Rhineland, and Saarland immediately removed from the authority of the Allied Control Council; they wanted reparations regardless of the state of the German trade balance; they wanted capital dismantling in the Ruhr to continue on the Potsdam schedule, even though the area had been internationalized and in spite of the likely economic problems it would cause in the Ruhr; and they thought that "rump" Germany would just have to "make [the] necessary adjustments" to deal with the inevitable foreign-exchange deficit.[24]

The French plans struck the Americans as unworkable. An OSS study had demonstrated that the French plan would strip Germany of its chief export-earning area, leading to an additional payments deficit so large (1.645 billion 1936 RM) that the Potsdam reparations schedule would have to be scrapped or the United States engage in the rebuilding of an industrial base for the rest of Germany.[25] A French counter-estimate of a mere additional RM 500 million deficit struck the Americans as "seriously in error."[26]

Simultaneous talks in Washington (13–20 November 1945), led

23. Director of the Office of European Affairs (Matthews) to secretary of state, 25 October 1945, *FRUS*, 1945, v. 3, p. 887; Caffery to secretary of state, 31 October 1945, *FRUS*, 1945, v. 3, pp. 88990; Caffery (Angell) to secretary of state, 31 October 1945, *FRUS*, 1945, v. 3, p. 893, n. 57; Caffery to secretary of state, 3 November 1945, *FRUS*, 1945, v. 3, pp. 890–91; memorandum of conversation by the chief of the Division of Central European Affairs (Riddleberger), 5 November 1945, *FRUS*, 1945, v. 3, pp. 891–92; Caffery to secretary of state, 6 November 1945, *FRUS*, 1945, v. 3, p. 892, n. 49; minutes of meeting of the secretaries of state, war, and the Navy, 6 November 1945, *FRUS*, 1945, v. 3, pp. 982–93; secretary of state to Caffery, 8 November 1945, *FRUS*, 1945, v. 3, pp. 893–994.

24. Caffery (from Angell) to secretary of state, 18 November 1945, *FRUS*, 1945, v. 3, pp. 895–96.

25. Secretary of state to Caffery (for Angell), 21 November 1945, *FRUS*, 1945, v. 3, p. 908.

26. Caffery (from Angell) to secretary of state, 24 November 1945, *FRUS*, 1945, v. 3, p. 910.

by Maurice Couve de Murville for France, were equally sterile. Although authorized to agree to central administrations if the Ruhr and Rhineland were excluded from their authority, the French diplomat found the Americans unresponsive to French military security concerns and determined to forge ahead with the creation of central administrative agencies to implement the Potsdam agreements. Secretary of State Byrnes told the French emissary that the United States had decided to make common currency, transportation, and administration arrangements with the British and Russian zones and to disregard the French, if the other powers wished to join with the Americans.[27]

In the aftermath of Couve de Murville's trip to Washington, Chauvel admitted to Caffery that the State Department's questions had forced the French to consider the likely economic impact of their plans on Germany in addition to the security benefits to be derived from the Ruhr and Rhineland. Alphand, Couve de Murville, and Jacques Rueff had a final session with the American experts on 27 November 1945. The economic aspects of political separation continued to be the key issue. Customs and monetary separation, which Alphand defended as "essential to success of [the] plan," would disrupt the prewar pattern of "invisible" exports to the Ruhr-Rhineland from the rest of Germany. The only means of balancing the accounts of "rump" Germany would be to allow the prewar pattern to continue. This, in turn, meant that the western territories could not be politically and economically severed from Germany.[28] When the French pressed for an international conference on their proposals, Byrnes reaffirmed his position: the Americans would stand by the Potsdam Agreements and would join with the British and Russians to circumvent the French obstruction of central administrations if necessary.[29]

27. Caffery to secretary of state, 13 November 1945, *FRUS*, 1945, v. 3, p. 892, n. 49; report on Franco-American conversations held in Washington, 13–20 November 1945, concerning the future status of the Rhineland and the Ruhr, 20 November 1945, *FRUS*, 1945, v. 3, pp. 896–906; memorandum of conversation by the secretary of state, 20 November 1945, *FRUS*, 1945, v. 3, pp. 907–8; secretary of state to Caffery (for Angell), 21 November 1945, *FRUS*, 1945, v. 3, p. 908.

28. Caffery to secretary of state, 28 November 1945, *FRUS*, 1945, v. 3, pp. 911–12; Caffery (from Angell) to secretary of state, 30 November 1945, *FRUS*, 1945, v. 3, pp. 912–13.

29. Memorandum of conversation by James W. Riddleberger, chief of the Division of Central European Affairs, 5 December 1945, *FRUS*, 1945, v. 3, pp. 915–16; secretary of state to Caffery, 6 December 1945, *FRUS*, 1945, v. 3, p. 916. Greatly distressed, Bidault protested that central administrations would just put Germany under the Soviet thumb. *FRUS*, 1945, v. 3, p. 916, n. 81.

Rejection of the French proposals did not mean victory, however. France continued to obstruct four-power control of Germany, driving the War Department to renew its demand for more effective pressure on the French. The British would not finally reject the French proposals until March 1946. The Russians also had shifted their stance openly to oppose the American proposals for trizonal cooperation without France. Apparently puzzled about how to proceed, the State Department stalled the War Department.[30]

December 1945 and January 1946 were months of great uncertainty in the Franco-American relationship on several levels. The Foreign Ministry's German-oriented strategy had encountered serious obstacles. Alphand's group realized that they would have to think far more constructively and profoundly about the economic aspects of the Franco-German relationship if they were to impose their demands on the Americans. France's territorial claims had been decisively rejected as impractible. It had been excluded from the inner circle of decision at the Moscow CFM once more.[31]

On the other hand, it may well have seemed to de Gaulle that he had achieved a standoff with the Americans on the future of Germany. No central administrative agencies could be created by the ACC, and the American scheme to circumvent the French through interzonal agreements had so far been rejected by the British and the Russians. De Gaulle took Anglo-American actions after the Moscow CFM as a sign that they were weakening sufficiently in the face of his policy of intransigence to satisfy his demand for political control as well.[32]

Monnet's strategy for economic recovery gained headway as France prepared to balance its own acceptance of American commercial policy against a grant of $4 billion.[33] Monnet's memoran-

30. Secretary of war to secretary of state, 10 December 1945, *FRUS*, 1945, v. 3, pp. 916–19; Greenwood, "Bevin," pp. 205–6; acting secretary of state to secretary of war, 12 December 1945, *FRUS*, 1945, v. 3, pp. 919–20.

31. Franco-Russian discussions of Germany and the French reaction to the Moscow CFM are reported in: memorandum by the deputy director of the Office of European Affairs (Hickerson) to the chief of the Division of Central European Affairs (Riddleberger), 15 December 1945, *FRUS*, 1945, v. 3, p. 920; Caffery to secretary of state, 18 December 1945, *FRUS*, 1945, v. 3, pp. 921–22. Acheson confessed the impregnability of the current French position in early January 1946; acting secretary of state to secretary of war, 12 January 1946, *FRUS*, 1945, v. 3, pp. 923–25.

32. De Porte, *De Gaulle*, pp. 266–68.

33. Margairaz, "La mise en place," pp. 21–22.

dum to de Gaulle of 4 December 1945 had linked a long-term reconstruction plan to foreign credits, foreign credits to rapid modernization, rapid modernization to increased production, and increased production to national economic independence. This, more than anything else, probably gave the plan an appeal to de Gaulle. Events all through 1945 had repeatedly brought home to the general that France would be excluded from the inner circle of decision so long as it lacked the real resources of a great power. The American credits would allow France to rebuild her power swiftly. At the same time, Monnet's scheme had the great advantage of conforming well with de Gaulle's own style of bargaining large things for large things on the basis of one-time exchanges. Just as de Gaulle sought to trade the French veto on four-power control of Germany for separation of the Ruhr and Rhineland, so France would trade acceptance of American international economic policy for the resources necessary to modernize its economy. If de Gaulle expected to return to power soon after his resignation with a victory over the divisive domestic opposition, he may also have felt a certain confidence that he would be able to improve France's international standing substantially. The reality, of course, proved very different since American aid actually dried up in mid-1946 and the Americans proved more unyielding on Germany than expected as the cold war deepened. But the most prescient statesman could not have foreseen the developments of the next twelve months – or of the next twelve years.

❖6❖

Harry S. Truman and Charles de Gaulle

Irwin M. Wall

It is hard to conceive of two more dissimilar men who were called on to lead their respective countries at critical points in their histories. Truman was a small-time merchant and an old-style machine politician; de Gaulle was a military man who had contempt for petty-bourgeois politicians and despised the interplay of political parties and local politics. Truman was a skilled practitioner of local and national politics, a party loyalist, and a neophyte in foreign affairs; de Gaulle subordinated internal affairs to foreign policy, in which he saw the achievement of French grandeur. For Truman, the amateur historian and constitutionalist, the American Constitution was the essence of the state and government; de Gaulle's conception of the state, and eternal France, elevated these abstractions above the constitution or the government of the day. Neither man had an extensive knowledge or deep understanding of the culture or politics of the other's country. De Gaulle had never been to the United States before the war. Truman had spent a year in France, first in the trenches of World War I, and then in various places while awaiting demobilization and shipment home. During most of that time, Truman played cards, but he spent three agreeable days in Paris in December 1918. In his autobiography, Truman remarked on virtually nothing he saw, noting only that he went to the opera to see *Manon Lescaut* and attended the *Folies Bergères*, which he found "a disgusting performance."[1] When the two men met in Washington for the first time, on 22 August 1945, Henri Bernstein, who tried to interpret the Gaullist Free French movement to Americans during the war, sought in vain for similarities

1. The Autobiography of Harry S. Truman (Boulder, 1980), pp. 50–51.

between the two men. The best he could do was to note that both were deeply religious, yet shared a sense of realism.[2]

Neither man was particularly kind in his memoirs to the other. Truman said of de Gaulle that he was "a man of dedicated courage who had rendered important services to France in 1940 at a time when French morale had hit bottom." This understatement is followed by three pages of complaints about de Gaulle's "methods of championing French national causes" in Stuttgart, the Val d'Aosta region of Italy, and Syria-Lebanon.[3] De Gaulle was more generous to Truman, finding him "equal to his task, his character firm, his mind oriented toward the practical side of affairs – in short a man who promised no miracles but could be counted on in a crisis." But de Gaulle attributed American opposition to French actions in the same incidents to be the result either of British machinations (Syria and Lebanon) or the American desire for hegemony (Val d'Aosta). And he criticized Truman's approach to world problems as stemming from a viewpoint that "simplified everything"; for a nation to be happy it needed only a democracy, as in the United States.[4]

Privately, both were even more acerbic toward each other than in their published work. During the Stuttgart incident, Truman said of de Gaulle, "I don't like the son of a bitch." During the Val d'Aosta crisis, when Secretary of War Stimson suggested that de Gaulle was a psychopath, Truman replied that this was his opinion, too. Following the Syria-Lebanon affair, Truman exclaimed, "Those French ought to be taken out and castrated." Truman remarked to his staff that "de Gaulle had insulted President Roosevelt and his troops had killed Americans and he (Truman) could not forgive him for these things."[5] Where Truman got the idea that de Gaulle's forces had killed Americans is not clear, unless he was confused about the North African landings, but the insult must have referred to de Gaulle's refusal to see Roosevelt in Algiers. De Gaulle is said to have remarked that if he had led the United States during the immediate postwar period, he would have used the threat of the atomic bomb to force the Russians to back down; Truman, "le marchand des bretelles

2. *The New York Times*, 23 August 1945.
3. *Memoirs*, by Harry S. Truman, vol. I, *Year of Decisions* (New York, 1955), pp. 238–42.
4. Charles de Gaulle, *Memoires de Guerre*, T. 3, *Salvation* (Paris, 1957).
5. Robert J. Donovan, *Conflict and Crisis: The Presidency of Harry S. Truman, 1945–48* (New York, 1977), p. 58.

(merchant of suspenders)," had missed his opportunity. When Truman fired MacArthur for advocating nuclear war in Korea, de Gaulle said, "C'est le quart d'heure des petits hommes, des éternels capitulards (This is the hour of little men, the eternal capitulators)." Truman was a petty politician who was afraid of elections, de Gaulle said; thus had a turning point in history been missed.[6]

Truman's messages to de Gaulle had a brutal frankness, to which de Gaulle never replied in kind. At Stuttgart, which was taken by French forces, de Gaulle ordered a French occupation administration established, thus marking out a claim for what was to become the French occupation zone of Germany. Eisenhower ordered the French to withdraw, but de Gaulle instructed General de Lattre to hold firm. Eisenhower was willing to accept the situation, but Truman wanted the French out. He wrote de Gaulle that he was "shocked by the attitude of your government in this matter and its evident implications," and warned of a "storm of resentment" in American opinion should the public become aware of French actions. If the French government persisted in obliging its army to carry out its political instructions, then "an entire rearrangement of command" would be necessary. Truman said he "should deplore such a crisis and I am certain it would be deeply regretted by you and your government." The text of the message was actually suggested to Truman by Secretary of War Stimson, who was not very adept at diplomacy. Truman used it verbatim.[7]

De Gaulle replied to Truman "in the same spirit of frankness that you were pleased to address me," expressing the hope that "such unfortunate incidents may be avoided," and asserting that they would be if France were regularly consulted on matters that concerned it. Yet Truman was the one who felt insulted in this exchange; according to Margaret Truman, de Gaulle was "almost as insulting to Dad as Marshal Stalin had been to President Roosevelt." Churchill is said to have urged Truman to release the messages to the public, "knowing that it would have finished de Gaulle politically in France," but Truman refrained from this drastic step, fearing that the Communists might succeed de

6. Raymond Tournoux, *Le Feu et la Cendre: Les années politiques du général de Gaulle*, 1946–1970 (Paris, 1979), pp. 25–26, 72, 155.

7. Harry S. Truman Library (Independence, MO), Naval Aid Files, Stimson to Truman, May 1, 1945. For the full text as sent, Foreign Relations of the United States (hereinafter FRUS), 1945, Vol. IV, France, May 1, 1945, p. 682.

Gaulle.[8] Actually, de Gaulle was very conciliatory the next day to American Ambassador Jefferson Caffery, telling him of his fears that the Russians were powerful enough to take over the whole European continent. "I would much rather work with you," de Gaulle said, "but if I cannot . . . I must work with the Soviets in order to survive even if it is only for a while and even if in the long run they gobble us up too." De Gaulle complained that the Americans appeared to have written off France, thinking it was again going to collapse: "and perhaps you are right, but she would not fall if you helped her."[9] Caffery replied that the United States was aware that a strong and prosperous France was in its interest, if only because of "our desire to export and we cannot export if you are not prosperous enough to buy." De Gaulle's difficulty with the Americans comes through here starkly, even in these conciliatory words: he thought geopolitically, and they in terms of economics.

In the Val d'Aosta, a French-speaking region of Northern Italy, the Americans accused French occupation troops of spreading annexationist propaganda, and demanded that the area be turned over to the American military government pending a postwar peace treaty, which would settle its fate. De Gaulle claimed he was only interested in minor frontier rectifications and autonomy for the region as a whole, but French troops were again ordered not to withdraw, as if to test the Americans. This time Truman lashed out:

> [I note] the unbelievable threat that French soldiers bearing American arms will combat American and allied soldiers whose efforts and sacrifices have so recently and successfully contributed to the liberation of France itself. I beg you to withdraw . . . before I acquaint the people of the United States with this situation. While this threat is outstanding against American soldiers I regret . . . no further issues of military equipment or munitions can be made to French troops.[10]

It is not clear whether French troops would have fired on the Americans, but they did have orders to resist American occupation of the region. In the meantime, the French deployed additional troops in Syria and Lebanon, hoping to induce those nominally independent countries to agree to treaties protecting special French privileges in education, trade, and military bases. The

8. Margaret Truman, *Harry S. Truman*, (New York, 1973).
9. FRUS, 1945, IV, France, 5 May 1945, pp. 68587.
10. FRUS, 1945, IV, France, 6. June 1945, p. 735.

result was an outbreak of rioting against the French, who responded with an attempt at repression and briefly shelled the city of Damascus. The two former protectorates appealed to the United States and the nascent United Nations for help, and Winston Churchill, welcoming an opportunity to pose as defender of the Arabs, ordered the French to cease fire and sent in British troops to establish order.

A new burst of anger at de Gaulle occurred at the American State Department, where the French actions were compared to the Japanese invasion of Manchuria in 1931. Truman gave his full support to Churchill's ultimatum, and in the face of far superior British power, de Gaulle was forced to order a cease-fire and withdraw. But not before he called for a five-power conference on the Middle East, including Moscow, in a vain effort to "throw a pebble in the Anglo-Saxon pond."[11] Between this crisis and the Val d'Aosta, Churchill was genuinely exasperated, sending a message to Truman to the effect that "we cannot deal with de Gaulle." De Gaulle in fact suspected that the Anglo-Saxons, counting on the lack of support for his policies in France, were scheming to overthrow him. The Americans were encouraged by Marshall Juin, who, in negotiating a solution in the Val d'Aosta, told them that de Gaulle's position was "unreasonable and impetuous," and all the cabinet, including Georges Bidault and René Pleven, were out of sympathy with him. But Churchill sadly concluded that if de Gaulle were to be overthrown, "it has to be by the French people themselves and not by outsiders."[12]

Yet a higher sense of mutual interest ultimately prevailed in Franco-American relations, and neither man, despite his dislike of the other, would permit those relations to deteriorate to the point of impeding necessary cooperation between them. On 18–19 May 1945, Foreign Minister Bidault stopped in Washington on his return from San Francisco, where the meeting establishing the United Nations had taken place. Truman certainly raised the American grievances against the French, but these were not allowed to dominate the talks. The president made a point of stressing that American aid to France continued despite shortages and privations suffered by the American people themselves. Truman told Bidault that he wished to see France restored, because a "strong France is a gain to the world." The president said he supported French participation in the forth-

11. De Gaulle, *Memoires de Guerre*.
12. FRUS, 1945, IV, France, 9 June 1945, 740.

coming talks in Berlin with the British and Russians, and would take the matter up with Churchill and Stalin. The French request to participate in the Pacific war was referred to the American military for consideration. Most importantly, Bidault had the opportunity to argue the French case for the postwar treatment of Germany, setting forth in great detail the French position on integration of the Saar with France, separation of the Rhineland, and internationalization of the Ruhr. German territory having already been amputated in the East, Bidault said that equally strong measures were required in the West. Truman, interestingly, said he saw no difficulty in ultimately arranging matters in Germany as the French desired. But Acting Secretary of State Joseph Grew corrected the president; the United States would not commit itself to the French theses on Germany beyond the promise to grant the French a zone of occupation, to be carved out of the projected American and British zones, as had been agreed with the Russians at Yalta.

Finally, Truman invited de Gaulle to visit the United States at a mutually convenient time.[13] The French press responded enthusiastically to news of the meeting. Caffery reported that the President's reception of Bidault "as the representative of a great power" was of particular importance in view of the French "inferiority complex," and that the mention of a French occupation zone in Germany was a "masterful touch." One wonders whether this brief euphoria might have led to a longer-lasting improvement in relations had the Val d'Aosta and Syria-Lebanon crises not intervened, and whether a more accommodating French attitude on both issues would have encouraged Truman to press harder for French participation in the Pacific war and the Potsdam meetings, or to accommodate the French a bit more on Germany. De Gaulle quickly responded favorably to Truman's invitation, offering to see the president either in provincial France, Paris, "any other town that would suit you," or Washington, if Europe was not on Truman's immediate itinerary. Of course Europe was on the president's itinerary, and perhaps nothing would have helped to cement relations so much as a triumphant visit by Truman to Paris, where popular enthusiasm, pent up for five years, for Franklin Roosevelt, the GIs, and

13. National Archives and Records Administration (NARA), Record Group 59, State Department Main Decimal File, 711.51/5-2045, 20 May 1945, 711.51/5-2145, 21 May 1945, memoranda of Truman-Bidault conversations, 19 May 1945, Washington, D.C.

the United States in general would no doubt have been showered on the American leader. But de Gaulle accompanied his invitation with the condition that any meeting between the two men not take place either immediately before or after the forthcoming meetings in Potsdam between the president, Churchill, and Stalin; only thus could Truman be received in France "with full confidence and joy," for reasons de Gaulle was sure the president would understand. But the President did not understand any such reasons. De Gaulle feared that a separate meeting with Truman would dramatize French absence from a conference of the big three, but this concern seemed petty in Washington, and precluded a visit by Truman to Paris. Truman set the meeting instead for late August, 1945 in Washington.[14]

The exchange was ironic, because similar considerations on de Gaulle's part had led to the earlier misunderstanding between de Gaulle and Roosevelt. In February 1945, Roosevelt had sent Harry Hopkins to see de Gaulle in the genuine hope of clearing up misunderstandings between the two leaders. Hopkins told Bidault that the president would like to see de Gaulle, and Bidault replied that it could not be before or after Yalta. Hopkins realized Roosevelt would not like this response and told Bidault he would prefer not to have to transmit such a reply to Washington. The next day, Bidault told Hopkins that, on the contrary, de Gaulle would be happy to meet the president, any time and any place. Hence the President's invitation to de Gaulle to come to Algiers. De Gaulle rejected the invitation as a "summons" to a city under French sovereignty, to which he should have invited the president rather than the reverse. De Gaulle must have known that raising the same objections in relation to Potsdam, as at Yalta, risked a similar misunderstanding with Washington.[15]

By the time of de Gaulle's visit to Washington, which took place from 22–24 August 1945, the minor irritants between the two countries had been settled. De Gaulle was received with pomp, circumstance, and extreme courtesy: a tea, a state dinner, one night at the White House and then the use of Blair House (traditional for visiting heads of state), wreath laying at Arlington National Cemetary, a visit to Annapolis, 21-gun salutes, etc. – nothing was missed, the protocol was handled with extreme

14. FRUS, 1945, IV, France, 29 May 1945, Bonnet to Truman, p. 701. Truman's reply to acting secretary Caffery, 2 July 1945, pp. 701–2.

15. FRUS, 1945, IV, France, 2 February 1945, p. 669. Also Ministère des Affaires Etrangères (MAE), B Amérique, 119, Bonnet to Bidault, 3 May 1945.

care. As a parting gift, the president presented de Gaulle with a C54 passenger airplane, for which Truman took some criticism in Congress, since it was not clear whether he had the authority to do so without legislative appropriation of funds.[16] De Gaulle turned the plane over to the French air force, and after his resignation it was kept available to him for his personal travels. There were some humorous aspects, which took place unperceived by the French visitor, to the visit. Truman was reportedly in an ebullient mood at the state dinner, and at one point told some of his friends that he had missed his calling, that he would have preferred to be "a piano player at a whorehouse." One wonders how this sort of self-deprecating humor would have gone over with the austere French visitor.[17] In a letter to his cousin Nellie the next morning, Truman described de Gaulle as "a real 'highpockets.' 6 ft. 6 in. tall and a pinhead really. Looks to me like he wears a 6-5/8 hat, but I may be mistaken."[18] De Gaulle was perhaps right that Truman remained a haberdasher at heart.

The French had a charged agenda in Washington: they hoped to secure American acquiescence in their return to Indochina, acceptance of their plans for the Rhineland and Ruhr, reparations, food supplies, and coal. But most importantly, Bidault told Caffery, was "our desire to wipe the slate clean of the past, start afresh and work with the U.S. as closely as we possibly can in the international field." In some respects, the visit could be judged a success. Truman told de Gaulle that the United States would not object to a French return to Indochina, and he showed sympathy for the French economic plight, promising to do what he could to make available foodstuffs and coal. To this end, loan negotiations were begun so that supplies to France under a previously canceled lend-lease program could be continued. The loan of $550 million was concluded by Jean Monnet in December. The French immediately thereafter requested talks, during which they could discuss with Washington the totality of their needs over the next four years, as developed according to the Monnet plan. The results were the Blum-Byrnes accords in 1946 and the Marshall Plan in 1947. In effect, de Gaulle's visit began a continuous, pro-

16. Truman Library, President's Personal File, De Gaulle Visit, 22-24 August 1945. The President eventually explained that he had presented the same gift to Churchill, Chiang Kai-shek, and the king of Saudi Arabia under the War Powers Act, and that the United States had more of these planes than it could use, while these countries needed them.

17. Donovan, *Conflict and Crisis*, p. 146.

18. *Letters Home by Harry Truman* (New York, 1984).

longed, and troubled history of American assistance to France that continued until 1954, by which time de Gaulle had become thoroughly disgusted with its effects (but this is another story). As far as "wiping the slate clean," the visit, to some extent, did that, and the two men parted on better terms. *The New York Times* reported that a "turning point" had been achieved in French policy: "France's face is turned toward the west and she will not again refuse to enter any doors that are opened to her." The official communique of the meetings referred to a "fundamental harmony" in aims between the two countries.[19]

But all was not sweetness and harmony. Truman had received reports of criticism of the United States in the French press, and he took the occasion to complain about it to de Gaulle. The president also rebuked some dozen or so French journalists who accompanied the de Gaulle party to Washington for failing to treat the United States fairly in their stories. There was a good deal of consternation about this among the French. De Gaulle excused the press as new and "inexperienced," but also pointed out that it was free and that his government had no desire to control it. Publicly, de Gaulle felt compelled to say that France was not always favorably treated in the American press either. But most importantly, the sympathy and consideration shown Bidault regarding French aims in Germany the previous May was no longer evident. This could have reflected a shift in American policy or, simply, a better command by President Truman of the basics of his country's foreign policy, in which he was still being guided by the State Department. De Gaulle repeated the French arguments: Germany had lost territory in the east, but nothing was being said of the west. As a result Germany's center of gravity was displaced toward France. The Rhineland was France's security frontier, its separation from Germany a geographical guarantee and a "psychological necessity" for the French people. The Potsdam decisions, to which France had not been party, provided for the creation of a central German authority; a reunited Germany might gravitate to the Slavic bloc and thus provide a more serious threat to European and French security. The Rhineland must be separated from Germany and the Ruhr internationalized. Truman replied that French fears of a revived Germany were exaggerated, since he had been to Germany and seen the extent of the devastation. At Potsdam it was

19. *The New York Times*, 26 August 1945.

agreed to limit German industrial production, making any military danger remote. The United States would not repeat the errors of the last war and finance German reparations. Security in the modern world lay not in territorial acquisition, Truman said, but in the new system of international security as manifested in the United Nations.[20]

Byrnes was even more blunt with Bidault. The United States would not recommence the errors of the previous war or spend one dollar to finance German reparations payments. No government could expect to recover its war costs. Byrnes complained of a high rate of exchange for the franc, and said that France had built high tariff walls around itself. Bidault upheld the French views that Germany must be amputated in the west as well as the east and refused to discuss the rate of the franc, but he did say that France repudiated economic autarchy and would adopt "a regime of [economic] freedom in the modern sense of the word, that is to say tempered by discipline."[21] The next day, Byrnes repeated to Bidault that the United States was opposed to internationalization of the Ruhr, which would bring the Russians into the center of Germany. Instead, the Americans were willing to consider guaranteeing French security and coal supplies for a period of 25 years. Bidault was cautiously favorable to this suggestion. In economic discussions with the Americans, Hervé Alphand noted a distinct sense of pessimism in Washington about the evolution of the French economy; the Americans accepted the French need for a transitional period of controls, but feared that the French were moving toward high tariffs, discrimination, and autarchy. But the Americans assured the French that "the existence of a strong France is a present axiom of American policy," and it was clear that the Americans wanted to consolidate the government in France, fearing that the only alternative was one of the extreme left.[22]

There was no meeting of the minds on the German question

20. Truman Library, President's Secretary's Files, Subject File, Foreign Affairs, France (178), notes by Jefferson Caffery on de Gaulle-Truman conversations, 22 August 1945.

21. "Dès que nous en aurons la possibilité nous adopterons certainement un régime de liberté du sens moderne du mot, c'est à dire tempéré par la discipline." Archives Nationales, AP 457, Papiers Georges Bidault, 735 (1), Etats Unis, Account of Bidault Byrnes conversations dated (sic) 13 August 1945. This conversation took place on August 23.

22. A.N., AP 457, Papiers Georges Bidault, 735 (1), "Résumé des Conversations de M. Alphand à Washington," 26 August 1945, and "Conversations à Washington et à New York sur certains problèmes européens," 31 August 1945.

during the remainder of de Gaulle's hold on power, and in fact no significant evolution could be discerned until late 1947. Only the Marshall Plan and the North Atlantic Treaty would alleviate French economic and security concerns sufficiently to permit the reconstruction of the German economy and polity.[23] During late 1945, the French began systematically using the veto, granted them at Potsdam by virtue of their membership on the Allied Control Commission, to prevent the creation of centralized agencies for certain services in Germany. In exchange, General Clay and the British, in whose zone the Ruhr was located, did little to facilitate German coal deliveries to France. Indeed, in November 1945, the Americans, British, and Russians agreed to reduce the French coal allotment from the Ruhr from 1.2 million to 900,000 tons monthly. When the French complained, they were told that the problem was lack of sufficient transportation in Germany, a problem created by their own refusal to permit the establishment of a combined transport authority.[24] There was interzonal friction as well, and the American military did not hesitate to create an espionage unit in Germany for the purpose of providing information about the French zone, where the influence of French Communism was very much feared. It was later discovered that Klaus Barbie, the infamous "Butcher of Lyon," was employed for this purpose, and when the French tried to extradite him to Germany in 1951, the Americans arranged for his escape down the "rat hole," the pipeline to South America for ex-Nazis.[25]

Simultaneously, de Gaulle sought to improve relations with the United States, paradoxically seeming to draw closer to the Americans in the aftermath of the October 1945 elections, in which the Communists gained 26 percent of the popular vote and laid claim to roughly one-third of the cabinet posts. On 20 November 1945, Colonel Dewavrin, alias Passy, de Gaulle's intelligence chief, called on Jefferson Caffery with a message affirming the general's desire to eliminate Franco-American misunderstanding. De Gaulle now understood that French foreign policy must draw close to that of the United States' if France was to survive. France, like it or not, had to get along with the U.S. and the

23. See John Gimbel, *The Origins of the Marshall Plan* (Stanford, 1976) and Timothy Ireland, *Creating the Entangling Alliance: The Origins of the North Atlantic Treaty Organization* (Westport, 1981.)

24. MAE, Y 1944–49, Internationale, Charbon, 89, dispatches of 3, 8, 12, 17, 19 November 1945.

25. *Klaus Barbie and the United States Government: A Report to the Attorney General of the United States*, presented by Allan Ryan, Jr. (Washington, 1983).

German question, which was "secondary to the Russian," would not be allowed to interfere. Dewavrin explained that de Gaulle would not allow the Communists any undue influence in the government, noting that they had been kept out of the "key" ministries concerned with foreign affairs. In Washington, this was appreciated as a "remarkable solution" to the Communist problem. On December 4, René Pleven, de Gaulle's minister of finance, called to say that the nationalization of French banks would not have any effect on American interests. France signed an aviation convention with the United States, agreeing not to raise tariffs and quotas pending international negotiations on liberalized trade and payments, as had long been insisted on by the United States. On 9 December 1945, Guillaume Guindey, a high French treasury official, told Caffery that France was prepared to ratify the Bretton Woods agreements and consider devaluation of the franc.[26] Turning his attention to economic questions, de Gaulle appointed Jean Monnet to head the Commissariat du Plan, which he attached directly to the office of the head of government's office, in part to keep it out of the range of Communist influence. Monnet concluded negotiations with Washington on the lend-lease loan of $550 million, and informed the Americans that France wished to open negotiations on French economic needs for the next four years, as outlined in the Monnet plan, then under preparation. Monnet was thinking of a loan on the magnitude of one recently concluded with Great Britain: $3.75 billion. Monnet said that France would only then participate in talks dedicated to a general international agreement on trade and payments, as Washington wished. It fell to de Gaulle's successor, Felix Gouin, to appoint Léon Blum to head the mission to Washington, which included Monnet, but it was under de Gaulle that the move toward Washington was begun.[27]

On January 18, Gaston Palewski informed Jefferson Caffery that de Gaulle planned to resign. It is a measure of how far things had evolved that Washington was genuinely regretful of de Gaulle's departure. Of course, Washington was to regret almost every cabinet crisis in the history of the Fourth Republic, with the

26. NARA, RG 59, 851.51/11-2045, 20 November 1945; 851.51/12445, 4 December 1945; 851.51/12-945, 9 December 1945. MAE, B Amérique, 119, 26 November 1945.

27. See Philippe Mioche, *Origines et Genèse du Plan Monnet*, and Irwin Wall, "Les Accords Blum-Byrnes, la Modernisation de la France et la guerre froide," *Vingtième Siècle*, no. 13 (Janvier-Mars, 1987), pp. 45–63.

exception of the fall of Mendès-France in 1955, and almost every new government that was formed in the unstable political situation in Paris was correspondingly greeted in Washington with a sigh of relief. But in the case of de Gaulle, the Americans believed he would return, and were generally reluctant "to accept the possibility that General de Gaulle, who had weathered so many grave situations in his country, might actually step aside in this latest upheaval." In an unusual tribute to de Gaulle, *The New York Times* said that he had opposition from the politicians but support from the people; and that by handing power over to the politicians, he wished to see whether they were capable of exchanging their policy of obstruction for one of responsibility. De Gaulle was a "towering figure, physically and morally. That France is whole today is due to his single-minded, inflexible faith." His work was great, he might well be recalled to power, and his departure left a vacuum in Europe.[28]

By 1947, Washington had rallied behind the Third Force, and the Americans remained more reluctant to accept the idea that de Gaulle might return to power than they had been to accept his resignation. The RPF was now feared in Washington as authoritarian, perhaps even fascistic. Caffery accepted the analyses of various Third Force politicians, according to which, if the general returned to power, a civil war might ensue in which the Communists would emerge victorious. Yet late in 1947, the Americans could not avoid the conclusion that the Ramadier government was failing and the regime imperiled. A series of negotiations during the bitter and protracted strikes of November-December 1947 focused on the conditions under which de Gaulle might return to power with American aid.[29] However, de Gaulle did not then seek power, and it fell to Truman's successors to deal with his later return to power at the head of a restored France. Despite his strong will and fiercely independent spirit, and the distinctly objectionable aspects of his period in the opposition, de Gaulle always remained, for Washington, a viable – though less preferable – alternative, in case the Fourth Republic could not be stabilized in the long run.

28. *The New York Times*, 24 January 1946.

29. I have gone into this in detail in *L'influence américaine sur la politique française* (Paris, André Balland, 1989).

Comment

Jean Lacouture

LET ME GO BACK, if you will, to Mr. Wahl's remarks concerning what was said in the preceding session. Because these papers focused more on the negative aspects – as well as on the people who intervened negatively – in the relationship between Free France and the United States during the war, we should remember, it seems to me, that several men intervened in a more positive way. Mr. Burin des Roziers has reminded us of how much de Gaulle lived in the constant hope that things would improve, that the clouds wouldn't last forever. He believed it with a certain naiveté, a word seldom used to describe de Gaulle.

But there were those bizarre conversations at Casablanca and especially at the White House which were subject to differing interpretations. Each time, de Gaulle hoped that the conversation had gone well. Indeed, his war memoirs are a striking testimony to this for Roosevelt's portrait in them is exceptionally laudatory. But ponder the fact that after each conversation Roosevelt cruelly joked that the man took himself for either "Joan of Arc" or "Clemenceau."

Despite these heavy clouds and the men who, for various reasons, have been presented in the papers here, there also were understanding people who tried to improve the situation. In London, for instance, we know that Ambassador Wynant and Admiral Stark (and their counterpart, René Pleven), tried to reconcile those very different points of view. We also should not forget that Eisenhower constantly tried to understand de Gaulle's views. Their relationship was good not only after 1958, but also during the war, when Eisenhower was a military leader who obeyed the political authority and orders that came from Washington. He did obey the orders, but he tried to give them a positive interpretation, favorable to Free France and de Gaulle. I think this should be remembered.

I also want to make another observation, which has not been made, about Roosevelt and his collaborators' fundamental mistrust of de Gaulle's democratic sentiments. This mistrust is understandable, although the intervention of a general in history could not altogether surprise the Americans, since several of the greatest American presidents were generals who had fought in the recent past. So, a general is not necessarily hostile to democracy. We Frenchman acknowledge the services rendered by the U.S. to our freedom, and we can almost grasp the reasons for their mistrust. However, there was the strange indifference with which President Roosevelt reacted to the following event: while Léon Blum was in prison in 1943 – but still in constant contact with the resistance through his family, who came to see him, and especially through Daniel Mayer and Renée, his step-daughter – he wrote a solemn letter of near supplication to Winston Churchill, who didn't need to be convinced, but also to President Roosevelt to say: "Go for de Gaulle, he is democracy." Coming from Léon Blum, it was striking, since few things tied de Gaulle to Léon Blum and their only meeting before the war had not been very favorable. Considering that Léon Blum was as symbolic of French democracy as Mr. Herriot, who also intervened on de Gaulle's behalf, it now seems strange that Roosevelt didn't take into account Blum's strong and positive defense of de Gaulle's links – spontaneous or not – with democracy.

Now, let me talk about the second part of the session, especially about Mr. Wall's remarkable paper. It seems to me that the colonial question was a crucial factor in the misunderstandings between France and the United States after World War II. This has been addressed in several papers, particularly in Mr. Munholland's paper concerning New Caledonia, but I think the Indochinese case was the more crucial.

I was very involved with Indochina since I was there immediately after the war, when important things were happening. It is true, and it is very interesting, that two months before he died, President Roosevelt modified his view about Indochina. I was very interested, like Prof. Funk, to know why Roosevelt changed his mind about the role France could play in Indochina. We know that he was opposed to the colonial principle, with good reason. We also know that he thought Indochina, like Dakar, could be a sort of base for an international police force, in which the U.S. would play an important role. There is not much to say about this, except to note his change, which is confusing.

Roosevelt was less severe about British colonial performances; but maybe, after all, the difference can be justified. I bring up the British because I am convinced that if he changed his position toward Indochina just before his death, it was, for the most part, because of British interventions. Although Roosevelt was perfectly capable of resisting British pressure – and we saw it during the war – I believe that Churchill, Mountbatten, MacDonald, and the English groups in Southeast Asia at this time intervened very actively in Washington, saying that English interests in Asia could not be maintained if they weren't flanked, so to speak, by a policy defending French as well as Dutch interests. I remember, by the way, that contacts between the English and French in Indochina were very close and positive, however different the problems of India and Burma were from those of Indochina. After all, we French people, leaving for Indochina in September 1945, were transported on the *Orontes*, a British ship, and, when we arrived in Saigon, welcomed by Gurkhas, which is to say, soldiers of the British. And we know about the intimacy of the relations between the British, who were responsible through the Postdam conference for maintaining order in southern Indochina, and the French military in this part of Indochina. So I am convinced that there were multiple British interventions to persuade the American government to treat the French well in Indochina. French and English interests were really linked in this part of the world, if not in the Middle East.

I would also like to recall that for those of us who were living there, right before the Indochinese war, when it still seemed possible to negotiate with the Vietminh, how much we were haunted by the American game there. We knew, especially since the coming to power of President Truman, that Washington was less hostile to the French position on and presence in Indochina. But it was obvious that if there was an official policy in Washington, there was a rather different policy implemented in Indochina; the American representatives in Indochina were much less understanding of the French. We were fascinated by the role played by the OSS. Mr. Wahl rightly recalled the role of the OSS in these circumstances, General Donovan's so-called personal policy, and the action, especially in Hanoi, by people like General Gallagher, Major Patti, and Major Helliwell. I was not at all conservative, I was even critical regarding French colonies. But I understood General de Gaulle's point of view when he said, and which he didn't say very often: "If we have to leave Indochina. . . ." What he didn't want was for France to be replaced in Indochina by any other power. It was very clear that he felt that in the Indochina affair (including the expansion of the Vietminh), there was, even more than a Soviet one, an American game, a trick to supplant the French, maybe even to put their Chinese friends in power.

Finally, there was a matter that made de Gaulle completely suspicious. Even for those who were less attached to France's power in the world, and to a neo-imperial power, it is certain that the American game in Indochina was quite ambiguous. It also certainly played a negative role in the psychological atmosphere at the end and immediately succeeding de Gaulle's time in power. This is not to mention that de Gaulle's main representative in Indochina was Admiral d'Argenlieu. It is true that d'Argenlieu, given his experience in New Caledonia, was particularly suspicious of any American move in Indochina, and he, alas, had a great influence on General de Gaulle. I am sure that all of this contributed to complicate the relationship between France and the United States at that time.

Comment

Melvyn Leffler

JEAN LACOUTURE HAS SPOKEN primarily about colonial and Indochinese issues, and I'm going to speak more about problems in Europe, particularly with regard to Germany. Both papers are interesting because they stress that there was a potential for a Franco-American accommodation in 1945 based on France's need for American financial aid and de Gaulle's recognition of this need. Yet the key stumbling block in 1945 was the German issue. In turn, both authors emphasize that the German issue was related to different conceptions in worldview and to contrasting conceptions about national security. However, Prof. Hill really doesn't explicate the differences in these larger conceptions. Prof. Wall does, saying that de Gaulle thought geopolitically while the United States thought economically.

I wonder whether this familiar dichotomy is an appropriate one with which to understand Franco-American differences. Economics and geopolitics were intimately interrelated, and de

Gaulle himself understood this. In his memoirs, he wrote that his chief motive was to restore the power of France, "which henceforth would depend on the economy." And indeed, his support of the Monnet plan was related to this realization.

U.S. officials, in turn, also grasped the relationship between power and economics. The men who guided America's postwar foreign policy were profoundly aware of the interconnections between military power, resources, and industrial productivity. In their view, German power inhered in Germany's capacity to mobilize the coal, steel, and metallurgy of the Ruhr and the Rhine for aggressive purposes. The most significant lesson that American policy-makers had learned from World War II was that no future adversary should be allowed to control the resources of Europe, and particularly the resources of the Ruhr and the Rhine.

Similarly, American officials believed that the open door world, symbolized by the Bretton Woods agreements, would not only enhance U.S. economic interests and expedite world recovery, but would also comport with U.S. strategic imperatives. Bilateralism and autarchy had been skillfully used by Nazi Germany and imperial Japan to both gain leverage over critical resources and build up artificial power. In contrast, an open door world would confer enormous advantages on nations (like the United States) that enjoyed comparative advantages in machine tools and heavy industry as well as on nations (again the United States) best equipped to export capital for investment in critical resources overseas.

The United States was in a uniquely favorable position at the end of the war. The only military threat that existed – and it was a potential threat, not an actual threat – was that emanating from the Soviet Union. De Gaulle incisively realized during his talks with Truman in August 1945 that the president and his advisers were not fearful of Soviet military power. De Gaulle saw the U.S. industrial capabilities and the U.S. atomic monopoly infused American officials with a great sense of military security. But Americans, de Gaulle realized, understood that their security was endangered by the "devastation, poverty and disorder" that afflicted so many parts of the world and particularly Europe.

More precisely, from Washington's perspective, the threat in Europe was twofold. Communists in Italy, France, and elsewhere might capitalize on the postwar unrest, gain power, and take their countries into the Soviet orbit. They might then sign bilateral treaties with the Kremlin, or extend air transit privileges, or perhaps even give the Kremlin base sites. The second was that an aggrieved Germany might choose to orient itself eastward. Either German leftists might capitalize on postwar turmoil, or just as likely, indeed more likely, German rightists might seek to fulfill national, economic, and political aspirations through an association with the Kremlin, which, after all, could offer markets, territory, and perhaps even unification.

The Franco-American dispute that emerged over Germany in 1945, therefore, did represent different conceptions of security. But these differences did not stem from the American penchant to think economically while the French thought geopolitically. Both nations fused economic and geopolitical considerations. De Gaulle defined French security in terms of gaining access to Ruhr coal and thwarting the revival of Germany power. He wanted to detach the Rhineland, establish international control over the Ruhr, and create a decentralized, federal Germany. He was willing to look either East or West "to contract the necessary alliance . . . without ever accepting any kind of dependency." Furthermore, he hoped to persuade the states along the Rhine, the Alps, and the Pyrenees to form a political, economic, and strategic bloc. In de Gaulle's view, this could constitute "One of the three world powers and should it become necessary, serve as the arbiter between the Soviet and Anglo-American camps."

The implications of de Gaulle's conception of French national security were incompatible with American conceptions of U.S. national security. It was already clear to policy-makers in Washington as early as July 1945 that German coal would have to be used to rebuild all of Western Europe. The production of 25 million tons of coal became the number one goal of occupation policy in Germany. In American eyes, Western Europe could not revive and Western European Communists could not be defeated without resuscitating German coal production and related industries.

But to win Germany's long-term loyalties to the West, one had to elicit its consent and cooperation. And the men who ran the U.S. Army in the summer of 1945 – Henry Stimson, John McCloy, Robert Lovett, and Robert Patterson – possessed a much larger conception of American interest than Prof. Hill implies in his paper. They opposed severing the Rhineland because they believed the "rump" of Germany would move politically and economically eastwards. They also believed that an autonomous Rhineland would remain a permanent sore point in Western relations with Germany. And they and their counterparts in the State

Department opposed the internationalization of the Ruhr because they feared Soviet participation and chicanery.

Now, some observers might think that this framework imposes too much bipolarity on the fluid situation that existed in the summer and fall of 1945. But de Gaulle himself certainly believed that such bipolarity already existed. The new president, de Gaulle wrote of Truman, "had abandoned the plan of world harmony, and admitted that the rivalry between the free world and the Soviet bloc now dominated every other international consideration."

Indeed, this explains the central point of Prof. Wall's paper. He stresses that despite the inherent tension between the United States and de Gaulle, American officials were sorry to see him leave office. They were sorry because they dreaded that without de Gaulle, the French Communists would maneuver their way to power. Yet U.S. policy-makers could not make concessions to de Gaulle on German issues because their own geopolitical conception made it imperative to stymie Soviet inroads in Germany as well as to co-opt German resources for the revival of the whole of Western Europe.

Reconciling western Germany's rehabilitation with France's security and integrating both France and Germany into a U.S. orbit required enormous imagination, patience, determination, and financial and military power. Over time, as Prof. Wall suggests, these goals would be worked out through the Marshall Plan, the North Atlantic Treaty, the Schuman Plan, and other institutional mechanisms. Although policy-makers in Washington in 1945 still did not define the Soviet Union as an enemy, prudence demanded that another totalitarian power must not be permitted to gain indirect control over the resources of Western Europe, either by outsmarting the Americans in Germany or by capitalizing on indigenous support of Communism in France. So de Gaulle was valuable as a counter to France's Communist Left, but his outlook toward Germany and his quest for an independent French policy made him an undesirable partner for an American government that was seeking to fulfill its own interrelated economic and geopolitical goals.

These goals, let me emphasize in conclusion, amounted to the establishment of a strong and stable France, invulnerable to a Communist takeover; the co-option of latent German power; and the creation of a multi-lateral trading order over which the United States would exercise a hegemonic role. In so doing, American officials hoped to assure a configuration of power compatible with U.S. strategic interests, and also sought to create a commercial order compatible with its economic interests. By keeping these points in mind, we can better understand what Prof. Hill means when he alludes to the different American and French conceptions of security. By keeping these points in mind, we can also understand why Prof. Wall is right when he says that American officials lamented de Gaulle's departure in 1946. Indeed, their fears for the future were very real. But their fears were not the result of their penchant to think economically while the French thought geopolitically. For officials in both nations, geopolitics and economics were inextricably linked – but in different configurations and with different implications for the future of Germany.

Comment

Nicholas Wahl

JUST A VERY SHORT FOOTNOTE to this period. It was not only Washington that had de Gaulle in mind as a guarantee against a Communist take-over in France, but also American business. During the year I did my first research on Gaullism, and especially the Gaullist party, I was interested in getting information the French hate to give, even today, to political scientists: the source of financing for political parties. I was interested in finding out how the RPF (*Rassemblement du Peuple Français*) was financed through party membership, and by occasional "friends" of the RPR. But one thing is certain, the RPF said, no money came from abroad. I finally found someone who admitted that some money did come from abroad, especially in 1947, the year the RPF was launched. It was no one less than the younger brother of the leader of the RPF, Pierre de Gaulle, who, partly because of naiveté, and partly because he was a little more removed from the events in 1953 than he had been in 1947, admitted that American business was interested in helping the only political party that, in the autumn of 1947, seemed strong enough to measure itself against the Communist party – and that was the RPF. De Gaulle's political party had, in one year, recruited close to a million members, and therefore seemed like the most solid anti-Communist force. As an American, it seemed perfectly normal to me that American business should support an anti-Communist party. I was surprised that the French were so reticent about it. Pierre de Gaulle went beyond this to say that his "great friend," Bill Bullitt, prewar ambassador in France, was the principal agent for raising money from big companies such as Union Carbide and others. Then, after some time, I was able to contact Ambassador Bullitt who, alas, in the late 1950s, was not in very good health. He said, "I can't remember clearly, but probably in those days I was raising money for lots of anti-Communist organizations, and I probably raised some money for de Gaulle's organization. I had great respect for General de Gaulle."

Part II
The United States and de Gaulle's Policy of Grandeur

CHAPTER 3

DE GAULLE CONSTRAINED BY THE ALGERIAN WAR, 1958–62

7

Dulles and De Gaulle

Richard Challener

"The first elementary steps for Americans is to give De Gaulle the courtesy of a clean-slate judgment. Up to now he has gone down in our political memory book as a professional 'intransigent,' a 'fanatic,' a stiff-necked authoritarian. . . . A lot of things have happened since 1953 when De Gaulle walked off France's political stage. It is wrong to conclude that he has lived in suspended animation ever since, as unforgetting and as unlearning as a 19th century Bourbon. . . . We *can* expect that De Gaulle will make some objections about the way NATO is now conducted. The greatest mistake the U.S. could make is to reject his complaints out of hand and insist on NATO in its present form. . . . The risk for France and for the U.S. is obvious. But the reward of even partial success would be great. The Gaullist deputy Jacques Soustelle last week expressed this hope well. 'France and De Gaulle may not be easy allies, but France will be a strong ally. In the long run a strong ally is better than a weak one.'"

So ran the editorial in the 9 June 1958 issue of *Life* magazine, an article written by its publisher, C. D. Jackson.[1] He received an immediate reply from his friend and sometime associate, Secretary of State John Foster Dulles: "I read the *Life* editorial about De Gaulle. It very much reflects my own viewpoint, and I am glad you have hit this note."[2]

The relationship between John Foster Dulles and Charles de

1. *Life*, XLIV, Pt. 3 (9 June 1958), 6.

2. Papers of John Foster Dulles, Mudd Library, Princeton University. General Correspondence and Memoranda Series, Box 3. John Foster Dulles to C. D. Jackson, 5 June 1958 (hereafter abbreviated as JFD Papers).

Gaulle, which began in the late spring of 1958, was of short duration. In the following February, Dulles went back to Walter Reed Hospital for the last time, resigned as secretary of state, and died of cancer in May. Moreover, prior to 1958, the two men had met only once and briefly in December 1947 when Dulles, then a Republican adviser to the American delegation at the London meeting of foreign ministers, made a highly controversial weekend visit to Paris to discuss with de Gaulle the political future of Europe and, especially, of Germany. Even a cursory examination of the transcripts of the many Eisenhower-Dulles phone calls in 1958 and early 1959, or the secretary's memoranda of his White House conversations with the president, will indicate that Franco-American relations were not high on the agenda of either man. For Eisenhower and Dulles, the crucial issues of 1958 and early 1959 were the many crises of that period: Lebanon, the "offshore islands" of Quemoy and Matsu, and, above all, Berlin. These, as even de Gaulle recognized, absorbed the attention of the Eisenhower administration. Even so, during the eight months de Gaulle dealt with Dulles, the French president raised virtually all the significant and troublesome issues that would set the agenda for Franco-American relations in the 1960s and come to a head during the Kennedy-Johnson years: control of nuclear weapons on French soil, French dissatisfaction with the structure and functioning of NATO, and, above all, de Gaulle's insistence that France be recognized and treated as a world power – his politics of *grandeur*. Dulles and Eisenhower did attempt to grapple with these issues, though their effort was sporadic, never definitive, and without real comprehension of the full thrust of the Gaullist agenda. What kept Franco-American differences from becoming as divisive as they were to be in the Kennedy-Johnson years was the Berlin crisis, which erupted in November 1958. And on Berlin the French president would, though for his own particular reasons, appear more hardline and unyielding than that stern Presbyterian moralist and defender of the West, John Foster Dulles.

The United States, albeit unwittingly, had played the role of precipitant in the sequence of events that led to the May 13 episode in France, the toppling of the Fourth Republic, and the return to power of the exile of Colombey-les-Deux Eglises. Early in February 1958, the French airforce, angered by Tunisian support for the Algerian rebels, had struck the Tunisian border town of Sakiet-Sidi-Youssef. The attack, in which the French used American-built aircraft, killed some 75 civilians, of whom 30 were children in a local school.[3] There was immediate outrage in the United States, not only in Congress, but especially in the White House and Department of State. Dulles exploded on the phone to Eisenhower: "bombing an open town on market day, slaughtering women and children was bad business." He wondered "where we are going from here, the French proving incapable of dealing with the North African situation. We started out with people in Morocco and Tunisia who wanted to be with the West, but are being driven into the other camp." The secretary, well known for his ability to paint ominous worst-possible-case scenarios, warned, "If the conflict could not be settled, we shall probably lose Tunisia, Libya, Morocco, the whole northern tier. . . . It was a question of trying to save that or trying to save NATO." Congress, he suggested, might well revolt "over our trying to pull France out of [their] financial hole without doing anything for North Africa." The basic problem, Dulles concluded, was that the government in Paris was so weak that "it does not dare to be bold and liberal."[4]

Eisenhower concurred. He immediately authorized his secretary of state to inform the French ambassador, Hervé Alphand, that the Gaillard government "should disavow the action and offer to pay reparations." Additionally, Dulles was to warn Paris that "we could not carry out our fiscal policies to France without, in the last analysis, having Congressional support, and we are in a rapid way to losing that." Dulles, however, did worry that "to take it out of their [French] hands would have such a bitter reaction in France that it would destroy NATO."[5]

Thus, the Eisenhower administration found itself caught in the same dilemma that it had faced little more than a year earlier over Suez: the need to support a NATO ally versus the strong desire to encourage decolonization and, above all, to prevent

3. On the Algerian question, see Dorothy Pickles, *Algeria and France* (New York: Praeger, 1963). For an account of de Gaulle's return to power and his ideas about foreign policy, see Alexander Werth, *De Gaulle: A Political Biography* (New York: Simon and Schuster, 1965), 238–42; Don Cook, *Charles De Gaulle: A Political Biography* (New York: Putnam, 1983), 313–25; and, especially, Alfred Grosser, *Affaires Extérieures: La Politique de la France, 1944–1989* (Paris: Flammarion, 1989), 137–61.

4. JFD Papers, Telephone Conversation Series, Dulles to Eisenhower, 9 February 1958. See also JFD's calls to his brother, Allen Dulles, head of the CIA, and Senator William Knowland on the same date (hereafter abbreviated as Tel Con).

5. JFD Papers, Tel Con, Allen Dulles to JFD, 9 February 1958.

newly independent nations from succumbing to Communism.[6] Eisenhower, moreover, felt deeply about Tunisia and admired President Bourguiba – not only anti-Nasser but also, in Eisenhower's later words, "a true friend of the West . . . an enlightened leader of his people."[7] In the aftermath of Sakiet-Sidi-Youssef, since neither France nor Tunisia wanted to take the issue to the U.N., the United States (with British assistance) sponsored a "good offices" mission to seek a negotiated settlement. But the chosen American representative was Under Secretary of State Robert Murphy, whose selection, to put it mildly, outraged Gaullists in both Algeria and France. They remembered Murphy blackly as one of the foremost American architects of the infamous deal with Admiral Darlan in 1942 and a heavy participant in the Roosevelt administration's effort to bypass de Gaulle and the Free French in favor of General Henri Giraud. The selection of Murphy not only played into the hands of the Gaullists, but added to the furor in the National Assembly, where memories were long and bitter about the American role in the Suez crisis. Premier Gaillard was accused of permitting the United States to intervene in what conservative and Gaullist deputies claimed was a domestic affair. The premier was overthrown on a vote of confidence in mid-April, immediately opening the doors to May 13 and the "revolution" that swept de Gaulle back into power.[8]

The attitude of the United States in the weeks of French crisis that followed May 13 was ambivalent – in part because of Dulles's own feelings about France, and in part because of numerous Franco-American difficulties that had arisen between 1953 and 1958.

John Foster Dulles, it should be remembered, had once been considered something of a Francophile. He had studied philoso-

6. On the eve of Suez, and just after the French had seized a Moroccan plane containing Algerian leaders, Dulles told Eisenhower of his "great concern lest the British and the French commit suicide by getting deeply involved in colonial controversies in an attempt to impose their rule by force on the Middle East and Africa." JFD Papers, White House Memoranda Series, Box 4, Memorandum of Conversation with the President, 24 October 1956.

7. Dwight D. Eisenhower, *The White House Years: Waging Peace, 1956–1961)* (Garden City: Doubleday, 1965), 488, 507–8.

8. Robert Murphy, *Diplomat Among Warriors* (Garden City: Doubleday, 1964), 394–96. Murphy, in his memoirs does show some sensitivity to the problem raised by his selection, but the various Dulles phone calls on the Murphy mission reveal none. Rather they contain unstinting praise for Murphy's handling of what Dulles termed "an impossible situation." See, for example, JFD Papers, Tel Con, various conversations on 13 April 1958 with Jandrey, Houghton, Elbrick and Palmer.

phy at the Sorbonne for a year following his graduation from Princeton in 1908; in the 1920s he had been sympathetic to French complaints about war debts and reparations; and in the immediate aftermath of World War II he had apparently thought it possible to structure the new European order around France. He had certainly been slow to jump on the German bandwagon; it took, in fact, the determined efforts of John McCloy and General Lucius Clay to "educate" him on the German potential and to introduce him to Konrad Adenauer, from which his famous friendship with Der Alte would slowly evolve.[9] Even so, when he attended the Moscow meeting of foreign ministers in 1947, Dulles unsuccessfully pressed for internationalization of the Ruhr, both as a way to aid European recovery and prevent Germany from ever again becoming a menace to European security.[10] In a lengthy memorandum, he argued that the unification of Germany would drive France into the Soviet bloc. A unified Germany, moreover, "will almost certainly be dominated by a spirit of revenge and ambition to recover great power status and, as after World War I, would align herself with the dynamic element of the disrupted wartime coalition" (i.e., the Soviet Union). Dulles's ominous conclusion: "If a united Germany can be created which initially will be independent of east and west, it would have enormous bargaining power which, if skillfully used, can give Germany the mastery of Europe."[11]

Details of what Dulles discussed with de Gaulle on his weekend in Paris in late 1947 are sketchy. The secretary's later recollection that he and the general had talked about de Gaulle's fear of a reunited Germany would suggest that he had by no means abandoned all of the premises of the above cited memorandum, which he had given to George Marshall at Moscow the preceding spring.[12] But the visit itself had been a near disaster. Georges Bidault, as well as segments of the French press, suspected that Marshall was using Dulles in a backdoor attempt to make contact with the Gaullist opposition. But Foster Dulles, as a Republican adviser to the American delegation – and, more importantly, as

9. Dulles Oral History Project, Mudd Library, Princeton University. Transcripts of interviews with Lucius Clay and John McCloy (hereafter abbreviated as DOH).

10. Forrest Pogue, *George C. Marshall: Statesman, 1945–1959* (New York: Viking, 1987), 174.

11. JFD Papers, Box 31, Memorandum for the Moscow Conference of Foreign Ministers, 7 March 1947.

12. Bernard Ledwidge, *De Gaulle et les Américains: Conversations avec Dulles, Eisenhower, Kennedy, Rusk, 1958–1964* (Paris: Flammarion, 1984), 21–22.

the principal foreign policy adviser to Governor Tom Dewey, the leading Republican presidential aspirant – always had freelance tendencies. Despite his claims that Marshall had approved his weekend jaunt, he had gone on his own initiative. (The "cover story" was that Mrs. Dulles wanted to go to Paris to buy a hat!) Marshall was annoyed. As soon as he got word of the controversy, he sent specific instructions to Dulles that he should either cancel his meeting with de Gaulle or, if he went ahead with it, should precede his talk with the former leader of the Free French by making contact with other leaders of the French political opposition, such as Leon Blum, Jouhaux, and even Maurice Thorez. Dulles, at a hastily called press conference, ducked the question of whether he intended to visit de Gaulle. (There is also a story, possibly apocryphal, that when Dulles returned to London and told Marshall that he had successfully arranged a meeting with de Gaulle, the secretary of state was monumentally unimpressed. He retorted that Dulles could have checked into a third-class hotel in Paris and that a representative of de Gaulle would have been waiting to see him in the lobby next morning.) Clearly, Foster Dulles's weekend in Paris had been a fiasco – unless, of course, Janet Dulles found a fashionable chapeau.[13]

All of this, to be sure, happened in 1947 when de Gaulle, out of political power for nearly two years, did not figure prominently in American foreign policy planning. But in 1958 – at the time of the May 13 crisis – John Foster Dulles, as Dwight Eisenhower's secretary of state, was now firmly committed to a policy that would bind Adenauer's Germany to the West. It was, indeed, one of his strongest objectives. A May 1954 memorandum, prepared for the president, had laid out his four principal foreign policy goals. Objective three was: the restoration of Western strength "by closing the Franco-German breach which for a century has caused the West to war with itself and expend its vigor in internecine strife."[14] But from 1953 on, Dulles had come to believe that the many and transitory governments of the Fourth Republic were responsible for frustrating many of his European objectives. There is no need in this article to provide yet another "agonizing reappraisal" of the many points of discord which had

13. DPH, McCloy interview and JFD Papers, Box 31. Memorandum dictated by JFD, 8 December 1947 and attached newspaper clippings.

14. For a detailed discussion, see my chapter, "John Foster Dulles: Theorist/Practitioner," in L. Carl Brown, ed., *Centerstage: American Diplomacy since World War II* (New York: Holmes and Meier, 1990), 328–48.

emerged between Washington and Paris after 1953: over the failure of France to ratify the one goal – the European Defense Community – which Dulles had relentlessly and single-mindedly pursued from the outset of the Eisenhower administration; over the French defeat at Dienbienphu and subsequent French unwillingness, despite offers of direct American assistance, to turn the "colonial war" in Indochina into a war for independence; over alleged French "softness" at the Geneva conference that, from Dulles's perspective, threatened to scatter dominoes across all of southeast Asia. To cap the climax, there had been French complicity in the abortive attack on Suez in 1956.

A no less important and constant irritant in Franco-American relations was Washington's annoyance at French policies in Tunisia, Morocco, and, above all, Algeria. This arose not simply from America's much proclaimed commitment to anti-colonialism, but, more significantly, from perceived cold war imperatives – the need to keep the Arab world out of the clutches of both Nasser and Krushchev, an objective deemed all the more important in the aftermath of Suez and the Middle Eastern resolution that had promised American assistance to all nations in the region that were threatened by those noxious forces. Thus, as previously noted, Dulles's outburst that the bombing of Sakhiet might drive the Arab world into the enemy camp. Indeed, two of the secretary's close associates recalled that the only time they witnessed Foster Dulles completely losing his temper was over hostile criticism from Paris in the late fall of 1957, when the United States shipped 500 rifles to the Tunisian government. Dulles was furious because he believed that Paris had reneged on a prior agreement to approve the shipment.[15]

But without question, his greatest frustration was over the instability of government under the Fourth Republic. The French, or so it seemed to official Washington, could never put together a cabinet strong enough to remain in office long enough to come to grips with colonial problems. Each cabinet, as one frustrated American official put it, simply exhausted itself in the process of forming the coalitions necessary to secure its parliamentary majority.[16] Dulles fully concurred with the assessment of the British ambassador, Sir Harold Caccia, that the Algerian situation was the direct consequence of French policies or "more

15. DOH, Interviews with General Lauris Norstad, Amory Houghton.
16. DOH, Interview with Horace Torbert.

accurately the lack of policies."[17] Nor did the Eisenhower administration appear to have much recognition of or sympathy for the internal politics that immobilized successive governments in Paris. In the later harsh words of Amory Houghton, the American ambassador to France, the problem of French political instability was "the problem of the dictatorship of the Assembly."[18] The French were fully cognizant of this attitude. As former premier Christian Pineau later observed, the United States simply did not understand the domestic politics that prevented Paris from developing an effective Algerian policy.[19] Moreover, stung by American criticism of France's role in Suez, many French politicians, well before de Gaulle's return to power, had begun to question French dependence on the United States and NATO. Indeed, the movement to create an independent French nuclear capacity – which de Gaulle eventually translated into his famous *force de frappe* – had picked up its momentum after Suez. The British, by contrast, had read the lesson of Suez as the need to restore their prized "special relationship" with the United States. Harold Macmillan, who succeeded Anthony Eden as the new British prime minister, capitalized on his wartime friendship with Eisenhower by moving swiftly toward cooperation with Washington – a cooperation symbolized both by their joint intervention in Lebanon and by the amendment to the MacMahon Act, which permitted the exchange of nuclear knowledge and materials with Great Britain.[20]

John Foster Dulles seems to have been genuinely surprised by the turn to de Gaulle in the spring of 1958. He was, one of his aides recalled, "flabbergasted" by the report of a special State Department task force which, in early 1958, had predicted a revolt in the French army that would shake France to such an extent that Charles de Gaulle would emerge as the only possible savior.[21] He was, of course, familiar with de Gaulle's criticisms of NATO, just as he had been annoyed by his previous opposition to EDC. Dulles anticipated difficulty with de Gaulle over the alliance as well as over de Gaulle's frequently expressed desire to

17. JFD Papers, General Correspondence and Memoranda Series, Box 2, Memorandum of Conversation with Sir Harold Caccia, 7 April 1958.

18. DOH, Interview with Amory Houghton.

19. DOH, Interview with Christian Pineau. See also interviews with Charles Yost and Livingston Merchant.

20. McGeorge Bundy, *Danger and Survival: Choices about the Bomb in the First Fifty Years* (New York: Random House, 1988), 471.

21. DOH, Interview with Julius Holmes.

restore France's status as a world power. But he knew little of de Gaulle's intentions towards Algeria – a matter on which, to be sure, he was far from being alone. But as his letter to C. D. Jackson clearly implied, and, as Amory Houghton later expressed it, Dulles welcomed the Gaullist order "with a sense of relief that the long and futile Fourth Republic had ended and at last there was strong leadership." Or as one of his closest associates, Assistant Secretary of State John Hanes, Jr., observed, "All of us felt a tremendous sense of relief" at the accession of de Gaulle as it promised stability in French political life.[22]

❖

During the long and drawn out process whereby de Gaulle received his "call" from the French people, the United States remained officially silent. Dulles, faced with a press conference shortly after May 13, wondered about the advisability of making "a friendly statement." But both he and his brother, CIA chief Allen Dulles, agreed that the last thing de Gaulle wanted from the United States was "a friendly push."[23] He and Eisenhower agreed that it was extremely important to make an official and friendly contact with the general as soon as he was officially in office. Eisenhower was particularly insistent. When U.N. Ambassador Henry Cabot Lodge, recalling his own wartime association with de Gaulle, volunteered his services, the president made it abundantly clear that he wanted Dulles for the job and offered the presidential plane for the mission.[24]

By early June, the arrangements were in place, and the secretary of state met the new leader in Paris on 5 July 1958. The two men, as previously noted, would meet twice again – at the NATO meetings in the late fall and again in early February 1959, when Dulles went on his last mission to Europe to coordinate the western response to Krushchev's Berlin ultimatum. Additionally, there was de Gaulle's famous memorandum to Eisenhower and Macmillan in mid-September, in which he outlined his demand that France be included in a new triumvirate of France, Great Britain, and the United States to develop common policies toward world problems and the employment of nuclear

22. DOH, Interviews with John Hanes, Jr., and Amory Houghton.
23. JFD Papers, Tel Con, JFD to Allen Dulles, 19 May 1958.
24. JFD Papers, General Correspondence and Memoranda, Box 5, Henry Cabot Lodge to JFD, 20 May 1958 and JFD to Lodge, 22 May; White House Memoranda, Box 6, Memoranda of Conversations with the President, 2 and 4 June 1958.

weapons. But most of the major Franco-American issues – including, though tangentially, the "tripartite question" – came up at their first session on July 5. It therefore makes little sense to analyze the Dulles-de Gaulle relationship – and the relationship between the two countries – in a strict chronological framework. The remainder of this chapter, therefore, will focus on the issues that arose at their first meeting and how these evolved in the coming months.

John Foster Dulles went well prepared to his July 5 meeting. His collected papers at Princeton contain various drafts of a so-called "talking paper," a memorandum of points he intended to cover in his discussions with de Gaulle. Moreover, the secretary carefully went over his nuclear proposals in Paris with both Ambassador Houghton and General Lauris Norstad, the commander of NATO.[25] The "talking paper" covered a wide range of subjects, from nuclear questions to attempts to reassure the French president that the United States had no intention of trying to supplant them in Africa. There was to have been, however, a harsh message to de Gaulle that, in the opinion of the United States, French policy in Algeria "had been designed to produce hostility and ultimately the alienation of North Africa from Western Europe." Also – a "given" in any Dulles presentation – was an extended discussion of the ideological, military, and political threat that Soviet and Chinese Communism presented to the West. Of particular significance was his intention to emphasize the importance of "engaging" the Federal Republic of West Germany to the Western Bloc. Although the "talking paper" was not actually used, and though Dulles (at least according to the official transcript) wisely decided to say next to nothing on Algeria, most of the points in it were fully covered at the July 5 meeting.[26]

To Dulles the nuclear issues were by far the most significant. He was well aware of the French effort to develop their own

25. JFD Papers, Selected correspondence, Box 127, Memorandum of 4 July 1958. Various versions of the "talking paper" are in the same box.

26. The complete State Department transcript, translated into French, is printed in Ledwige, *De Gaulle et les Américains*, 14–33 who obtained it and other materials, via the Freedom of Information Act. However, in a cable that he sent to Adenauer immediately following his meeting with de Gaulle, the secretary maintained that he had told the new French leader that France's role as a world power "would come about automatically if greater internal stability could be consolidated in France and problems such as Algeria and the external financial debt could be successfully resolved." JFD Papers, Selected Correspondence, Box 127, JFD to Konrad Adenauer, 7 July 1958. No such comments, however, are to be found in the transcript printed in Ledwige.

nuclear capacity, but he clearly hoped to persuade de Gaulle not to do so. His case was all so delicately put. Every nation, as the secretary carefully phrased it, had the right to decide for itself if it wished to become a nuclear power. But, he went on, such an effort would be costly, wasteful, inefficient – and unnecessary because the United States arsenal was more than sufficient. Moreover – and one wonders how well Dulles had gauged his man – the secretary even suggested that France might wish to take the initiative within NATO to get all its members to agree not to develop an independent nuclear capacity. Both ideas were complete non-starters. De Gaulle made it forcefully clear that France was determined to have nuclear weapons even though the effort would not be comparable to the United States and might take twenty-five years to achieve. On the "offer" to persuade NATO, de Gaulle did not even deign to respond.[27]

More serious were Dulles's attempts to get the French to agree to the stationing of Intermediate range ballistic missiles (IRBMs) on French soil. It was scarcely six months since the Soviets had launched Sputnik; they had developed and were about to install intercontinental ballistic missiles (ICBMs); and already there was a growing controversy in the United States about an alleged "missile gap" between the two countries. Moreover, Dulles was acutely aware – the ever-fearful Adenauer had long since made the point – that Europeans might conclude that the United States, knowing that the Soviets had the capability of striking directly against American soil, might not respond to a Russian attack on Western Europe. Moreover, Dulles was aware of French sensitivities about locating missiles on French soil. As early as the fall of 1957, in a discussion with Adenauer about the establishment of nuclear sites in Western Europe, Dulles had agreed that, on the issue of control, "a measure of concurrence" must be given to the French.[28]

In his July meeting, therefore, Dulles put forth a carefully reasoned argument. First, he claimed that, given its great advantages in manned bombers, the United States would have clear superiority over the Soviets for at least five years. Second, he

27. For de Gaulle's version of the meeting, see *Memoirs of Hope: Renewal 1958–62* (London: Weidenfeld and Nicolson, 1971), 207–9. For a sympathetic interpretation of both de Gaulle's foreign and atomic policy, see McGeorge Bundy, *Danger and Survival*, 472–82.

28. JFD Papers, General Correspondence and Memoranda Series, Box 1, Memorandum of Conversation with Adenauer, 14 December 1957.

emphasized, America had both the will and the determination to employ its nuclear power. The problem, he contended, was not American intentions, but whether or not both allies and enemies believed the United States. Fear of nuclear war, he added, would increase if a condition of stalemate between the two powers was reached. Moreover, if neither side was willing to accept the consequences of nuclear war, the danger of a localized war would increase. It followed, therefore, that the immediate problem was the need to develop regional defenses – above all, regional defenses organized in such a way that "nations threatened by a Soviet attack would not have to fear that their defenses depended upon a strategic armament under the control of another power, which might not be prepared to employ it in case of necessity."

Dulles then proposed to de Gaulle the stationing of tactical nuclear weapons, IRBMs (small, clean, tactical were the buzz words) on French soil. No less important, he added, was the need to develop ways and means to guarantee that these weapons would be employed according to plans worked out in advance and not dependent upon a political decision "in a far-away country." The Eisenhower administration, he averred, was prepared to examine these matters with the French in order to make certain that "in the case of a major attack against French or American forces in Europe, the nuclear weapons at the disposition of NATO would be employed immediately without having to wait on a political decision in the United States" – a decision, Dulles conceded, about which the French "could have some doubts." Additionally, the United States stood ready to assist the French in training their troops to use the new weapons and adapt French equipment for their use. This was, it should be noted, a concept that had been under consideration in Washington since the previous fall and in which General Norstad had been heavily involved. As Bernard Ledwige has pointed out, it anticipated certain aspects of the concept of "graduated deterrence" that Defense Secretary MacNamara would develop for John Kennedy.[29]

But there were severe restrictions. Everything, Dulles admitted, would have to be done in accordance with existing American law and within the context of NATO.[30] And the nuclear war-

29. Ledwige, *De Gaulle et les Américains*, 35. See also DOH, Interview with Lauris Norstad.

30. Norstad has insisted upon the point. See JFD papers, Selected correspondence, Box 127, Memorandum of 4 July 1958.

heads themselves would have to remain under strict American control. Additionally, Dulles had to concede that his proposal was still quite tentative, had not yet received full staff preparation in Washington. Indeed, much more thought would have to be given to the matter before anything more precise could be said about implementing the new concept.

Here again was an impasse. De Gaulle's response indicated that he had seen through the restrictions. That the concept would be carried out "within the context of existing American law" meant to de Gaulle that the French would not get the same favored access to nuclear information that the British had just attained through the amendment to the MacMahon Act. "Within the context of NATO" simply meant that the American commander in Europe would make the critical nuclear decisions. Not surprisingly, de Gaulle responded – and emphasized in his later meeting with Dulles – that France would have no interest in such proposals as long as the final decisions had to be made either by the American president or the American commander-in-chief in Europe. He would, he emphasized, accept nuclear weapons on French territory – whether in American hands or as part of NATO – only if France had complete control over them and the right to decide about their employment.

Foster Dulles had rightly assumed that de Gaulle would express not only his displeasure about NATO, but would also demand that France be treated as a world power. Hence, in his own presentation, he argued that the United States was committed to the idea NATO could succeed as a military alliance only if it took political issues within its purview. Great powers, he argued, always did have particular responsibilities, but in the modern age it was also important to recognize and respect the equality of all nations. There could not, he stressed, be unity without equality. Therefore, any attempt by a few great powers to get together and dictate to the lesser would only backfire, create dissent, shatter the unity that was necessary in the face of the Soviet threat. Dulles was, in effect, rejecting in advance de Gaulle's later demand for a triumvirate of France, Britain, and the United States to determine world politics and strategy.

Again, it hardly needs to be said, this was not sufficient for de Gaulle. The thrust of his criticism – first expressed in July, elaborated in greater detail in his letter to Eisenhower and Macmillan as well as at the December NATO meeting – was that the structure of NATO was unsatisfactory. It had been conceived in 1949, at a time when the only major threat was in Europe and at a time when American monopoly of nuclear weapons seemingly justified American control of the nuclear deterrent. But, de Gaulle argued, the times and the weapons had changed. Threats and dangers now emanated from Africa, the Middle East, and the Far East, areas not covered by NATO. French interests in these areas simply could not be handled within the existing NATO framework. The development of intermediate and intercontinental ballistic missiles had outmoded the NATO system of security. At the minimum, the French president insisted, NATO must be extended to North Africa and the Middle East and its command structure must be altered. At all times there was the constant theme that France had always been – and would always remain – a world and not just a European power, that France must be treated as an equal, that France expected to have a major role in shaping the flow and pattern of world politics.

This – the politics of *grandeur* – was spelled out in de Gaulle's September letter to Eisenhower and Macmillan. The French president was both blunt and specific:

> It appears necessary . . . that on the level of world policy and strategy that there be set up an organization composed of the United States, Great Britain and France. It would be up to this organization, on the one hand, to take joint decisions on political questions affecting world security and, on the other, to establish and if necessary to put into effect strategic plans of action, notably with regard to the employment of nuclear weapons.[31]

With time, too, came evidence that de Gaulle had some very definite ideas about how his proposed triumvirate would operate. In December, at the NATO meetings, he speculated to Dulles that, if the three Western nations had developed a common policy toward Morocco and Tunisia, the current situation in both countries would be far different. Moreover, he implied that a common policy toward Morocco and Tunisia would "inevitably have been a French policy." This clearly suggests that, in de Gaulle's ideal world, each nation would have a free hand – and the support of its allies – in those areas where its own interests were predominant. France would back the United States on the offshore islands of Quemoy and Matsu; the United States and Britain would support France in North Africa. There was, it

31. JFD Papers, White House Memoranda series, Box 6, de Gaulle to Eisenhower and Macmillan, 17 September 1958.

should be emphasized, no place for Adenauer's Germany in de Gaulle's world order. Germany, he stressed in December, was not a world power. She was still a divided nation, her final boundaries had yet to be determined, and she was still subject to certain external controls. Germany, he pronounced forcefully, "cannot speak with the same authority as the other three powers."[32]

❖

On his return from Paris in July, Dulles chose not to emphasize the differences that had emerged at his first meeting with the new French leader. In a soothing message to Adenauer, he chose simply to state that problems would inevitably arise over France's desires to play a larger role in NATO and the world and de Gaulle's attitude about stationing nuclear weapons in France. But his conclusion was weak: "We may both need to be conciliatory and helpful."[33] On the nuclear issue Dulles remained hopeful: "something mutually satisfactory . . . can be worked out." He seems not to have done much except brief Eisenhower about his visit. The president, in turn, merely dispatched a short, conventional, and (even for Eisenhower) bland note to de Gaulle. In it Eisenhower simply expressed his pleasure at the state of de Gaulle's health, his delight that his secretary of state and the general had had an opportunity for "a frank and honest discussion of our respective points of view," and his hope of "working with you closely in trying to resolve together the great problems of the world."[34] In the following weeks, there was virtually no mention of Franco-American relations (except with reference to French attitudes toward a summit meeting on the Near East that Krushchev had demanded after the intervention in Lebanon and about which de Gaulle was, if anything, less enthusiastic than Dulles.) About all that the records show are sporadic comments about "the importance of trying to get the French back into line."[35]

But Franco-American differences, whether taken lightly or seriously, were almost immediately obscured by the Lebanese

32. Ledwige, *De Gaulle et les Américains*, 46–58, official transcript of de Gaulle's meeting with Dulles on 15 December 1958.

33. JFD to Adenauer, 7 July 1958 as cited in Fn. 26.

34. JFD Papers, White House Correspondence, General, Box 7, Eisenhower to de Gaulle, July 1958.

35. JFD Papers, Tel Con, Harold Macmillan to JFD, 25 July 1958 and White House Memoranda, Box 7, Memorandum of Conversation with the President, 29 July 1958.

intervention in mid-July 1958 and by the second Quemoy-Matsu crisis that burst on Washington at the end of the summer. De Gaulle was shut out of the former, not consulted on the latter, and angered by both. At their July 5 meeting, Dulles and de Gaulle had discussed the Far East only in broad generalities, but Dulles had been quite specific in telling the French president that, should intervention in Lebanon be required, the United States did not favor a French presence. This, to be sure, was not directed against de Gaulle. Well before he returned to power, the Department of State had concluded that France should not be involved in any Lebanese operations. The reasons: Frances's ties with Israel and the danger that the Algerian situation would be involved. The French, Dulles told Eisenhower, "particularly are a great liability."[36]

At their July meeting, de Gaulle tried to force the issue. He bluntly told Dulles that, if the Anglo-Americans intervened on behalf of Chamoun, "France will be present. . . . France has many interests to protect in Lebanon, and if the western powers intervened, France would do the same thing." Dulles, in response, recited the same reasons earlier developed by the State Department – ties to Israel, the Algerian connection – and argued that a French presence would only complicate the situation.[37]

During the summer and fall, the United States continued to fry its own anti-colonial fish in North Africa. When Guinea opted for independence rather than accepting the Gaullist offer of association, the United States quickly backed the new African state for membership in the United Nations. When a resolution endorsing Algeria's right to independence came to the floor of the U.N., the United States simply abstained instead of siding with de Gaulle and voting against it. And while Dulles ceased to make suggestions about how France should deal with its Algerian problem, he clearly believed that the only viable outcome was independence.[38] Moreover, the available Eisenhower-Dulles documenta-

36. JFD Papers, Tel Con, JFD to Eisenhower, 13 May and 15 June 1958.

37. At the time of the actual intervention in Lebanon in July of 1958, the French press complained bitterly that de Gaulle had been misinformed by Dulles at their July 5 meeting. But these charges, as the transcript reprinted by Ledwige clearly shows, are inaccurate – though Dulles was something less than ingenuous in his many statements to de Gaulle that the best solution for Lebanon was for no one to intervene. Certainly he never told the French president about the extent to which, for many months, the Eisenhower administration had been seriously planning for a possible intervention in Lebanon. See Ledwige, *De Gaulle et les Américains*, 38.

38. JFD Papers, Tel Con, JFD to Christian Herter, 2 December 1958. See also Ledwige, *De Gaulle et les Américains*, 41–42.

tion, admittedly scant, does not suggest any new sensitivity to the French position. Rather, there are light-hearted comments about the fact that a delay in the U.N. vote on Guinea will not be a problem since, after all, the United States did not as yet have a specific ambassador in mind. To which Eisenhower joked that maybe this time we could just settle for a minister.[39]

De Gaulle was not pleased. His September memorandum was blunt and direct: "Recent events in the Middle East and in the Straits of Formosa have contributed to show that the present organization of the Western Alliance no longer corresponds to the necessary conditions of security." He underscored his point: "The sharing of risks incurred is not matched by indispensable cooperation on decisions taken and on responsibilities." Not surprisingly, at the December NATO meeting de Gaulle lectured the secretary on American policy at the U.N. Why, he asked pointedly, had the United States been in such haste to recognize Guinea, the one former French colony that could be expected to side with France's enemies? In a similar vein he noted that, while France had been consulted neither on Lebanon nor on Quemoy and Matsu, she had endorsed both actions. To strengthen his case against NATO, he argued that both Lebanon and the off-shore islands demonstrated, Berlin notwithstanding, that the real dangers to world peace arose in areas outside the jurisdiction of NATO. Moreover, he insisted, these same events increased the need for the triumvirate he had called for in September. And he was threatening. France would contribute nothing more to NATO and would refuse to accept IRBMs on French territory as well as any other American or NATO weapons with nuclear capability.

By late fall it must certainly have been clear to the French president that the Eisenhower administration was interested in neither his restructuring of NATO nor his concept of a three-power directorate to oversee global strategy. Charles Lucet, then serving in the French embassy in Washington, correctly recalled that when he and Ambassador Alphand handed de Gaulle's September letter to Dulles, "we knew from the start that he was not interested in the idea. . . . He never said so frankly and clearly . . . said it was necessary to study it, but we had the impression he was really not interested."[40] Dulles's brief report to Eisenhower certainly sustains Lucet's impression: "I told the French ambas-

39. JFD Papers, Tel Con, JFD to Eisenhower, 31 October 1958.
40. DOH, Interview with Charles Lucet.

sador that this memorandum raised very major problems and would probably require considerable study both by the Department of State and the Department of Defense."[41]

There was, nonetheless, considerable discussion within the administration about how to deal with de Gaulle's unwelcome proposals. NATO meant much to Eisenhower who, as its first commander in chief, had presided over its creation. Both Eisenhower and Dulles agreed that de Gaulle's proposed reforms would destroy NATO, and that there could be no restructuring in which three nations would be superior to the other twelve. Perhaps, they speculated, he could be satisfied by more consultation within NATO on political matters. His ideas on nuclear decision-making violated American principles of command and control.[42] Other NATO allies immediately objected. As soon as Rome got wind of de Gaulle's tripartite scheme, the Italian government dispatched its ambassador to the White House to make a strong protest.[43]

Both president and secretary, as well as subordinate officials in the Department of State, were exceedingly reluctant to open any discussions at all with de Gaulle over the proposals contained in his September letter.[44] Eisenhower, having heard the objections, made it clear that he "sided with the boys who advised caution." But he finally did authorize talks provided they were at the subsecretary of state level, with the further restriction that West Germany and Italy be informed, well in advance, "that the meeting was for the purpose of *discussing* the plan and was *not* the beginning of *carrying into effect* the De Gaulle plan."[45] Eisenhower facetiously suggested that the ideal solution would be if the representatives of the three countries held their discussion at dinner during a U.N. session when no one would know what they were doing.[46]

41. JFD Papers, Presidential Handling, JFD to Eisenhower, 25 September 1958.

42. For a discussion of the command and control issue, see Andrew J. Pierre, "Conflicting Visions: Defense, Nuclear Weapons and Arms Control in the Franco-American Relationship During the De Gaulle Era," paper read at the de Gaulle and the United States Conference, Columbia and New York Universities, New York City, 6–8 April 1990. (See chapter 12, pp. 275ff.) In his few public statements about the De Gaulle proposals, Dulles was extremely cautious. See, for example, his remarks at a 7 November 1958 press conference (JFD Papers, Department of State Press release No. 676) and the *New York Times*, 16 December 1958.

43. JFD Papers, White House Memoranda, Box 7, Memorandum of Conversation with the President, 2 October 1958.

44. JFD Papers, Tel Con, Eisenhower to JFD, 16 October 1958.

45. JFD Papers, White House Memoranda, Box 7, Memorandum of Conversation with the President, 13 October 1958. Underlinings are in the original document.

46. JFD Papers, Tel Con, Eisenhower to JFD, 16 October 1958.

Dulles's underlying skepticism runs through the transcript of an early November telephone conversation with Robert Murphy: "The proposal that came from De Gaulle is unacceptable. . . . Secretary said he would be inclined to ask the French first what they were up to . . . said all De Gaulle wanted was to crystallize the tripartite relationship. He tells us one thing, he tells others something else. He wants to dramatize before the world France's gradual emergence as a great power. Anything that will bring this result, he will accept. If we ask him just what his program is, he will be hard put to come up with something."[47] To Adenauer he relayed the message that the United States continued to be "perplexed" about the French proposals, then added, "They also speak of themselves as a 'potential' nuclear power. However, the mere fact of having an isolated explosion in the Sahara Desert will not make them a nuclear power. There is no free world nation except the United States that has the resources to be a significant nuclear power in relation to the USSR."[48] He later confided to CBS correspondent David Schoenbrun that what really disturbed de Gaulle was not that he wasn't consulted or informed, but that "we simply do not agree with him."[49]

Yet there were few immediate consequences of the Franco-American impasse. De Gaulle was, like the Americans, preoccupied – with efforts to find an acceptable Algerian solution and with the details of the constitution of the Fifth Republic. Moreover, since he was clearly aware of America's lack of interest in his tripartite proposal, it has been argued that his letter to Eisenhower and Macmillan was basically an attempt to build a public record which would demonstrate that the Anglo-Saxons were unwilling to accept France as an equal power.[50]

Regardless of de Gaulle's possible motivation, what kept French and American differences from coming to a head was the

47. JFD Papers, Tel Con, JFD to Robert Murphy, 8 November 1958.

48. JFD Papers, Chronological Series, Box 16, JFD to Adenauer, 31 October 1958. He was perplexed, Dulles wrote, because "The French Ambassador has just left me and has presented the matter somewhat differently than heretofore. He now suggests that the French proposal does not relate to NATO at all, but is designed to establish a relationship between the US, UK and France as regards world politics and military plans in non-NATO areas such as Africa, the Middle East, and the Far East."

49. DOH, interview with David Schoenbrun.

50. See the discussion on this point in Bundy, *Danger and Survival*, 476, who disagrees with the conventional wisdom.

Berlin crisis, touched off in November 1958 when Krushchev demanded that Berlin be turned into a free city – with the additional warning that, unless agreement was reached in six months, he would turn control of Berlin, as well as access to the city, over to the East Germans. Not only did Krushchev's demand raise the threat of a second Berlin blockade, but, for Dulles, it opened the ugly prospect of having to deal with (and at least implicitly recognize) the East German regime. Dulles and de Gaulle met twice – in mid-December and early February – in sessions at which Berlin was the first order of business. At both de Gaulle emerged as the most militant, the most unyielding.[51] In December the general said flatly that "If the Soviets threatened a war, we should accept the challenge even if it might involve a war. The only way to stop war was to accept the challenge, and we should make ourselves clear." In February he promised that by May 27 the French would be ready to use force as soon as the Soviets had completed the transfer to the East Germans. For Dulles's benefit, Foreign Minister Couve de Murville drew the lesson of the Rhineland in 1936: the need to act immediately without prior mobilization. "He felt that we should be prepared to act quickly with our military force to any Soviet or GDR interference with our access to and from Berlin."[52]

But John Foster Dulles, the very model of the modern "cold warrior," came through, on both occasions, as less provocative. In December, for example, he responded to de Gaulle by observing that he did not think that the Russians actually intended war and were, in fact, only testing the diplomatic waters. In February he argued that, before taking any action that might lead to shooting, it would be preferable to mobilize public opinion through the U.N. He also told de Gaulle that he did not think that Krushchev really sought a solution to either the German or the Berlin problems; rather, his objective was simply to compel the West to recognize the East German regime. With regard to de Gaulle's statement about being ready to use force at the end of

51. For the February meeting, see Ledwige, *De Gaulle et les Américains*, 64–71. Ledwige was not able to get a copy of the transcript of the February meeting but he did secure heavily excised copies of cables that Dulles dispatched after his meeting with de Gaulle and also the text of his full report to Eisenhower.

52. JFD Papers, General Correspondence and Memoranda series, Box 1, Memorandum of Conversation with Couve de Murville, 7 February 1959. considering how the French government had actually responded to the Rhineland occupation in 1936, it is more than a little ironic that Couve de Murville would make this particular historical reference.

May, Dulles wondered, in his report to Eisenhower, if the French had really thought through the implications of their statement.

This is not to imply that either Dulles or Eisenhower were not prepared to meet the Soviet challenge. It is easy to assemble another series of quotations from the record that demonstrate Dulles's commitment to firm resistance. In a memorandum, "Thinking Out Loud," prepared in early 1959, the Secretary argued that yielding on Berlin would destroy American credibility.[53] Concerned that Harold Macmillan's well publicized intention to visit Moscow presaged a British attempt to make a dangerous compromise, he tried to convince the British leader that, if the West yielded to Soviet pressure on Berlin, then the entire fabric of American policy in Europe would be endangered. Indeed, on numerous occasions in the spring of 1959, he speculated that Macmillan was prepared to accept the Soviet agenda, maintained that there were increasing differences between the British and American understanding of the nature of Communism, and claimed that the British, anxious to avoid a confrontation over Berlin, were about to abandon the close Anglo-American cooperation that had developed since Suez.[54] On his death bed in Walter Reed Hospital, he argued that the United States should not attempt to buy its way out of the crisis "by making concessions rather than standing firm and relying on our deterrent power to keep the peace." A March memorandum to Christian Herter contended that "if we show that we are prepared to use whatever force may be required to assure our rights in respect to Berlin, and if the Soviets have no doubts about this, then we will not in the event have to use that force."[55] Nonetheless,

53. JFD Papers, White House Memoranda series, Box 7, Memorandum, "Thinking Out Loud," 26 January 1959.

54. JFD Papers, Tel Con, JFD to Christian Herter, 10 April 1959 and Robert Murphy to JFD, 19 April 1959; General Correspondence and Memoranda, Box 1, Memorandum of Conversation with Harold Macmillan, 5 February 1959; Special Assistant's Chronological Series, Box 14, Memorandum by Joseph N. Greene, Jr. of conversation with JFD, 20 February 1959 and Greene memorandum of telephone conversation with JFD, 20 March 1959. Indeed, one of the last memoranda that Dulles prepared, dated 21 April 1959, focused on the differences between the British and American perceptions of the Soviet Union. The British, Dulles maintained, saw the Soviets as simply following the old Tsarist line and, therefore, believed "dependable agreements" were possible. The Dulles view, needless to say, was the opposite. See Special Assistant's Chronological File, Box 14, Memorandum of Conversation in Walter Reed Hospital between Dulles, Herter, Dillon, Murphy, Merchant and Greene. The JFD memo, in outline form, is attached.

55. JFD Papers, Tel Con, JFD to Christian Herter, 10 April 1959; Special Assistant's Chronological File, Box 14, Joseph Greene Memorandum for Christian Herter, 6 March 1959.

Eisenhower was willing to consider (provided Adenauer agreed) the prospect of a totally free Berlin, and both men doubted that the American public would support a war over the issue of recognizing East Germany.

Given his fears for Western solidarity over Berlin, Dulles, especially in February, welcomed de Gaulle's support – all the more so because, contrary to expectation, the French president had not raised the issues that separated France and America. On his return, he informed de Gaulle that the visit had given him a feeling of new confidence and that he was "particularly grateful that our thinking is so close to yours."[56] From Dulles's perspective, de Gaulle had proven reliable on the gut issues of the cold war. He did not, I believe, suspect that de Gaulle had other objectives – that his stance on Berlin was part of his larger European strategy of winning Adenauer for Paris and away from Washington. Indeed, while both de Gaulle and Dulles sought to support Adenauer on Berlin, their underlying motivation was far different.

The German question had first been raised at the initial Dulles-de Gaulle meeting in July of 1958. At that time, as previously noted, the American had emphasized the need to bind the Federal Republic firmly to the West. He had stressed that there were only three possibilities for Germany: (1) to be absorbed by Communism and tied to the Soviet Union, (2) to become neutral, or (3) to be bound to the West. The second possibility – neutralism – was probably worse than the first. He had, Dulles told de Gaulle, closely studied Germany's behavior after World War I when liberalism had not survived. Then – in a statement which, over a decade later, echoed his 1947 proposal at the Moscow Conference – Dulles continued: "A disengaged Germany would constitute an element between the two blocs which would use bargaining and blackmail for its own ends, which could very well lead to another war." He reminded de Gaulle of their first meeting in 1947 when, he recollected, the French president had worried about the same possibilities. No, he emphasized, the only acceptable policy was to bind Germany so firmly to the West that "German nationalism cannot again become an independent force." John Foster Dulles, in short, always pursued a policy of "double containment." His objective was not simply to contain Soviet expansion, but also to contain the latent force of German nation-

56. JFD Papers, General Correspondence and Memoranda series, Box 117, JFD to Amory Houghton, 9 February 1959.

alism. Adenauer *was* his friend, but he was also the vehicle for carrying out the Dulles policy of double containment.[57]

In July de Gaulle chose not to reveal his own larger intentions for Germany and Europe. In response to Dulles's lengthy disquisition, the new French president merely stated that there was no longer any rivalry between his country and Germany. Moreover, "the current situation did not worry him." At their December meeting, as earlier noted, he had made clear his belief that Germany was at best a European power, but not to be included in the ranks of nations with world responsibilities. But de Gaulle had already started his German initiative, his attempt to win Adenauer for Paris and away from Washington. The Krushchev ultimatum had come at an inopportune time; it arrived just two days before his scheduled second meeting with Adenauer, thus interrupting the flow of his German initiative. But de Gaulle fully understood just how much Berlin meant to Adenauer and, above all, how much the German chancellor always feared that the West would make a deal with the Soviets at the expense of the Federal Republic. Consequently, it was essential for de Gaulle to take an uncompromising stand on Berlin, thereby demonstrating to Adenauer that Paris could always be trusted. De Gaulle, indeed, put himself in a position where he could maintain that he had been more adamant than the Americans and that he had, in effect, helped to force them to maintain a strong stand. His German policy was far different from that of Dulles, whose double containment sought not only to bind the Federal Republic to the Western alliance, but also to contain German nationalism. De Gaulle, by contrast, wanted to make West Germany less dependent on Washington as an integral part of his larger objective – that of making Western Europe a third, and more autonomous force, a Western Europe in which the voice of Paris would be the strongest. Moreover, since he also intended to exclude Great Britain from the Continent, support for Adenauer contributed to his goal of winning German approval for the exclusion of Great Britain from the Common Market.

Thus, the full implications of the Gaullist demands on the United States – control of any nuclear missiles in France, the re-

57. For an interesting discussion, from the German point of view, see Wolfram Hanrieder, *Germany, America, Europe: Forty Years of German Foreign Policy* (New Haven: Yale, 1989), esp. 6–11, 142–43. See also Gordon Craig's review of Hanrieder and other recent books on Germany in *The New York Review of Books*, November 1989.

structuring of NATO, the establishment of a French-British-American triumvirate in world affairs – were postponed by the Berlin crisis during which both Dulles and de Gaulle supported Adenauer, but for widely divergent reasons. Indeed, in February, de Gaulle had downplayed Franco-American differences on these issues to such an extent that Dulles left Paris with the impression that the French president was satisfied, though grudgingly, with the progress of talks in Washington about giving France a larger voice in world affairs.[58]

It is interesting to speculate on what might have happened if Foster Dulles had not succumbed to cancer. His friendship with Adenauer was real, and the German leader, whatever his suspicions and fears, did have faith in him. Dulles, moreover, was an artist in stroking Der Alte. His letter to Adenauer, written after his July meeting with de Gaulle, was a masterpiece, with its soothing argument that nothing would ever develop in Franco-American relations that would weaken the bond between Washington and Bonn. Similarly, his communication to the chancellor after de Gaulle's September proposals sought to assure Adenauer that the United States did not believe that "present French thinking is along sound lines."[59]

But Dulles passed abruptly from the scene almost immediately after his February meeting with de Gaulle. Thereafter, it was Christian Herter who guided American policy through the Berlin shoals. The French president, while remaining just as firm on Berlin, now began some of his anti-NATO measures. The French fleet in the Mediterranean was removed from NATO command, and in April de Gaulle demanded that all American nuclear material be removed from French territory as well as those aircraft capable of carrying them.[60] It was left to Eisenhower, in September of 1959, to visit Paris and once again defend the American position: that while there should be more consultation within NATO, its organization could not be changed and that, while France and the United States should freely consult on world issues, they must, at all costs, avoid anything that suggested a tri-

58. It should be noted, however, that in February French Prime Minister Michel Debré had made the point that the French wanted more freedom of action for their fleet because neither the British nor the Americans had supported them on Algeria. But in his report to Eisenhower, Dulles noted only that de Gaulle had not brought up the Algerian issue.

59. JFD Papers, Chronological Series, Box 16, Dulles to Adenauer, 31 October 1958.

60. Ledwidge, *De Gaulle et les Américains*, 77.

partite arrangement to run the world. Eisenhower, for whom NATO meant so much, was unwilling to grant de Gaulle a special voice within the organization. Thus, the underlying disagreements were ultimately left to John Kennedy and the men of the New Frontier.[61]

Too much has been written about de Gaulle's policies as being the result of his underlying resentment of Britain and America because of the way they treated him and the Free French during the war and his long standing desire to free his country from alleged Anglo-American domination. Too much has also been written about his politics of *grandeur*. There is, to be sure, little question about the depth of his feelings on these matters. Nor is there any doubt that de Gaulle believed that an independent nuclear capacity was the key to autonomy in foreign policy. Nonetheless, as even his American critics conceded, France, under de Gaulle, did act with greater vigor; there was no longer the waffling, the indecision, the uncertainties that had marked the unstable coalition governments of the Fourth Republic. And by settling the Algerian problem – albeit to the fury of those of his supporters who had believed him to be the partisan of *l'Algérie française* – he put an end to the most divisive issue in French politics just as Richard Nixon's equally controversial policies ended the Vietnamese war, which had similarly polarized his society.

Viewed from the perspective of the early 1990s – with the cold war at last having become history – de Gaulle appears as the first, and most spectacular, of many political leaders both in Europe and elsewhere who sought to enhance the national interest of their countries by moving the world from bipolarity to multipolarity. For all his rhetoric of world power and French *grandeur*, de Gaulle believed that French national security would be enhanced in a multipolar world. He sought a greater and more independent voice for Europe, to be sure a Europe from which Britain would be excluded and in which France would be predominant. But West Germany, after Adenauer, would begin to pursue its own independent Ostpolitik. And perhaps coincidentally, just at the moment when de Gaulle was returning to power in France, the Chinese Communists were beginning to resist various Soviet

61. Bundy, *Danger and Survival*, 477–81.

efforts to coordinate Soviet and Chinese naval efforts. Mao Tse-Tung was informing Krushchev that the Russian terms for cooperation infringed upon Chinese sovereignty.

De Gaulle, as he had done immediately following World War II, would make his own overtures to the Soviet Union. Indeed, though they had no immediate policy implications, his interchanges with Dulles at their various meetings indicated that the two men had differing interpretations of the roots of Soviet behavior. When, for example, Dulles in July of 1958 delivered his standard peroration about the threat of Soviet ideology, the new French president, in response, talked about historic Russian expansionism established in the years of the Tsars. In December Dulles described Krushchev as more dangerous than Stalin because he was not "cold and prudent but a braggart, full of himself." De Gaulle, by contrast, spoke of Krushchev's insecurity because he had not yet consolidated his power.

Thus, Charles de Gaulle, for all his dedication to the will-'o-the-wisp of French grandeur, was but the first prominent European to break with many of the orthodoxies of the cold war. Neither Dulles nor Eisenhower could fully appreciate this. Indeed, they tended to believe that palliatives – such as greater political consultation within NATO – might suffice. But given their commitment to NATO and their policy of using NATO to tie Germany to the West, they simply could not respond positively to the French president. In the context of the cold war of the 1950s, de Gaulle's proposals seemed outrageous, a threat to the Western unity and cohesion they sought. But the full implications of the policy differences between Washington and Paris did not fully emerge because of the Berlin crisis in which de Gaulle and Dulles did cooperate but, ironically, for different purposes.

❖8❖

Kennedy, De Gaulle, and the Challenge of Consultation

Frank Costigliola

Among the somber Allied leaders who marched down Pennsylvania Avenue during John F. Kennedy's funeral, Charles de Gaulle stood out because of his height, his military uniform, his seniority among Western rulers, and, most significant, because he had presented the greatest challenge to Kennedy's direction of the Western Alliance. The basic issue between Kennedy and de Gaulle concerned whether and how to share power in the making of decisions. The Kennedy administration opposed de Gaulle's aspiration for a major, privileged voice in such alliance decisions, and then, when de Gaulle's quest failed, the Americans disapproved of the general's bid for significant independence in French foreign policy. In addition to the central question of decision sharing, Kennedy and de Gaulle disagreed over the governance and structure of the West's nuclear deterrent, the response to the Berlin crisis, policy on Germany and Vietnam, the nuclear test ban treaty, long-range cold war strategy, and monetary affairs. Although both leaders tried to limit these disputes to preserve the basic alliance, relations between Paris and Washington became frosty.

The two men began with different perspectives on global affairs. Educated before 1914, de Gaulle saw a world of competing states, where national interests often proved more enduring than ideology. De Gaulle looked ahead to the indefinite future when Russia might throw off its Communist ideology and rejoin Europe, perhaps in association with France, as in the past. Kennedy grew up in the 1930s and 1940s, decades rife with ideological combat, and perhaps that experience made it harder for him to imagine a world after the cold war. In any case, Kennedy remained the pragmatist interested in immediate prospects, not in the misty future. Kennedy shared the assessment of his ambassador to France, Charles "Chip" Bohlen, that de Gaulle's thoughts of post-Communist Russia were a "fantasy."[1] Although wary of Soviet power and possible aggression, de Gaulle fundamentally disliked the cold war because it limited French independence and ability to maneuver. While Kennedy felt the heavy burdens of tension with the Soviet Union, it was easier for him and other American presidents to accept the cold war stalemate that clarified diplomacy, helped create a domestic political consensus, tended to keep the allies in line, and legitimized U.S. leadership of the Free World.

Despite their differences, however, Kennedy and de Gaulle respected each other. President Kennedy had grown in de Gaulle's eyes from a "fumbling," "over-eager" "novice"[2] to a "vigorous" statesman whom the general complimented for thinking "like a European."[3] JFK esteemed de Gaulle as a great man who had restored French honor in World War II and who was reconciling France to the painful necessity of giving up Algeria. "De Gaulle had a curious fascination for President Kennedy," recalled Bohlen; JFK "was always trying to find out what made the man tick."[4] Yet Kennedy "also was irritated by De Gaulle's intransigence . . . his insistence on going it alone," remembered close adviser Theodore Sorensen.[5] Both superb politicians, the American and French presidents appreciated each other's ability to generate popular enthusiasm. After de Gaulle's stunning success in the 1962 French elections, Kennedy inquired of the American embassy in Paris what lessons he might learn from the general's campaigning techniques.[6] On the day of JFK's funeral, de Gaulle commented that "President Kennedy was extremely popular with the French people."[7] French citizens did mourn deeply

1. Bohlen, "Continuing Elements of de Gaulle's Foreign Policy," enclosed in McGeorge Bundy to the President, 30 August 1963, Box 72A, National Security File (hereafter NSF), John F. Kennedy Presidential Library (hereafter JFKL).

2. Charles de Gaulle, *Memoirs of Hope: Renewal and Endeavor* (New York: Simon and Schuster, 1971), 254.

3. De Gaulle to British Ambassador Pierson-Dixon, reported in Bohlen to Secretary of State, 25 November 1963, No. 1975/93F, Declassified Documents Reference Service (hereafter DDRS).

4. Charles E. Bohlen Oral History, JFKL.

5. Theodore Sorensen Oral History, JFKL.

6. McGeorge Bundy to Charles Bohlen, 29 November 1962, Box 71A, NSF, JFKL.

7. Memorandum of Conversation between President Johnson and President de Gaulle, "Franco-American Relations; Forthcoming Visit of General de Gaulle to the United States," 25 November 1963, No. 1975/94A, DDRS.

for Kennedy. "I felt a great choke," a French woman wrote to Mrs. Kennedy.[8] Not even "the Fall of France and the death of President Roosevelt . . . compared to the loss felt by the common man," observed Jean Médecin, mayor of Nice since 1938.[9] Bohlen reported that French officials "act almost as if they had lost their own head of state."[10]

Yet personal esteem and popularity did not translate into warm official relations. While attesting to Kennedy's appeal among French citizens, French Foreign Minister Maurice Couve de Murville also recalled that during the Kennedy years "Franco-American relations . . . had really deteriorated."[11] One measure of that breakdown was the paucity of direct contact between Kennedy and de Gaulle. The French president played the gracious host during John and Jacqueline Kennedy's 31 May to 2 June 1961 visit to Paris – indeed, he turned on the charm during meetings with every American president from Franklin Roosevelt to Richard Nixon. De Gaulle found Jacqueline Kennedy "dazzling and cultivated" as she displayed her command of French language and history. Meanwhile, John Kennedy quoted back to de Gaulle passages from the general's war memoirs. The French leader was less impressed with the policies JFK enunciated in Paris. "Kennedy offered me . . . a share in his projects," de Gaulle recalled; as usual, the Americans "could not conceive of their policy ceasing to be predominant or of ours diverging from it."[12] According to the general, one major divergence already threatened to split the Western alliance. At Paris, de Gaulle stressed his doubts whether Kennedy or any other American president would risk destruction of U.S. cities to oppose a Soviet attack on Western Europe. Kennedy's repeated assurances of America's nuclear credibility did not convince de Gaulle. Within months after the June meeting, French and American policies also diverged on the Berlin crisis. After signaling his resolve with a tough speech and a military build-up, JFK was determined to negotiate with the Soviets over Berlin. De Gaulle disagreed,

8. A.J. Rebeillard to Jacqueline Kennedy, 27 November 1963, Box 14, Condolence File, Robert F. Kennedy Papers, JFKL.

9. Reported in Paul F. Duvivier (Nice) to Department of State, 29 November 1963, No. A- 36, EX FE 3-1/Kennedy, John F., Oversized Attachments, White House Central Files, Lyndon B. Johnson Presidential Library, Austin, Texas (hereafter LBJL).

10. Bohlen to Secretary of State, 23 November 1962, No. 2517, ibid.

11. Maurice Couve de Murville Oral History Interview, JFKL.

12. De Gaulle, *Memoirs of Hope*, 255.

insisting that such talks would only alienate the West Germans and signal Western weakness.

The June 1961 summit proved to be the last time the two men would meet. De Gaulle put off Kennedy's repeated invitations to come to the United States until he finally agreed to visit JFK in March 1964. The March 1964 meeting would have been the second Kennedy-de Gaulle get-together in three years, as compared to the seven meetings in less than three years that took place between Kennedy and British Prime Minister Harold Macmillan. Even West German Chancellor Konrad Adenauer, who was nearly twice Kennedy's age and who never enjoyed rapport with JFK, frequently visited the White House and hosted the president in Germany in June 1963. In contrast to the frequent telephone calls between Kennedy and Macmillan, there was apparently only one call between JFK and de Gaulle. In December 1961, when France refused to approve a NATO communique endorsing negotiations on Berlin, Kennedy in exasperation called the general. Assistant Secretary of State for European Affairs William R. Tyler, who served as interpreter in the conversation, recalled that he transposed rather than translated, "for if Kennedy's remarks had been interpreted literally to de Gaulle, it would have caused trouble."[13] By late 1961, it appeared to both Kennedy and de Gaulle, but particularly to the French leader, that direct contacts with each other made little sense since there existed basic disagreements between American and French foreign policy.

The most fundamental difference was over consultation. American and French officials differed even on the meaning of the word "consultation." The U.S. readily discussed issues such as the Berlin crisis with the allies, informed them of American thinking, considered modifications of policy, invited European comments and suggestions, and sought allied unity. This is what the Americans meant by "consultation." If, however, some of the allies remained unpersuaded by the main thrust of U.S. policy, the Americans often went ahead anyway. For example, when the French and Germans remained opposed to negotiations with the Soviets over Berlin, Kennedy told Secretary of State Dean Rusk that the allies "must come along or stay behind. . . . [W]e cannot accept a veto from any other power."[14] French officials defined "consultation" or "coordination" of policy far differently;

13. "Background for 1000 Days," 12, Box W-13, Schlesinger Writings, Arthur M. Schlesinger, Jr. Papers, JFKL.

14. Kennedy to the Secretary of State, 21 August 1961, Box 82-98, NSF, JFKL.

indeed, de Gaulle sought an influential voice in decision-making and a veto on matters of vital interest to France. "Consultation should take place before a position is rigid," explained Hervé Alphand, the French Ambassador.[15] Yet sharing in basic decision-making was rare, partly because of the exigencies of controlling nuclear weapons, the ambivalence of many Europeans about wielding power, and the inherent difficulties of reaching consensus among proud, often fractious allies. But also standing in the way of shared decision-making was the Americans' conviction that their power and insight gave them the right to lead. Kennedy administration officials, like their predecessors and successors, were forever talking about improving consultation and consultation procedures, but despite their professions of good intentions, they remained reluctant to share power in deciding fundamental questions.

The consultation issue went back at least to 25 September 1958, when de Gaulle transmitted to President Dwight D. Eisenhower what became a famous memorandum. Noting that a nuclear war between East and West threatened France with annihilation without representation, de Gaulle demanded a significant voice in directing the Western alliance. He urged "that an organization comprising the United States, Great Britain and France should be created and function on a world-wide political and strategic level." This tripartite directorate "would make joint decisions in all political [and military] questions affecting global security . . . especially as regards the use of nuclear weapons."[16] When de Gaulle's proposal for a formal organization met adamant opposition from the Americans, British, and other allies, he pressed for an informal but binding tie. "De Gaulle actually wants a veto power over the use of our Strategic Air Command," noted an unsympathetic General Lauris Norstad, the Supreme Allied Commander in Europe.[17]

15. McGeorge Bundy, "Memorandum of conversation with Ambassador Alphand, Mr. Nitze, and Mr. Pelen, French Counselor," 8 May 1961, Box 70, NSF, JFKL.

16. De Gaulle letter in Alfred Grosser, *The Western Alliance* (New York: Vintage Books, 1982), 187; see also Michael M. Harrison, *The Reluctant Ally* (Baltimore: The Johns Hopkins University Press, 1981), 87-88, 95; Jean Lacouture, *De Gaulle Le Souverain 1959–1970* (Paris: Editions du Seuil, 1986), 358-63; McGeorge Bundy, *Danger and Survival* (New York: Random House, 1988), 476-79; Maurice Vaïsse, "Aux origines du Mémorandum de septembre 1958," *Relations internationales*, No. 58 (Summer 1989); 25368.

17. "Memorandum of Conference with the President, 9 June 1959 – 2:00 PM," No. 1986/3509, DDRS.

De Gaulle sought at least three benefits from tripartite consultation: a share in decision-making over such vital matters as nuclear war and peace, the German issue, and relations with the Soviet Union; American and British support for French policy in parts of Western Europe and Africa, areas the general saw as within a French sphere of influence; and, if these first two benefits proved largely unattainable, at least the appearance and prestige of French leadership as one of the Western Big Three. In meetings with Americans from 1958 to 1962, the haughty general – who hated to ask for anything – repeated this request for a central role in governing the Western alliance. Like Kennedy after him, Eisenhower was not about to share with either Britain or France real control over American nuclear or foreign policy, especially since such a tripartite arrangement would alienate West Germany, Italy, and other allies. Eisenhower tried to stall de Gaulle by setting up a middle level committee with the French and British for, in John Foster Dulles' words, "*discussing*" but "*not . . . carrying into effect* De Gaulle's plan."[18]

When Kennedy became president, de Gaulle tried again to win the U.S. to tripartite arrangements. "The trouble with de Gaulle was that he always returned to his September 1958 letter on the *directoire*," complained Douglas Dillon, a top official in both the Eisenhower and Kennedy administrations.[19] On 10 March 1961, Jacques Chaban-Delmas, president of the French National Assembly, arrived in Washington on a "personal mission" from the general. A "fundamental reconstruction" of the Atlantic Alliance had become essential, he argued to Kennedy. France wanted "intimate coordinat[ion]" through "decisions taken beforehand at the level of the conception of policies and not belatedly at . . . their implementation." Chaban-Delmas urged that the U.S. recognize that Paris's ties with Bonn and other neighbors made France the "natural channel for the coordination of policies on the [European] continent."[20] In short, de Gaulle wanted two things which the U.S. government opposed: equality with Washington in the decision-making of the Western Alliance, and a general deference to France in Western European issues.

18. John Foster Dulles, "Memorandum of Conversation with the President," 13 October 1958, Box 7, White House Memoranda Series, John Foster Dulles Papers, Mudd Library, Princeton University, Princeton, N.J. (Emphasis in original).

19. C.L. Sulzberger, *The Last of the Giants*, (New York: The Macmillan Company, 1970), 707–8.

20. Chaban-Delmas in "Tripartite Consultation between France, the United States and the United Kingdom," 10 March 1961, Box 70, NSF, JFKL.

Bundy and Assistant Secretary of Defense Paul Nitze alluded to such differences when they reminded Ambassador Alphand that "strategic cooperation requires a broader basis of political agreement than we now have."[21] De Gaulle pressed on anyway, telling former Secretary of State Dean Acheson, an important though unofficial advisor on European affairs, that multilateral talks within NATO had little appeal for France. However, "it was most important for France, Britain and the U.S. to discuss matters together and then together attempt to influence the course of events," the French leader maintained.[22] De Gaulle and his representatives repeated this refrain many times in the months after Kennedy took office, but in January 1962 the general enunciated perhaps most clearly how his view of organized consultation differed from the ad hoc or uncommitted discussions favored by the Americans:

> Unless there is an organized system, there is clearly no engagement for a common policy. We need a permanent cooperation of the three main western powers. The others . . . would have to follow us. What could Germany do except follow? Anyway, Germany had no world interests, no world obligations, no political undertakings.[23]

De Gaulle aimed to subordinate Bonn, whether as part of a tripartite arrangement that allotted West Germany and Western Europe to France, or with a Paris-Bonn axis, under French leadership and around which the rest of Western Europe might coalesce. When it became clear that the Americans rejected his version of consultation, de Gaulle refocused his ambitions to making France the predominant power in a united Europe, largely independent of the U.S., though under the protection of the American and French nuclear umbrellas. The Kennedy administration objected to this Gaullist ambition too, taking issue with both the content of de Gaulle's vision and his effort to get U.S. support for it through tripartite consultation.

After France detonated its first atomic bomb in February 1960, de Gaulle eased his demand for a veto over the use of American nuclear weapons. If France could not win a direct voice in Washington's nuclear decision-making, France could at least reduce its attractiveness as a Soviet nuclear target; and so de Gaulle did not

21. Bundy to Lucius Battle, 9 May 1961, Box 70, NSF, JFKL.
22. Dean Acheson to the President and Secretary in James Gavin to the Secretary of State, 21 April 1961, ibid.
23. Sulzberger, *Last of the Giants*, 842-43.

allow U.S. nuclear warheads to be based on French territory. As many French and American analysts argued, the independent *force de frappe* gave France possible leverage to launch U.S. nuclear forces. A top French defense official claimed that in the event of a Soviet assault on Western Europe, France's "limited nuclear force" could trigger an American attack on the Soviet Union by starting a nuclear conflict that the U.S. would have to finish.[24] A State Department paper essentially agreed: "The US has accurately seen the French *force de frappe* as threatening control of our own weapons"; French or other European nuclear weapons "put the all-important American nuclear force automatically at the service of Europe *as a deterrent*, whatever American policy might be in the matter."[25] Sorensen recalled that Kennedy "did not want De Gaulle having an independent nuclear force which could bring into play United States nuclear forces."[26] Aside from its possible role as a detonator, the *force de frappe* appealed to de Gaulle as a means of enhancing France's independence and prestige, its superiority over non-nuclear West Germany, and its right to share significant decision-making in the Western alliance.[27]

De Gaulle's bid for an independent nuclear force and hegemony in Western Europe challenged basic policies of the Kennedy administration. Led by Secretary of Defense Robert McNamara, the Administration wanted to concentrate control over the West's nuclear deterrent in Washington, not share it with national nuclear forces. Centralized crisis management was essential to the strategic doctrine of flexible response, an effort to replace the Eisenhower administration's policy of massive retaliation with a more adaptable, graduated escalation employing, first, beefed-up conventional forces and then, if necessary, selective use of nuclear weapons.

Kennedy hoped to reverse Eisenhower's policy of a special nuclear relationship with Britain and persuaded London to trade in its independent nuclear deterrent for membership in the proposed Multilateral Force (MLF), in which the U.S. would have a

24. James Gavin to Department of State, "U.S.-France Military Problems," 18 May 1962, Box 71, NSF, JFKL.

25. Thomas L. Hughes to Secretary of State, "Possibilities and Limitations in Dealing with de Gaulle," 6 April 1963, Box 72, NSF, JFKL (emphasis in original).

26. Sorensen Oral History, JFKL.

27. Jean Klein, "La stratégie de dissuasion de la France et la stratégie des Etats-Unis dans l'Alliance atlantique," in *L'Aventure De La Bombe* (Paris: Plon, 1985), 175–88.

major voice including probably a veto.[28] Conceived in 1960 by consultant and former State Department Policy Planning chief Robert Bowie, the MLF evolved into a proposal for a fleet of surface ships, manned by a mix of NATO nationalities, armed with nuclear missiles, and under NATO command. Its American backers, concentrated in the State Department, believed that the MLF would encourage European unity and head off nuclear proliferation by giving West Germany and other allies greater participation in the West's deterrent apparatus. If the British deposited their nuclear weapons with the MLF, this would set a precedent for France, perhaps post-de Gaulle, to abandon its separate nuclear weapons program. The U.S. ambassador to NATO explained that *any* truly "independent" nuclear deterrent – British, French, or European – was "dangerous." "We simply have to be in it."[29] Not surprisingly, the French opposed the MLF because it would strengthen American influence in Europe while weakening the distinction, vital to de Gaulle, between nuclear-armed France and non-nuclear West Germany. American and French officials agreed on the need, as a top U.S. diplomat put it, "to contain and provide a creative outlet for . . . West Germany,"[30] but they differed on who would control the reins on Bonn. De Gaulle wanted a Franco-German entente directed from Paris. The Americans sought to reinforce both ties within the U.S.-dominated NATO alliance and ties within the Common Market, the latter institution to be strengthened and kept open to American influence through the admission of Great Britain.

Differences over Germany involved the concern, especially strong among State Department analysts, that France's development of a national nuclear force might stimulate West Germany's nuclear aspirations, particularly after the retirement of the iron-handed chancellor, Konrad Adenauer. The mere prospect of German nuclear weaponry "would shake NATO to its foundations" and inflame East-West tensions, Secretary of State Dean Rusk feared.[31] Believing that the *force de frappe* set a bad example for Germany and complicated the problem of centralized deterrent

28. Kennedy to James Gavin, (n.d. but early 1962), Box 116, President's Office Files (herafter POF), JFKL.

29. Robert Estabrook Interview with Elbridge Durbrow, 2 November 1962, Box 1, Robert Estabrook Papers, JFKL.

30. Memorandum by David Bruce, 9 February 1963, Box 49-56, Theodore Sorensen Papers, JFKL.

31. Rusk to James Gavin, 5 May 1961, Box 70, NSF, JFKL.

management, the Kennedy administration adhered to Dean Acheson's advisory recommendation of 21 April 1961 not to sell or give to the French any information or equipment that would help their nuclear program.[32]

Although the administration never reversed the ban on nuclear aid to France, on several occasions it considered doing so if – and this was the key issue – de Gaulle would agree to what Bundy termed some "limitations on [the] freedom of action" of the French force and some "commitments to [the] common defense."[33] De Gaulle would not even discuss this issue of fetters on the autonomy of the French nuclear force. Since compromise on independence seemed impossible to de Gaulle, he avoided negotiating the question, frustrating such officials as Bundy who continued to hope for some workable deal.

Washington's escalating differences with de Gaulle in 1962 to early 1963 touched the style as well as the substance of alliance relations. "The heart of our problem with the French is that de Gaulle is playing a lone hand," Bundy wrote Kennedy in early October 1962. "This shows up all over the world, but it is most dangerous in Europe, and especially with respect to a Berlin crisis."[34] From Washington's perspective, de Gaulle had mounted a systematic challenge to U.S. leadership of a unified Free World. Couve de Murville expressed the French view: "We do not blindly follow U.S. policy. That is the real crisis."[35]

In contrast to de Gaulle's longing for privileged, shared decision-making among the Western Big Three, Kennedy officials preferred to conduct much of their European diplomacy within the larger, multilateral context of NATO, which institutionalized, facilitated, and legitimized U.S. leadership. NATO operated as more than a military grouping directed by the U.S.; it functioned also as an arena in which the European allies contained each other through what one State Department analyst termed a "subbalance of power" rivalry. Though this rivalry hampered Wash-

32. An exception was the sale to France of tanker planes to refuel the projected fleet of French nuclear bombers. These tanker planes would not significantly boost French nuclear capabilities, Americans calculated, since in the missile age "aircraft are phasing out as an effective Europe-based system for delivering nuclear weapons." See "Instruction for Ambassador Bohlen" enclosed in Rusk to the President, 16 October 1962, Box 71A, NSF, JFKL.

33. Bundy to Raymond Aron, 24 May 1962, Box 71, NSF, JFKL.

34 Bundy, "Memorandum for the President," 9 October 1962, Box 71A, NSF, JFKL.

35. Sulzberger, *Last of the Giants*, 882.

ington's long-held goal of European unity, the State Department paper explained, Europe's quarreling also "offers certain advantages to the United States," for "as one state moves into disagreement with specific American policies . . . the others tend to move nearer the US."[36] NATO meetings were, then, assemblies for venting – and diluting – what Americans perceived as the narrow, nationalist concerns of the European allies. NATO also served as a friendly forum in which Washington put forth its broader, alliance-wide interests, interests that generally prevailed because of America's superior power, Europe's division, and the North Atlantic consensus on the Soviet threat. NATO offered a final advantage to the U.S., according to Dean Acheson, who had done much to set up the organization: the NATO Council offered a place where "national policies . . . could be more easily harmonized by men who knew one another and were accustomed to working together."[37] Of course, that pattern of fraternal and accustomed harmony presumed U.S. leadership. "The US had a curious tendency to wish always to act as a member of some sort of group," commented de Gaulle.[38]

Of course France had its own group, the European Common Market. Although opposed to any submergence of French sovereignty or identity in a "supranational" organization, de Gaulle appreciated the Common Market as a vehicle for expanding and modernizing the French economy and for mobilizing Western Europe behind France. American officials looked differently at the Common Market. Although the U.S. faced some trade discrimination from the customs union, Washington officials, especially those in the State Department, appreciated the organization as a step in building a strong, integrated, "supranational" Western Europe able to tamp down nationalism, anchor West Germany, and assist Washington in combating poverty and Communism in the Third World.

American officials promoted Great Britain's admission to the Common Market, believing that the island nation, with its ties to America and its worldwide trading interests, would help keep the market a liberal, outward-looking bloc receptive to U.S. ideas, investment, and trade. Although many Kennedy officials

36. Thomas L. Hughes to Secretary of State, "Possibilities and Limitations in Dealing with de Gaulle," 6 April 1963, Box 72, NSF, JFKL.

37. Dean Acheson to the President and Secretary in James Gavin to the Secretary of State, 21 April 1961, Box 70, NSF, JFKL.

38. Ibid.

hoped to phase out Britain's special nuclear relationship with America, they appreciated the closeness of London's other ties with Washington. As a top official explained, "we hoped that if England went into Europe, it would take a sense of 'special relationship' with it, and that we would then have a 'special relationship' with Europe."[39] De Gaulle saw Britain's adherence in much the same light – and concluded that Britain in the Common Market would be America's Trojan horse.

In 1962, as negotiations for Britain's admission to the Common Market got bogged down over London's reluctance to sacrifice economic ties with the Commonwealth, Franco-American relations soured further. Unless a war broke out, "the US should stay out of [the] affairs of Europe," particularly in matters of European unity, de Gaulle bluntly told Ambassador James Gavin in May.[40] Stung, Kennedy instructed Gavin that "General de Gaulle really cannot have both our military presence and our diplomatic absence, and you should make this point with emphasis."[41]

Persistent payments deficits and shrinking gold reserves also threatened the American position in Europe, Kennedy worried. The president told the National Security Council that "if we cannot keep up our export surplus, we shall not have the dollar exchange with which to meet our overseas military commitments. . . . We must either do a good job of selling abroad or pull back."[42] Meanwhile, France rang up the world's largest balance of payments surplus. The French twitted the U.S. for spending beyond its means, especially in buying up French businesses. This criticism sparked concern by Kennedy and others that Paris might attack the dollar. Although Bonn agreed to purchase sufficient U.S. conventional military equipment to offset the U.S. balance of payments drain resulting from stationing GIs in West Germany, Paris refused such an offset agreement to cover the $320 million cost of keeping the 30,000 U.S. troops in France – unless Washington agreed to sell weapons-grade uranium, compressors, and other items for the *force de frappe*. "You don't want to sell us what we want to buy," concluded an exasperated General Lavaud after a nearly fruitless purchasing mission to Wash-

39. Quoted in David Nunnerly, *President Kennedy and Britain* (London, 1972), 11.

40. Gavin to Secretary of State, 16 May 1962, Box 71A, NSF, JFKL.

41. The President to Gavin, enclosed in McGeorge Bundy to William H. Brubeck, 18 May 1962, Box 71, NSF, JFKL.

42. "Summary of the President's Remarks to the National Security Council – 18 January 1962," Box 313, NSF, JFKL.

ington.[43] France did give short-term help to the U.S. balance of payments by early repayment of post-World War II loans, $470 million worth in 1962.[44] This discharge of past obligations to the U.S. fit de Gaulle's policy of French independence better than did purchases of American-made conventional weapons.

Still, de Gaulle's real independence remained limited, as the Cuban missile crisis dramatically showed. Paris remained dependent on strategic decisions made in Washington without significant input from France or from other allies. On 22 October 1962, Kennedy publicly announced a blockade of Cuba and demanded that Moscow remove its missiles from that island; on the 27th, probably the tensest day of the confrontation, Kennedy's Executive Committee (ExComm) debated whether to accept, either explicitly or implicitly, Nikita Khrushchev's proposal that the U.S. remove its Jupiter missiles from Turkey in return for Soviet removal of missiles from Cuba. On both occasions, U.S. actions could have started a chain of consequences leading to conflict in Europe and general nuclear war; yet the ExComm did not share basic decision-making with the allies on either issue. From the American perspective, bringing the Europeans into the process would have greatly complicated the ExComm's decision-making, negotiations, and military planning while compromising its secrecy. From the viewpoint of France and other allies, however, Washington's unilateral actions painfully underlined the Western Europeans' helplessness, their reduction to what the pro-American commentator Raymond Aron called "protectorate nations."[45] In a more egalitarian alliance, Washington might have accepted the costs of shared decision-making to arrive at a policy to which all of the NATO nations might have contributed.

As the ExCom debated what response to make to the Soviet missiles, Dean Acheson reminded Kennedy that since the United States was not going to consult with the French president, it should at least inform him "in an impressive way." Perhaps thinking that Acheson was as impressive as anyone and that his

43. Memorandum of Conversation with General Lavaud, Mr. Nitze, General Wehle, Mr. Kuss, Colonel Cocke, and Lt. Colonel Hoffman, 13 March 1962, Box 71, NSF, JFKL. See also "Balance Sheet of U.S. and French Requests in Military Field," 5 March 1962, ibid.; Gavin to the President, 9 March 1962, *ibid.*; President to Gavin, [n.d., draft], ibid.

44. Department of State to Bundy, "French Foreign Economic Policy in Relation to Trade Negotiations," 22 March 1963, Box 72, NSF, JFKL.

45. *Washington Post*, 20 December 1962.

hard-line stance in the crisis more suited the mood in Paris than in Washington, Kennedy asked the elder statesman to go to France. De Gaulle greeted Acheson with the premier question: "In order to get our roles clear . . . [H]ave [you] come . . . to inform me of some decision taken by your president – or have you come to consult me about a decision which he should take[?]" When Acheson replied, "I have come to inform you," de Gaulle dropped the issue of consultation, but he did not forget it. Argument was undignified and pointless.

France also lacked some of the technological capabilities necessary to act with independence in such a crisis. This deficiency was underscored when Acheson showed the general the aerial photographs of the missiles in Cuba. The American emissary remembered that de Gaulle was impressed when he looked at the pictures and asked, "from what height were these taken?" When Acheson replied "65,000 feet," the proud general started to say "We don't have anything . . . " – then caught himself, and remarked that he was not familiar with photography. The French leader agreed with Acheson that Khrushchev probably was bluffing and would withdraw the missiles. But whatever happened, he declared, "France will support [Kennedy] in every way in this crisis." The general did not expect to have to make good on this promise, but it fit his image of France as an ally independent but loyal in wartime. Moreover, he was setting a precedent for American loyalty in a European crisis.[46] Acheson also informed the NATO Council of the crisis – a few minutes before Kennedy made his October 22 speech.

Later, after the emergency, administration officials stressed the problem of security leaks if the allies had been consulted before Kennedy imposed the blockade. At a then-secret U.S. Senate hearing, Rusk said that making the Cuban crisis a NATO affair would have aggravated the danger of the Soviets moving on West Berlin. Further, Rusk testified, "we could not be sure *in advance* what the response of our NATO allies would be."[47] Kennedy officials did not want an exchange of opinion. During the crisis, Bundy commented that discussing the problem of Cuban missiles with the NATO nations meant getting "noise . . . from our allies saying that they can live with Soviet MRBMs,

46. Dean Acheson OH Interview, JFKL.

47. U.S. Senate, *Executive Sessions of the Senate Foreign Relations Committee 1963*, 15 (Washington, GPO: 1986), 6–7 (emphasis added).

why can't we."[48] Rusk later explained to the Senate that rather than ask the Europeans whether they "agree[d] with American actions," it was "simpler" and "easier" to poll them: "Do you in this situation of danger support the United States?"[49] NATO leaders said yes, but de Gaulle was not the only one to resent what one U.S. diplomat acknowledged as "consent-building notification after the fact." The British, West Germans, Italians, Canadians, Belgians, Dutch, and Turks all reportedly fumed at the lack of consultation.[50]

Even after the crisis, Rusk and other officials stuck to the official story that the U.S. had rejected Khrushchev's proposed deal to withdraw his missiles from Cuba in return for America's withdrawal of its missiles from Turkey. Of course, on October 27, at the height of the tension, Robert Kennedy had orally assured Soviet Ambassador Anatoly Dobrynin that while there could be no such explicit or public trade, the Americans would in fact remove the obsolete missiles from Turkey after the crisis. Kennedy officials decided to keep the implicit agreement secret lest Turkey and the other NATO allies complain that missiles supposedly protecting them were being removed by Washington, under Soviet pressure, to safeguard U.S. security.[51] The ExComm's unwillingness to share decision-making on this issue was heightened by the realization that although some NATO allies would favor removing the missiles in Turkey in return for eliminating those in Cuba, others, including the Turks, would oppose the swap. Americans viewed the allies as too fractious and too emotional to arrive at a sensible, cogent policy on this vital matter. The fear that Washington would sell out allied interests was "irrational and . . . crazy, but it's a *terribly* powerful fact," Bundy told the ExComm.[52]

48. "Cuban Missile Crisis Meetings, October 16, 1962," Presidential Recordings Transcripts, Item 1, 16, JFKL.

49. U.S. Senate, *Executive Sessions of the Senate Foreign Relations Committee 1963*, 15 (Washington, GPO: 1986), 6–7.

50. For an account based on declassified Dutch documents, see Cees Wiebes and Bert Zeeman, "'I don't need your handkerchiefs': Holland's experience of crisis consultation in NATO," *International Affairs* 66 (January 1990); 97–99.

51. Bundy, *Danger and Survival*, 434–36. A quarter century after the missile crisis, Bundy thought that probably NATO could have successfully handled an open discussion of the Turkish missile issue. The security issues here were complex; when the Cuban crisis seemed about to explode into war, Defense Secretary Robert McNamara suggested disarming the missiles in Turkey so as to protect Turkey from being an attractive Soviet target. See McGeorge Bundy (transcriber) and James G. Blight (editor), "October 27, 1962: Transcripts of the Meetings of the ExComm," *International Security*, 12 (Winter 1987/88), 72–75.

52. Bundy and Blight "October 27, 1962: Transcripts of the Meetings of the ExComm," 39.

Also on the 27th, a surface-to-air missile shot down an American U-2 reconnaissance plane over Cuba. This increased the danger of fighting breaking out over Cuba and spreading to Europe. Kennedy decided that "we'd better have a NATO meeting tomorrow." The president was not thinking of a conference to determine policy for the alliance, but a meeting that would provide the Europeans "an up-to-date briefing," make them "feel that they've a part of it . . . feel that they know," and warn them that the Soviets could attack in Berlin or elsewhere.[53] Rusk stressed the importance of consulting Europe, by which he meant taking allied views "into account before we decide what has to be done here in this Hemisphere." When Rusk suggested explaining to the NATO representatives the ExCom's preferred strategy for dealing with the missiles, Kennedy cautioned that "even if we want them to end up that way, we don't want to look like that's where we urged them." He worried that overt efforts to "steer" the allies could lead to recriminations if the crisis "goes bad, which it may well" do.[54] Khrushchev's agreement on October 28 to withdraw the missiles from Cuba made a NATO war meeting unnecessary. Europeans were relieved, but many were also daunted by their limited say in the life and death crisis. One British diplomat complained that "the lesser Powers, to which we . . . belong, have little influence on the policies and actions of the nuclear giants. Cuba made that very clear." Prime Minister Macmillan, who prized a special relationship more special to Britain than to the U.S., responded by trying to move even closer to the American giant.

For a short while, de Gaulle apparently tried to do the same. French embassy officials attempted, in a conciliatory way, to revive the consultation issue. Ambassador Alphand reported de Gaulle's view that "the Cuba crisis had to be handled without consultation, but this technique could not work in a Berlin [or other European] crisis." Alphand urged that we "move as soon as we can on the problem of political consultation; and the initiative for it should come from Washington." Moreover, de Gaulle was now willing to accept West Germany "as an equal of the Big Three."[55]

53. Bundy and Blight, "October 27, 1962: Transcripts of the Meetings of the ExComm," 71–72, 83.

54. Typescript of transcription of tapes recorded in the Cabinet room on Saturday, 27 October 1962, 68–69.

55. Memorandum of Conversation between Hervé Alphand and W. W. Rostow, "Political Consultation," 9 November 1962, Box 71A, NSF, JFKL.

Soon after this conversation, another French embassy official elaborated that "the way to make progress with Paris in alliance matters – until the questions of British accession to the Common Market and European political institutions are settled – is in this low key, concrete, and practical way" of quiet, serious discussions among the Western Big Four.[56]

Instead of improving consultation with de Gaulle, however, Kennedy approved a nuclear deal with Macmillan that aggravated French resentment of both the "Anglo-Saxon" powers. On December 10, Secretary of Defense McNamara announced that the U.S. would no longer develop for itself the airborne Skybolt missile, which the Eisenhower administration had promised to sell to the British for their national nuclear force. On December 14–16, Macmillan met with de Gaulle at Rambouillet and explained the Skybolt problem and his intention to ask the Americans for the submarine-launched Polaris missile. The prime minister also stressed Britain's desire to enter the Common Market. De Gaulle was offended at Macmillan's intention to put one foot in Europe while edging closer to the United States on military matters. The general apparently suggested that instead of asking for Polaris, Britain might join with France to develop a missile to replace Skybolt.[57] Macmillan deflected this proposal, aware that Washington officials opposed what one U.S. senator termed an "unholy alliance."[58] De Gaulle may have decided at this point to block London's admission to the Common Market; in any case, ensuing events confirmed his view of Britain as an American satellite.

A few days after Rambouillet, Macmillan flew to Nassau to meet Kennedy; there he pressed for the sale of Polaris missiles to Britain. JFK was torn between the need to demonstrate to the Germans and others his commitment to the MLF and the need to support the pro-American prime minister. The Kennedy administration was also sharply divided. Fervent MLF advocates like George Ball, Henry Owen, and Walt Rostow calculated that with-

56. Memorandum of Conversation between W. W. Rostow and Jean-Claude Winckler, "Consultation within Alliance, Suggested Dialogue Between President and General de Gaulle; Multilateralism," 29 November 1962, ibid.

57. See Konrad Adenauer, *Erinnerungen 1959-1963* (Stuttgart: Deutsche Verlags- Anstalt), 201–02 for de Gaulle's account. See also Lacouture, *De Gaulle Le souverain*, 333–34.

58. The quotation from Stuart Symington in U.S. Senate, *Executive Sessions 1963*, 622; see also Kennedy to Gavin, 14 June 1962, Box 71, NSF, JFKL; "De Gaulle and Great Britain," *espoir*, 42 (June 1983), 83–84, 91.

out Polaris, Britain (and, in the post-de Gaulle era, France) would have to fold its independent deterrent and accept the MLF. This would head off any German aspirations for nuclear weapons. Others, like McNamara, remained dubious about MLF and favored multinational integration in NATO. This latter alternative meant putting the British (and eventually perhaps the French) national deterrents under a centralized NATO command.[59]

Kennedy finally decided to sell Polaris missiles – but not warheads or submarines – to the British on the condition that they commit the missiles to the proposed MLF and/or the integrated NATO command. Macmillan agreed to assign the British Polaris missiles to MLF and/or NATO, but insisted on a broad escape clause providing for independent use for reasons of "supreme national interests." Of course, this was the only justification to employ such weapons. The deal was purposely ambiguous, allowing Macmillan to come away claiming that he had saved Britain's independent deterrent and allowing the different contenders in the Kennedy administration to claim that the multilateral or the multinational solutions had won out.[60] "The MLF is dead," Bundy reportedly told Henry Kissinger on returning from Nassau.[61] Meanwhile Ball and others continued pushing the scheme.

Although Kennedy officials debated what to do with the bundle of contradictions that was Nassau, they agreed that, in the words of an unpublished study written by Richard Neustadt and commissioned by Kennedy, "de Gaulle stood at the center of all questions."[62] Unlike Macmillan, who had probably already written off Common Market admission, the Americans, imperfectly informed about Rambouillet, hoped that Nassau was compatible with getting Britain into the market. Kennedy sent de Gaulle a

59. Tyler and Rostow to the Secretary, 17 December 1962, Box 19, Richard E. Neustadt Papers, JFKL; Rostow to the Secretary, 21 December 1962, ibid.; Bundy to the President, 29 December 1962, Box 71A, NSF, JFKL; George W. Ball, *The Past Has Another Pattern* (New York: Norton), 1982, 259–68; John D. Steinbruner, *The Cybernetic Theory of Decision* (Princeton: Princeton University Press, 1974), 234–38.

60. Richard E. Neustadt report to Kennedy, "Skybolt and Nassau," 15 November 1963, pp. 94–95, Box 319-324, NSF, JFKL.

61. "Background for 1000 Days," 16, Box W-13, Schlesinger Writings, Schlesinger Papers, JFKL.

62. Neustadt, "Skybolt and Nassau," 97. Neustadt later published an account of Nassau that did not include the classified policy documents quoted in the unpublished version. See *Alliance Politics* (New York: Columbia University Press, 1970), 30–55.

letter offering the Polaris missile on "similar" terms as the British.[63] Yet France had neither the submarines nor the warheads to make use of Polaris. Would the Kennedy administration now reverse its policy and supply the nuclear aid to enable France to use Polaris?

Both Paris and Washington officials were unsure, and the latter saw advantage in the uncertainty. McNamara hoped French Polaris missiles (assigned to NATO but with the escape clause) would lure the *force de frappe* into NATO. Once in NATO, the force's independence could be whittled away through integrated military planning. Such nuclear aid, McNamara hoped, could free French military spending for additional conventional forces.

Neustadt reported that Ball and the other MLF enthusiasts "saw all this differently." The Polaris deal "was worth offering the French since a negotiation might entangle them in such a way as to assure complaisance toward the British" getting into the Common Market. "But once the British had got into 'Europe,' we should . . . work our way back to the safe ground of a 'truly' multilateral solution – MLF. Otherwise, the German problem would remain to haunt us."[64] The key point here was that both the MLF opponents and advocates wanted to enmesh de Gaulle in negotiations that would limit his autonomy.

The degree to which the Americans were willing to compromise with de Gaulle was important because although the French had, as Bundy reported to Kennedy, "a very sour view of Nassau,"[65] the general asked his representatives to ascertain what the Americans would offer and at what cost. The general may have been disappointed, but he was probably not surprised. On December 29, Alphand found Kennedy, as Paris officials reported, "non-committal" about warheads.[66] On December 28, Rusk told his deputies he expected a considerable price for nuclear aid to France, namely "a considerable alteration in . . . [French] policy, especially toward NATO and the multilateral force."[67] Most American officials assumed that discussions with France over Nassau would go on quite a while, and, as Neustadt put it, while the general was talking, "he could not, at the same time, be beastly to the British."[68]

63. Ibid., 97-98.
64. Ibid., 101.
65. Bundy to the President, 29 December 1962, Box 71A, NSF, JFKL.
66. Neustadt, "Skybolt and Nassau, 103.
67. Ibid., 104.
68. Ibid., 105.

Washington officials underestimated de Gaulle's anger, acumen, and independence. According to visitors present when the general learned of the Nassau agreements, he flew "into a tremendously violent temper" – directed mostly at the British, whom he denounced for "betraying Europe" and as "no longer worthy of being considered a free country."[69] Already impatient with British obstinance on trade issues in the Common Market negotiations, he would not begin another entangling talkfest with the "Anglo-Saxons." "The French are so very suspicious," Bundy noted.[70] De Gaulle's suspicions were probably heightened by Alphand's report and by Ball's trip to France and Germany "explaining" Nassau – with a decided slant toward the MLF.

On 14 January 1963, de Gaulle demonstrated that he could raise the ante on non-consultation. In a dramatic press conference, the French president poked a hole in the Kennedy administration's policy toward Europe by rejecting both the Nassau formula and Britain's admission to the Common Market. If Britain entered the Common Market, the grouping would dissolve into a "colossal Atlantic Community dependent upon and controlled by the United States." De Gaulle criticized American predominance in nuclear as well as in economic matters. Mocking American efforts to centralize the West's nuclear deterrent, he observed that "in strategy . . . as in economics, monopoly . . . appears to him who holds it as the best possible system." The Cuban crisis had demonstrated that America, without consulting its allies, might initiate nuclear war to protect its interests. No one could say whether the U.S. would risk the same for Europe. Thus, France had to have an independent deterrent. In effect, de Gaulle declared irrelevant the internal American debate over whether to integrate existing national nuclear forces under NATO or create a mixed-manned nuclear unit under NATO. He saw both alternatives as threats to French independence. De Gaulle understood – and rejected – that which attracted the Americans to integrated forces: the resulting "web of liaisons, transmissions and interferences" such that the *force de frappe* would lose its independent capability, escape clause or no.[71] While rebuffing the British and Americans, de Gaulle snuggled closer to the West Germans. Despite warnings from Washington and from more Atlantic-

69. Memorandum on de Gaulle enclosed in Klein to Bundy, 18 April 1963, Box 72, NSF, JFKL.

70. Bundy to the President, 29 December 1962, Box 71A, NSF, JFKL.

71. *New York Times*, 15 January 1963.

minded officials, such as Foreign Minister Gerhard Schroeder and Economics Minister Ludwig Erhard, Adenauer signed a friendship treaty with France a week after the general's bombshell.[72]

De Gaulle's January 14 pronouncements were a slap in the face to the Kennedy administration. At first, Kennedy feared the rebuffs might signal a seismic shift in France's position between East and West in Europe. Theodore Sorensen, one of Kennedy's closest advisers, recalled that the president received from British intelligence a report "that De Gaulle was contemplating some sort of master negotiation with the Soviet Union." Sorensen remembered that for a short while Kennedy was "extremely concerned" about what such a Franco-Russian deal might portend for "our posture of world leadership."[73] On 31 January 1963, Kennedy drew up a list of "questions to be settled in the coming months," an enumeration that expressed his concern with de Gaulle's challenge: "What kind of a deal can de Gaulle make with the Russians which would be acceptable to the Germans[?]"; "Will de Gaulle top us" with the Germans?; "How can we improve the American line from the various embassies so that there will not be as much [sic] pro-de Gaulle stories[?]"; "What defense can we build with the dollar[?]"; and so on.[74] The siege atmosphere soon lifted when it became apparent that there was no Franco-Soviet deal afoot. Although the U.S. could do little about getting Britain into the Common Market, it still had to contend with de Gaulle's treaty with Adenauer and the general's subversive projection to Western Europeans of a future Europe largely independent of the U.S.

At this juncture, Kennedy commissioned David Bruce to review U.S. postwar policy toward Western Europe. The Ambassador to London, Bruce ranked as a highly-respected, long-term veteran of various diplomatic missions. He responded to Kennedy's request with a succinct statement, widely discussed within the administration, which emphasized that the U.S. should continue its postwar policy of promoting Europe's unification and close ties with Washington. Bruce argued that, particularly in an era of chronic payments deficits, "the US needs Euro-

72. Bruno Bandulet, *Adenauer zwischen Ost und West* (Munich, 1970), 199-208; Ball, *The Past Has Another Pattern*, 272–73.

73. Sorensen Oral History, JFKL.

74. "Questions to be settled by the United States in the coming months," 31 January 1963, Box 62, POF, JFKL.

pean resources to promote the defense, security, and trade of the free world." He continued: "We cannot accept the prospect of the US and Europe going their separate ways. . . . A fragmented or adventurist Western Europe might make all manner of trouble for us, quite apart from the danger of Communist takeover. In a nuclear age, especially, we must have a voice and play a stabilizing role in European affairs." De Gaulle, of course, would have read this memorandum as further evidence that America intended to preserve its dominion over Western Europe. Bruce recognized that although many Europeans disliked the idea of French hegemony on the continent, they agreed with de Gaulle's criticism of American predominance. Bruce blamed much of the "considerable anti-Americanism in Europe" on the "growing fear that we may want to control a strong and united Europe by smothering it in the Atlantic Community." To break the vicious cycle between "European dependence" and "US predominance," the experienced diplomat urged that Washington build a "true partnership" with a uniting Europe on the basis of the Multilateral Force in which the U.S. would relinquish its veto and on meaningful political and strategic consultation.

Bruce's analysis was probably more realistic than was his prescription. "True partnership" was problematic for several basic reasons: most U.S. officials, including Kennedy, remained unwilling to give up the American veto in the proposed MLF (though they talked about doing so to encourage Europeans to take the scheme seriously); Europe remained divided; and genuine sharing of decision-making with an autonomous partner remained difficult for Americans to swallow. Even Bruce, after all, thought it dangerous if Europe played "a role independent of the US."[75]

Meanwhile, for Kennedy, the combined impact of de Gaulle's blunt assertion of French independence and the sobering experience of the Cuban crisis had clarified wonderfully his sense of U.S. self-interest. A week after de Gaulle's press conference, Kennedy expressed his long-held resentment that the French and other Europeans were getting an easy ride from American defense efforts. He told the National Security Council that "we should consider very hard the narrower interests of the United States." "We have been very generous to Europe," the president

75. Memorandum by David Bruce, 9 February 1963, Box 49-56, Theodore Sorensen Papers, JFKL; for the memorandum's impact, see Arthur Schlesinger, "Background for 1000 Days," n.d., Box W-13, Schlesinger Papers, JFKL.

asserted, "and it is now time for us to look out for ourselves." Kennedy valued the MLF proposal not as a means to "true partnership" in Bruce's sense, but rather as a device that "will increase our influence in Europe and provide a way to guide NATO and keep it strong." He would "push for a multilateral force which will weaken de Gaulle's control of the [Common Market] Six."[76]

In the months after de Gaulle's press conference, the Kennedy administration pushed the MLF while ensuring that West Germany remained in the American orbit. The president appointed skilled diplomat Livingston Merchant to direct negotiations for the MLF and decided to include Germany in a trip to Europe. When a top German Foreign Office official visited in February, Kennedy reportedly gave him a "real dressing-down" over the de Gaulle treaty.[77] Administration officials, assisted by Acheson and John J. McCloy, both 1940s godfathers of the Federal Republic, lobbied Atlantic-minded German leaders to append to the treaty with France a *Bundestag* resolution reaffirming the primacy of Atlantic relations.[78]

By mid-1963, the January crisis had passed and new developments made Western European problems appear relatively less important. On May 16, the German parliament ratified the Franco-German treaty with a preamble emphasizing Atlantic ties. Kennedy's hugely successful June 1963 German visit helped undercut de Gaulle's dream of a Paris-Bonn axis. A public opinion analysis of the JFK tour indicated that "you beat de Gaulle in a close election in Germany," Bundy told Kennedy.[79] The MLF now seemed less urgent, especially since Europeans, other than the Germans, remained cool toward the proposal. Especially cold to the scheme were French leaders, including some otherwise pro-American Paris officials. The Soviets, who opposed the MLF but now seemed amenable to a limited nuclear test ban treaty, added an important element. In an era of budding détente, the

76. "Remarks of President Kennedy to the National Security Council Meeting of January 22, 1963," No. 1986/2274, DDRS.

77. "Background for 1000 Days," 34, Box W-13, Schlesinger Writings, Schlesinger Papers, JFKL.

78. McCloy to Adenauer, 4 February 1963, Box 31, ibid.; Acheson to Kurt Birrenbach, 19 February 1962, Box 3, Dean Acheson Papers, Sterling Library, Yale University, New Haven, Conn.; Acheson, "Memorandum of Conversation with W.A. Menne, 3 May 1963," Box 68, ibid.; author interview with George Ball, 24 June 1986.

79. Bundy to Kennedy, "Week End Reading," 19 July 1963, Box 318, NSF, JFKL.

U.S. should not appear "as the nuclear rearmers of Germany," Bundy advised the president. Kennedy accepted his suggestion to stop pushing so hard and to let the Europeans press for the MLF if they wanted it.[80]

This decision was part of Kennedy's partial shift away from European concerns. "What made things interesting to Kennedy," Bundy recalled, was the "prospect that you *could* do something or that you *must* do something."[81] With British admission to the Common Market stalled, the Berlin crisis eased, and the de Gaulle challenge contained, Western Europe fit neither category. In foreign policy, Kennedy focused instead on the promise of a nuclear test ban treaty and on the precariousness of South Vietnam.

In both these areas, the U.S. and France stood at odds. The established nuclear powers – the United States, the Soviet Union, and Britain – negotiated the test ban treaty of July 1963, intending that, once signed by most of the world's nations, the accord would slow nuclear proliferation. The treaty permitted only underground tests – more expensive and more difficult to monitor than atmospheric explosions. Americans hoped that other nations would hesitate to go nuclear if they had to pay the huge costs and face negative world public opinion. "The central problem," Rusk remarked, "is France."[82]

Despite Kennedy's personal plea to de Gaulle and sincere offer to help France conduct underground tests (though where and on what terms JFK apparently did not specify), the French leader declared there was "no chance" of signing the treaty. De Gaulle bluntly told Bohlen that he did not believe Kennedy could supply France with the needed technical information; that he "doubted whether Kennedy seriously wished to do it"; and that even with such data France would have to test itself to verify the workability of a hydrogen bomb.[83] De Gaulle's obstinance undercut a main purpose of the treaty – to mobilize a global coalition against the development of independent nuclear capabilities in the People's Republic of China and (a less serious danger) West Germany. Asked in a secret Senate hearing whether the Soviet Union would join in "coercive action against China," Rusk

80. Bundy to the President, 15 June 1963, Box 23, NSF, JFKL.

81. Author interview with McGeorge Bundy, 21 January 1988. Emphasis in original.

82. Rusk in Senate, *Executive Session 1963*, 435.

83. Bohlen to Secretary of State, 30 July 1963, Box 72A, NSF, JFKL; see also Kennedy to de Gaulle, 24 July 1963, Box 73A, ibid.; David Klein to Bundy, 30 July 1963, ibid.

replied: "[I]f we got everybody but China to sign . . . we could . . . take some action along this line."[84]

De Gaulle further undermined efforts to isolate China by increasing trade and other contacts with Peking. In August 1963, he angered Washington officials by publicly criticizing U.S. involvement in South Vietnam. Kennedy and other White House officials became apprehensive about French efforts to mediate between North and South Vietnam.[85] Bohlen commented that Southeast Asia was an area "where de Gaulle has really caused us trouble."[86] After Kennedy's death, U.S. involvement in Vietnam would become a major irritant between Washington and Paris.

A few weeks before his death, Kennedy himself offered an assessment of his relations with Gaullist France. After meeting with de Gaulle's foreign minister, JFK told a journalist: "We confirmed, Mr. Couve de Murville and I, that we agreed on nothing, but we agreed that this total lack of accord should not harm Western countries." Kennedy could speak with such confidence because his Administration had contained de Gaulle's challenge, affairs in Western Europe seemed less pressing than those in other parts of the world, and the general remained committed to the Atlantic alliance though not to the NATO organization. De Gaulle and Kennedy both accepted the split between them, though they saw it differently. In Kennedy's view, "de Gaulle's strategy [of independence], which I do not understand very well, requires a certain tension with the United States" – a summation that suggested that the general had manufactured tensions to justify French autonomy.[87] However the record of the Kennedy years suggests that de Gaulle had the more accurate perspective: tensions arose primarily because American officials believed that French independence conflicted with U.S. interests.

Kennedy expressed the broad consensus within the U.S. Government on how to deal with de Gaulle. Like both the Eisenhower and Johnson administrations, the Kennedy administration

84. Rusk in Senate, *Executive Session 1963*, 436, 470; see also Gordon H. Chang, "JFK, China, and the Bomb," *The Journal of American History*, 74 (1988); 1287–1310.

85. CIA Memorandum, "Gaullist France and Communist China," 23 October 1963, enclosed in Chester L. Cooper to Bundy, 24 October 1963, Box 73, NSF, JFKL.

86. "Background for 1000 Days," 73, Box W-13, Schlesinger Writings, Schlesinger Papers, JFKL.

87. *New York Times*, 11 December 1963. See also Maurice Couve de Murville, *Une politique étrangère* (Paris: Plon, 1971), 105.

tried to contain and defuse de Gaulle's challenge by pushing America's own agenda while minimizing public acrimony, offering Europe a counter attraction, and waiting for the succession of a more amenable French leader. No Kennedy official favored de Gaulle's bid for the tripartite directorate or independence in foreign and strategic policy, in part because the other allies also had apprehensions about the general's program. But even though de Gaulle's demand for consultation and his stubborn independence stemmed from his concern with French national interests, they also flowed from a broad Western European yearning for a larger and more independent voice in governing Western affairs. The Kennedy administration's reluctance to share real power over decision-making reflected America's historic difficulty in actually treating the European nations as equal partners – instead of just talking about such equality. De Gaulle's difficulty in making good on his ambitions illustrated another historic difficulty – the problems Western Europeans, whether as individual nations or as a coalescing group, have had in mobilizing the power necessary to deal with America as an equal. What Bruce described as the vicious circle of American predominance, European dependence, and mutual resentment has long operated. But if the Western alliance is to prosper in the radically changed environment of the 1990s and beyond, it must successfully meet the challenge of building an egalitarian relationship. For all his fierce nationalism, this was a challenge de Gaulle could understand.

❖9❖

The American Economic Challenge: De Gaulle and the French

Richard F. Kuisel

De Gaulle's France was unique among West European nations in resisting American investment during the 1960s. There may have been grumbling in West Germany and Britain about the unprecedented flow of dollars, but only in France did a government try to control, and even discourage, this influx of foreign capital.[1] Nowhere else was public opinion so excited, disturbed, and involved with the issue. Nowhere else did the mid-1960s witness a comparable expression of anti-Americanism.

The French encounter with American capital under de Gaulle's presidency raises important historical questions. Why was France so different from other West European nations who welcomed American firms and dollars? Why, on the level of both public policy and public opinion, did France respond to American investment as a challenge rather than as a boon? From a different perspective, who was responsible for the policy of *contrôle*, how did the policy evolve, and what were its consequences?

French resistance is especially puzzling since the nature and magnitude of American investment in France was not more threatening than it was elsewhere within the European Community. In a quantitative sense, the American challenge was not strong. In fact, France received only a relatively small share of dollars compared to other Common Market countries, yet it made the greatest effort at controlling them.

Direct American investment in France in the 1960s was relatively modest in volume and limited in scope. After reaching a peak between 1961 and 1964, the rate of inflow slowed until 1969

1. For European reaction see: Alfred Grosser, *The Western Alliance* (1980), pp. 224–25; Christopher Layton, *Trans-Atlantic Investments*, The Atlantic Institute (1968), pp. 44–48.

when it resumed under the presidency of Georges Pompidou. By 1963, of total United States investment in the Common Market, 40 percent went to West Germany, 25 percent to France, and 15 percent to Italy.[2] By the end of 1967, the stock of direct United States investment in France was $1.9 billion, but this was much less than (in billions) Great Britain's $6.1 or West Germany's $3.5, and not much above Italy.[3] On a per capita basis, France was about average for the European Community.[4] At the sectoral level, dollars may have been focused on French growth sectors, but levels of control were no more concentrated than in West Germany or elsewhere within the Six.[5] Moreover, while the rate of American investment in France slowed in the mid-1960s, it continued to grow elsewhere in Western Europe, at least until 1966. In the decade from 1959 to 1969 the distribution of American capital among the Six shifted to France's disadvantage.[6]

If quantitative measurements of the magnitude, velocity, and concentration of American investment fail to explain French resistance, then what is the answer? It was a matter of politics and perceptions. At the crux of the phenomenon, besides Gaullist foreign policy, were perceptions of American power and American business as well as French fears of economic backwardness. This paper is about both French policy and the consensus that supported it.

President de Gaulle initiated the policy of resistance and he dramatized and politicized the issue of American investment. He may have even persuaded some to adopt a less accommodating stance than they would have done otherwise. Just as he did in his grander policy of trying to end the American "protectorate," de Gaulle led public opinion. To the extent that his American policy enjoyed wide support, the president helped build it. He exploited popular misgivings about American influence, especially the stationing of American troops in France, and he capitalized on grievances about how the United States had treated France and French interests since the war. At the peak of troubles between

2. Louis Manuali, *La France face à l'implantation étrangère* (1967), pp. 11–13.

3. Robert B. Dickie, *Foreign Investment: France a Case Study* (1970), p. 20.

4. For example Benelux received $47, West Germany $37, France $30, and Italy $16 according to Jean Meynaud and Dusan Sidjanski, *L'Europe des affaires* (1967), p. 77.

5. Gilles Bertin, *L'Industrie française face aux multinationales* (1975), pp. 50–51.

6. French share fell in this decade from 28.7 percent to 21.2 percent. West Germany's share advanced from 35 percent to 41.7 percent (Rainier Hellmann, *Puissance et limites des multinationales* [1974], p. 41–42).

France and the United States, the French, when asked whether de Gaulle's policy toward the United States was too harsh, too conciliatory, or *comme il faut*, half said it was *comme il faut*.[7] If America was generally liked, it was the president who shaped and mobilized opinion to adopt a more anti-American stance in the mid-1960s.

De Gaulle's motives and the evolution of his policy toward the American economic challenge (defined here as a question of investments and excluding trade and tariffs) fit the conventional interpretation of Gaullist foreign policy. While Gaullist resistance to American capital was often couched in socio-economic reasoning, such as that dollars went to buying profitable firms without bringing any advantage, or American subsidiaries did not play by the rules of the game, his motivation was political. He reasoned that the flow of capital represented outside – worst of all, American – control over vital economic sectors. French independence was at risk when decision-making rested with corporate headquarters located across the Atlantic. From his perspective, there was danger in allowing industries, especially those essential to national defense, to fall under American control. The fact that in 1963 Washington blocked the sale of a special computer deemed vital for the French nuclear program demonstrated the consequences of such technological dependence. On these issues, and in general with respect to the main lines of economic policy, President de Gaulle made the decisions.[8]

In addition, the trend of de Gaulle's policy toward American investment roughly paralleled his broader policy toward the United States. At the outset of his presidency, he welcomed American dollars, but shifted to a tougher posture in 1962–63, when he also launched his general offensive against Washington. The peak of antagonism over this issue came in the mid-1960s, the same years he quarreled with Washington over nuclear policy and NATO, and the affair faded as his tenure came to a close.

De Gaulle may have led the way in combating American

7. IFOP polls of 1964 and 1965 cited in Jean Charlot, *Les Français et de Gaulle* (1970), p. 268. Only 18 percent thought de Gaulle's policy toward America was too harsh. Other polls show a rising disapproval of his policy towards the U.S. from 1962 to 1966, but even at the nadir of its popularity (April 1966) 41 percent approved, 29 percent disapproved, and 30 percent voiced no opinion (Charlot, p. 267).

8. This interpretation of the General's interest and responsiblity can be found in the account of one of his closest financial advisers Alain Prate (*Les Batailles économiques du Général de Gaulle*, 1978, p. 18).

investment, yet there was a broad consensus based on ambivalence about American capital that supported his quasi-protectionist policy – at least until the government's screening efforts proved unsuccessful. Agreement existed that American capital constituted a challenge that had to be confronted. Foreign investment was seen as a source of growth and modernization, yet at the same time it bore certain undesirable consequences and thus should be screened or channeled. American capital should not be free to do as it pleased. Dollars were welcome, but only on French terms. De Gaulle, his government and advisors, those economic interests most directly affected such as business, and even the political Left agreed on the need to guide foreign investment.

This consensus of ambivalence, which supported de Gaulle's restrictive policy and marked French difference, derived from three deeply held popular aspirations or fears. There was, first, an unrelenting national assertiveness. Postwar France yearned for a greater measure of independence vis-à-vis the United States. This sentiment had been expressed, sometimes in strident ways, during the Fourth Republic, and the de Gaulle regime both nurtured and excited it. In this instance, national assertiveness translated into a refusal of American domination via investment. A second element of this consensus was a fear of American capitalism. American business had a mixed reputation. The interwar years left a caricature of gigantism, impersonality, regimentation, and ruthlessness, which lingered despite the propaganda of the Marshall Plan years. The ways of American capitalism were antithetical to some presumed more humane French way of business behavior. The French Left added an ideological gloss that stressed the exploitive, expansive, and "colonizing" aspects of the American system. A final ingredient of this consensus was a fear of economic decline. In the race for international competitiveness, postwar French worried about falling further behind the leaders. The United States was both an agent and a reminder of this relative retardation. In the midst of unprecedented economic growth there were doubts that France was abreast of its rivals and fears that Americans would like to keep France in a subordinate position by controlling its dynamic sectors. This consensus dampened enthusiasm for the capital boon from the New World and provided de Gaulle with support for his intervention against the dollar.

In sum, the sources of French exceptionalism with respect to American capital were due not only to de Gaulle's drive for independence, but also to French perceptions and fears about American economic power, behavior, and intentions. A closer examination of the evolution of Gaullist policy and the anti-American consensus supporting it should amplify and substantiate this interpretation.

After several years of official hospitality, the Fifth Republic reversed itself in early 1963 and adopted a hard line toward American investment. By then France was running a surplus in its balance of payments and had much less need for foreign capital than it did at the beginning of de Gaulle's presidency when American investors were eagerly sought. A few sensational events precipitated this reversal. During the previous summer, General Motors and Remington-Rand laid-off hundreds of workers which, according to a government spokesman, violated more humane French procedures in handling unemployment. These layoffs also demonstrated that the locus of decision-making lay in cities like Detroit. Then came Chrysler's surprise take-over of Simca in mid-January 1963, which irritated de Gaulle and his government.[9] This about-face also corresponded with the early stage of the president's diplomatic offensive against Washington. Almost simultaneous with Chrysler's move, de Gaulle announced his opposition to British entry into the Common Market. The principal reason for his veto was to protect the European Community from losing its identity and coherence in a vast Atlantic free-trade area dominated by the Anglo-Americans. Two weeks later, the minister of finance, Valéry Giscard d'Estaing, announced he would try to persuade his fellow European ministers to take up the question of protecting important economic sectors within the community. When Giscard encountered opposition from his colleagues, Paris tried to exercise control at the national level. Rather than risk an open clash with either the European Community or the United States over existing treaty obligations, which required liberalizing capital movements, the Pompidou government simply tightened existing procedures. In effect, requests for authorization by American investors gathered dust at the finance ministry and dollar investments slowed.

If the influx of private American capital in the 1960s, as has been argued, was weaker in quantitative terms than elsewhere within the Six, there were more than enough dollars to give rise to the perception of an alleged American take-over. Of the total

9. De Gaulle, shortly thereafter, upon meeting the PDG of Simca at an Elysée reception, supposedly rebuked him by saying, "Vous auriez pu prévenir." (*L'Express*, 30 May 1966, p. 45).

stock of foreign investment, which reached about $5 billion as of 1965, over half came from the United States.[10] Over three-quarters of this took the form of "direct" rather than portfolio investment, meaning that it carried some form of continuing control by the investor, such as a substantial share of equity ownership or transfer of patents, technology, machinery, or management. Most of this inflow had arrived recently and the number of transactions was relatively large. Most important, it was concentrated almost entirely in manufacturing, and much of this was in the most dynamic industrial sectors. Whether it was a *secteur de pointe*, like computers, or a traditional sector, like food processing, the targets for American capital were the growth industries of the day.[11] From the perspective of national interest, some of the sectors where American firms attained a "dominant" position, such as computers and communications equipment, were vital, but others, such as razor blades, were not.[12] Moreover, much of this new investment transgressed the so-called traditional boundaries of American presence. For subsidiaries of Standard Oil or IBM to raise their capital stock was acceptable. But for new entries to expand outside traditional implantation, as Chrysler did entering automobile manufacture or Libby McNeill did with food processing, made it appear like the Americans had cast off all restraint.

The policy of strictly screening foreign investment that functioned through 1965, and in this case foreign investment largely meant direct American investment, encountered little domestic opposition. It enjoyed a consensus. Within the government, the partisans of *rigueur*, such as the *ministères de tutelle*, especially the

10. Report of the Ministry of Industry in "Les Investissements étrangers dans l'industrie française," *Perspectives*, No. 949, 9 October 1965, p. 2. Data on direct investment on a country basis can be found in the annual volumes: US Department of Commerce, Bureau of the Census, *Statistical Abstract of the United States* (Washington, D.C.).

11. One source estimates 84 percent of foreign investment between 1960 and 1964 went to four sectors: chemicals, mechanical-electrical, oil, and farm machinery-food processing (Erick Schmill, *Les Investissements étrangers en France* [1966], p. 44).

12. American investors followed the same strategy as other foreign investors in this respect. Some sectors where Americans acquired a "dominant" role were: synthetic rubber, petroleum, office machines, tractors, photographic supplies, sewing machines, elevators, telegraph and telephone equipment, and computers. Data on sectoral investment can be found in numerous studies. See for example: Manuali; Schmill; Layton; Gilles Y. Bertin, *L'Investissement des firmes étrangères en France 1945–1962* (1963); Jacques Gervais, *La France aux investissements étrangers* (1963); Allan W. Johnstone, *United States Direct Investment in France* (1965).

ministry of industry, and the *Elysée* were more strict in their assessments of specific proposals than the finance ministry and DATAR (Délégation à l'aménagement du territoire). The latter agency championed regional development and eagerly sought foreign investment, but its stance was exceptional. The Commissariat Général du Plan stood in between the extremes advocating a liberal policy in principle but endorsing restrictions for strategic sectors, like electronics. If there was disagreement over certain authorizations, the screening policy was generally accepted by the administration. Ultimately, selection was in the hands of Pompidou, Giscard, and de Gaulle. Together they often rejected positive nominations from below. With the exception of DATAR, ministers and officials agreed with the president's policy. In practice, while many requests for authorization won approval, a substantial number were also rejected and many more faced frustrating bureaucratic delay.

Looking outside the offices of the ministries in Paris, it is difficult to generalize about how major interest groups such as business or labor – much less the French people – viewed American investment. Reactions were immensely varied, sometimes derived from personal experience with an American firm. But it is evident that there was no important opposition to Gaullist restrictions, at least at first. Criticism grew only as monitoring and stalling turned into a de facto freeze.

Peak employers' associations like the CNPF (Conseil National du Patronat Français) and the CGPME (Confédération Générale des Petites et Moyennes Entreprises) adopted no official stance. Given their diverse constituencies, this is no surprise. The closest approximation of a position were the declarations of Georges Villiers, the head of the CNPF. If at one time this confederation encouraged American investors, by 1964–65 Villiers more carefully weighed the pros and cons and tactfully asked Americans to respect certain limits. Speaking at a reception for the United States ambassador, Villiers, after praising the benefits of this capital influx, stated that it was in the interest of neither country that this movement develop in "an excessive manner." French industry, he declared, needed to adapt by itself to international competition, and it would be harmful if the sources of technical progress or the centers of decision were to be concentrated in the United States. Sounding a political note, the president of the CNPF remarked that the magnitude of this financial and technical movement "threatens to produce economic and social effects, and, by rebound, political effects out of proportion with the amounts involved, and that we must try to avoid."[13]

Similarly, when presidents of several American subsidiaries like Ford-France met to exchange views with heads of major French firms in 1964, the latter accepted the Americans' arguments in principle yet expressed certain misgivings. While the Americans stressed France's need for dollars and warned that if France closed the door they would go elsewhere within the European Community, the French PDGs spoke of an unequal struggle. General Electric, they pointed out, produced 200,000 different products and General Foods, should it want, could merely cut its prices 10 percent and force out every French candy manufacturer. Outside capital was wanted, but Americans must respect certain limits. They should, for example, invest in existing companies without demanding control and make full use of French cadres, French techniques, and French sub-contractors. Otherwise, the French industrialists warned, there might be a nationalist reaction.[14]

Still other businessmen disapproved of the way American subsidiaries allegedly violated the Gallic code of behavior especially with respect to competition and personnel practices. Instead of accepting the status quo, Goodyear and Firestone, for example, tried to win a foothold in the original-equipment tire market by offering unparalleled discounts to French auto-makers.[15] Other subsidiaries ruthlessly replaced managers and fired workers without helping them re-locate. Gallic anxiety about the "savage" aspects of American business, which had been repressed in the 1950s, emerged a decade later when American subsidiaries "misbehaved" and showed their true colors.

The business or financial press stressed the several advantages of American investment and warned against xenophobia, yet accepted the need for vigilance.[16] This press, like business itself,

13. Villiers, "Le CNPF s'adresse aux industriels américains," *Patronat français*, No. 253 (July 1965), p. 30. Also: Villiers, "Face à la concurrence américaine, les entreprises européennes devront souvent concentrer leurs moyens," *Patronat français*, No. 243 (August-September 1964), pp. 2–15.

14. "Pour ou contre les investissements américains en France?", *Entreprise*, 26 September 1964, pp. 41–51.

15. Richard Austin Smith, "Nationalism Threatens U.S. Investment," *Fortune*, August 1965, p. 131.

16. Jean Luc, "Les Investissements étrangers," *Le Journal des finances*, March 1963; "Faut-il refuser les investissements américains en Europe?", *Entreprise*, No. 387 (9 February 1963), p. 13; Paul Deroin, "Les Investissements américains en France," *L'Economie*, No. 948 (12 February 1965), pp. 10–12. Also: Manuali, p. 67; Smith, *Fortune*, pp. 128-29; *New York Herald Tribune*, 10 December 1964.

also complained that American capital targeted certain sectors, some of which were vital to national independence. They reported the "brutal" layoffs at Remington; the contracts required by Libby McNeill's new cannery in the Languedoc, which made farmers work "à l'américaine"; and American penetration into the food industry, which threatened artisanal manufacture. For these observers, it was the colossal size of American enterprise that raised anxiety. The press reported that while the turnover of the entire French electronics industry was 5.5 billion francs, that of General Electric alone was 27 billion. Chrysler, which ranked only third among American auto-makers, reportedly turned out more cars than the entire French automotive industry. Profit margins for big business were estimated to be on the average double that of their French counterparts. The daily volume of transactions on the New York Stock Exchange was 30 times that of the Paris Bourse. One of the most common comparisons was that General Motors' annual sales exceeded the Dutch GNP by 10 percent.

These journals tended to disapprove of the melodramatic way the government presented the problem and the political and anti-American overtones of its policy, yet they urged the Americans to keep their level of investment moderate and to avoid seeking controlling interest. They opposed a severe protectionist policy, and looked to Europe, either at the level of European-wide mergers or European Community regulation, for a solution. But as many experts advised and as *Le Capital* declared, "France has the duty to protect itself against oversized American investments."[17]

By the mid-1960s, the American challenge acquired some popular notoriety. Foreign investment no longer provided dull reading in economic journals. General interest periodicals carried the story, and the topic assumed some national stature with affairs like the General Electric take-over of the computer company Machines Bull. One report said that although the man in the street had learned to accept Mobil Oil, Coca-Cola, Gillette, and O'Cedar, American acquisition of companies making automobiles, snacks, and other foods evoked "a sort of distrust."[18] Public opinion surveys are inconclusive except for verifying a substan-

17. Pascal Arrighi, "La Puissance américaine et l'Europe," *Le Capital*, 2 December 1964. Among the experts who also favorably assessed American investment yet counselled vigilance are: Gervais; Manuali; and Bertin (1963). Far more critical of de Gaulle for politicizing the issue is Schmill.

18. *L'Opinion*, 2 December 1966.

tial degree of reserve about foreign investment among the French – more so than their neighbors.[19] This rather latent anxiety about Yankee subjugation was to emerge fully in 1967 with the publication of Jean-Jacques Servan-Schreiber's *Le Défi américain.*

Politically, the issue, except for discussion of the Fifth Plan, became the subject of a major debate in the National Assembly, but the Left tried, half-heartedly, to use it against de Gaulle.[20] The Communists attacked the government for selling out French industry to the Americans, and the Socialists asserted that the Gaullist regime favored class interests over national ones. François Mitterrand reproached the Pompidou government for authorizing "the colonization of France by foreign capital."[21] Gaston Defferre, who made a bid to be the Left's candidate for the presidency in 1965, denounced the government's handling of the Simca and Bull affairs, and accused it of accepting American colonization. He called the Bull affair "the most striking event of 1964, by its symbolic value and its practical consequences . . . it means, in effect, that we abandon a sector which controls the future of all the most advanced enterprises."[22] Defferre blamed the Gaullists for mistakenly seeking a French solution to a problem that could only be resolved at the European level. Gaullist errors, the Socialist candidate declared, were leading not to independence but to economic and political "enslavement."[23]

But trying to outbid the Gaullists by playing the nationalist-protectionist card did not work because the aims of the Gaullists

19. To the query: "A votre avis, est-ce que tout compte fait, les investissements américains en France sont un bien ou un mal pour notre pays?", 39 percent said "un bien," 27 percent answered "un mal" and 34 percent had no opinion in 1970. The principal nay-sayers were those identified with the Communist Party and farmers and workers ("Investissements américains: les Français sont pour," *Les Informations industrielles et commerciales*, 9 March 1970). Opinion surveys from the mid-1970s indicate that French attitudes toward multinationals were similar to most West Europeans, except that the French people expressed more anxiety – for political reasons – and declared themselves slightly less favorable. The French, more than other nationalities, also tended to identify multinationals with America, and while praising them for their technical and managerial leadership, also criticized them as "incontrôlables" (Jacques Attali *et al.*, *L'Opinion européenne face aux multinationales* [1977], pp. 47, 71, 75).

20. Olivier Brault, "Indépendance nationale et investissements américains: la politique française à l'égard des investissements directs américains sous les présidences du Général de Gaulle et de Georges Pompidou," mémoire de maîtrise, Université de Lille III, 1986, pp. 158–63.

21. Quoted by Hellmann, p. 76.

22. Gaston Defferre, *Un nouvel Horizon* (1965), p. 99.

23. *Journal officiel*, débats de l'Assemblée nationale, 26 November 1964, p. 5588. The Gaullists (Maurice-Bokanowski in *Le Monde*, 25 June 1965) chided Defferre for trying to outbid them on this issue.

and the Left converged. The government was already doing what almost everyone wanted, that is, it was monitoring foreign investment, and the Left had no real alternative to offer other than Europe and Europe had refused to cooperate with de Gaulle. The Gaullists allowed the Left little space for its outflanking maneuver. All that could be asked was for a more effective screening policy. In the end, foreign investment was not even a marginal issue in a campaign that earned de Gaulle his re-election in 1965.

Whatever the merits of the attempt by the Gaullist regime at channeling investment were, the policy was not successful. In 1966 it was overhauled. What went wrong? First, France received no help from the European Community. There could be no "European" policy when France's partners welcomed American companies. Faced with interminable bureaucratic delays, Phillips Petroleum and Rhône-Poulenc, for example, chose Antwerp as the site of their new plastics factory rather than Bordeaux. And Ford shifted its proposed new plant from Metz to the Sarre. In this way France lost jobs, tax revenue, technology, exports, and research facilities – and American products rolled across its borders anyway. Second, the government had difficulty devising criteria to distinguish "good" from "bad" investments and procedures for granting authorization were slow and seemingly arbitrary. American executives complained that they could not understand what government policy was other than submitting to the pressure of special interests.[24] Discouraged in advance by ministerial arbitrariness and delay, companies ceased even to apply for authorization. This deprived the government of its option of screening applications and approving "good" investments.[25] Third, time after time the government failed to find a "French solution" to a proposed takeover because of weaknesses in French industrial structure and capital markets. Ministers often found it impossible, as in the case of the General Electric's offer to Machines Bull, to find sufficient domestic sources of capital, technology, and management skills to substitute for the American offer. Structural weaknesses of the French economy also helped stymie Gaullist policy.

As a result, what purported to be a policy of selection became a de facto freeze – to France's disadvantage. At this point criticism

24. "Business en France," *Le Monde*, 18 June 1965.

25. Jonathan Wise Polier, "Indépendance nationale et investissement étranger, une étude de cas: la politique française à l'égard des investissements américains, 1945–1967," mémoire, Fondation nationale des sciences politiques, 1967, p. 106.

emerged. Reports commissioned by the government in 1965 stated that foreign investment was not excessive and, in fact, was declining.[26] These reports argued that in highly competitive international markets it was better to have a French company compete, even if it were under American control, rather than have the firm disappear waving the tricolore. The real issue was not foreign investment, according to these reports, but technological leadership, and in this respect France was lagging behind. They recommended against "uniform ostracism" and saw foreign investment as a means of closing the technological gap.

Early in 1966, following a reorganization of the Pompidou government, Michel Debré became finance minister and all but discarded the restrictive policy that had been followed for three years. Debré retained the principle of selection and spoke of the necessity of maintaining a reserved zone that excluded foreign domination, yet at the same time he streamlined procedures and once again welcomed American investors. De Gaulle consented to this shift in policy rather than ordering it.[27] The way the problem was now perceived was less political, less a matter of outside control of French industry, and more economic and technological than it had been previously. France seemingly faced a "technological gap," which the Americans could help remedy. It was no coincidence that 1966 also marked the start-up year of the Fifth Plan. One of the plan's major goals, which de Gaulle fully shared, was to raise the economy's global competitive stature. Yet the planners faced declining total investment levels. The answer was to once again open France to those who could bring both cash and technology. Debré observed: "from the perspective of the Plan, which guides governmental action . . . American investments are better than no investments at all. It was rather hard to imagine that national investments would come forth to replace them."[28]

When quizzed about American investments, Debré acknowledged that the government was not entirely free to respond because of its commitment to competition and because of the

26. Conseil Economique et Social, "Investissements étrangers en France dans le cadre de la Communauté européenne," rapport présenté au nom de la Section du plan et des investissements par Louis Charvet, 10 May 1966. A summary of this report is: "Les Investissements étrangers dans l'industrie française," *Perspectives*, pp. 1–9. A commentary is: Michel Herblay, "Investissements américains, la France sait-elle ce qu'elle veut?", *Direction*, No. 123 (December 1965), pp. 1134–37, 1164–73.

27. Prate, p. 215.

28. Cited by Brault, p. 68.

warm reception given dollars within the Common Market. Moreover, Debré said, France lagged in technology and its financial market did not match the level of its industrial ambitions.[29] Debré also complained that if the government refused foreign investors, the political opposition would accuse it of "blind nationalism."[30]

Despite the more liberal policy that Debré introduced in 1966–67, Paris was unable to increase the diminished flow of American capital. In 1958, France and West Germany received dollars at about the same level, but a gap steadily opened so that France received only $163 million and West Germany $349 in 1965. Between 1963 and 1966, France alone among the Six had a falling annual rate of American direct investment.[31] The domestic turmoil of 1968 discouraged foreign investment and rates did not revive until 1969. By the time de Gaulle resigned, only one of every five dollars invested in the European Community went to France. In 1970, even after further steps had been taken to encourage American investors by de Gaulle's successor, a poll of the heads of American and European multinationals confirmed the reputation of France as the least hospitable country in Europe for foreign investment.[32] It seems probable that the Fifth Republic's restrictive policy had a considerable effect on restraining capital flow.[33] This is the price France paid for trying to control foreign investment on a national basis.

There is another story about Gaullist attempts at combating the American economic challenge that cannot be narrated here. It need only be noted that while the Fifth Republic tried to channel American investors through controls, de Gaulle also led a struggle against the alleged source of these dollars by attacking the Gold Exchange Standard, which awarded the dollar the privileged status of a reserve currency. From 1965 to 1967, de Gaulle publicly denounced the Gold Exchange Standard which, among

29. Interview with Debré in *L'Entreprise*, No. 552 (7 April 1966), p. 27.

30. *Combat*, 24 May 1966.

31. Direct annual investment in France between 1963 and 1966 (in millions of dollars), according to US Department of Commerce figures (*Statistical Abstract of the United States*), fell from 210 to 149 while it rose from 304 to 646 in West Germany, from 114 to 169 in Italy, from 70 to 146 in Belgium and Luxembourg, and from 70 to 173 in the Netherlands.

32. *L'Express* (2–8 March 1970, p. 86) reports this survey.

33. There were, to be sure, other reasons for France's falling share of dollars. The rate of return on investment fell in the mid-60s and Washington acted to curb the outflow of private capital by such measures as the Interest Equalization Tax adopted in 1963.

its alleged negative consequences, permitted the free financing of American investment abroad. In its place he offered the gold standard, or at least some form of monetary discipline, that brought all nations under the same rules. In this case, as with the issue of direct investment, de Gaulle was less concerned with strict economic or monetary questions, less committed to the gold standard per se, and more motivated by French rank in international affairs. A former official at the Quai d'Orsay, who later served as the governor of the Bank of France, observed that it was de Gaulle's foreign policy rather than his assessment of financial problems that led him to intervene in monetary affairs.[34] Indeed, the campaign against the dollar seems, in retrospect, to have been less a genuine debate about money than it was a Gaullist tactic to curtail American economic penetration of Europe and elevate France and Europe vis-à-vis the Anglo-Americans in running the international monetary system. But without much cooperation from his European partners, and faced with an aggressive policy from Washington, which offered its own solution (Special Drawing Rights) to problems in the international monetary system, de Gaulle submitted. In the end, he obtained very little of what he wanted in this affair and, while personally displeased with the outcome, let the matter drop.

In the fall of 1967, bookstores displayed a new title. By Christmas, Jean-Jacques Servan-Schreiber's *Le Défi américain* had sold 400,000 copies and the book went on to become the best-selling title in France during the 1960s. The popularity of *Le Défi* and its author, who was no Gaullist, testifies to the national consensus about resisting subjugation to America that supported Gaullist policy. It also demonstrates the shifting conception of the problem during the closing years of de Gaulle's presidency.

Explaining why a book becomes a best-seller is hardly a scientific enterprise, but among the reasons for the enormous popularity of *Le Défi* was the anxiety that made Gaullist policy French policy in the 1960s. To be sure, part of the book's success was due to the glamour of its author, i.e., his courageous stance during the Algerian war, his success at remaking the weekly news review, *L'Express*, his Kennedy-like appearance, and his associations with eminent politicians like Pierre Mendès-France. Equally important was the novel way the book was marketed, using

34. Olivier Wormser, "Le Général de Gaulle et la monnaie," *Etudes gaulliennes*, Nos. 3 and 4 (July 1973), p. 148.

means similar to those perfected by American publishers to create publicity and excite and sustain interest.[35] But there was also the message.

Le Défi sounded an alarm. It was the eleventh hour and unless the French, and the Europeans, launched an immediate counterattack, it would be too late and Europe would become a satellite of the United States. Europeans were on the verge of forfeiting their last chance of staying abreast of the technology and skills that accounted for America's dynamism. In a generation, if Europeans remained passive to the challenge, the United States and a few other countries, like Canada and Japan, would have attained the rank of "post-industrial societies," while Europe would fall to the status of an underdeveloped region. European firms would become mere subcontractors of American subsidiaries. The decisions about how Europeans worked, lived, and even learned would be made in cities like New York and Chicago.

This warning touched a common Gallic fear – that the Americans were taking over France and Europe. Evidence had been accumulating that France might be slipping into the American orbit and the Gaullists had politicized the incursion. But Servan-Schreiber dramatized the issue in a book that combined a catchy title with the drama of an apocalyptic warning, the authority of some carefully selected economic statistics, and the consolation of obvious solutions. He addressed both aspirations for independence and fears of economic backwardness. He struck what was worrying a nation.

Following in the government's footsteps, Servan-Schreiber shifted attention from a preoccupation with American capital to technology and management. He noted that "putting an end to American investment . . . will only weaken us further."[36] The problem by 1967 was one of organization, of research and development, of innovation and creativity. The problem was human capital, not investment capital. More important, the answer lay, at least in part, in imitating the Americans. Servan-Schreiber advocated doing as the Americans did with respect to scale of enterprise, management methods, spending on research and development, and close relations between industry, government, and academia.

Like the Gaullists, Servan-Schreiber also evoked the taste for

35. Diana Pinto, in an unpublished paper of May 1983, has analyzed the commercial success of *Le Défi*.

36. Jean-Jacques Servan-Schreiber, *The American Challenge* (1968), p. 30.

independence – but within a European context. Thus, *Le Défi* criticized Gaullist policy for being too timid and defensive in facing the challenge, and for trying to meet it on the national rather than the European level. The bestseller attacked de Gaulle for his opposition to further European integration and thoroughly antagonized the Gaullists by warning that:

> We can no longer sit back and wait for the renaissance. And it is not going to be evoked by patriotic rhetoric or clarion calls left over from the age of military battles. It can come only from subtle analysis, rigorous thought, and precise reasoning. It calls for a special breed of politicians, businessmen, and labor leaders.[37]

It should come as no surprise then that when President de Gaulle was asked at his press conference for his opinion of *Le Défi*, he answered, "ici, on ne fait pas de publicité littéraire."[38]

Virtually every review of Servan-Schreiber's book agreed that there was a dangerous American challenge, and that he had correctly formulated it as a lag in technology, management, and research rather than capital. The disagreement came over solutions. The most common response was to accept at least some measure of his Americanizing therapy. Among the celebrities who nominally endorsed *Le Défi* were: Louis Armand, François Bloch-Lainé, Michel Drancourt, Raymond Cartier, Albin Chalandon, Marcel Dassault, Jean Fourastié, Pierre Lazareff, and Jean Monnet. Giscard d'Estaing, who had once forcefully resisted American investment, adopted *Le Défi*. The former minister of finance had only praise for Servan-Schreiber's analysis and his solutions.[39] Others, mainly on the Left, criticized Servan-Schreiber's remedies. Such critics were quick to fault *Le Défi* for preaching Americanization as the way to resist America.[40] A few on the Left, like Gaston Defferre, who had been the candidate of *L'Express* for president in 1965, praised the book. And François Mitterrand, then head of the Federation of the Left, echoed the alarm *Le Défi* sounded, but objected to finding a solution in a liberal rather than a socialist Europe.[41] Others agreed that Servan-

37. Servan-Schreiber, p. 277.

38. *Le Monde*, 29 November 1967.

39. Valéry Giscard d'Estaing, "Solitaire Europe," *Le Figaro*, 7 December 1967. Giscard discussed the book with Mitterrand on Europe No. 1 (*Le Monde*, 23 October 1967).

40. Manuel Brindier, "La Réponse socialiste au défi américain," *Le Progrès de Lyon*, 5 March 1968.

41. Mitterrand, "Seule une Europe socialiste . . .," *Fédération Champagne*, 1 April 1968.

Schreiber's conception of Europe was too "capitalist" to assure either independence from America or a social democratic future. The Communists likened the European Community to a capitalist club and saw no solution in merging French monopolies with other European monopolies.[42] The proper response, for the Communists, was to build socialism on a national basis.

Le Défi's notoriety was brief. The events of May-June 1968 overshadowed it. For several months the book could not even be sold, and the public's attention shifted to domestic, social, and political issues raised by the students and strikers. While the best-seller exposed and expressed the national anxiety about American economic hegemony, it appeared after the major wave of dollars had subsided and just as the issue was assuming the character of a gap in technology and human resources. And, importantly, it proposed to answer the American challenge with a dose of Americanization.

Resisting the American challenge remained the Gallic consensus at the end of de Gaulle's presidency, but the conception and answer to the problem had changed. American subsidiaries still stirred French fears of dependence and economic decline, and the Fifth Republic, even under liberal President Pompidou, continued to protect strategic sectors. But American investments were now welcomed because the need for modernization took precedence over worry of outside take-overs. Economic priorities precluded a restrictive policy that blocked foreign investment. American investment was beneficial and if the challenge was to be met, it would have to come not through selection and protection, but by making French manufactures more competitive. Thus, the way out for the French was, paradoxically, to adopt American ways, e.g. import dollars, management techniques, and technology, along with fostering mergers and homegrown research to stay abreast of and maintain independence from the Atlantic colossus. Even a more open society, which Servan-Schreiber preached, free of the rigidities that obstructed the free movement of resources, might be necessary. Just as even de Gaulle himself by 1967 continued to complain about the dollar but accepted economic priorities, so French attitudes moved toward accepting American investment and, more important, certain American techniques as the means of resistance and inde-

42. The Communist response is in: *L'Humanité*, 25 November 1967; Charles Fiterman, "Pour une Europe indépendante, démocratique et pacifique," *Cahiers du communisme*, April 1968, pp. 14–26; *Le Monde*, 17 January 1968.

pendence. Gaullist policy and national consensus both advanced toward a more pragmatic, less politicized stance that incorporated a certain measure of Americanization.

In retrospect, what does the American economic challenge explain about President de Gaulle? It confirms that he believed in *politique d'abord*. His motives in resisting American investment and in reforming the international monetary system were primarily political. At risk was French control over its economic future and parity in decision-making with France's allies. The timing and development of economic-financial policy also corresponds to the contours of the president's grand foreign policy aimed at ending the American "protectorate." Resistance emerged in 1962–63, peaked in 1964 to 1966 and then receded. Second, the attempt to meet *le défi* places de Gaulle at the center of economic decision-making and disputes the cliché that he was uninterested and indifferent to economic questions. Third, the decision in 1966, which allowed Michel Debré to adopt a more flexible approach, affirms the president's pragmatism. He set aside politics and accepted economic priorities, including American capital and technology. Of course this was a tactical concession toward a strategic political goal, for in welcoming American investors de Gaulle was trying to close the economic and technological gap with France's competitors in order to one day behave more independently. The Americans could remedy the very weakness that made the French dependent. Finally, in trying to resist the American economic challenge, de Gaulle employed both a French and a European strategy. When his European partners proved uncooperative he tried a "French solution." But in whatever direction he looked he encountered restraints. From Europe there were legal, diplomatic, and economic restraints, and at home there was economic and financial weakness and by 1966, mounting criticism. Denied either a national or a European solution, de Gaulle and the French moved toward accepting American transfers.

Comment

William James Adams

I AM PERHAPS THE TOKEN ACADEMIC ECONOMIST here at the conference, a grateful status, let me say to the organizers. But it will come as no surprise to you that I know more about direct foreign investment than I do about either Foster Dulles or Fitzgerald Kennedy. As a result, I plan to focus my comments on the paper of Richard Kuisel. I am delighted to do so, moreover, because I am the careful and repeated reader of his books, which have led me to expect a perceptive understanding of French actors, on the one hand, and a thorough examination of French sources, on the other. And I can tell you, having read this paper, that I have not been disappointed. I feel that it is a masterful treatment of the subject at hand. I want to organize my comments this afternoon around three headings: the first is that of motives. What exactly motivated French responses to the so-called American challenge? Second, what were the economic effects of France's response to the so-called American challenge? And finally, although it is somewhat outside the scope of this conference, I want to talk briefly about some of the potential parallels between the French response to the American challenge and today's concern over the American response to the Japanese challenge.

So, first of all, let's talk about motives. I think that Richard Kuisel is fundamentally correct in the two different lines explored in the paper, only one of which is represented in his oral remarks. In his oral remarks, he has suggested that de Gaulle's fundamental preoccupation was one of foreign policy, or security policy, rather than one of economics. Surely this does not mean that he was uninterested in economics; it simply means that the economics was a tool toward a foreign policy and a security policy end. Second, and it is the point that does not come from his oral remarks, is the fact that there is some diversity of opinion within France as to why there must be a response to a so-called American challenge. I think this is brought out very cleverly in the subtitle of Richard Kuisel's paper, where de Gaulle is distinguished from the French, and it is clear that there are many different factors playing to the general concern with American investment in France. In this sense, it is very useful to make reference to the *Défi Américain*, which certainly suggests that, at least for some important elements in France, it is not the foreign policy end that is paramount, but the future of the French standard of living which is truly paramount. And I think this is more central to the concern of Servan-Schreiber and Stoléru, who is also writing in this period. The other notable book expressing this point of view, the *Impératif Industriel*, was published two years after the *Défi Américain*. So the real question is, to the extent that politics is driving this subject and economics is not, what is it that has motivated the politics? Here I will ask for your indulgence to speculate a little on what is underlying the politics. I do this because I am confident that those who will succeed me here – that is, the witnesses – will immediately correct any misperceptions I might raise. With respect to what underlies de Gaulle's politics, it seems to me that there is an important missing element in what we have discussed so far, and that is the central role that is played by the Common Market. After all, this is a period when France is opening substantially to foreign competition, not simply in the form of American investment, but in the form of exports from other Common Market countries and, indeed, from foreign investment from other sources within Europe. Given the fears in France that are very accurately summarized by Richard Kuisel – first of all, a fear of big capitalism, and second, a fear that France will no longer be able to emulate big capitalism – it is entirely possible in this period that public opinion could potentially turn away from the Common Market and opt out of economic competition with Germany. And yet, Germany was the cornerstone of de Gaulle's foreign policy during this period. The point of the Common Market was not to improve French standards of living, but to keep Germany close at hand and to engage in a special relationship with Germany. That special relationship – or at the very least, the opportunity to keep Germany close at hand – would have been called into question had France been subjected to internal political pressure to leave the Common Market. So, rather than identify the threats of economic competition with Germany and the problems that might be created in terms of resentment of Germany, why not deflect that onto the United States? Why not associate the fears of economic competition with a power outside the community that would leave intact the political possibility of continued French participation in what was, after all, a foreign policy exercise for the president?

Second, I believe the Common Market also explains, in some measure, the efforts of those like Servan-Schreiber, and even more the efforts of people like Stoléru, who were more directly involved in economic activity within the government. Because just as the Common Market was creating competition, it was also removing many of the traditional levers of French economic policy from the hand of the policy-makers. No longer were tariffs an option within the community, no longer were regulations in the form of quotas an option within the community, no longer were foreign exchange controls an option within the community, and that left a very substantial policy community without many levers to pull. It required, in those circumstances, a rethinking of what economic policy should be, what it was that should be done other than to dismantle the policy-making machinery of the various ministries. That, I think, is also important in trying to understand why one sees flowing from these pens a profound economic liberalism, but at the same time a call for continued government participation in the economy. It is an attempt to find a new basis for economic policy under change and political constraints.

What can we say about the effects of France's regulation of American investment? Richard Kuisel has presented us with a variety of examples of investments America intended to make in France, investments which were refused by the French government. He accurately portrays the policy of the period as being less one of prohibition that of procrastination, leading Americans simply to abandon requests for location in France. I have tried to systematize that by looking carefully at the evidence of American investments in France, going through the entire postwar period, from 1951 to 1980, substantially. And what I have done for three different variables, which I will describe, is to examine the trend in American involvement in the French economy through foreign investment. The first of these is simply the percentage increase in the stock of American foreign investment in France at the end of the year related to the previous year. The second, following Richard Kuisel, is the share of the increment of American investment in Europe that is attributable to France, that is, what share France got out of the increment of the United States within Europe. And the final variable is the share of France in American new investment within the original European community, that is, the original six members. What I have been able to do, then, is to look at how particular years deviate from that trend. In other words, rather than just look at what has happened in one year relative to the next, I have looked at the whole trend to see which years deviate from that trend and in which particular direction. There are some very interesting things that flow from this analysis.

The first conclusion is that the period of the late 1950s to mid-1960s is a period when American investment in France is systematically above trend. That is, it is a period when the percentage increase in American investment is above its long-term trend. It's a period when France is getting more than its trend share of American investment in Europe.

Similarly, the period from 1965 through 1969 is a period when France is getting less that the trend. And then once again from 1970 to 1975, France is getting above the trend. This certainly seems to accord with the view that there is some effect on American investment in France that is occurring as a result of the policies of the mid-1960s. But before we rush to that judgment, it is important to look at the specifics of the years involved. Quantitatively speaking, there is one year that dominates the whole series, and that year is 1968. During 1968, American investment in France is dramatically below trend, and one might well question whether the rules of 1964 and 1965 are the principal explanation of the pattern of American investment during that year.

We can go beyond the pattern of United States investment in France to look more broadly at the effects of American investment and French policy toward American investment on French growth and on the French standard of living. Here I think it is safe to say that whatever impact we can detect of that French policy on American investment, it seems to have had very little impact, for better or for worse, on French economic growth and the French standard of living. The 1960s were the golden age of French growth, a period of extremely rapid growth, not simply by pre-World War II standards, but relative to Germany and Italy. It is France's shining hour in the growth standings of the large nations of Europe. And it is clearly the case that however effective French policy was in curbing American investment, it was certainly not the case that it had a deleterious impact on French growth. Moreover, one can say that it is not even clear that in the longer run, France's policy severely affected France's ability to compete in competitive world markets. It is at least possible that American investments in France did have some of the anti-competitive effects that certain French economic commentators worried about. In fact, other calculations that I have made suggest that there was indeed a systematic relationship between the degree of competition on a particular French market and the presence of American firms in that market. To say, therefore, that curbs on American investment were necessarily anti-competitive is a hypothesis that needs further study.

The last set of comments that I wish to make relate to the potential parallel with the American situation today. For, after all, twenty years after the *Défi Américain* was published, one hears very little indeed about the American challenge. Rather, one hears a great deal about the Japanese challenge, and one hears about that Japanese challenge in the United States as one does in Europe. Just as earlier, as Richard Kuisel points out, there were allegations in Europe of unfairness on the part of the Americans, so in the United States as well as Europe, we now hear about the lack of level in the playing field vis-à-vis Japan. So now that the shoe is on the other foot, and the United States is in the position that France was in during the 1960s, how do we measure up in the United States? Is the analysis in the United States any more sophisticated than it was in France during that period? I want to suggest to you in closing that the United States does not measure up at all well. In fact, the French approach of the 1960s makes a good deal more sense, even to me as an economist, than does the present United States' policy. For the United States has essentially matched protectionist rhetoric with protectionist policy, and protectionist policy that has had protectionist effects. The United States is in an isolated position in the world, economically speaking, and so any kind of protectionist measure is likely to reinforce that degree of insulation from world markets. On the other hand, the genius of Gaullist strategy, intended or unintended, was to talk protection but to practice – however incompletely, however imperfectly – openness. Because the commitment of a quasi-permanent nature to participation in the European Economic Community guaranteed that, whatever the rhetoric of French policy, whatever the desire of certain interest groups within France, the policy towards United States direct foreign investments in France would not tilt France in a fundamentally protectionist way. Unfortunately, I detect no such genius in American foreign policy.

Comment

Ernest May

ALL THREE OF THESE PAPERS HAVE A COMMON THREAD. They argue that the differences, the controversies, the near conflict between the United States and France during the presidency of General de Gaulle were not rooted in serious conflicts of interest. They are not to be explained in terms of conflicts of strategic interests, of political interests, or even economic interests. Nor are they to be explained in more trivial terms of personal animus or prejudice. Conflicts during the Eisenhower, Kennedy, and Johnson administrations were, at base, results of differences in two kinds of perception. One is self-perception: the perception of the nation, on the American side and on the French side. The other is perception of the international system, or perception of the trend lines in the international system.

Through this period, American leaders tended to think of the United States as the leader of the alliance and the natural leader of the Western world. They thought the United States more disinterested than the European members of the alliance and hence, though willing to consult and to take account of the interests and attitudes of its European allies, entitled in the end to leadership if it chose to exercise it. And these Americans were guided by a vision of a United States of Europe, not identical with a United States of America, but with some points of similarity, ultimately cooperating internally and then cooperating globally with the United States of America.

General de Gaulle, by contrast, saw France as an independent nation whose power happened at the moment to be significantly inferior to that of the United States, but not necessarily perpetually. He had seen the United States with comparable indices of power in the 1920s play a relatively small role in the world scene. He saw this discrepancy. He thought of the United States and France as simply separate nations. He saw France and other European states as having interests that were not necessarily parallel with those of the United States and not lastingly identical with one another. His vision of the future resembled the past.

These seem to me unassailable generalizations. The papers themselves are admirably done. They are well documented and carefully argued. Since I do not take issue with any of the papers, let me use this opportunity to make a complementary point, which is that one element of explanation for these differences in perception is a difference in salient experiences.

During the last few years, an American, British, French, German Nuclear History Program has been gathering documents and memories related to the general subject of the role of nuclear weapons in American-European-Russian relations since World War II. It has been striking how often individual recollections do not jibe with the documentary record. These are not just discrepancies about what happened when, but discrepancies in emphasis and in the total resultant picture.

Of relevance here is the fact that documents suggest a constant, concentrated debate between Americans, on the one hand, and French and other European leaders, on the other hand. But when Americans and Europeans report their recollections, Americans talk in one time frame, Europeans in another.

Americans thinking about the American-European relationship and the American-French relationship more specifically, tend to see the highlights as in the early 1950s. That was when they confronted the great issues: whether the United States would be committed to the defense of Europe; whether once there was a retreat from the Lisbon force goals the United States would be willing to commit itself to sacrifice Chicago for Hamburg (as the phrase went); whether it would be possible to begin the integration of Germany into Europe and thus to create a system in which there would be no future European civil war. Americans feel that the great issues had largely been resolved by 1955, or thereabouts. Issues that arose subsequently, complicated though they might have been, concerned details. They had to do with fixing the structure and making sure that what had been created in the earlier period was maintained.

For Europeans, on the other hand, the salient events are of a later date. The great issues they remember arose in the latter part of the 1950s. This is particularly true of the French, given that the coming to power of President de Gaulle represented a break with the past not experienced by other Europeans. The great events for them were the open decision to develop nuclear forces and the struggles with Washington and London over the degree of independence of America's allies.

To add this point is not to take exception to the argument that differences were not rooted in interest or personality. It is simply to embellish the proposition that key differences were rooted in differences in perception of national status and visions of the future. These differences in perception were simply evidenced as a result of the fact that American and French leaders looked back to different reference points in their experiences of the 1950s.

Comment

Pierre Mélandri

MY POSITION IS VERY DELICATE because after the three excellent papers, there were three excellent comments. I would be tempted to give up my time, but I won't do that.

First, I would like to talk about Mr. Kuisel's paper, to say that I completely agree with his analysis, and that, to me, two things seem particularly interesting. Mr. Kuisel first insisted on the essentially political aspect of de Gaulle's motivation, and at the same time he showed the independence and autonomy of politics from investments. In the political sphere, the period from 1965 to 1968 was rather tense. Yet the paper shows that, after Mr. Debré became Minister of Finances in 1966, Gaullist pragmatism decided on a much more flexible policy regarding investments. This is, I think, a very interesting point.

I would say that the other interest of this paper is to remind us of the expression "American challenge," of the fact that the French leaders were worried about the risk of economic conquest, so to speak, by the Americans, although it is now clear that during this period, the second half of the 1960s, there appeared many of the difficulties that would contribute to the decline of American power as it had been perceived in the early 1960s.

Now I would like to talk about the two other papers, which seem to me to cover the decisive period from 1958 to 1963.

First, I will attempt to recall the historical origins of the French demand for a three-power directory. Second, I will try to explain why the context was so particular and forms, in itself, a unique phase in Franco-American relations.

Let us first examine this three-power directory proposal. Professor Challener was right to say that it is necessary to go back as far as 1949 to understand the situation within the alliance. The French asked, through Ambassador Henri Bonnet, that a military organization similar to the "combined chiefs of staff," with worldwide competence, be created in which they, the Americans, and the British would be included. The American answer was very nuanced. The American military didn't think it was possible because France didn't have worldwide responsibilities comparable to those of the Americans and the British. At the same time they realized that a negative answer would politically jeopardize the alliance that was being created. So Charles Bohlen proposed a compromise: "To give France full membership in whatever was the real controlling body from the military point of view of the Pact, but at the same time confine the functions of any of the organizations under the Pact to the immediate question of the implementation of the Treaty." It is not surprising that throughout the Fourth Republic (beginning in 1951 with Mr. Pleven who asked Mr. Acheson for it), the French urged the worldwide extension of this regional scheme of three-power cooperation.

Of course it was refused. With de Gaulle, however, things were a little bit different, even if we cannot deny the historical background I just mentioned. The first difference was de Gaulle's personality. A request by General de Gaulle didn't have the same weight as those made by the governments of the Fourth Republic, well known to be unstable. The second difference was, I believe, that in de Gaulle's mind, the goal was not exactly the same. I think that the Fourth Republic wanted, above all, to be treated on an equal basis with Great Britain. And I believe its leaders were obsessed by the feeling that they were being lumped with the Italians, as certain allies had intimated. On the contrary, de Gaulle clearly asked for equality with the Americans.

And finally the third difference is the context, and this is my last point. To understand the context of this period, 1958 to 1963, which, in my opinion, was the period when discussions about the possible and desirable redistribution of responsibilities within the alliance were the most important, I would like to start, a little illogically, with the end.

The year 1963 is an important American date. It is the tragic date of the assassination of President Kennedy, but I will say that in fact, it is both in 1964 and 1962 that we must see the conclusion of the period. To me, 1964 begins a new period, when hitherto non-existent possibilities opened for General de Gaulle to accomplish one of his main objectives: to get rid of what he considered the Yalta system. He wanted (it is mentioned in Prof. Challener's paper) to establish a more multipolar distribution of power and also, as Mr. Costigliola said in his paper, to return to the kind of concert between states that had existed before the blocs, especially the period before World War I. But, before 1964, it was very difficult to go in this direction because of an obstructive outside element: the deliberately provocative attitude of the Soviet Union. Trying to negotiate under such conditions could only appear to be an admission of weakness, and I think that in de Gaulle's opinion, it was out of the question to negotiate with Krushchev, who had been taking legally unjustified initiatives concerning Berlin. That is what explains General de Gaulle's intransigence concerning Berlin; his other motive being, as Prof. Challener explained to us earlier: the desire to lay the groundwork for a French-German reconciliation. So there was only one possibility: to work inside the Western bloc and to make it less monolithic, allowing other countries besides the U.S. to assert their own interests.

In this context, it is necessary to evoke 1962. In my mind, the end of 1962 marked an acceleration of this process because a certain number of elements made the task easier for de Gaulle. First, the elections in the fall of 1962 marked the end result of an effort to redress domestic affairs, which we don't need to belabor, but which should not be forgotten. Second, 1962 was the end of the Algerian war. I think this is an essential point because it freed de Gaulle from the burden he called his "boite à chagrin" (box of sorrows); also because in French-American relations (Mr. Lacouture mentioned it about Indochina), colonial questions were a raw nerve, particularly concerning Algeria. Mr. Challener described to what extent the Sakiet-Sidi-Youssef affair had envenomed French-American relations. After the Sakiet-Sidi-Youssef affair, there were demonstrations in front of the French Embassy in the U.S. (which was very rare), just as there was a movement of popular anger in France after the delivery of American weapons to Tunisia.

Michael Harrison said, basically, that the end of the Fourth Republic was characterized by an orgy of anti-Americanism. When de Gaulle returned, things became more serene but still,

Algeria was a very serious problem between the French and the Americans. I have the feeling that America's United Nations vote in 1959 not to support the French on the question of Algeria, although de Gaulle had talked to President Eisenhower in advance about his plans of self-determination, counted for a lot. Ambassador Alphand noted: "Something seemed to be broken that would be difficult to fix."

Finally, on the international level, 1962 meant two things. The end of 1961 was precisely the moment when the Berlin crisis ceased to be a privileged forum for three-power discussions and became a source of real friction (with regard to the problem of negotiations.) Second, it was also the year of the Cuban missile crisis. It seems to me that, according to recently published interviews with Robert Kennedy (published in the U.S. at the same time), President Kennedy himself expected French-American relations to worsen as the Russians emerged weakened from this triumphal encounter, thus giving General de Gaulle more freedom to maneuver.

What I noticed in Mr. Costigliola's paper is that despite everything, de Gaulle decided to revive the question of consultations immediately after this crisis, which raises the following question: What precise interest did de Gaulle have in this three-way directory? Was it to show that reshaping the Atlantic alliance was impossible, or did he hope that something could come out of what he was proposing?

I would say, in conclusion, that this revival of the negotiation process underlines a reality about which we must say a few words. This leads me to talk about the first date: 1958. By some sort of trick of history, or by pure coincidence, de Gaulle's return coincided with the first signs of a long term weakening of the American position. In October 1957, the Sputnik was launched, and the two papers reminded us how, from then on, people started questioning whether American dissuasion could, in actual fact, be extended to Europe.

The year 1958 also marked the first serious deficit of the American balance of payments. That is why, when we draw a balance sheet for this period, even if nothing was urgent, there was, nevertheless, the relative possibility that roles might need to be redistributed, which is to say that the burden might need to be shared. I was very sensitive to a few sentences in Mr. Costigliola's presentation, when he said that Kennedy knew that the situation had changed. He explained: "We have been very generous to Europe and it is now time to look out for ourselves." There lies the sign that the era of postwar American hegemony was over. But if one wants to share the burden, one must offer to share the decisions and responsibilities. I have the feeling that President Kennedy was not intellectually hostile to that. One day he said to Walt Rostow, according to one of the latter's books, that "in the 1950's the United States spent its time collecting nuclear bombs, while Europe had been rounding up gold." Wasn't it possible to try to redistribute the whole thing? Yet the problem was that "Europe was split: 'I'm the president of the United States, but who's the president of Europe?'"

The problem, too, was that the (very relative) economic decline implied a forbidden idea: the eventual erosion of the American strategic situation. I mean that the reaction to the Sputnik was the policy of flexible retaliation. It was the fear of independent national forces, publicly portrayed as unfriendly, and privately as intolerable. Far from opening up to France, said Mr. Costigliola, there was a will to end (Nassau would change this) then, or in the near future, British-American nuclear cooperation. Basically, multinational and multilateral concepts weren't adapted to the nuclear domain, whereas they fit quite well in monetary and economic spheres. I would like to conclude by using the chess term "pat," or "stale-mate" as you say in English, to describe this blocked situation, where the French succeeded in preventing what was originally the most dangerous for them (the multilateral force), but where, conversely, because they were also confronted with the problem of sharing nuclear decisions, they weren't able to convince their European allies to go as far as they wanted toward a new definition of a European identity.

Nevertheless, and this will be my last word, with the American refusal of the three-power directorate on the one hand (which was explicable since a French veto on American nuclear weapons didn't seem, understandably, a priority for Washington), and the definition of a European defense on the other (at the time when the policy of French independence seemed to exclude a European nuclear defense), couldn't there have been, in light of this blocked situation, a third option? Nuclear cooperation with the British could have been one answer. Were there any serious projects on either the British or the French side? Was the American veto explicit or implicit? Perhaps this is more a question about history as it could have been than a question about history as it was; still, this question is perhaps at the heart of the issue.

Witness

Robert R. Bowie

HAVING HAD ONLY THE CHALLENER PAPER in advance, I will comment on that from the perspective of the Eisenhower administration. Although I had left government before de Gaulle took office, I was still a consultant.

Let me start by agreeing with two propositions of Challener's. The first one is that U.S.-French relations had a somewhat low priority in the full agenda of the Eisenhower administration from 1958 on. This was due partly to the number of crises Challener mentioned: Lebanon, Berlin, Quemoy/Matsu, and so on. Moreover, Eisenhower was very much concerned with trying to improve relations with the Soviet Union in discussions with Khrushchev, arms control efforts, and so forth. And finally, there was at home the defense debate, including the supposed missile gap that turned out to be a fiction. So in comparison with the Kennedy administration, the amount of top level concern with U.S.-French relations was considerably less. In the Kennedy period, the Algerian albatross had been shed so that de Gaulle had a freer hand for pursuing his objectives and perhaps the Kennedy administration for objecting to some of the moves that de Gaulle was making.

The second proposition on which I agree with Challener is that both Eisenhower and Dulles had a positive reaction to de Gaulle's coming back to power. I think Eisenhower, in particular, although he had had lots of frictions with de Gaulle, nevertheless had a considerable personal respect and regard for him. And in policy terms, they hoped that de Gaulle would be able to resolve the Algerian problem, which had been not only a source of turmoil within France, but also a source of friction with the United States (because the United States had not been willing to back the French to the degree they felt appropriate). And finally, I think that the Eisenhower administration hoped and thought that de Gaulle would be able to restore French self-confidence and enable France to play a more active role in the Western alliance.

Very soon, however, as was indicated, conflict arose on specific issues. Two of the issues were particularly important. One was obviously the proposed Directorate with France and Great Britain, which called for a veto of the use of U.S. nuclear forces and for worldwide consultation. I think it would be fair to say that Eisenhower and Dulles thought such a scheme was completely out of the question. They did not think it appropriate that the U.S. should accept a veto by France, or anybody else, on its use of nuclear weapons, especially outside of the NATO area, but at the same time they were anxious to have cooperation and consultation. From the perspective of the United States, the claim of French (or British) equality was rather hollow because the United States was carrying so much more of the burden worldwide compared with either France or Great Britain. And while Great Britain seemed to enjoy a somewhat privileged position, it didn't have anything remotely like a veto on the use of U.S. forces, or actually enjoy the kind of relation that de Gaulle seemed to conceive. Indeed, de Gaulle did not ask for just equality with Great Britain, but for equal status in the Directorate of three. And as I said, this was not acceptable. It was also seen as destructive of the NATO alliance itself, which Dulles and Eisenhower thought was extremely important not just for the defense of Europe or for the Europeans, but for American security. They considered that the cohesion of all the allies was what was important, and that preferred status for one or two would be disruptive and create problems with respect to Germany.

On the second question raised by de Gaulle, U.S. help for nuclear weapons, I think the record would show that Eisenhower was somewhat more sympathetic to the possibility of giving nuclear help to allies, in keeping with what he conceived to be the proper relationship among allies. (In 1960, Eisenhower espoused the Multilateral Nuclear Force.) But the Joint Atomic Energy Committee in Congress was very powerful at that time. While willing to amend the statute in 1958 to permit help once more to the British, Congress was not willing to go beyond that to provide a basis for assistance to the French or others. I think that Eisenhower did not like this result, but felt that he could not achieve any further opening up of the statute.

More broadly, my sense is that, in spite of these disagreements with de Gaulle, neither Eisenhower nor Dulles fully took in the extent of the conflict between the Gaullist vision and their own conceptions of international order and Western strategy. It seems to me that this conflict was very basic, perhaps emerging more clearly as time went on as compared to the early stage. First, with respect to NATO, the conception of Eisenhower and Dulles of NATO and collective security as essential for all the allies, including the United States, was fundamentally incompatible with de Gaulle's notion of the independence of France. And Eisenhower did not accept at all the Gaullist argument that a nation can rely only on its own forces for its security. Somewhere Eisenhower recalled a conversation with de Gaulle in this period in which de Gaulle was making this argument and Eisenhower said, "Well, maybe so, but when we were fighting World War II and liberating France it didn't seem to work that way. The morale of the allied forces was perfectly adequate for the assignment." In any event, the view of de Gaulle that the nation was the only basis for effective security was clearly not bought by Eisenhower.

The second fundamental divergence was with respect to the European Community. Eisenhower and Dulles both favored the European Community and the development of a strong, unified Europe. Their reasons were partly parallel to what de Gaulle said he wanted: namely, they felt that the degree of disparity between the United States and the other members of the alliance was unhealthy. They did not enjoy this supposed hegemonic relationship; they thought that inevitably it would be a source of friction and tension. Therefore, the soundest basis for Atlantic relations would be a united Europe able to act effectively in its own interest. Moreover, they deeply believed that an integrated Community offered the best hope for avoiding the tragic European rivalries of the past and ensuring stable peace in Europe. They were not so naive as Mr. Kissinger suggested as to think that this meant that under all circumstances the United States and a united Europe would find themselves in tandem with no problems. They knew it would create problems when a united Europe would be much more capable of formulating its own interests and of asserting them and demanding that they be taken into account. But they did believe that there was a fundamental parallelism of interests with respect to security and economic wellbeing. While there would be divergences, they would not be as fundamental or as apparent as de Gaulle thought. I would stress that they were strongly for an integrated European community. The Gaullist conception of a coalition of independent states each unconstrained with respect to its freedom of action was wholly inadequate to achieve these purposes. They feared that when the cold war ended, or sooner, such a loose structure would run the risk of returning to the pre-World War II relations, which inevitably degenerated into balance of power rivalry and hostility. And that would jeopardize the Franco-German reconciliation within an integrated Community, which they saw as one of the key postwar achievements – and vital for European stability and peace. Thus, in weakening or undermining the Community, de Gaulle's course would conflict with their view of the basic interests of both Europe and the United States.

Witness

Jean-Marcel Jeanneney

I was not solicited, understandably, for a professorial lecture on the relationship between de Gaulle and the U.S., but rather for a testimony. So please excuse the somewhat unstructured nature of my remarks.

I would like to help explain the deeper reasons for the difficult relationship between de Gaulle and the U.S. I saw de Gaulle for the first time at the end of August 1944, when he summoned my father, whom I accompanied, to ask him to become a member of the provisional government. I closely followed de Gaulle's actions during the whole period of his temporary government, since my father was minister of state and I was his cabinet director. I saw him for the last time in 1969 when I was invited, with my wife and Jean-Noël Jeanneney (whom some of you know), to La Boisserie, where he shared his thoughts with me about what had happened, and what was likely to happen, asking me to keep everything to myself. I wrote them down, put them in a vault, and never published them. However, this doesn't keep me from drawing on them for some of these remarks.

I believe that in order to understand these relations, one must always keep in mind (regardless of the events one is commenting upon) that General de Gaulle, who was in love with France, its history, and its legend, considered that France wasn't France if it wasn't independent, and if its leaders didn't consider themselves responsible in their actions towards France and its affairs. That is why, of course, he was "allergic" to anything that appeared to encroach on this independence and on his responsibilities. This attitude manifested itself in his disagreeable comments and behavior during the war towards his allies. It also manifested itself immediately before the Liberation. In order to understand more fully his idea of independence and responsibility, I will recall a significant event, briefly mentioned this morning.

De Gaulle had learned that the American government intended, as France was being progressively liberated by American and many British troups (and thankfully a few French ones), to organize the French administration by charging American officers (who, by the way, had been specially trained for this purpose in American universities) to replace the prefects and administer France. For the General de Gaulle, this was absolutely unacceptable! And this is the reason for which he clandestinely sent Michel Debré to choose and designate prefects for all French departments with one absolute order: They had to be right in front of the Prefecture, more or less hidden in a house or an apartment, so as to be able, the moment the Germans left, to take over the office of the prefect and say: "I am the state!" Michel Debré recalled a few rather picturesque scenes, which actually went quite well, between these badly dressed civilians from the Maquis who took over the office of the prefect, and the American Commander who arrived right after, saying: "But I am in charge of administering. . . ." Well, I am not only recounting this for its picturesque quality, but also because it is utterly symbolic. The idea that the French be governed in their daily life by anybody other than themselves, even for one day, was totally unacceptable, even if this refusal meant shortages in supplies and a worse material situation.

I will give you another example of what I would call "symbolic susceptibility" since de Gaulle, like all great men, attached much importance to symbols, insofar as they represented something to his people. If I am not mistaken, it happened in December 1944. I remember it well because de Gaulle had left for Russia in order to negotiate with Stalin, and my father was responsible for the interim government in de Gaulle's absence. My father had learned that de Gaulle was going first to Algiers, then from Algiers to the Middle East to take a Russian train, since few French planes could fly safely over the Mediterranean Sea. There was a danger of a crash, so my father personally went to see de

Gaulle to tell him: "Please, general, I know that the American embassy is offering you an American plane. Accept it. Don't take any chances, we are worried!" General de Gaulle responded: "Don't worry, everything will be fine. Anyway, could you possibly see me taking an American plane to go see the Russians?" I remember accompanying my father to Le Bourget, where the ground was all muddy. General de Gaulle got into the small plane with one or two collaborators (I don't remember who they were), but I will always remember my father's worried look as the plane was taking off. But in the end everything went well. These are all anecdotes, but since I am here as witness, I tell them because they convey a certain "état d'esprit," or atmosphere.

We recalled earlier that the feelings and thoughts of the men in charge are very important to explain history. I think this is absolutely true. But with Charles de Gaulle, we shouldn't take into consideration individual friendships. I remember one day during a Ministerial Council (Messmer and Guichard must remember), one minister said, regarding a matter I have forgotten, "our friends." I don't know whether these friends were American or British, but de Gaulle stopped talking and said: "Do not forget that in international relations, one does not have any friends." Indeed, he believed that self-interest on the one hand, and power on the other, guided international relations. So, knowing whether or not he was angry at Roosevelt, Churchill, or any other person, is interesting anecdotally, but doesn't help in any way whatsoever to explain his political positions. Maybe the only man for whom, in spite of their differences, he had real affection was Winston Churchill, because, unlike others, he welcomed and understood de Gaulle as early as June 1940, and gave him the means, albeit limited, to begin his action. I also remember that in 1944, or the beginning of 1945, my father told me about a lunch to which de Gaulle had invited Churchill, to give him the French Military Medal. Some intense and emotional words were exchanged there, but this was perhaps the only time.

I will now comment in more technical detail on the papers I have read. Mr. Wall states in his paper that, in February 1945, an important debate took place at the Council of Ministers, to choose between the so-called "Mendès-France thesis," and the "Pleven thesis." The paper explains that, in the end, Mendès-France's thesis did not win, because an agreement had just been signed in which the Americans agreed to supply us with coal, food, etc. De Gaulle and the other ministers allegedly said to each other: "Well then, the policy of austerity that Mendès-France proposed is no longer worth it since the Americans are going to supply us with what we need." This is typical of the kind of abstract reasonings historians make, which absolutely don't correspond to reality. God knows how truly helpful American aid was, but really one had to have lived through the winter of 1944–45 in France to know that, no matter how much aid was received, the austerity was not going to end. I will remind you that during the winter of 1944-45, we were in Matignon, using the coal that the Germans had left behind. In January, we ran out of coal, the Seine was frozen, and new coal wasn't arriving. I remember that in my office, which was next to my father's, the temperature was 5 degrees Celsius. It was a very harsh winter. As I was saying, there were certain advantages to this situation: when I had an undesirable visitor, he didn't stay for very long. And I remember René Mayer angrily saying: "A government that can't heat itself isn't a government."

And this is the question I have debated with Lacouture, and if we didn't choose the Mendès-France plan, it is not at all for those reasons. His plan was perfect. As an economist, I entirely approved of it, as would have any economist. Unfortunately, it was inapplicable, because first, it implied an exchange of currency that we didn't have because we hadn't printed any yet, and second, because the exchange had to take place everywhere, on all liberated territory on the same day. But we didn't have any trucks and the roads were still cut off because of blown-up bridges. So this was impossible. Moreover, this very well designed plan implied a normal economic administration. For instance, if we wanted to carry out a similar plan in France today (thankfully, we don't have to), we have an administration capable of doing it. But we must consider what the French administration was at that time! One part of it had been purged, another part was made up of people from the "maquis," who had just been demobilized and were working in unheated offices. In addition, one could barely communicate with the provinces. Therefore, for these particular reasons, the plan was inapplicable. By the way, Mendès-France eventually came to realize this fact. But this was another trait of de Gaulle's: he perfectly accepted propositions from his collaborators that called on theoretical economics. He would listen patiently to you and then say: "So, practically speaking, what can we do?" And practically, there were many things we couldn't do in 1944–45, but which had nothing to do, by the way, with our relations with the United States. But since one of the papers touched upon these questions of domestic French policy, I am just trying, as a witness, to reestablish what I believe was the truth.

A quick word now on American investments. Here again, I am very surprised by the historians, because they say that Michel Debré was more favorable to American investments than Valéry Giscard d'Estaing (in other words that Michel Debré was less nationalistic than Giscard d'Estaing). Anyone who knows both of these politicians knows that it is the opposite. Indeed, when Michel Debré was nominated Minister of Finances, he asked Pompidou for the responsibility of the Committee of Foreign Investments, because he thought he would be a little tougher than Pompidou. I sat on this Committee. So what then was the real problem? It was no different from the preceding years. I don't believe there was a break. De Gaulle's idea, his collaborators' and everybody else's, was that American investments were useful, to the extent that they could bring us new techniques. But at the same time, we noticed that they weren't necessary to equilibrate our balance of payments. The latter – and this is important – was equilibrated by the monetary Reform of 1959. Thanks to our own effort, we had a positive balance of payments. Thus, we didn't have the same reason to have American investments as there is for the U.S. today to have Japanese investments. This reason didn't exist for us.

It is also said that, in 1966, there was a lot more investment in Germany than in France. This is true and while, as an economist, I am favorable to investments, everything depends on the context. These heavy American investments in Germany, in 1966, led to an economic overheating (perhaps there were other reasons), which forced Germany to put a terrible brake on its economy in 1967, which, by the way, plunged it into a recession. Therefore, I believe it is too simplistic to think that the more foreign investments there are in a country, the better off it is. No! Everything depends on the type of investment and on the economic situation of the moment.

Finally, I will say a word on what has been said about the relations between Kennedy and de Gaulle. One the one hand, de Gaulle was manifestly charmed by this young brilliant man who had many ideas. He was charmed by him and also by his wife. But we shouldn't forget that among all the European allies, he was the toughest whenever there was a serious crisis. Everyone recognized this. But insofar as Kennedy seemed to be the man of new frontiers who wanted to re-establish American authority of sorts in the world, de Gaulle couldn't possibly agree with him. This is evident.

I was quite amused by what has been said, that according to Kennedy, de Gaulle's ideas about what could happen after the cold war were fantasies. In fact, he told us what he thought would happen after the cold war. It wouldn't be with containment, with the cold war, that Communism would be collapse. Obviously, it had to be contained if they tried to invade Europe. But Communism would collapse from the inside, when a generation of technicians would be born that would no longer bear the yoke. And in this, you will agree, he was more prophetic than Kennedy, who believed these were fantasies.

Witness

Bernard Tricot

DURING THE PERIOD WE ARE DISCUSSING, I had a precise and very interesting role, but one which didn't expose me to international affairs. I was one of Pierre Messmer's administrative and financial collaborators, and my task, Mr. Prime Minister, was mostly to help you find a way to finance the strategic nuclear force. I would like to intervene rapidly on two points.

First, an anecdote to confirm what Mr. Jeanneney said earlier about de Gaulle's feelings towards Winston Churchill, and about the possibility that, nevertheless, they may have had some influence on public affairs.

My little story is about the "Soames affair." You may remember this conversation between the British ambassador in Paris, Mr. Soames, to whom General de Gaulle, in the beginning of 1969, confided his ideas on the future of Europe, the desirable creation of a small directory or organism (with a few important countries), that would have a predominant influence in Europe, and which could perhaps be a future solution for Europe. He wasn't saying it was THE solution, but that if the British were interested in an arrangement of this type, then maybe we could talk about it. But of course, the matter had to be discussed discretely, and thought through calmly. At that moment anyway, it was only an off-hand idea. And you know that Mr. Soames quite normally informed his government of this talk, which had delighted him. In any case, he couldn't hide it from his government and kept discussing it with de Gaulle. The British government, and especially the Minister of Foreign Affairs, had nothing better to do than to go tell the story to our European partners: "You see, de Gaulle is building something behind your backs and trying to get an agreement with us, Germany and perhaps Italy but excluding Belgium, the Netherlands and so on. . . ." So, in this affair, I often wondered if de Gaulle had not been a little careless, if it was really so urgent to mention it to Soames, and if he really had taken the necessary precautions to explain to Soames that it was just brainstorming, that we would think about it more seriously later. Then it occurred to me that the reason he had been so imprudent (and that happened to him several times in his life) was that he got along well with Soames, and that, à priori, he enjoyed talking with him. Why? I remember that when we found out that the British government was going to propose Mr. Soames as ambassador, de Gaulle was delighted. When I showed some surprise at this sudden burst of enthusiasm, he said to me: "Well you know, he is Mrs. So and So's husband." (I admit that I forgot Mary's name). I was still puzzled, so he said: "Come on! She is Churchill's daughter." I suddenly realized that through Mary and Mr. Soames, he had found his great partner again. And there was certainly, on his part, the pleasure to come in contact again with the atmosphere surrounding the great partners of the international scene.

I would also like to go back to what Mr. Jeanneney said earlier about the factors which, for de Gaulle, dominated international relations. I was late here today because of another conference in Montreal. I hope you will accept my apologies. This morning, in Montreal, where Mr. Lacouture was also present, someone, speaking once again, of course, about "Long Live Free Quebec" and about the Pnomh-Penh speech, said: "I believe that de Gaulle's exclusion from the Yalta conference left him with a deep wound, and when he found the opportunity to get even with the U.S., by irritating and bothering the Americans (with the Pnomh-Penh affair), or by encouraging the independence movement in

Quebec, which could be detrimental to American interests (though this case seems less evident to me), he was happy to do so." I am still indignant, several hours later and in a different country, at such an argument. I say this because the argument is sometimes made that de Gaulle took international positions in order to take his revenge, or to get even, or simply because he still hadn't overcome his bitterness and his anger. This way of reacting was so contrary to his psychology, to his way of dealing with things, that those who knew him have an obligation to emphasize that this accusation has no leg to stand on. Concerning the affair of "free Quebec," he deeply believed that they were French – "French people from Canada," as he used to call them – but who were French anyway, a part of the French people. And he thought that France hadn't done for them what she should have (and especially since the 1763 treaty when France abandoned not only French territory but also French people), and that there was a debt to be paid. Lacouture described this perfectly in one of his books.

De Gaulle felt that the Quebecois were becoming more aware of their individuality, that they were making progress economically, intellectually, in industry, science etc. . . . and he wanted to acknowledge it and encourage them. That was fundamental. Lumping this basic idea with Yalta is a mistake. Although Yalta did have, in my opinion, unfortunate consequences for Europe, it is a completely separate problem. As far as Phnom-Penh, he also had the feeling that with regard to weak peoples (even if in the end they won wars), like those of the Indochinese peninsula, powerful nations shouldn't behave as we did in the past, or as the United States was being called upon to. I also believe that the advice he gave to America, to find solutions other than war that would respect the freedom and dignity of the peoples of this country, which (as we had in Algeria) the Americans were being drawn into, was good advice. If it had been followed, it would have saved human lives and also gained time in solving important international issues. This, at least, is my opinion. But these things cannot be explained by grudges. General de Gaulle was above that.

Witness

Etienne Burin Des Roziers

I BELIEVE MR. MÉLANDRI ASKED if there had been more than a passing attempt at cooperation between the British and French concerning nuclear defense. The answer is positive, there were attempts. But we must understand that in 1962 this couldn't go very far, since France didn't yet have any operational nuclear warheads. And it was out of the question to ask our British friends to cooperate in this area, because they themselves were bound by the dispositions of the [American] MacMahon Law. Moreover, de Gaulle always considered that he shouldn't ask for foreign help in this domain. He never agreed to sign the nuclear non-proliferation treaty, but at the same time, he always said that a state that bore the formidable responsibility of possessing nuclear weapons should not share them with anyone. Therefore, he never criticized the U.S. or Great Britain, or even expressed regrets on that issue. Therefore, cooperation couldn't be very extensive, although serious talks had started in the area of vectors, that is, in rockets.

This question was addressed by de Gaulle and Mr. Macmillan on two visits the latter made to France in 1962, first in the beginning of June at Champs, and then at the end of the year in Rambouillet. The first time they talked about this question, there was no real objection by the French, in principle, to the idea of cooperation. It was even encouraged. Later, at the end of the year, in Rambouillet, the problem was brought up again, but the circumstances had changed. Mr. Macmillan himself raised the issue. He said that he had long counted on the "Skybolt" rockets to increase the range of British aircraft, allowing them to aim nuclear explosives at enemy territories. But he had just learned that the United States government had decided not to pursue the production of Skybolts. Therefore, he told us, he was in a very difficult position and, in fact, he had an appointment with President Kennedy a few days later to examine the problem. Then, he said that he would certainly be offered "Polaris" rockets in exchange for Skybolts, and that he would probably accept. Let me add that he emphasized the fact that when a state buys rockets with cash, it has control over them and no one can contest its sovereignty over their use. So the conversation was not pushed any further. Mr. Macmillan continued his trip to Bermuda, where he met President Kennedy, and there they laid the groundwork for their multilateral force plan. I learned about it almost immediately through the American Chargé d'Affaires, who brought me the text that Kennedy and Mr. Macmillan had agreed upon, which we were also invited to accept.

This invitation, contrary to what has been said, was not dismissed out of hand without any study. The Council of Ministers (and I am sure Mr. Messmer remembers the discussion on this project) examined this proposal, but it was established that it didn't suit our purposes because, as I already mentioned, we didn't have at that time any nuclear warheads. So we were offered Polaris rockets to launch nuclear warheads we didn't have. Perhaps at a later date, if and when France had its own nuclear warheads, the problem would have been completely different. Perhaps, by that time, France would have had its own rockets. Thus, on a technical level, this proposal was of no immediate relevance for us. More importantly, the project called for these Polaris rockets to be made available to Great Britain, and eventually to France, as part of an international force, over which we would have no control. This international force, like NATO, would be under American command, therefore we wouldn't have any power in it. Granted, there was a clause stating that in grave circumstances (in case of national survival), we could use this force. But de Gaulle said he couldn't quite see how, in an apocalyptic case of nuclear war, we would be able to separate our nuclear power from this international force. Therefore, we had the best reasons not to accept. But the most serious reason was a matter of principle, which was that it placed French nuclear power, then under construction, largely out of our own sovereign control.

CHAPTER FOUR

DE GAULLE AT APOGEE, 1963–68

❖10❖

De Gaulle and the Monetary System: The Golden Rule

David P. Calleo

In his own time, when bipolarity and American hegemony were riding high, even some of de Gaulle's admirers saw him as an atavistic obstacle to progress. Now he is more often admired as a prophet. While he was always celebrated as a master tactician, today his ideas seem the real foundation for his success as a statesman. In the great quarrels of his career, de Gaulle was generally right and his opponents often wrong. In the 1940s, he foresaw better than Roosevelt the needs of the postwar European order. And in the 1960s, he understood better than the Atlanticists or the "Good Europeans" the essence of the new European confederation and the principles that should govern its long-term relations with America and Russia.

De Gaulle's positions reflected a certain general vision of international order – a vision with three fundamental elements. These might be described as struggle, leadership, and balance. Struggle was manifest in de Gaulle's vision of history – a sort of Bergsonian competition where diverse nations, each with its own personality, strove to flourish and realize their potential. To succeed required visionary leadership exercised through a strong state with institutions able to mobilize the nation's strength. Finally, along with competition and leadership was balance – the need for national policies to be governed by measure and self-restraint in what was an inextricably interdependent world system.

It is easy enough to link de Gaulle's abiding policies to these elements of his philosophical vision. His sense of struggle in history made him resolute to assert France's interests and to safeguard her self-determination, even against close friends and protectors. His corresponding faith in the need for a strong state inspired the long campaign to reform French political institutions. And despite his emphasis on will and grandeur, his respect for measure informed his actual policies to a notable degree. He had no desire to emulate Napoleon, whose career, for all its genius, illustrated the "tragic revenge of measure." He wrote more approvingly about the *Ancien Regime*, whose policy was:

> that of circumstance, careful to avoid abstractions, but savoring of realities, preferring the useful to the sublime, the opportune to the resounding, searching, for each particular problem, not the ideal solution, but the practical one, not very scrupulous as to the means, but grand, all the same, by the observation of the right proportion between the object pursued and the forces of the state.[1]

De Gaulle was sometimes rash enough to claim measure as a particular French virtue:

> In a French garden, no tree tries to stifle the others by its shadow, the flowerbeds make the best of being geometrically arranged, the pond does not yearn to cascade, the statues do not seek to thrust themselves up individually for admiration. Occasionally, one senses a noble melancholy. Perhaps it comes from the feeling that each element, if isolated, could have shone more. But this would have been to the detriment of the whole, and the stroller is glad for the rule which gives to the garden its magnificent harmony.[2]

It was perhaps this third element in de Gaulle's vision that was the most prevalent in his view of the postwar international system. He could hardly claim a monopoly on the concept of interdependence, but his interdependence was rather different from that popularized on this side of the Atlantic. It dictated a system not where all were equally dependent on American leadership, but where everyone – including the Americans – obeyed the same rules. Such a system, de Gaulle believed, could only be sustained by an effective balance of power, not by hegemony. Thus, in the face of a bipolar Europe and America's Atlantic and global hegemony, de Gaulle held up the vision of a balanced multipolar system. In the global context, he greeted the rising Third World giants, like China, and within the West, he championed a Europe

1. Charles de Gaulle, *La France et son armée*, Paris: Plon, 1938, p. 47.
2. Charles de Gaulle, *La discorde chez l'ennemi*, Paris: Berger-Levrault, 1944, p.x.

of States to counterbalance American economic and political power. In the face of bipolar reality, he envisioned a disintegrating Soviet Empire, with a Westernized Russia joining a Europe stretching from the Atlantic to the Urals.

Nowhere is de Gaulle's taste for measure more clearly revealed than in his stance on international monetary questions. De Gaulle was often said to be uninterested in economics, but any survey of his public utterances shows him to have been greatly preoccupied with economic issues. As he well knew, France's political aspirations had long been handicapped by her relative lack of economic prowess. From his early years as a military planner, de Gaulle had preached the need to rejuvenate France's technocratic traditions in order to rebuild her strength in the world. His years in power amply reflected that early ambition. The economic restructuring of the 1960s is hardly the least part of his legacy.

De Gaulle's concern with international monetary relations should not, therefore, be surprising. Nor, indeed, should his mastery of the technical issues. While de Gaulle obviously relied on his advisers, most notably Jacques Rueff, few public utterances by a head of state, or any leading politician anywhere, can equal the lapidary exposition of monetary principles to be found in the famous 1965 press conference. That brief exposition not only reflected technical mastery of the gold question, but was imbued throughout with de Gaulle's fundamental views on the nature of the international system. The gold standard became a metaphor for the requirements of a healthy international order – one based, that is, on interdependence without hegemony.

The remainder of this paper, reconstructed from some of my earlier writings, examines de Gaulle's monetary position and reflects on its implications for the plural world system that he favored.[3]

The Gaullist Critique of the Bretton Woods System

De Gaulle's criticism of Bretton Woods in 1965 reflected the slow undermining of the dollar's credibility that had been occurring ever since convertibility had actually come into effect in 1958. As early as 1960 there had been a dollar crisis in the London gold

3. David P. Calleo, *The Imperious Economy*, Cambridge: Harvard University Press, 1982, chapters 3–5.

market. Thereafter, a series of *ad hoc* measures had failed to reverse the continuing American payments deficit. With the tax cut of early 1964, and with the Great Society and Vietnam in the wings, the prospects for controlling American inflation began to deteriorate. The world's currency markets were growing uneasy.

The domestic boom year of 1965 saw the first serious attack on the dollar since the gold crisis of 1960–61. Signs of domestic price inflation were occurring even before any significant increase in defense expenditures for Vietnam. The 1965 crisis indicated not only the growing technical weakness of the dollar but an increasing politicization of the international monetary issue. The Western alliance was in the midst of a major quarrel between the French and the Americans that covered the whole range of foreign policy. De Gaulle seemed determined to frustrate the grand designs of the Kennedy administration. He continually attacked American detente policy as a new "Yalta" and sought to promote his rival version of a Europe that stretched from the Atlantic to the Urals. By 1965, de Gaulle was growing openly critical of American involvement in the Vietnam War. In 1966, France withdrew formally from the integrated commands of NATO.

Economic issues took a prominent place in the quarrel. By 1963, de Gaulle's veto of Britain's application to the European Economic Community had already blighted the Kennedy administration's hopes for trade liberalization. By 1965, he had forced the EEC to adopt the Common Agricultural Policy and had dashed hopes for a Europe wide open to American farm products.

In 1965, de Gaulle also attacked U.S. monetary policy. The American deficits, he charged, were exporting inflation to Europe. In his celebrated press conference that dealt with the monetary question, held on February 4, de Gaulle attacked the whole reserve-currency system. By permitting endless American deficits, he argued, the system was unsound as well as unfair. The exported dollars were pumping the world full of inflation and, as American debts began to exceed American reserves, building financial instability that threatened "world-wide upset." Stability, according to de Gaulle, could be restored only by returning to the gold standard, a system without special privileges. Everyone would then be required to settle external imbalances promptly in a neutral medium, not in a fiat currency that one government could issue at will.

De Gaulle also touched on the political aspects of the question. Under the gold-exchange standard, American deficits that other countries were expected to hold made those countries, in effect, America's unwilling creditors. This involuntary extension of credit coincided with heavy American direct investment abroad. Certain countries were thus experiencing "a sort of expropriation of some of their business firms," take-overs that they were themselves financing by holding the surplus dollars. In broad terms, America's monetary hegemony reflected a political relationship between Europe and America that was growing increasingly inappropriate. Without being unfriendly to America, European states, in the nature of things, wished "to act independently in every field of international affairs." Arrangements natural in the period following Europe's postwar debilitation appeared "inadequate, even abusive and dangerous," as the European states recovered "their substance." Changes should be made before the monetary and political problems grew unmanageable.

De Gaulle's notion of exported inflation reflected a critique of the reserve-currency system put forward by the Bank of France in the 1920s and revived after World War II. The economist most closely connected with this critique was Jacques Rueff, prominent both in the prewar theories and their postwar revival. After de Gaulle's return to power in 1958, Rueff became his close economic adviser. Rueff had long ago concluded that monetary stability was incompatible with the use of reserve currencies. The gold-exchange standard had amply demonstrated its failings in the 1920s, Rueff argued. It had nevertheless been reborn in the Anglo-American arrangements of Bretton Woods.

The rebirth was not a coincidence. The reason for the use of the dollar as a reserve currency after 1945 was the same as for its use after World War I. After each war, the world's economies, save for the United States', lacked sufficient monetary reserves to restore normal international business. To do so required large credits in dollars, the only currency with sufficient gold backing to be acceptable for international transactions. After World War I, the United States obliged with huge public and private loans. The British managed to restore the credibility of sterling and, by the mid-1920s, were themselves pumping "liquidity" into the international economy. Under the circumstances, it was not surprising that countries kept dollars and pounds as monetary reserves. The system broke down when the British could no longer sustain the pound's convertibility in 1931. The system's ruin was sealed by Roosevelt's defection from the gold standard in 1933. The situation of the international economy was even more desperate after World War II. American loans again came to the rescue. Hence, the return of the gold-exchange standard, with dollars the principal reserve currency.

As Rueff saw it, such an international system would inevitably break down once again. Any gold-exchange standard was doomed to fail, Rueff believed, because permitting the use of national currency as a reserve in place of gold precluded those corrective adjustments that, under the classical gold standard, had worked automatically to restore equilibrium. Without these automatic tendencies toward adjustment, the international monetary mechanism led ineluctably to inflation and collapse.

Rueff's analysis based itself upon a classic monetarist model. Under the gold standard, Rueff noted, a United States running an external deficit would automatically have had to cover that deficit with gold. The gold transfer, while lowering the money supply and hence aggregate demand in the United States, would have raised the money supply and aggregate demand in the countries receiving it. With demand thus lowered in the United States and raised abroad, Americans would have been induced to export, and their imports would have fallen. Trade would have made the necessary adjustment to equilibrium.

Under the reserve-currency system, by contrast, dollars flowing abroad increased demand outside the United States, but without reducing it inside. When the United States was in deficit, foreign central banks, instead of receiving American gold, held dollars in the form of U.S. Treasury instruments. This influx of dollars resulted in the corresponding increase in the national money supply on the European side, as the European central bank issued its own currency in return for the dollars brought to it. The Treasury instruments given to the foreign central banks were simply added to the American national debt, with no loss required for the U.S. monetary base. Consequently, no reduction followed in America's national money supply. The outflow of dollars produced no corresponding reduction in domestic American demand and hence no corresponding impulse to export in compensation. In short, under the gold-exchange standard, whatever the United States acquired abroad did not have to be extracted from domestic U.S. resources.

Considerations of equity aside, the system was relentlessly inflationary. Surplus dollars flowing into Europe caused European money supplies to grow too rapidly and made inflation inevitable. American debts would pile up higher and higher,

Rueff reasoned, until the system would become so unmanageable that countries would have to abandon fixed parities and protect themselves by capital and trade controls. The international economy would disintegrate and the 1930s return.

Rueff was convinced that only the gold standard could restore stability, and he outlined a series of practical steps leading to its return. De Gaulle's own defense of gold, while no doubt perfectly genuine, could also be taken as symbolic. In practice, as long as national reserve currencies were eliminated, any objective standard not subject to extensive manipulation or wide fluctuation would do. Nothing in de Gaulle's pronouncements, for example, ruled out using some multilaterally determined unit as the international standard of value and reserve in place of gold. Revaluing gold by multilateral agreement, Rueff's blueprint for returning to the gold standard was not, after all, so different from creating "Special Drawing Rights" (SDRs) by agreement in the International Monetary Fund (IMF). It was essential, however, that the creation of new international money not be inflationary, and therefore not be controlled by the United States in particular or by debtor countries in general. In the end, it was difficult for the French to imagine any arrangement as satisfactory as gold. As a commodity, it had a real value of its own, determined by the cost of increasing its supply. It also had many sources, and its price was therefore not easy to manipulate over a long period of time. Furthermore, after a lifetime as odd man out in various clubs dominated by the Anglo-American special relationship, de Gaulle was disillusioned with the possibilities of multilateral management.

Rueff's views were widely misunderstood at the time, even among the monetary experts. In fashionable opinion, defending gold represented atavistic nationalism and antediluvian economics. Keynes' strictures about the foolishness of digging gold out of the ground and then putting it back into vaults could always be used to give a sophisticated gloss to arguments that, in effect, evaded the essential issue. That real issue was whether the United States was serious about ending its balance-of-payments deficit and whether it could expect to do so without a much stricter international discipline over its domestic and foreign policies. Even if conventional American official thinking in the mid-1960s still imagined a return to equilibrium, an international order that would seriously constrain the United States to do so was instinctively rejected. American rhetoric may not yet have adopted the frankly hegemonic arguments popular among the

British, to the effect that the world system requires a leading country whose special responsibilities give it special rules. But American thinking was drifting in that direction.

THE AMERICAN RESPONSE

Ironically, instead of taking on the real issues of adjustment raised in the gold question, contemporary American academic discussion preoccupied itself with resolving the problem of "world liquidity," a difficulty that was expected once the American deficit was stopped. In the late 1950s, a Belgian economics professor at Yale, Robert Triffin, had formulated the liquidity problem into what became known as the "Triffin Paradox." Triffin took it for granted that a weakening dollar would sooner or later force the United States to end its balance-of-payments deficits. What would happen, Triffin asked, when U.S. deficits finally did stop?

Had the United States ended its deficits as Triffin assumed, his liquidity problem would doubtless have become real enough. In this respect, Triffin's analysis was more realistic than Rueff's. Returning to Rueff's gold standard would have required a whole series of other domestic and foreign changes, requiring a more rigid self-discipline from modern nation-states than was probable, at least without the intervention of some universally traumatic experience with inflation. But as events actually transpired, Triffin's concern was misplaced. Since the United States was never to end its payments deficit, the problem of liquidity was its actual excess rather than its putative deficiency. Under these circumstances, creation of new liquidity by the IMF had a practical appeal to American policy for quite opposite reasons from what Triffin had intended. Since the United States dominated the IMF, had by far the largest IMF quota, and would presumably also be the major recipient of the new reserve units, the Triffin scheme seemed an ideal way to finance dollar deficits in the future. In effect, Triffin's concern for a hypothetical liquidity shortage, after the dollar deficit was ended, provided the rationale for a new multilateral way to finance a continuation of that deficit.

Though creating SDRs was not to prove very significant in itself, the whole initiative and debate marked a notable step toward bolder conceptions in American strategy. As the American government began to face up to the intractability of the payments deficit, it started to rethink its commitment to fixed exchange rates, the very foundation of the Bretton Woods system. The drift of American thinking was reflected in the semiofficial "benign neglect" arguments that began to be found among academic experts in the late 1960s. Countries unwilling to absorb more dollars, the experts argued, ought to be willing to revalue their own currencies upward. Psychologically and technically, the occasional revaluation of one or two allied currencies would be far less disruptive than some across-the-board dollar devaluation. This line of thinking gradually gained ascendancy inside the beleaguered Treasury and prefigured Nixon's revolution in 1971. It had the advantage of shifting the onus for the action away from the United States to the surplus countries, who could be isolated and singled out for particular pressure.

The SDR campaign indicated not only more radical American views on monetary questions, but also a growing willingness to use power to make these views prevail. As America's economic strength diminished, its political power came into more obvious use. U.S. international monetary policy became more frankly hegemonic. Defense of the dollar in the late 1960s came to depend primarily upon direct political pressure applied on America's major creditors.

In early 1968, the Johnson administration's luck nearly ran out. The domestic economy's "pause" in 1966 had temporarily calmed the dollar's international troubles. Thereafter, the Federal Reserve, under severe congressional pressure, had relaxed its tight monetary policy. Domestic expansion quickened in 1967, but Great Britain's sterling crisis inhibited again raising U.S. interest rates, lest the pound be weakened still further. Prime Minister Harold Wilson's long struggle to sustain the pound finally collapsed in late 1967. Speculation began to turn directly against the dollar. Passage of the tax increase in early 1968 induced the Federal Reserve to relax monetary policy still more.

The administration tried to head off the crisis. In the State of the Union Address in January 1968, Johnson finally imposed mandatory controls on direct investment abroad and again asked Congress to remove the domestic gold cover and thus make the entire gold stock available to defend the exchange rate. The storm broke with the announcement of the 1967 balance-of-payments figures in February 1968. The payments deficit in 1967 had risen to $3.7 billion and was rising especially rapidly in the last quarter. Political factors were also undermining confidence in the dollar. The war in Vietnam was convulsing the United States with political dissent and economic dislocation. The war was widely believed to cause, in itself, a large outflow of dollars. No end seemed in sight. The American commander, General William Westmoreland, was asking for yet another "escalation." By March, an enormous rush had developed in the gold market. On March 14, the United States gave up supporting the gold pool, and Johnson asked Wilson to close London's gold market. In effect, the United States defaulted on its obligations under the gold-exchange standard.

Gold, of course, had always been the weak link in Johnson's hegemonic monetary policy. Whereas the United States had an infinite supply of dollars, it had only a limited supply of gold. As long as foreign dollar holders had the right to ask for gold, the United State might at any time be faced with bankruptcy. Though central banks might be pressured, the private gold market was harder to control. An American policy moving toward open hegemony naturally drifted toward renouncing the gold commitment. In late 1966, an internal Treasury memorandum had already suggested untying the dollar from gold. In 1967, the United States had extracted from the Federal Republic of Germany a pledge not to ask for payments in bullion. By March 1968, when the great run developed in the private gold market, the administration was psychologically and intellectually prepared to "demonetize" gold.

America's traditional hegemonial style, however, required that unilateral repudiation be dressed up as multilateral reform. By solemn international agreement, the empty gold pool thus became the "two-tier" gold market. Under the new arrangements, the United States would maintain its hypothetical commitment to pay out gold at the official price to central banks, a pledge that American political power and economic weakness had already emptied of substance. In the private market, however, the gold price would henceforth be left to fluctuate. In other words, America's hegemony over its allies was no longer to be mocked by the private market. Gold was effectively demonetized. The world was on a *de facto* dollar standard.

From breaking the link to gold, however, it was only a short step to the end of fixed exchange rates altogether. Bretton Woods still committed the United States to sustaining the dollar's parity against other currencies, but with the gold tie to the private market out of the way, private holders grew less and less inclined to accept dollars for strong foreign currencies except at a discount, that is, at higher and higher interest rates. When those interest rates were no longer available, the flood of dollars into foreign central banks became unbearable. By the time of the next great run on the dollar, in 1971, the psychological barrier to breaking the dollar's parity had already given way. Europeans had lost their faith; the United States had lost its desire. Benign neglect was blossoming into a defense of floating rates.

The Johnson administration was spared this last step by a series of domestic changes and foreign catastrophes. The Federal Reserve's abrupt switch to tight money in 1968 removed the immediate pressure after the March crisis and gave foreign dollar holders the high interest rates they demanded. Moreover, within two months of the March run in the gold market, fortune favored the dollar with a series of political and economic explosions in Europe. The May events in Paris nearly toppled the Gaullist regime, and the Russian invasion of Prague in August forcefully reminded the Europeans of their military dependence. The French franc came under strong pressure, and a great flow of European capital moved to the United States. The fall of the dollar, like the fall of Vietnam, was left to Nixon, but the trends leading to the dollar's collapse in August 1971 were the same as those that had steadily weakened the dollar throughout the 1960s. Nixon's dollar crisis was, in effect, a resumption of Johnson's.

Nixon's revolutionary solution meant the end of the Bretton Woods system and, ultimately, a new regime of floating exchange rates. In some respects, American hegemony was even more blatant than before. Under prevailing conditions, the new regime was, in effect, a pure dollar standard. But like the Americans, the Europeans had also learned something from the monetary crises and debates of the late 1960s. While European opinion outside France was still slow to evolve toward radical solutions, the monetary debates and general turmoil pushed European political leaders toward a more conscious awareness of their common interest. While Americans contemplated floating, Europeans began thinking about a monetary union of their own.

MONEY AND GEOPOLITICS

Looking forward as well as backward from 1971, what was the general political and economic significance of America's abandoning the Bretton Woods system? What, in retrospect, were the geopolitical implications? How well did de Gaulle's monetary critique relate to his broader geopolitical vision?

The roots of complex practical problems can often be found growing in the ambiguities of theory. The concept of a balance of payments, for example, carries elusive and contentious economic, political, and even moral assumptions. To begin with, the very notion of balances between countries implies a nationalist definition of the world economy. Each national economy is taken as a discrete entity, a common household whose accounts should be kept in relation to the rest of the world. A more cosmopolitan view might argue that with the world increasingly a "global village" of free men and multinational enterprises, the whole concept of national balances is an impediment to progress. No one, after all, keeps a formal balance between New York and Texas. Flows do occur, but the adjustments take place through the movement of goods, capital, and labor – without anyone reckoning a formal monetary balance that the governments of New York and Texas feel they must somehow act to regulate. Why should the same not be true of monetary flows between the United States and West Germany?

To anyone with a Gaullist view of international affairs, the answer seems obvious. The United States and Germany are sovereign nation-states, whereas New York and Texas are not. Having a balance of payments is an attribute of national sovereignty, for, in the present world, sovereignty extends to economic as well as political self-determination. Governments of modern nation-states are expected to regulate their domestic economic environments to provide stable prosperity. They are also expected to do their best to ensure a favorable international context for that domestic prosperity. To meet these expectations, governments normally seek to regulate the national money supply and to promote an exchange rate favorable to domestic development.

Economic conditions in New York and Texas, of course, are not deprived of this governmental solicitude. The two states share together the policies set by the U.S. Treasury and Federal Reserve. So, it might also be argued, does the German Federal Republic. In some respects, much of the capitalist world does form an integrated monetary union with a common money supply. With America's special reserve role in the postwar international monetary system, the huge size of its economy, and the growing interdependence of capital markets, monetary conditions in the United States have had a powerful influence on monetary conditions in West Germany. Some find this monetary integration part of a general world progress toward political integration. In this view, the Federal Reserve should quite properly play the role of world central bank.

Again, however, nationalist reality intervenes. American monetary institutions are part of the American political system. American monetary policies are made mainly with American preferences in mind. They reflect the complex conditions of the American economic, social, and political scene. Germans are not willing to hand over the management of their economic environment to Americans. In particular, postwar Germans do not care for American inflation rates. Germans thus insist, as best they can, that their monetary policies be made by institutions that reflect the particular nature of their own economic, political, and social community. Hence the Germans and Americans keep a balance of payments between them.

Not only does the concept of a balance of payments suggest a nationalist international system, but it also traditionally implies a certain balanced relationship among the members of that system. The word "balance" is itself ambivalent. Balance may mean simply a reckoning of pluses and minuses. But it may also mean an equilibrium, as when accounts are "in balance." Such a notion of equilibrium applied to international payments suggests that a country ought ideally to have neither a surplus nor a deficit. Behind this prescription is the vision of a system with a natural law or an inner harmony, attainable if governments behave properly. Liberals, with their faith in free markets, see equilibrium achieved by a "hidden hand," the natural result of unspoilt competition. But not everyone shares such a liberal view of the international order. A Hobbesian view sees instead states in a ceaseless competition where some flourish and others decline. Order is the product not of artless nature but of conscious power. Laws and rules are simply instruments of domination and perhaps exploitation as well. In more strictly economic terms, a traditional mercantilist view sees a payments surplus not as a disequilibrium to be adjusted but as a superior competitive performance to be sustained.

In summary, the very concept of a balance of payments is loaded with ambiguous and arguable implications, toward which governments and analysts themselves have shifting and ambivalent views. The lack of real agreement on these fundamental questions is reflected in the inability of states to formulate and sustain any durable international monetary regime. This lack of agreement does not represent merely a perverse incapacity of economic experts from different countries to resolve technical problems. Mercantilists have hold of a fundamental point. In the end, an international monetary regime, like domestic monetary institutions, reflects an overall balance of political and economic power. A monetary system with special rules for one power reflects a group of states dominated by that one power. The system will last as long as the hegemony. A system characterized by equal rules equally obeyed reflects, by contrast, an integrated group of states with a plural diffusion of power among them. Even the biggest states in such a system cannot break the rules with impunity. A pluralistic liberal system of this sort lasts only as long as the political balance that it reflects. Integrated monetary regimes come apart when the member states neither feel constrained to accept hegemony nor share sufficient interests, perceptions, or institutions to consent to common rules. In this situation, a pluralistic international system without consensus, the world's monetary regime tends toward a series of distinct monetary blocs, separated by floating rates and controls.

Not only does an international monetary system reflect the relative power of states, but it also reflects the domestic economic, social, and political character of its principal members. For no international monetary regime is likely to survive unless the domestic economic and social order in each participating country is in harmony with the international regime. The classic gold standard, as Rueff imagined it, needed not only a plural world system in which the major powers were constrained to follow the same rules, but also, within those major powers, domestic societies dominated by social classes interested in monetary stability.

De Gaulle once described American policy as the will to power cloaked in idealism. A similarly cynical view would find American balance-of-payments policy the will to power cloaked in academic economics. The will to power does seem to provide the one consistent thread to American payments policy and the theories that have informed it since the early 1960s. Ignoring the capital markets, harping on the hypothetical liquidity shortage, inflating the International Monetary Fund, demonetizing gold, floating – all have reflected a basic urge to dominate the monetary system so that no external constraint can limit the expansive impulses, at home or abroad, of the American political economy. The upshot has been to make the world subject to American monetary policy and to make that monetary policy, in turn, not subject to any external constraint.

Hegemonic monetary systems are hardly novelties in history. A powerful case can be made for a hegemonic power with a special role in managing a collective system. That role is presumably justified for others by a close and self-evident identity of the hegemon's interest with that of the system as a whole. But since the United States is rather different from most other economies in the system, and far more autarchic, the U.S. Federal Reserve is perhaps not very well suited to be a monetary Vatican City. In the perspective of the other powers, what results from American predominance is less a dutiful management of the collective economic interests than a nationalist exploitation of power. From this perspective, the insensitivities of American academic analysis might, to a foreigner, seem more plausibly explained by nationalism than by ignorance.

An American, of course, might find no lack of national interest in the theories of his European colleagues. True, in retrospect, the French monetarists, like Rueff, appear more reliable analysts of the real world than their American counterparts. Rueff's argument that the use of reserve currencies in the gold-exchange standard was inexorably inflationary seems difficult to fault in the light of subsequent experience. Moreover, since the switch to floating rates in 1971, Rueff's case for some version of a gold standard has certainly not lost its force. The vast increase in dollar credits after the oil crisis, the spread of other reserve currencies, and the liberated credit-creating powers of international banking have all relentlessly assaulted monetary stability. A huge overhang of speculative debt and credit weighs more and more heavily on the future of the liberal world economy. The technical case for gold – for some standard tied to real values and less subject to manipulation – has grown more and more intellectually compelling.

The weakness of the French analysis in de Gaulle's time was the reverse of the American. American analysis was wrong but predominant. French analysis was correct but impractical. For a gold standard, like any other plural but integrated system, ultimately depends upon there being enough power dispersed throughout the system to force even the biggest state to obey the rules. Beyond, it depends upon domestic regimes among the member states willing both to support and to accept for themselves the external restraint. In short, a gold standard rests on politics. It depends upon an international equilibrium of power among the states in the system and a domestic equilibrium favoring monetary stability within each of the major states. Neither condition prevailed. In this perspective, Rueffian analysts were no less nationalist than American, but their nationalism was that of a middle power, unable itself to pretend to hegemony but seeking to escape from the damaging hegemony of another.

The problem with the French analysis was that France lacked the power to enforce it. If the American domestic economy exploited Europe as the French maintained, it was because the Americans could get away with it. Europe's monetary weakness stemmed from its geopolitical weakness – its disunity and hence dependence upon its American protectors. Under these circumstances, American exploitation of the monetary system was natural. Europeans should have blamed themselves rather than the Americans. As de Gaulle often noted, those who cannot mobilize their own strength generally suffer the fate they deserve. In view of their temptations – the domestic pressures and foreign ambitions – the Americans could have been a good deal worse. All of this, moreover, needs to be put in its proper geopolitical context. That Americans have so long carried such a disproportionate defense burden has surely been a major cause of their perennial inflation. Under the circumstances, it ill behooves the rich protectorates to complain of the monetary hegemony that has made their protection possible. Until the affluent allies can combine the will and resources for a political equilibrium within the capitalist system, they should expect to adjust to policies made for the convenience of others.

But if power has its own rules, economics also has some laws of its own. Key among them is the deleterious effect of bad money. Thus, the triumph of American policy has, more and more, become the ruin of American prosperity. The problem with American economics is not an excessive concern with the national interest, but an inability to define that interest properly over the long term. That is the lesson writ large in the decades that followed Nixon's revolution. As de Gaulle would have seen it: inflation is the revenge of measure, the economic price for political hubris.

In its fashion, balance has been reasserting itself. America's overextension and consequent economic decline have helped hasten that evolution toward the more plural global system that de Gaulle foresaw and professed to prefer. At the same time, the

American monetary excesses that de Gaulle complained of have gradually encouraged the recreation, in the European Monetary System, of the sort of disciplined regime that Rueff would doubtless have approved of. For what seem good Rueffian reasons, today's French leaders are pressing hard for a European Monetary Union that they expect will confirm, among other things, the domestic monetary stability so painfully achieved in recent years.

This European Monetary System, however, has not been able to avoid its own elements of hegemony. Until now, at least, Europe's monetary hegemon, the Federal Republic of Germany, has been content to exercise its leadership in the general interest of monetary stability rather than to finance national geopolitical ambitions beyond national resources. A Germany, divided and contained by Cold War bipolarity, has lacked the scope for economically ruinous grand designs. Now that Germany has slipped out of its bipolar straight jacket, it remains to be seen whether German monetary hegemony will remain so exemplary. To be sure, French statesmen since the war – de Gaulle not least – have been weaving European structures for the day when the changing postwar order might permit a resurgent Germany. Perhaps their time of real testing is at hand.

Europe's new German problem reveals an old anomaly in the Gaullist vision. Gardens planned by committees are not necessarily harmonious. Above all, it is difficult to have a French garden without a gardener.

❖ 11 ❖

Lyndon Johnson and De Gaulle

Lloyd Gardner

In the funeral procession following John Kennedy's casket, France's Charles de Gaulle towered over other foreign dignataries. It would be too much to say that de Gaulle towered over Lyndon Johnson's foreign policy problems as well, but he was a presence in all of them. During the funeral weekend, de Gaulle was singled out by Kennedy's National Security Advisor, McGeorge Bundy, for a special private meeting after the general diplomatic reception. "In some ways your meeting with him, for purely symbolic reasons," Bundy advised the new president, "may be the most important of the lot."[1]

The hastily prepared briefing paper for Johnson's use in the de Gaulle conversation stressed that "atmospherics" were the most important element in this encounter. "The President must convey to the General an air of confidence that he can, intends, and will cope with the major problems facing us and, like President Kennedy, intends to exercise to the fullest United States' responsibilities of leadership."[2]

Johnson later recalled that he heard that the French leader had said America was slow to come to Europe's aid, and could not be counted upon unless there was something like Pearl Harbor. But de Gaulle took another tack. "While changing forces called for certain adjustments in our respective roles," de Gaulle supposedly said (according to Johnson's memoirs), "the important thing was that Frenchmen knew perfectly well they could count on the United States if France were attacked."[3]

1. "Memorandum for the President," 24 November 1963, *The Papers of Lyndon Baines Johnson*, Johnson Presidential Library, Austin, Texas, National Security File, Bundy Memos to the President, Box 1. (Hereafter, *Johnson Papers*, followed by file identification.)
2. Undated Memo, "President's Conversations With," [25 November 1963], *Johnson Papers*, Declassified from Unprocessed Files, Box 1.
3. Lyndon Baines Johnson, *The Vantage Point* (New York: Popular Library, 1971), p. 23.

The actual minutes of the meeting, surrounded as it was by the emotions of the time, have de Gaulle stressing that the difficulties that had developed between the two nations were really minor questions, resulting from a change in the relative military and, to a certain extent, the political positions of the two nations. De Gaulle then went on to say what France was trying to do: "It is to organize Europe – continental Europe – from an economic point of view and after this is done, perhaps also from the political point of view." When this was completed, Europe would open negotiations with the United States on economic questions. Europe did not want autarchy, he concluded, but would take a very liberal attitude.[4]

These words, however carefully put, foreshadowed deep concern in Washington about de Gaulle's ultimate intentions. As it happened, however, the major message conveyed by the French leader got reduced to a minor tiff over whether de Gaulle had promised to return soon to Washington for substantive talks. Several times during the conversation, Johnson had pressed de Gaulle about another visit as soon as February. De Gaulle never said yes exactly, but he did not say no, either. Afterwards the tiff was blown out of proportion by speculations that de Gaulle felt the president, being the newest world leader, should pay his respects first in Paris to the oldest Western statesman. In succeeding years, it grew into a legend and came to symbolize the conflict between the two men. What developed into an argument over who promised to meet whom really involved the State Department's advice that Johnson should stress America's determination to "exercise to the fullest United States' responsibilities of leadership," and de Gaulle's assertion that "changing forces called for certain adjustments in our respective roles."

Hurrying from his meeting with de Gaulle, Johnson addressed a group of state governors, telling them that although his conference with the French leader had lasted longer than he expected, they had not finished. "So we have another meeting set up for early in the year when he comes back to this country."[5] Hearing about Johnson's statement as he was about to depart, de Gaulle sent word to State Department officials that he had not meant to

4. Memorandum: French-American Relations; Forthcoming Visit of General de Gaulle to the United States, 25 November 1963, *Johnson Papers*.

5. "Remarks to State Governors," 25 November 1963, Office of the Federal Register, *Public Papers of the Presidents, Lyndon Baines Johnson, 1963–1964* (Washington: Government Printing Office, 1965), p. 4. (Hereafter, *Public Papers*, followed by year.)

say that he was coming back next year, but the American president would be welcome in Paris.[6] Over the next five years, the subject of a de Gaulle-Johnson meeting came up again and again. Various intermediaries offered their services to arrange such a tête-à-tête, even to the point of White House annoyance. "Tell Rusk and all interested," Johnson scribbled on a 1966 memo describing one of these efforts, "thanks much but I prefer to do my own planning on conferences with de Gaulle."[7]

The diplomatic minuet these two danced around the issue of a face-to-face meeting also served the very useful purpose of avoiding what neither wanted: an opportunity for their domestic critics to seize upon their differences to achieve other ends. At Adenauer's funeral in April 1967, the "visit" issue was reprised one last time. The keeper of the president's daily diary recorded the event as follows:

> The President talked to DeGaulle at the luncheon on Tuesday. . . . The two were extremely courtly and courteous to each other. There was virtually nothing of substance except for some elegant fencing on who should invite whom to what country. The duel ended in a draw: no visit decided upon as of this moment. De Gaulle offered the President the biggest chateau outside of Paris, and the President countered by saying he would always be glad to see him sometime, perhaps when de Gaulle comes through en route to Expo '67 – in other words, no hits, no runs, and no errors – no ball game.[8]

NO BALL GAME : THE MLF FIASCO

De Gaulle evaded him, Johnson would complain. "President De Gaulle was the hardest to get to," he confided to Doris Kearns. "I always had trouble with people like him, who let high rhetoric and big issues take the place of accomplishments."[9] LBJ ordered an end to sniping at de Gaulle by lower level officials, nevertheless, hoping that somehow the famous "Johnson Treatment" would work its magic on the French president. It never had a chance.

The real stimulus to America's original proposals for a multi-

6. Phillip Geyelin, *Lyndon B. Johnson and the World* (New York: Praeger, 1966), p. 4. The misunderstanding is also discussed in Jean Lacouture, *De Gaulle* (3 vols., Paris: Editions du Seuil, 1986), III, p. 370.

7. Walt Rostow to Johnson, with the latter's comment, 20 May 1966, *Johnson Papers*, National Security Files, Rostow Memos to the President, Box 7. (Hereafter, NSF.)

8. *Johnson Papers*, Daily Diary, 25 April 1967, Box 11.

9. Doris Kearns, *Lyndon Johnson and the American Dream* (New York: Harper & Row, 1976), p. 195.

lateral nuclear force (MLF), for example, had been Washington's growing unhappiness about the independent nuclear capabilities of its allies. The "Johnson Treatment" might persuade a wavering senator, hoping for some advantage for his constituents in return for a "yea" or "nay," but de Gaulle was immune to such blandishments. A memorandum prepared in McGeorge Bundy's office during the summer of 1963 contrasted the different political motivations in London and Paris for an independent force: London supposedly desired the weapons as insurance that Great Britain would always have a seat next to the United States in Western nuclear councils, whereas, it was asserted, de Gaulle wanted them for exactly opposite reasons – to convince his people that the Americans were unreliable and not to be trusted with Europe's safety, or otherwise to determine its future.

The French attitude was far more dangerous to American hopes for the alliance:

> Thus the entire French effort has come to constitute a continuous challenge of the central premise . . . namely, that the unity of the Alliance is indispensable to the defense of all its members. Unless that unity is in doubt, the usefulness of the French force remains in question, even to Frenchmen. Unless and until it is related in some new way to the Alliance as a whole, the French nuclear force must constitute a standing challenge to the basic principle of the Alliance . . . if France under de Gaulle were to seem justified in its lonely nuclear effort and be elected by its firmness and foresight to Continental leadership; and if the United States were to make no effort to demonstrate that its necessarily lonely course in [the] Cuba[n missile crisis] was the exception, not the rule – if these things should happen, then indeed the Alliance might begin to come apart.[10]

Growing out of these concerns was a closely related issue: the problem of German nuclear capability. If the French force was not integrated into the alliance, how would it be possible to continue denying Bonn membership in the nuclear club? At this point, the American interpretation of the French position was that while Paris would not participate, it also would not oppose the plan. "Couve de Murville [the French Foreign Minister]," read a briefing paper for Johnson, "has recently discussed MLF as likely to come into being, with other countries as members."[11]

10. "The Multilateral Force, Where it Came from – what it is – and what it is not," 24 June 1963, *Johnson Papers*, NSF, Subjects, Boxes 25-27, pp. 10–11, 16.

11. "Notes on the MLF: Status and Needed Decisions," 6 December 1963, *Johnson Papers*, NSF, Subjects, Boxes 22-23.

But de Gaulle's presumed "benevolent neutrality" (if that was ever the case) toward MLF had turned to active opposition. In one sense it could be argued, as has Alfred Grosser, that de Gaulle's position had been determined by the Cuban missile crisis. On the one hand, Cuba had displayed American unilateralism and a desire to "inform" its allies rather than to "consult"; on the other, Cuba represented a great victory over Russia, so much so that it permitted de Gaulle to take an increasingly independent role in dealings with both West and East.[12]

But de Gaulle also had been rankled by hedges the Bonn parliament put into the Franco-German treaty signed in early 1963, hedges that spoke of the Federal Republic's superior obligations to "multilateral treaties."[13] Having denied Great Britain entrance to the Common Market, de Gaulle may well have feared the Americans had switched stalking horses, and were now attempting via the MLF to sneak back in through Germany.[14] In any event, the German-American embrace threatened a number of his projects. On another level, for example, it has been asserted that de Gaulle wished to play the middle-man between Russia and Germany, assuring Bonn that German wishes would get a better hearing through him speaking to Moscow, and the Russians that he held the key to containing German adventurism.[15]

However de Gaulle weighed these various factors, by the spring of 1964 he had become an outspoken opponent of MLF.[16] Given de Gaulle's opposition, British lack of enthusiasm, Congressional concerns, and a doubting Defense Secretary Robert McNamara, it is perhaps surprising that Johnson continued to plan strategies for securing acceptance of MLF.

Yet he did – at least for a time. By now, however, the emphasis had swung to the German part of the problem. At one planning session, Acting Secretary of State George Ball, a leading "integrationist" in the State Department, put the German point first to Johnson, "emphasizing the need for giving the Germans a legiti-

12. Alfred Grosser, *The Western Alliance: European American Relations Since 1945* (trans. by Michael Shaw, New York: Vintage Books, 1982), p. 199.

13. W. W. Kulski, *DeGaulle and the World* (Syracuse, NY: Syracuse University Press, 1966), pp. 276–77.

14. The relationship between de Gaulle's veto of British entrance into the Common Market and the Franco-German Treaty of 1963 is treated suggestively in Grosser, *Western Alliance*, p. 207.

15. John Newhouse, *De Gaulle and the Anglo-Saxons* (New York: Viking, 1970), p. 33.

16. Geyelin, *Johnson and the World*, p. 167.

mate role in the defense of the Alliance, but 'on a leash.'" Even McNamara admitted that doing nothing – now that the genie had been let out – might lead the Germans to demand medium-range missiles under a two-key system – a much worse alternative.[17]

De Gaulle's related actions, such as withdrawing French naval forces from NATO command and prohibiting the stationing of American nuclear weapons on French soil, and his policies elsewhere, especially his call for the neutralization of Vietnam, made some Washington policy-makers impatient with the French nation for putting up with "Le Grand Charles." As Philip Geyelin observed in the *Wall Street Journal*, however, there were still fears in Washington that the "deluge" after de Gaulle might be worse than suffering the worst the general could do. The likely successor to de Gaulle was a socialist who would come to power with Communist support – hardly a promising development from Washington's standpoint.[18]

So it was best, as Johnson kept saying, not to rile the general's supporters by giving them additional reasons for opposing American plans. De Gaulle, Johnson would sometimes say, was like a reactionary senator, requiring special handling to keep him from leading others into damaging the great causes. "To have attacked de Gaulle," he said in his memoirs, "would only have further inflamed French nationalism and offended French pride. It also would have created strains among the nations of the European Common Market and complicated their domestic politics."[19]

For his part, de Gaulle was quoted as saying that "Kennedy was a mask on the face of America while Lyndon Johnson *was* America."[20] That somewhat ambiguous comment suggested, of course, that behind all the sophisticated "Atlanticists" in America – even at the time JFK's "Grand Design" was being developed – was the reality of an America out to dominate the world.

If de Gaulle could not be confronted, he could be surrounded. Former Secretary of State Dean Acheson affirmed his belief that

17. Ball's and McNamara's comments may have been at different sessions because Phillip Geyelin (*Johnson and the World*, p. 168) cites a Saturday morning meeting in April, where the Defense Secretary gave his opinion, while a memorandum featuring Ball's comments in the *Johnson Papers*, NSF, Subjects, Boxes 22 and 23, "Memorandum of Discussion of the MLF at the White House," is dated Friday, 10 April 1964.

18. *The Wall Street Journal*, 21 February 1964, p. 8.

19. *The Vantage Point*, p. 305.

20. Merle Miller, *Lyndon* (New York: G.P. Putnam's Sons, 1980), p. 344.

the power of the United States to shape the "inevitable" for General de Gaulle was "immense." And Rusk told Belgian statesman Paul-Henri Spaak that the issues now facing the alliance were greater in complexity than those of earlier years, and that de Gaulle's position was capable only of producing contradiction and confusion. "How, for instance, can there be [a] European atomic force outside [the] NATO context and without European political unity? In [the] face of threatened NATO deterioration, now is the time to call [a] halt and see what happens. Even though direct confrontation should be avoided, now is the time to stand up and say no to destruction of NATO and let France see she is isolated."[21]

When the British muddied the waters still further with their own version of an MLF, some policy-makers began to feel that perhaps the best course would be to postpone MLF decisions until a more propitious time.[22] But the decision was to go ahead, making a special effort to convince the French that MLF was not designed against them, and that if de Gaulle could not see his way to joining, was it not possible for him to consider "at a minimum" cooperating with it. But since the telegram to Paris asking Foreign Minister Couve de Murville to think about these issues was not even clear about what shape MLF would finally take, it was hard to imagine a favorable response.[23]

As might be expected, the French foreign minister pointed out the ambiguities in the MLF proposals. What were the Russians to think, for example, of American protestations about nuclear proliferation if at the same time Washington awarded weapons to this new entity? And if it was argued that the United States retained a veto power of the use of the weapons, how did that square with other Washington statements and German expectations that MLF was only a first step toward full partnership?[24]

It was suggested that a special emissary be sent to find out exactly what it was that de Gaulle was after. Ball remarked at a White House meeting that he had had an agreeable discussion with de Gaulle about Southeast Asia the previous summer. Rusk added, yes, agreeable "and sterile." Someone suggested sending

21. Geyelin, *Johnson and the World*, p. 62; MacArthur to Washington, 11 May 1964, *Johnson Papers*, NSF, International Travel, Boxes 33-34.

22. Memorandum of Conversation, 19 November 1964, *Johnson Papers*, NSF, Files of McGeorge Bundy, Boxes 18-19.

23. Bundy draft of Rusk to Bohlen, 12 November 1964, *Johnson Papers*, NSF, Subjects, Box 24.

24. Bohlen to Rusk, 19 November 1964, *Johnson Papers*, NSF, Subjects, Box 24.

John J. McCloy, the former High Commissioner in Germany, but Johnson vetoed the idea, displaying a good deal of common diplomatic sense absent in much of the discussion. McCloy's closest association was with Germany, he remarked, which was not the best background for such a mission. "De Gaulle," besides, "might well conclude that there was no government operating in the United States, just bankers from New York. De Gaulle certainly was not going to succumb to a bunch of errand boys. He might react the way President Johnson would if de Gaulle started sending French bankers over here as his personal emissary."[25]

A presidential letter to de Gaulle was drafted, asking him to set forth his general and specific positions about MLF and the problem of controlling "this awesome power effectively at the service of peace and freedom." It was not sent, but given as an instruction to Under Secretary Ball to discuss with Couve de Murville. Bundy saw all this leading absolutely nowhere. On 25 November 1964, he sent a memorandum to Rusk, McNamara, and Ball: "I am reaching the conclusion that the U.S. should now arrange to let the MLF sink out of sight." The only issue was whether it should be done quickly or slowly. What was remarkable about this memo was that, in essence, it accepted many of the French objections, along with additional reasons for abandoning the effort to launch the plan. He could foresee only "a protracted and difficult Congressional struggle in which we would be largely deprived of the one decisive argument – that this arrangement is what our major European partners really want."[26]

In mid-December, Rusk traveled to Paris and had a series of talks with de Gaulle. When MLF came up, the general insisted that the changed conditions in Europe called for a rethinking of NATO. In the early postwar period, the United States had been the sole deciding voice, according to its own plans had placed troops and tactical nuclear weapons in European countries, "and had plans for escalation which would involve at a certain time under certain conditions, as yet unknown, the use of this nuclear power, but always on our choice." MLF was an outmoded and dangerous extension of that postwar view. Rusk countered with the standard Washington argument that MLF, to the contrary,

25. Memorandum of Conversation, 19 November 1964, *Johnson Papers*, NSF, Files of McGeorge Bundy, Boxes 18-19.

26. Draft letter, 24 November 1964, *Johnson Papers*, NSF, Country File, France, Box 170; Memorandum, "The Future of the MLF," 25 November 1964, ibid., National Security Files, Bundy Memos to the President, Box 2.

was the only way to satisfy German nationalism. But the major thing that emerged from the conversation was de Gaulle's insistence that, MLF or no, there would have to be discussions on coordination of nuclear strategy by 1967 or 1968, along with changes in the NATO organization itself – a portent that escaped full notice.[27]

At year's end, Johnson used a visit by British Prime Minister Harold Wilson to begin to back away gracefully from MLF. At a background press conference, he let it be known that the United States would not attempt to force mixed-manned missile carrying ships down the throats of its allies.[28]

"Just think of some of the things we could do without de Gaulle," one of Johnson's advisers was reported as saying by Philip Geyelin in the *Wall Street Journal*, beginning with MLF, which would move the NATO's military command to Germany, "where it logically belongs."[29] "The MLF is dead," de Gaulle was quoted as having boasted to Ambassador Alphand. "It is I who killed it."[30] But MLF sank instead, leaking from every portal and seam.

ABOUT AS MUCH AS LUXEMBOURG?

When France recognized "Red" China in early 1964, an American commentator remarked dismissively, according to Alexander Werth, that Paris "counted in South-East Asia for just about as much as did Luxembourg."[31] But in secret testimony before the Senate Foreign Relations Committee, Secretary of State Rusk expressed an altogether different view. If France extended diplomatic recognition to the "Peiping regime," followed by the French-speaking nations of Africa, the result would be the establishment of Chinese Communist embassies as centers of subversion in some of the most delicate Third World areas of that continent. Recognition would also breach the line in the United Nations, where the nations that recognized "Red" China had

27. In passing the minutes of the conversation to Johnson, for example, McGeorge Bundy noted there was nothing new except that De Gaulle had now "set a time at which he thinks he will be ready to talk about 'coordination of nuclear defense' – 1967–1968." Bundy to Johnson, 15 December 1964, with attachments, *Johnson Papers*, NSF, Country File, France, Box 170.

28. Ball to Rusk, 16 December 1964, *Johnson Papers*, NSF, Subject File, Box 24.

29. 13 November 1964, p. 14.

30. Bohlen to Department of State, 23 March 1965, *Johnson Papers*, NSF, Subject File, Boxes 25-27.

31. *De Gaulle* (New York: Simon and Shuster, 1965), p. 337.

already reached more than forty. "If that balance were to change quickly the question of membership there could be a very difficult one to manage indeed."[32]

Johnson recalled that before his meeting with the French leader at the time of the Kennedy funeral, de Gaulle had called for the "neutralization" of Vietnam. When de Gaulle said at that meeting that he was sure if France were attacked, America would respond, Johnson thought to himself both then and later that if the United States had "taken his advice to abandon Vietnam, I suspect he might have cited that as 'proof' of what he had been saying all along: that the United States could not be counted on in times of trouble."[33]

As the American involvement in Vietnam deepened, both Paris and Washington generalized the issue of European support for the war into overall approaches to the Third World. When he went on tours of Latin America and Asia, de Gaulle would contrast French offers of aid and assistance with American heavy-handedness and, by implication, militarism. Such "name calling" might not hurt the American war effort directly, but it provided a rallying point for European opposition opinion – especially valuable to the Left, of course, because it emanated from this classical conservative figure.

When de Gaulle began trading in his dollars for gold, however, the situation took on a new aspect. Determined not to abandon the Great Society programs, and loath to increase taxes, Johnson chose to pay for the war by printing dollars. As a reserve currency, the dollar had a fixed value in Europe. The discrepancy between the value of the dollar in America and in Europe produced a situation where Europe was, in effect, being "taxed" to pay for the American war in Vietnam. Surplus dollars returned for gold had a very sobering effect on international perceptions of the strength of the American currency, and American ability to meet all its various international and domestic responsibilities.

De Gaulle had dramatized the issue by sending Air France airplanes to pick up the gold, instead of leaving it in the American Federal Reserve Bank on deposit. In 1965 alone, he "cashed in" more than $300 million before calling for gold to be re-established as the international standard at $70 an ounce – a level that

32. United States Senate, Committee on Foreign Relations, *Executive Sessions of the Senate Foreign Relations Committee* (Historical Series), vol. XVI (88th cong., 2nd sess.) 1964 (Washington: Government Printing Office, 1988), p. 8.

33. *The Vantage Point*, p. 23.

would presumably stop American attempts to pay for the war with "greenbacks."[34] "This was one of several times when I was tempted to abandon my policy of polite restraint toward de Gaulle," Johnson wrote in his memoirs, "but I forced myself to be patient again."[35]

De Gaulle's "interference" in the American war effort began to be uncomfortable in 1964, when Senator Mike Mansfield, citing the French proposals for neutralization, wrote to Johnson about the pattern of military coups in South Vietnam, a pattern that gave little hope for a solid foundation on which to mount a successful war effort. "The de Gaulle approach to Southeast Asia," he wrote the president on 1 February 1964, "offers a faint glimmer of hope of a way to solution at a cost to us somewhere commensurate with our national interests in Southeast Asia. For this reason, it is most unfortunate that the new military junta in south Viet Nam has seen fit, as one of its first acts, to denounce it."[36]

Mansfield's views were treated with respect, but the problem, as it was then perceived, was to convince *everyone* that America was not about to back out of its "responsibilities." Retiring Assistant Secretary of State for Far Eastern Affairs Roger Hilsman, later a critic of the war, declared in his valedictory letter to Dean Rusk that the greatest need was to clear up doubts about U.S. intentions:

> De Gaulle, Lippmann, and Mansfield have set the neutralist hares running with self-fulfilling prophecies that dishearten those who wish to fight and encourage coup-plotting among both the true neutralists and the simple opportunists. But what gives these lofty, unrealistic thoughts of a peaceful neutralist Asia their credibility is, again, fundamental doubts about our ultimate intentions.[37]

Ambassador Bohlen, accordingly, was instructed to seek an early audience with de Gaulle, and to present him with a presidential letter outlining American reasoning and policy. "What we actually want from de Gaulle is a public statement, prior to SEATO meeting, that the idea of 'neutralization' does not apply to the attitudes or policies of the Government of Vietnam or its friends in the face of the current communist aggression." He was

34. Richard Barnet, *The Alliance: America-Europe-Japan, Makers of the Postwar World* (New York: Simon and Shuster, 1983), p. 250.

35. Ibid., 316–17.

36. *Johnson Papers*, NSF, Bundy Memos to the President, Box 1.

37. Hilsman to Rusk, 14 March 1964, *Johnson Papers*, NSF, Bundy Memos to the President, Box 1.

not being asked to abandon the idea for all eternity, only in the present time. Then this:

> You may use whatever argument or persuasion you deem most effective in the presentation of this demarche. But you should make it clear that we expect France, as an ally, to adopt an attitude of cooperation rather than obstruction in this critical area of United States interest.[38]

From an American point of view, disaster followed. At the April SEATO meeting, Couve de Murville refused to endorse the communique expressing support for American policy in Vietnam. "From that moment on, the French delegation stopped attending the sessions."[39] The most serious discussion of the issues, however, occurred between Under Secretary of State George Ball and President de Gaulle at the Elysee Palace on 5 June 1964. Ball, who actually agreed with de Gaulle's estimate of the situation, faithfully presented American arguments against attempts at "neutralization."

The Under Secretary was in a very difficult position, for he had to argue that the United States did not desire any permanent military standing in Vietnam, while at the same time insisting that successful negotiations with Communist powers always had to be backed by countervailing power – so obviously lacking in Southeast Asia. Ball's instructions had pointed up the dilemma. From what the French said at the recent SEATO meeting, de Gaulle's "neutralization" proposal would mean that all of Indochina would be barred from obtaining outside military aid – an unacceptable situation at that stage of affairs for Americans.[40]

De Gaulle's response to the Under Secretary was to stress that the world had changed since the Boxer Rebellion, when the West had imposed its will on Asia. He had told President Kennedy, the French leader went on, that Southeast Asia was a "rotten" territory in which to fight. France could not become involved in any way in a war in Asia. Perhaps the Americans really believed that they could outlast Ho Chi Minh without the situation escalating to a major war. Perhaps they could for an extended period. But they would never be able to bring the affair to an end. Once that realization set in, "we would have to make peace. This would mean peace with China and others in the area."

38. Johnson to Bohlen, 24 March 1964, *Johnson Papers*, NSF, Bundy Memos to the President, Box 1.

39. Grosser, *Western Alliance*, p. 239.

40. George S. Springsteen, "Draft Instructions for De Gaulle Conversation," 4 June 1964, *Johnson Papers*, NSF, Country File, France, Box 170.

De Gaulle argued, finally, that while the 1954 Geneva Conference had taken a long time – and not worked out in the end – a "vast diplomatic operation" such as he had in mind would make it impossible, he believed, for Ho Chi Minh to go on killing South Vietnamese. As Ball reported his words to Washington,

> This would provide the Vietnamese people – and he was not speaking of General Khanh [the current leader in Saigon] – with a sense of support and assurance for the future. He doubted that even Ho Chi Minh could continue to kill South Vietnamese while taking part in a conference. World opinion would make it impossible.

To Ball's counter-arguments along these lines, de Gaulle responded with a note at once sympathetic and rueful. After matters reached a certain stage, there was a tendency to blame others for all the difficulties incurred.

> France had done this in the past. Now the United States tended to blame France. He would like to ask how could France take any action when it had been eliminated from the scene and had no power for action?

Ball politely demurred, assuring the French president that whatever rumors might appear in the American press, everyone in the Johnson administration held him in the highest esteem. Ball departed Elysee Palace with the final comment that experience had taught Americans that aggression must be checked at an early stage – otherwise, the costs became progressively higher. Reporting to Washington, the Under Secretary added that he and Ambassador Bohlen thought de Gaulle was biding his time, waiting for the moment when the Americans would come to him to ask him to summon such a conference.[41]

At his 24 July 1964 press conference, de Gaulle asserted that the United States wanted to take France's place in Southeast Asia. The only solution, he said, was for an international conference, which would neutralize the whole area. The powers – France, China, the Soviet Union, and the United States – should resolve to be committed no longer.[42] Did de Gaulle believe such abnegation was really possible? Or was there some other motive behind his actions? The State Department's Intelligence and Research Division suspected that there was, suggesting to the White

41. Ball to Johnson, 6 June 1964, *Johnson Papers*, NSF, Country Files, France, Box 170.

42. Newhouse, *DeGaulle and the Anglo-Saxons*, p. 262.

House the possibility that the proposal had been developed in advance with China, North Vietnam, and the National Liberation Front.[43]

De Gaulle had made it plain in this press conference that he believed the problem began when the United States, against French wishes, had brought in Ngo Dinh Diem to run South Vietnam "and that in all fields, notably the fields of defence, economy, and administration, he placed himself in Washington's orbit." When Diem tried to extricate himself from this increasingly unpopular (with his own people) position, a military putsch brought forth a new government. And then another putsch and another government. "The guerrilla warfare and fighting . . . extends further and further over the territory while the population feels less and less inclined to support an authority and a cause which, whatever their opinions concerning communism, seem to them indistinguishable from those of a foreign state."[44]

On the verge of the fateful decisions to begin bombing North Vietnam in early 1965, Johnson had a long talk with Couve de Murville. Better put, Johnson lectured the French diplomat on American determination. Since he had been in the Oval Office, LBJ began, he had been careful not to try to throw American weight around, not to bully allies. But he was not going to run out on the commitment Eisenhower and Kennedy had made to the people of South Vietnam. Recalling the events since the Gulf of Tonkin incidents in 1964, the president declared that he was not going to write North Vietnam a "thank-you note" for an attack on an American compound:

> The President wondered what de Gaulle or Erhard or Wilson would do in similar circumstances. What we had done was to bomb certain of their staging and assembly points. Then the following night they had come and blown up a hotel and killed some more of our soldiers. So our planes went back and "sprinkled them a little." The President didn't think we had killed many of them. In fact he thought that our action had probably caused more concern in certain other parts of the world than it had in North Vietnam.

This was all vintage Johnson, as was his next comment that he had tried to find out what it was de Gaulle meant when he spoke out on Vietnam. He was told that the French leader favored a

43. Thomson to Bundy, 24 July 1964, *Johnson Papers*, NSF, Country Files, France, Box 170.

44. From a transcript in *Johnson Papers*, NSF, Country File, France, Box 170.

political solution. So did he. But how did he go about getting one? The United States would get out if South Vietnam's independence was guaranteed.

But there was not going to be any sanctuary as there had been in Korea, or unwise statements about what weapons would or would not be used:

> We were going to keep them guessing and use appropriate means in response to their aggression. We don't want to move to escalation, but if the others do it, we will do whatever is required on the basis of the wisest military judgment. We would like to have everybody else's help in our efforts and we haven't had much help from others.

Until the United States got that help, "we will never be able to explain our alliances satisfactorily to the American people." Then Johnson (in effect) warned the foreign minister, as if he were speaking to the other side, that so far he had not been "too sensitive" to demands for stronger action from people in this country. "In this connection he specifically mentioned Goldwater, Nixon, Scranton, Rockefeller and Lodge, who had all asked for greater military measures."

Against this barrage of cajolery, threats, and exaggerations, Couve de Murville simply replied that he understood the feelings of the president. "The essential problem was: how to get out." There was a "complete contradiction," he went on, between American and French information about the willingness of China and North Vietnam to negotiate. When pressed, the foreign minister admitted that the future of South Vietnam's government "was a risk which one would probably have to take. It was not possible to tell what the nature of a South Vietnamese government would be."

George Ball asked if it would not be one dominated by Hanoi? Ambassador Alphand then interjected that Belgrade was not Moscow. The discussion turned into a sparring match about the aggressiveness of Communist China, with de Murville pointing out that Russia had not become expansionist until World War II opened up the opportunities, and Americans arguing that China was already expansionist. Success by the Chinese, Johnson said, would be likely to increase their appetite. As in previous discussions, an impasse had been reached.[45]

Johnson had no intention of attacking Chinese "sanctuaries" or

45. Memorandum of Conversation, 19 February 1965, *Johnson Papers*, NSF, Country File, France, Box 171.

using atomic weapons, and his plea that the United States was not getting support from the alliance was hardly designed to encourage a change in French attitudes and actions. The only change or development was that on 1 March 1965, when Ambassador Bohlen reported that the French Government had now openly expressed willingness to work directly with the Soviet Union in seeking an international conference on the war. The announcement was designed to bring pressure on Washington, Bohlen added, and was especially unfriendly coming on the heels of Johnson's intimate talks with Couve de Murville, during which it was made "abundantly clear" that the United States did not think the time was propitious for a conference. "Looked at objectively, de Gaulle statement appears to violate spirit of NATO and certainly of SEATO which was conceived as coming together of like-minded nations for defense of Southeast Asia against communist aggression."[46]

Johnson's advisors were really at a loss to suggest any further means of countering de Gaulle's "shenanigans," except to note their very adverse impact on the "Alliance."[47] After Johnson's speech at Johns Hopkins University in April, Ambassador Bohlen described the American position to de Gaulle as now favoring negotiations without pre-conditions. It was too late, de Gaulle replied. Now that the bombing of North Vietnam had begun, the Chinese and North Vietnamese were no longer interested in negotation, but accepted with "oriental fatalism" the inevitable escalation of the war. "The issues were now engaged and there was very little that could be done." He was pessimistic and philosophical, "with a considerable measure of schadenfreude about the future in regard to Vietnam."[48]

Meanwhile, American policy-makers watched the progress of Soviet- French relations with considerable concern. A joint communique issued at the end of April, after talks with Russian Foreign Minister Gromyko, expressed an agreed position on Southeast Asia that was a "clear thrust" against the United States. And there were other agreements as well. The communique, a National Security Council aide informed Bundy, "puts the French in

46. Bohlen to Secretary of State, 1 March 1965, *Johnson Papers*, NSF, Country File, France, Box 171.

47. David Klein to McGeorge Bundy, 2 March 1965, *Johnson Papers*, NSF, Country File, France, Box 171.

48. Bohlen to Secretary of State, 4 May 1965, *Johnson Papers*, NSF, Country File, France, Box 171.

bed with the Soviet Union on a number of causes calculated to create discomfort in several places, including Washington, London and Bonn."[49]

There were ominous signs that de Gaulle was planning a formal break with NATO, at least to the extent of ordering foreign troops out of France. Secretary Rusk had ordered studies of the possibility of pulling out before ordered out. But Bundy's aide thought that was premature. "1969 is a long [way] away. The General is not young. And time might resolve many problems, including this one."[50]

But America's troubles in the Third World, not only Vietnam, were giving de Gaulle a platform from which he could denounce Washington's unilateralism and strengthen the case for an "independent" Europe. During a joint press conference with Gromyko, de Gaulle was asked about French motives in helping the Third World:

> Yes, we are helping these countries, and they like France as a result. In their view the contrast between us and the United States has become immense: while we are helping them, the Americans are using all their brillant new technological inventions to exterminate in the most horrible ways thousands of these poor long-suffering Vietnamese, who merely want to be left alone. And look what they are doing at San Domingo. . . . And I'm afraid this isn't the end yet. *L'appetit vient en mangeant*.[51]

At this same press conference, de Gaulle said that this subordination, known as "integration," "which hands our fate over to foreign authority shall cease, as far as we are concerned" in 1969.[52]

THE LETTER – AND AFTERWARDS

Nearly a year later, on 7 March 1966, de Gaulle sent Johnson a formal letter, made public at once, explaining that France was determined to assert full sovereignty over its territory. The other shoe had dropped. All foreign forces were to be out of France

49. David Klein to Bundy, 29 April 1965, *Johnson Papers*, NSF, Country File, France, Box 171.

50. Klein to Bundy, 5 May 1965, *Johnson Papers*, NSF, Country File, France, Box 171.

51. Werth, *De Gaulle*, p. 342. Alfred Grosser notes, however, that while de Gaulle was now posing as the savior of the Third World, he had acted in the same way in Gabon. *Western Alliance*, pp. 210–11.

52. Newhouse, *De Gaulle and the Anglo-Saxons*, p. 283.

within thirteen months' time. France would no longer place its forces at the disposal of NATO. In the event of a conflict, however, France would coordinate its plans and facilities with the other members of the alliance. De Gaulle's actions caused a furor inside France, leading to the most serious debate in the history of the Fifth Republic.[53]

But Johnson maintained his aloofness. "When a man asks you to leave his house," he told Defense Secretary McNamara, "you don't argue; you get your hat and go."[54] To de Gaulle he wrote back that he was puzzled by the expression that American troops were an infringement on French sovereignty, as they had been there as a result of an invitation. Be that as it might, the United States was determined to join with the other fourteen members of the alliance to preserve the NATO deterrent. These other nations did not take the same view of their interests "as that taken at the moment by the Government of France." "Indeed," he went on, "we find it difficult to believe that France, which has made a unique contribution to Western security and development, will long remain withdrawn from the common affairs and responsibilities of the Atlantic. As our old friend and ally her place will await France whenever she decides to resume her leading role."[55]

Behind the measured formal response to de Gaulle, American policymakers were both alarmed and angry.[56] It was comforting to think that the general was an old man who might soon be gone from the world scene – as Bundy's aide David Klein had said – but after him what? De Gaulle had, in policy-makers' view, unloosed forces that would be hard to contain. If France, as a result of de Gaulle's assault on NATO and efforts to re-imagine Europe from the Atlantic to the Urals, moved into a "neutralist" position, what then? Congress might refuse to put up the money for an "integrated deterrent," opined Walt W. Rostow, Bundy's successor as National Security Adviser. The Italians and Danes might also slide

53. Grosser, *Western Alliance*, pp. 214–16.

54. Ibid., 215.

55. Johnson to De Gaulle, 22 March 1966, Johnson Papers, Confidential File, Box 58.

56. Dean Rusk, so calm in front of the Senate Foreign Relations Committee, often spoke sharply to French diplomats. And when de Gaulle told him he wanted every soldier out of France, the Secretary shot back, "Does that include the dead Americans in the military cemeteries as well?" Thomas J. Schoenbaum, *Waging Peace and War: Dean Rusk in the Truman, Kennedy and Johnson Years* (New York: Simon and Schuster, 1988), p. 421.

toward neutralism, and the Germans would move towards bilateralism vis-à-vis both Washington and Paris.[57]

By his actions, de Gaulle had further damaged the possibility of ever integrating Germany into a politically calm and stable Western Europe. He had posed, for example, the question of French troops in Germany. Without NATO, these forces became an army of occupation, a situation the West Germans would not long tolerate. If only some variant of MLF had succeeded – but that seemed hopeless. "Now that France is no longer taking part in this joint effort – and, indeed, placing heavy pressure on German political life," read a proposed Johnson letter to Prime Minister Harold Wilson, "there is grave danger that the Germans will over time feel that they have been cast adrift. A growing sense of uncertainty and insecurity on their part could lead to a fragmentation of European and Atlantic relations which would be tragic for all of us."[58]

When Ambassador Bohlen next talked to de Gaulle in June 1966, it emerged that the French leader, who was about to depart for a major diplomatic effort in Moscow, was reasonably content with things as they were. He was not entirely happy with the German situation, either, but for very different reasons. The Franco-German Treaty might not have worked out quite as well as he wished, but he obviously felt he still had room to maneuver with both West and East.[59] A reunified Germany, he told Bohlen, which France favored in principle, would be dangerous if it came too quickly, because it would solidify the control of Moscow over its apprehensive satellites, and because of Western fears. But so far as the question of French troops in West Germany was concerned, they would stay only if the Germans wanted them.[60]

On 1 September 1966, he spoke before 100,000 cheering Cambodians in Phnom Penh, decrying the American military presence in Vietnam in his harshest language yet, and predicting there was no chance that the peoples of Asia would submit to the law of foreigners "from across the shores of the Pacific, whatever their intentions and however powerful their arms."[61]

57. Rostow and Francis Bator to Johnson, 18 May 1966, *Johnson Papers*, NSF, Rostow Memos to the President, Box 7.

58. "Draft Letter to Prime Minister Wilson," undated [May 1966], *Johnson Papers*, NSF, Rostow Memos to the President, Box 7.

59. Grosser, *Western Alliance*, p. 208.

60. Text of Bohlen Cable, 13 June 1966, *Johnson Papers*, NSF, Rostow Memos to the President, Box 8.

61. Barnet, *The Alliance*, p. 265.

It was American militarism, he said, that took root in Vietnam after 1954, and "simultaneously, the war rekindled there in the form of national resistance."

> Whereupon, illusions concerning the use of force led to the continuous build-up of the expeditionary force and to an increasingly extensive escalation in Asia, closer and closer to China, more and more provocative with respect to the Soviet Union, more and more condemned by many peoples of Europe, Africa and Latin America, and, in the last analysis, more and more threatening to the peace of the world.[62]

De Gaulle's opportunity to challenge aspects of American policy back in Europe as in Asia was vastly increased by the general situation resulting from the Vietnam War.

Those things having been said, it remains true that the French president's economic policies, especially his assault on the dollar and his dominance of the policies of the Common Market, worked against America's "Grand Design" from the Kennedy years through the Johnson era. NATO did not collapse, as many in Johnson's inner circle feared might happen, nor did German bilateralism disrupt the European scene. But things worked out differently from the way Washington had planned.

It had long been de Gaulle's view that British membership in the European Community was designed to further American economic domination of the continent – part of a pattern that would aid American capitalists to use inflated dollars to buy up European resources, at the same time denying French technology a chance to compete in the American market. The view was not, by any means, an exclusively "Gaullist" resentment. The popularity of Jean-Jacques Servan-Schreiber's *The American Challenge* indicated the breadth of interest and concern about France's economic future in an "Americanized" Europe.[63]

A second veto of British membership in the Common Market in 1967 gave Americans yet another opportunity, on the other hand, to focus on de Gaulle as their favorite nemesis. Treasury Secretary Henry Fowler summed up the impact of French policies at a National Security Council meeting on 3 May 1967:

> The French have been trying to use the Common Market structure for the past five years in an effort to diminish our economic, political and

62. Transcript in, *Johnson Papers*, NSF, Country File, France, Box 172.
63. Grosser, *Western Alliance*, pp. 220–223.

military influence. This French effort in Europe affects our ability to be effective in other parts of the world.[64]

President Johnson agreed that the economic situation was coming to dominate American-European affairs. "A showdown in this country is coming soon." If trade talks with Europe and financial discussions did not produce an agreement on sharing the costs of the American forces, he asked, "what do we do?" Besides the economic problem, noted Arthur Goldberg, Ambassador to the United Nations, other countries were following the French example of complaining that the United States did not consult, only inform. "We no longer have a solid bloc of western allies behind us." National Security Adviser Walt Rostow responded to all this with a short observation that, "Europe is neglecting the world. It is in an isolationist cycle. We should get one of our Senators to make this point in a major speech."[65]

Johnson agreed with the sentiment, but "what we need is a solution." And that was not easy. In the final months of the administration, the United States managed to avoid or, better put, to postpone the "showdown" the president feared over the balance-of-payments deficit, through a combination of tax increases and fiscal restraints. And, indeed, when the French faced a serious monetary crisis in the summer of 1968, ironically, Johnson was quickly able to come to de Gaulle's aid. But Richard Nixon would soon reap the fruits of what historian David Calleo called *"ad hocery"* in 1971.[66]

From the earliest moments of his presidency to the end, Lyndon Johnson was engaged with Charles de Gaulle in an ongoing "non-dialogue" about the future, the "Atlantic Community" and "Europe," world responsibilities of alliance members, hegemony, and independence. They talked past one another. Given their respective positions and roles, it could hardly have been otherwise. Through it all, Johnson maintained – and imposed on his advisors – a remarkable equanimity in his public and private musings about the general, especially in contrast to his reactions to domestic opponents. If he could not overcome the difficulties with de Gaulle's France on MLF or Vietnam, he kept them from

64. "Summary Notes of the 569th NSC Meeting," 3 May 1967, *Johnson Papers*, NSF, NSC Meetings, Box 2.

65. Ibid.

66. "American Power in a New World Economy," in William H. Becker and Samuel F. Wells, Jr., eds., *Economics and World Power: An Assessment of American Diplomacy Since 1789* (New York: Columbia University Press, 1984), pp. 391–447.

overwhelming American foreign policy at a critical time when things could have gotten much worse. And that in itself was perhaps not an insignificant achievement.

❖ 12 ❖

Conflicting Visions: Defense, Nuclear Weapons, and Arms Control in the Franco-American Relationship During the De Gaulle Era

Andrew J. Pierre

In his address to the officers of the senior military academies on 3 November 1959, de Gaulle noted that "in everything that constitutes a nation, and principally in what constitutes ours, nothing is more important than defense."[1] This guiding principle, ingrained in de Gaulle's life experience, was a key element of his policy of grandeur. Thus, it should not be surprising that issues involving defense and arms control were at the heart of much of the French-American discourse and often led to controversy and conflict.

Just as in the 1930s de Gaulle was convinced that the modernization of the tank corps was essential for an effective defense, in the 1960s the acquisition of nuclear weapons was seen by de Gaulle as critical to France's national security. Nuclear weapons were, moreover, basic to a nation's stature and political influence. "A great state which does not possess them, while others have them," he said in Strasbourg in November 1961, "does not command its own destiny."[2]

1. As cited in Alfred Grosser, *The Western Alliance: European-American Relations Since 1945* (New York: Continuum Books, 1980), p. 184.

2. Quoted by André Passeron, *De Gaulle Parle I* (Paris: Plon, 1962), p. 357, as cited by Wilfrid L. Kohl, *French Nuclear Diplomacy* (Princeton: Princeton University Press, 1971), p. 129. I have benefitted greatly from Kohl's detailed and excellent analysis. Other excellent works which address de Gaulle's relationship with the United States in defense include Edward A. Kolodziej, *French International Policy Under De Gaulle and Pompidou: The Politics of Grandeur* (Ithaca: Cornell University

THE FORCE DE FRAPPE

The national decision to build a French nuclear force was made before de Gaulle's return to power. In the background was an accumulation of more than a decade of decisions involving the atomic research program. As for delivery systems, in 1956 it was decided to build a Mirage IV tactical aircraft that could be modified to have a nuclear capability, and to commence research on a strategic ballistic missile. The government of Felix Gaillard made the actual decision to proceed with a nuclear force as such in 1957, and in April 1958, shortly before the end of the Fourth Republic, a 1960 target date was set for the first atomic test.

De Gaulle, nevertheless, substantially revised the policy aims and theoretical underpinnings of the *force de frappe*, and gave its development the highest priority. Under the Fourth Republic, the nuclear force was seen as a way of enhancing France's military position – *within* the NATO alliance. This would keep the nation involved at the cutting edge of technology in such a way as to be a more effective partner within the alliance's multinational framework. During the Fifth Republic, however, the *force de frappe* was to have a predominantly political role *outside* the alliance in support of an independent foreign policy.

The basic themes of Gaullist foreign policy are well known. The possession of a nuclear weapons capability was designed to serve and buttress these aims. Only a nation with a nuclear force could be a true world power, could have sufficient freedom of maneuver and flexibility vis-à-vis a superpower even though still aligned with it, could form the centerpiece of a "European" Europe, and could seek to reduce the existing Superpower duopoly. The British nuclear force was not seen as independent due to its reliance upon American technology and London's cooperation in targeting with NATO. As for West Germany, the important restrictions upon its military nuclear development denied it a place at the top diplomatic table and any claim to the leadership of Europe.

THE THREE-POWER DIRECTORATE

The first major clash between France and the United States, a few months after de Gaulle returned to power, came as a result of his

Press, 1974); Wolf Mendl, *Deterrence and Persuasion: French Nuclear Armament in the Context of National Policy, 1945–1969* (London: Faber & Faber, 1970); and John Newhouse: *De Gaulle and the Anglo-Saxons* (New York: Viking Press, 1970).

proposal for a new three-power directorate outside of NATO for managing the affairs of the West. In his memorandum to President Eisenhower of 17 September 1958, de Gaulle noted that events of the prior months in the Middle East and the Taiwan straits had demonstrated that the NATO alliance, with its geographical limitations, could not adequately deal with the worldwide security requirements of the free world. Moreover, within the Western camp, the United States no longer had a nuclear monopoly. "It therefore seems to France that an organization comprising the United States, Great Britain and France should be created and function on a worldwide political and strategic level," he wrote.[3]

De Gaulle was not only seeking to use the tripartite mechanism to participate in decisions on global problems, he was also demanding a role in the decision to use the West's nuclear weapons. This was tantamount to exercising a right of veto over an American decision, as Secretary of State Dulles uncovered on a visit to the Elysées soon thereafter.

Given the extravagance of this demand, Eisenhower's tempered response was an attempt to keep bridges open. Although Paris suggested that no response was given, in subsequent years it was revealed that the American president, while indicating that he could not agree with any proposal that would restrict the participation of other NATO allies in decisions affecting their security, was willing to consult on how to make NATO more effective under changing conditions that had to take into account a wider geographical zone.

This episode was central to de Gaulle's withdrawal from NATO in later years. Was it a tactical ploy on the part of the general who, knowing that it could not possibly be accepted, was creating the justification for subsequent foreign policy moves? A number of observers came to that conclusion, although de Gaulle must also have been influenced by the desire to make up for the slights he felt he had suffered at the hands of the Americans and British during the World War II.

AMERICAN NUCLEAR ASSISTANCE

While losing no opportunity to emphasize the independence of France's nuclear role, de Gaulle in his first four years directed his

3. *Espoir*, Revue de l'Institut Charles de Gaulle, No.15, Juin 1976, as cited in Grosser, op.cit. p. 352.

lieutenants to explore delicately the possibility of American assistance for the still fledgling *force de frappe*. Only once does he appear to have raised the assistance issue himself, in his meeting with Dulles a few weeks after returning to office. It was unfortunate timing, for only a few days earlier Eisenhower had signed the 1958 amendment to the U.S. atomic energy legislation (McMahon Act), which continued the restrictions on nuclear assistance except for countries that had "already made substantial progress" in the development of atomic weapons – a loophole that was intentionally designed to discriminate in favor of Great Britain. Dulles had little choice but to demur on the larger question of making American assistance available while nevertheless offering help in building a nuclear submarine. Even that, however, proved to be too much for the U.S. Congress's Joint Committee on Atomic Energy (JCAE), which at that time was all-powerful.

Over the next several years there were a number of attempts to find ways to provide American nuclear assistance. After the first French atomic test in 1960, Eisenhower declared in a press conference that he favored amending the McMahon Act so as to at least give the French what the Russians already knew. Once again his wishes ran afoul of the Joint Committee, which reiterated its firm opposition. Kennedy's ambassador in Paris, General James Gavin, having been instructed by the new president, who admired de Gaulle, to improve relations, also sought to remove this irritant in French-American relations. Gavin had a great deal of experience in the development of military technology, and he was convinced that it was impossible to withhold secrets for long. He proposed several forms of nuclear assistance that would have the added benefit of helping the United States in its growing balance of payments problem. In particular, he proposed American aid in the construction of the gaseous diffusion plant at Pierrelatte for the purpose of producing enriched uranium. In this he was supported by both General Maxwell Taylor, then a close military advisor to Kennedy, and by the Joint Chiefs of Staff, who wished to reduce the cost to the French of their nuclear program in order to encourage additional spending on conventional forces for NATO. But Gavin's efforts also failed, this time because of the growing concern in the State Department about avoiding any steps that could be viewed as encouraging nuclear proliferation.

NATO Nuclear Sharing Proposals

Although direct atomic assistance was proving to be difficult, some arrangement providing for French participation in nuclear sharing with the United States could nevertheless have been worked out. A number of proposals were made in the late 1950s and early 1960s that would have assured this. When Sputnik demonstrated in 1957 the unexpectedly rapid growth of Soviet missile power, Washington became concerned about Western Europe's vulnerability to Soviet nuclear forces. Equally on the mind of American strategists was the fear that in the wake of the declining credibility of the American nuclear umbrella, pressures would grow in Europe for new national nuclear forces. Of particular concern, of course, was West Germany.

In December 1957, the United States offered to place intermediate range ballistic missiles in Europe to be deployed and targeted under a "dual key" arrangement in accordance with the plans of SACEUR. Great Britain, Italy, and Turkey accepted, but once in office de Gaulle rejected this offer on the grounds that any nuclear weapons on French soil must be under her exclusive control. Similarly, de Gaulle turned down three related proposals each of which had been the subject of intense Alliance consultations, i.e., General Lauris Norstad's suggestion as Supreme Allied Commander, Europe (SACEUR) that there be a NATO nuclear force consisting of land-based medium range missiles; U.S. Secretary of Defense Thomas Gates's idea for deployment of such missiles on barges in European rivers and canals; and the more fully fleshed out proposal for a submarine-based multilateral nuclear force (MLF), which consumed over two years of alliance diplomacy.

None of these proposals were received with approbation in Paris. De Gaulle argued that they encompassed a limitation on French nuclear independence that was unacceptable. He was, moreover, moving in the direction of withdrawing from NATO's military command structure, whereas these concepts were construed by him as steps towards further integration. Nevertheless, his continuing interest in bilateral nuclear assistance led him to suggest that some French participation was possible if there was to be a quid pro quo of direct nuclear aid, but neither Eisenhower nor Kennedy thought that approval for this could be obtained from the JCAE.

The final denouement during the de Gaulle era with respect to possible American nuclear assistance to France came in the wake of the Nassau Agreement of December 1962 between the United States and Great Britain. After the failure of the British Blue Streak missile, the opposition Labor Party and many informed observers argued that the United Kingdom could no longer maintain a credible independent nuclear deterrent. As this issue became part of the still wider argument concerning unilateral nuclear disarmament, it rapidly became the key foreign policy question in the British political debate. The issue became even more heated when Secretary of Defense Robert McNamara canceled, for American budgetary reasons, the Skybolt missile, which the British had counted upon receiving from the U.S. as a replacement for their own Blue Streak. At their Nassau meeting, Macmillan won from Kennedy (against the advice of most of his administration) the promise of the sale to London of Polaris missiles.[4]

Mindful of the impact that this would have upon de Gaulle, Kennedy decided to make a similar offer to the French. Among his advisors who favored nuclear assistance to France, this was viewed as a golden opportunity to create a new nuclear tripartism. The sale of Polaris missiles to France, they thought, would open a bridge to de Gaulle that could lead to the restoration of a cooperative relationship within NATO.

But the Polaris deal, which was worked out on the spot in Nassau, had not been discussed with any of the Allies. Kennedy wanted to defer any public announcement until de Gaulle could be personally apprised of the offer of equal treatment for Paris and London, but repeatedly he was urged by Macmillan to make public the Polaris offer to Britain before the two leaders left Nassau, the Prime Minister claiming that his very political survival was at stake. Kennedy accommodated his friend in what proved to be a costly mistake. De Gaulle first heard of the offer through newspapers! He claimed that the offer of Polaris was irrelevant because France did not have the appropriate submarines and warheads, even though then U.S. Ambassador Charles E. Bohlen told him that American assistance for these could also be provided. The general further insisted that the British had given up their nuclear independence at Nassau by agreeing to coordinate their targeting plans with NATO. This was incorrect, as Lon-

4. Andrew J. Pierre. *Nuclear Politics: The British Experience with an Independent Strategic Force, 1939–1970*, (New York and London: Oxford University Press, 1972), pp. 217–51.

don's independence was in fact safeguarded when "supreme national interests" were at stake. A few weeks later, de Gaulle held his famous press conference of 14 January 1963 at which he strongly reaffirmed France's need to have her own unfettered *force de frappe*, rejected any military arrangements which constrained her national defense through integration, and vetoed British entry into the Common Market.

NUCLEAR PROLIFERATION

A number of fundamental differences between the United States and France over questions of defense and arms control had emerged by this time. The two nations were at odds over the risks of nuclear proliferation, the strategic doctrine by which atomic weapons could be employed, and the utility and desirability of arms control measures.

During 1962, anxiety grew within the Kennedy administration over the dangers of nuclear proliferation. In a widely noted speech at Ann Arbor in June of that year, McNamara described independent but limited nuclear forces as being "dangerous, expensive, prone to obsolescence and lacking in credibility."

Washington's quest for centralized nuclear control and a monopoly in the ultimate decision-making power may well have been in America's interest as it was seen at the time. But the questionable assumption was usually made that this was also in the interest of France, Great Britain, and any potential nuclear power. American strategists feared that independent forces, such as the *force de frappe*, might involve the United States in a nuclear war against its will, or make more complex, and therefore less controllable, the conduct of a war once it had commenced. Accordingly, they sought the prevention of additional nuclear forces within NATO (principally West Germany) and the eventual dissolution of existing ones. In many ways, therefore, the offer of Polaris to France went directly against the grain of American policy on nuclear proliferation – Washington would have far preferred that the French nuclear program be discontinued.

President Kennedy was deeply concerned that a world of many nuclear powers increased the risks of instability and of war. He was moving towards arms control initiatives with the Soviet Union, with a nuclear test ban as the initial agreement. Nuclear aid to France, in the words of his close advisor Theodore Sorensen, "would not win General de Gaulle to our purposes but only strengthen him in his." The view in the Oval Office, according to Sorensen, was that "while minor military benefits might have been received in return, the General's desire to speak for all of Europe, free from British and American influence, would not have been altered. His desire to be independent of NATO, and to form a three-power nuclear directorate outside of NATO, would only have been encouraged. And the West Germans, more pointedly excluded than ever, would surely have reappraised their attitude towards the Atlantic Alliance and toward the acquisition of their own nuclear weapons."[5]

STRATEGIC DOCTRINE

The strategic doctrine that underpinned the deployment of French nuclear weapons emerged chiefly through the writings of military intellectuals, principally Generals Pierre Gallois and André Beaufre. Although tailored to French circumstances, these writings often appeared to be targeted against American strategic thought.[6]

The purpose of the French force was to deter (the phrase *force de dissuasion* was later to replace *force de frappe*), but if deterrence failed, it was to strike at the most vulnerable targets, population centers, in what Americans termed a "counter-city" strategy. In contrast, the McNamara doctrine called for moving away from the "massive retaliation" doctrine of the 1950s towards a strategy of targeting enemy military installations and nuclear weapons in a "counterforce" strategy. This shift was designed to keep a nuclear war as controlled as possible, limiting its escalation and augmenting the war-fighting options available to policy-makers while seeking to be less genocidal. The American doctrine, however, presupposed a more varied and sophisticated nuclear weapons capability than the French had at their disposal at this time.

Another element of French strategy, as elucidated by General Gallois, was the concept of "proportional deterrence," whereby the French force only had to have the capability to inflict sufficient damage to an opponent to make it unworthwhile for him to engage in aggression against a small country like France. This

5. Theodore C. Sorensen, *Kennedy* (New York: Harper & Row, 1965), pp. 571–72.

6. See, in particular, General Pierre M. Gallois, *Stratégie de l'age nucléaire*, (Paris: Calmann-Levy, 1960) and André Beaufre, *Dissuasion et stratégie* (Paris: Armand Colin, 1964).

justified a nuclear force far smaller than that of the Superpowers. But understandably the Americans became nervous when it was also suggested that all France had to do was to be able to "trigger" (*un detonateur*) the American nuclear arsenal, the supposition being that the United States would be incapable of remaining apart if a nuclear war were to start in Europe.

Even more troubling for the United States – as well as for the other West European countries – were the statements made in the second half of the 1960s, as France withdrew from the integrated military command of NATO, that its nuclear forces were to be deployed in all directions ("*tous azimuts*"), as if no distinction was to be made between the nations to the East and the West. This new concept, espoused by Chief of Staff General Charles Ailleret, was accompanied by the decision to develop longer range, intercontinental ballistic missiles with thermonuclear warheads.

In addition to these differences in strategic doctrine for the use of nuclear weapons, there was a clash over the use of conventional forces. The Kennedy administration, in the aim of delaying the use of nuclear weapons in case of a conflict in Europe, sought a strategy of "flexible response." Conventional forces were to be built up so as to create a pause before the nuclear threshold was crossed. Most of the West Europeans were less than enthusiastic about this change, as it was based upon the assumption of a longer war on the Continent, but after some modification it was adopted as official NATO policy. De Gaulle, however, continued to reject the strategy as it implicitly devalued the utility of the *force de frappe*. In his view, the more immediate the threat of the use of the nuclear force, the greater its power of deterrence.

ARMS CONTROL

Given the conflicting approaches to defense, it was not surprising that there were contrasting views on arms control.

Arms control became a policy objective for the Americans in the 1960s in part as a result of the intellectual ferment that created some basic concepts for the limitation of arms and in part due to the growing awareness of the dangers posed by both the Soviet-American arms race and the spread of nuclear weapons capabilities worldwide.

De Gaulle, however, viewed arms limitation agreements with some suspicion, as they seemed to him designed to maintain the predominant nuclear positions of the two superpowers and discriminated against the lesser powers. He was also strongly opposed to all arms control regimes that could possibly restrain France's own nuclear development.

Accordingly, de Gaulle refused to have France sign the Test Ban Treaty of 1963, which prohibited nuclear tests in the atmosphere and underwater but not underground. Kennedy offered to give de Gaulle information on underground testing techniques and the option of conducting French tests at American sites in exchange for his signature, but the general would have none of it. He deemed the Test Ban Treaty to be of "limited importance." France's adherence, in his view, would prevent her from acquiring the nuclear capacities essential to maintaining the *force de frappe* and thereby preserving the nation's independence.

Similarly, de Gaulle refused to have France sign the Nuclear Non-Proliferation Treaty, which he saw as another measure of superpower arms control designed to maintain existing advantages. This said, the actual policies adopted by Paris on nuclear non-proliferation were pursued as if it were a signatory of the NPT.

France's approach towards arms control was perhaps best characterized by de Gaulle's insistence that the French seat at the eighteen-nation Disarmament Conference in Geneva be kept empty. He declared that the efforts there could only lead to false hopes. Only when the principal nations truly wanted to organize disarmament – and that meant the four atomic powers he quickly noted – would France occupy its rightful place.

France's Withdrawal From NATO's Military Structure

The culmination of the French-American controversies discussed above came with de Gaulle's announcement in March 1966 that he intended to withdraw all French forces from NATO commands and require the transfer out of French territory of all the alliance's bases and installations, including the headquarters of NATO, which were then located just outside of Paris. This was a unilateral step, undertaken without prior discussion. Only one year was allowed for such a massive move to take place.

Although de Gaulle had given many indications in the eight years since the start of his presidency of his dissatisfaction with NATO, the timing and scale of this declaration came as a surprise and led to protests and debate within the alliance as well as an unsuccessful motion of censure within France's National Assembly. The fact that, despite its military withdrawal, France was remaining a formal member of the alliance did not assuage many of its national members.

In citing the reasons for his action, de Gaulle argued that NATO no longer was attuned to the prevailing conditions of world politics. Since the inception of the alliance in 1949, the threat to Western Europe had diminished and the European nations had revived. Moreover, France was equipping herself with atomic arms, the very nature of which in his judgment precluded military integration. The focus of international crisis had shifted from the Atlantic world to Asia. De Gaulle suggested that the American involvement in Vietnam threatened to draw in the Europeans, and that in case of a widened conflagration, the integrated military command would make it difficult to remain apart. In justifying the government's action, Prime Minister Georges Pompidou listed a number of complaints about NATO that had a clear anti-American tinge. One was the switch in alliance strategy, upon Washington's urging, from "massive retaliation" to "flexible response." Another was the fact that the bulk of America's nuclear deterrent remained outside of NATO, whereas all of the French nuclear forces were to be integrated in NATO. This was a disingenuous argument, however, for under the NATO Treaty each nation was still free to decide what actions it would take in case of hostilities.

France's withdrawal from NATO's military structure marked the low point in Franco-American relations during the de Gaulle era. It came at a time when de Gaulle had turned his attention to promoting detente and improving relations with the Soviet Union. Separating himself from the United States and NATO would presumably assist him in his quest for a Europe from the "Atlantic to the Urals."

But as fate would have it, two unexpected turns of events destroyed de Gaulle's aspirations for improving relations with the Soviet Union and reduced the value of distancing from NATO. The revolution of May 1968 weakened de Gaulle at home and turned his attention to the nation's socio-political crisis. The Soviet Union's invasion of Czechoslovakia only a few months later forced a reassessment of Soviet intentions and made France's search for independence from allies less attractive.

In his last year in power, de Gaulle partially reversed gears and now encouraged a thaw in Franco-American relations. Quietly, military liaison with NATO in the Mediterranean was unofficially resumed because of a step-up of Soviet naval activity in the sea. A new French Chief of Staff, General Michel Fourquet, dropped the *"tous azimuts"* strategy and announced a new strategy of graduated military action that was closer to "flexible response." Discussions were held with the new SACEUR, General Lyman Lemnitzer, with the aim of coordinating the use of French tactical nuclear weapons with those of the alliance. And planned expenditures on the nuclear force were scaled back so as to free funds for domestic social and economic priorities.

The change in Paris fused well with the transition in Washington. President Nixon made the improvement of relations with de Gaulle a matter of priority, and he went to visit the general a month after his inauguration. The new national security advisor, Henry Kissinger, had frequently called for improved consultations with the European allies. Relations between de Gaulle and the United States on issues involving defense had been in a tailspin of deterioration for a decade, but in the general's last year unexpected events had led to a partial turn around.

CONCLUSIONS: LOOKING BACK, LOOKING FORWARD

France and the United States were in an almost continuous clash on the issues of defense and arms control during the entire de Gaulle era save the final year. Given the revisionist objectives that de Gaulle had in mind when he returned to power, and his steadfastness in maintaining them, this was all but inevitable. Neither Eisenhower, Kennedy, nor Johnson was willing to accept de Gaulle's vision of the world, and although Nixon may have been tempted, the de Gaulle-Nixon period was too brief. In the case of Kennedy, his vision of a "Grand Design" for the Atlantic relationship was in fundamental ways incompatible with that of the general.

De Gaulle wished to break up what he saw as a bipolar system of two blocs in order to move towards a new pan-European system. In his vision of a "Europe of States" there would be a new equilibrium on the continent from the "Atlantic to the Urals." This required a disengagement of the two superpowers from the European continent.

Persuading the Soviet Union to leave Eastern Europe was never fully addressed except in the vague formulation of pursuing a policy of "détente, entente et coopération." Most of de Gaulle's revisionist scheme was focused upon the changes that he saw as necessary in the organization of the West. In particular, he wished to see a curtailment of Western Europe's prolonged dependence upon the United States. This required a diminution of NATO, which de Gaulle clearly saw as being dominated by the "Anglo-Saxons."

France's withdrawal from the military structure of NATO therefore served a dual purpose: it weakened the mainstay of the American presence in Europe, and it was essential to the pan-European vision that de Gaulle wished to pursue. In his last memoirs, de Gaulle made clear that he viewed his 1958 demand for a three-power directorate as the first step towards a disengagement from, and a weakening of, the alliance.[7] If the demand were accepted, which he knew was unlikely, the directorate would supersede the alliance in significant ways: if rejected he would be justified in his attempt to give France a more independent role and to pursue his quest for a transformation of the bipolar world structure.

For the United States, NATO was a collective alliance that entailed joint responsibilities. It was the appropriate vehicle for seeking both defense and detente, as the Harmel Report recommended. In order to provide for a greater European role in the alliance, befitting the postwar economic and political resurgence of Western Europe, Kennedy's "Grand Design" called for a "twin pillar" or "dumbbell" relationship between the alliance's North American and European members. But within this concept, NATO was to remain its centerpiece.

The difficulty with Kennedy's vision – which was the most clearly articulated American vision of what should be the trans-Atlantic relationship during the de Gaulle years – was its total failure to address how the European pillar should be constructed in respect to defense and security. Kennedy was a recruit of Monnet's concept of a united Europe, and Washington became more supportive of the economic aims of the European Community during his presidency. But the devolution of power and authority to a United Europe that was envisaged was never spelled out in the defense realm.

The lack of support for a European identity in defense was particularly significant with regards to nuclear weapons. The notion

7. Charles de Gaulle, *Mémoires d'Espoir: Le Renouveau, 1958–1962* (Paris: Plon, 1970), p. 214–15.

of a European pillar based upon the British and French nuclear forces never received serious attention because it violated the centrality of command and control that Washington deemed necessary in the nuclear age. The Americans were not insensitive to the interest of the Europeans in having a greater role in their nuclear defense. This led to a variety of plans for nuclear sharing under "dual key" systems and multilateral nuclear forces such as the MLF. In each case, however, the United States retained nuclear control.

This was unacceptable to de Gaulle, and thus the clash was inevitable. In the general's thinking, France's independence in nuclear matters was absolutely critical to her status as a great power, as well as to her national security. Nothing had a higher priority than the promotion and development of the *force de frappe* as rapidly as possible. This accounted for his unwillingness to engage in arms control, since, in one way or another, it would limit France's flexibility.

De Gaulle's vision of Europe was one in which France, as one of the two nuclear powers and the only one not tied to the American apron strings, would be the leader. A nuclear-capable *Europe* would modify the bipolar, bloc structure and move it towards a multipolar system. A nuclear-capable *France* would form the basis of a New Europe, which could become a third power in world affairs.

De Gaulle's vision was never achieved. But might its greatest sin have been to be a generation too early? The revolutionary events of the past year suggest that this might well be the case.

With the removal of the Soviet hold over Eastern Europe and the emergence of democracies, we are rapidly moving towards a pan-European system not unlike what de Gaulle envisioned. A Europe from the "Atlantic to the Urals" is now becoming more likely. On the twentieth anniversary of the Yalta Agreement of February 1945, de Gaulle correctly foresaw that the key issue was the solution of the German problem, which in turn was dependent upon major changes within the Soviet Union. All this is now in the process of taking place. The unification of Germany is likely to be embedded in the thirty-five nation Conference on Security and Cooperation in Europe. What is different from what de Gaulle foresaw or wished is the continued involvement of the United States.

Similarly, Western Europe has in recent years moved towards greater economic and political cohesion. To what extent the new developments along the East-West axis in Europe will reduce the momentum towards European unity is not clear, but it is already evident that Western Europe has eliminated its dependency upon the United States in most matters. The notable exception is defense. In the coming decade, NATO is certain to be transformed – assuming it is not terminated – along lines with which de Gaulle would have approved. It will become a predominantly "European" alliance, with a drastically reduced American role, and it could be gradually replaced by a European defense identity based upon either the Western European Union, the European Community, or something new. As the military confrontation in Central Europe is eliminated, and negotiated restraints are placed upon the military forces allowed on German soil, France's geographical position will gain in importance. To the extent that military power remains relevant, might not the *force de frappe* gain the importance in the European context that de Gaulle ultimately wanted? And might not France return to NATO's integrated structure, this time with a SACEUR who is a French general?

❖13❖

Idées Simples and Idées Fixes: De Gaulle, the United States, and Vietnam

Anne Sa'adah

Charles de Gaulle, it could be said, had a critique of American policy in Indochina even before the United States had a policy in Indochina – and certainly before most Americans recognized the political importance of the American presence in South Vietnam. By the mid-1960s, the public controversy swirling around America's expanding involvement in the Vietnam War increasingly dominated domestic political debate in the United States. Disagreements about the war had also become a complicating factor within the "troubled partnership" of the Atlantic Alliance.[1] But Charles de Gaulle did not wait for the commitment of massive ground forces to the war, or for the initiation of a relentless campaign of aerial bombing against North Vietnam, to formulate a critique of American intervention in Southeast Asia. Nor was his criticism a product of the Europe-centered NATO disputes of the mid-1960s.[2] As early as 1961, the French president took exception to the logic of intervention he saw developing in Indochina.[3] What accounts for the early timing, the urgency, and

1. The phrase is Henry Kissinger's, *The Troubled Partnership: A Re-appraisal of the Atlantic Alliance* (Garden City, NY: Doubleday/Council on Foreign Relations, 1965, 1966). Ch. 2, in which Kissinger discusses American and Gaullist conceptions about international conflict, cooperation, and order, is relevant to this paper.

2. France withdrew her forces form the integrated military command of NATO in March 1966. For an overview of de Gaulle's foreign policy during the Fifth Republic, see Jean Touchard, *Le gaullisme, 1940–1969* (Paris: Le Seuil, 1978), ch. 7, and Edward A. Kolodziej, *French International Policy under de Gaulle and Pompidou* (Ithaca, NY: Cornell University Press, 1974). For an analysis to which the argument of this paper is particularly indebted, see Stanley Hoffmann, *Decline or Renewal? France since the 1930's* (New York: Viking, 1974), Part IV.

3. See discussion below.

the particular content of de Gaulle's critique of American policy in Indochina?

I will argue in this paper that American policy in Vietnam set what de Gaulle saw as an American *idée simple* – unity of interest in the Free World – on a collision course with what most people would see as a Gaullist *idée fixe* – national independence. The French leader's reactions to unfolding events in Southeast Asia were prompted by what previous observation had led him to identify as an unchanging pattern of American behavior in international politics: if the legitimate international interests of all democratic states were substantially similar (as American leaders asserted they were), and if American resources far outstripped those of any other state (as all conceded they did), then the United States was uniquely qualified to speak for all states dedicated to the establishment of a stable, democratic world order. European states might still be influenced by imperial memories, interstate rivalries, and the bitter heritage of centuries of strife and revolution. By contrast, America's isolationist past and peculiar path of political development would guarantee the impartiality of American leadership. Resistance – the assertion of an independent agenda by another state – could rightly be attributed to motives incompatible with democratic values and international stability.

De Gaulle had identified and contended against this pattern of American behavior in his capacity as leader of the Free French during World War II. In the *Mémoires de guerre* he wrote from political retirement in the 1950s,[4] de Gaulle pointed to repeated examples of the predicted behavior. He took exception to the American pattern on both intellectual and political grounds: American behavior conflicted with French interests, but it was also based on a faulty understanding of international politics. Americans, de Gaulle believed, were unable to accept the notion that international politics is an arena in which all states rightly and inevitably pursue their national interests through unceasing, though not necessarily violent, conflict. Convinced that all nations had a shared interest in an international common good, Americans were inveterately incapable of recognizing (much less legitimizing) their own hegemonic ambitions, and they regularly misread the motives and intentions of other powers. Misunder-

4. Charles de Gaulle, *Mémoires de guerre* (hereafter cited in the notes as *MG*) vol. 1, *L'Appel, 1940–1942* (Paris: Plon, 1954), vol. 2, *L'Unité, 1942–1944* (Paris: Plon, 1956), vol. 3, *Le Salut, 1944–1946* (Paris: Plon, 1959).

standing the nature of the international politics, they chased after illusory goals while failing to notice real opportunities. They were stubbornly disinclined to view world politics as a complex game of power whose results tended to be both ambiguous and temporary and whose processes required sustained and expert attention. The United States, de Gaulle succinctly and acidly remarked, "apply elementary sentiments and complicated politics to the resolution of weighty problems" (translations from the French by the editors).[5]

From the "Alice in Wonderland" AMGOT plan of 1944[6] to the Alliance and Anglo-French disputes of the 1960s, French independence was, in de Gaulle's view, a constant and intended casualty of America's complicated policies. At the same time, independence was de Gaulle's primary goal. As leader of the Free French and later as president of the Fifth Republic, de Gaulle exploited every opportunity to characterize and criticize the "sentiments élémentaires" that lay behind American policies. In de Gaulle's eyes, the American tendency to wrap hegemonic designs in unobjectionable ideological goals and then to refuse to see neutrality, or independence, as anything other than a cover for betrayal and hostility, was a perennial feature of American policy.

De Gaulle's critique of American policy in Indochina was simply the application of a previously elaborated analysis to a new set of circumstances. To de Gaulle, America's posture in the early 1960s was not a problem faced only by Souvanna-Phouma in Laos and Sihanouk in Cambodia, nor were its manifestations limited to obscure, if deadly, jungle encounters between ununiformed combatants. Rather, the American pattern was the central impediment to the success of de Gaulle's own foreign policy. In responding as he did to American policy in Indochina, de Gaulle

5. *MG*, vol. 1, p. 181. De Gaulle seems to associate "elementary sentiments" with undiluted popular politics, rather than more specifically with a hypothetical American "national character." Thus he writes in the preface to *Le Fil de l'épée* (Paris: Plon, 1971, 1944; originally published in 1932): "You can't move crowds except by elementary sentiments, violent images, coarse appeals." (p. 13).

De Gaulle's appraisal of America can be usefully compared to that of George Kennan, *American Diplomacy, 1900–1950* (Chicago: University of Chicago Press, 1951) and Stanley Hoffmann, *Gulliver's Troubles, or the Setting of American Foreign Policy* (New York: McGraw-Hill/Council on Foreign Relations, 1968). See also Hoffmann, *Decline or Renewal?*, ch. 11.

6. The qualifier is de Gaulle's; *MG*, vol. 2, p. 212. [Editors' note: AMGOT (American Military Government in Occupied Territory) was the military occupation regime that the American government prepared for Liberated Territories, including initially, France.]

was not, or not only, venting his frustration against a senior alliance partner, or playing to a potentially useful Third World audience, or appealing across conventional partisan cleavages to a nationalist constituency at home; he was responding consistently to a pattern of behavior he saw as inhibiting French independence.

When viewed in the broader context of his understanding of American statecraft, the vigor and lucidity of de Gaulle's precocious critique of American policy in Indochina seem less surprising. The substance and consistency of his logic also help explain the choices de Gaulle made in two other episodes apparently unrelated to any critique of American policy: de Gaulle's refusal, in 1947–48, to return to power and impose his constitutional preferences through a coup, and the evolution of his Algerian policy in the early Fifth Republic.

I will look first at de Gaulle's assessment of American statecraft as elaborated in the *Mémoires de guerre*, then examine the timing and content of de Gaulle's critique of American policy in Indochina. Finally, I will consider the sources and implications of de Gaulle's arguments about the use of force to achieve political ends in the international arena.

American Statecraft in the Mémoires de guerre

De Gaulle's account of American diplomacy during World War II focuses on three elements of American statecraft: the nature of American ambitions, American views of power and peace, and American assumptions about the domestic sources of democratic values and political stability. Together, these three elements added up to a pattern of policy – and de Gaulle's analysis of the pattern dictated a policy of French resistance, first in the 1940s and later in the 1960s.

De Gaulle's overriding objective after the defeat of June 1940 was to restore France to the status of a major international power. Absent such status, de Gaulle declared, France would not be France. France's national identity depended on her position in the international arena. As World War II progressed and the outlines of a new distribution of power in the international system began to emerge, it seemed to de Gaulle that, after Nazi Germany, the primary obstacle on the path of French independence was likely to be the new superpower, the United States. In contrast, Great Britain and the USSR appeared as potential resources: de Gaulle hoped to use either or both to counterbalance the enormous power of the United States and to prevent the resurgence of an expansionary German state in the heart of Europe. His analysis led him to focus warily on American moves, and what he saw only confirmed his anxieties.

To de Gaulle, American exceptionalism did not extend to the realm of international behavior. Whatever the peculiarities of her diplomatic style, America was a state like any other state. States, de Gaulle assumed, have interests and ambitions, and they pursue those interests and ambitions to the full extent of their material and political capacities – regardless of the ideological orientation of their regime. The political capacity of a modern state depended, in de Gaulle's view, on the cohesiveness of the national community, the institutional strength to the central state, and the quality of the nation's political leadership. Material capacity depended on geographic location, human and physical resources, industrial strength and economic performance, and the existing distribution of power in the international system. As restraints on these objective determinants of a nation's ability to project its own power, pronouncements of peaceful and altruistic intent were of little significance. De Gaulle read American ambitions as a function of American resources, and assumed that American statements invoking service to the common interest of the international community were at best examples of ideological self-delusion and at worst efforts at manipulative dissimulation.

De Gaulle identified the conflict between American power and French interests in 1941, even before the United States entered the war: "Confronted with the immensity of American resources and Roosevelt's ambition to make law and pronounce justice throughout the world, I sensed that independence was indeed at stake."[7] Domestic economic development and World War II had, de Gaulle believed, brought America's isolationist phase to a definitive end. In the American drive toward hegemony that began in earnest in 1941, France would be singled out as an early target because of her sorry performance in 1940. Britain and Russia could still pretend to American respect, but France was vulnerable. How could a country that had collapsed in six weeks demand equal treatment from her former allies? As de Gaulle himself put it, "To get up to their level, we were starting from a very low point."[8] De Gaulle might insist that France had never

7. *MG*, vol. 1, p. 182.
8. *MG*, vol. 3, p. 48.

left the war, but Washington persisted – for reasons de Gaulle understood only too well – in seeing the story differently. In the *Mémoires de guerre*, de Gaulle relates at length a conversation with Harry Hopkins. While he argued against Hopkins' conclusions, he wanted his compatriots never to forget the chain of events that had made the conclusions plausible. Roosevelt's aide explained why the United States was so reluctant to bet on the revival of French power, and therefore remained unwilling to take de Gaulle seriously. The source of tensions between the Free French and the American government lay in a past both de Gaulle and Washington deplored. As Hopkins put it:

> The source . . . is above all the amazed disillusion that France caused us in 1940 when we saw her collapse in disaster and then capitulation. The idea we had always held of her worth and vitality was upset in an instant. . . . Don't look any further for the profound reason for the attitude we have adopted toward your country. Judging that France is no longer what she was, we could not entrust her with a great role.[9]

De Gaulle believed the past could be overcome; Washington, for both interested and disinterested reasons, did not. The combination of American ambition and French weakness dictated, in de Gaulle's view, America's wartime vision of France's postwar future: "Fundamentally, the American leaders were convinced that France no longer counted."[10] The eclipse of French power would pave the way to American hegemony. If French submission could not be assumed – and all of de Gaulle's actions were calculated to disrupt visions of French dependence – American power would be used to obtain it.

American actions seemed to bear out de Gaulle's expectations. American leaders equated the realization of American ambitions with the establishment of a legitimate world order, failing even to distinguish between the two. Again and again, de Gaulle denounced what he saw as "the *idée fixe* of the President of the United States to make himself the arbiter of French destiny."[11] The consistent efforts of American political leaders to relegate France to the status of a dependent, client power explained, in de Gaulle's view, both the genesis and the content of the many crises of wartime relations between Washington and the Free French: the clash over St. Pierre and Miquelon, the American

9. Harry Hopkins, cited in *MG*, vol. 3, pp. 81ff.
10. *MG*, vol. 1, p. 181.
11. *MG*, vol. 2, p. 211.

preference for General Giraud over de Gaulle, the disagreements over invasion strategies, the AMGOT plan, the disputes over the liberation of Paris and the defense of Strasbourg, and the exclusion of de Gaulle from Allied summits and postwar planning. In each case, American political leaders sought to assert their control over France's political future; in each case, de Gaulle fought back with whatever meager means he could assemble.

De Gaulle believed that "the iron law of states is never to give something for nothing,"[12] and he concluded that Allied treatment would not change unless and until French power could force the U.S. to take French views into account. On 12 September 1944, urging the necessity of a strong external posture before an audience of eight thousand Resistance activists and government officials gathered at the Palais de Chaillot, de Gaulle condemned "the kind of official banishment," of which France was the victim in Allied councils.[13] It was in order to reverse that "official banishment" that on 26 March 1945, de Gaulle sent a telegram to General de Lattre de Tassigny, commanding the French First Army in the Allied advance on Germany: "My dear General, . . . you must cross the Rhine, even if the Americans aren't for it, and even if you have to use rafts."[14]

The material basis of American power was the constant object of de Gaulle's envy: if only he could command such resources, what a destiny France might achieve! Vast resources predictably and understandably generated vast ambitions. It was natural for great powers to expand – and equally natural for other powers to resist. In *La France et son armée*, de Gaulle described Europe's attitude toward France on the eve of the Revolution:

> [Europe] feared our vast designs. She envied our might. Whether she wanted it or not, our influence poured in through every kind of intellectual expression, and the current that bore us along therefore worried her all the more. By both hatred and rational calculation, our neighbors tried to take preventive action against us whenever they thought we were weak.[15]

12. *MG*, vol. 3, p. 4.
13. Speech cited in *MG*, vol. 3, p. 6.
14. Telegram cited in *MG*, vol. 3, p. 155. The First Army crossed the Rhine on March 30 and entered Stuttgart on April 20. De Lattre later commanded French forces in Indochina. He died of cancer in January 1952, thirteen months after assuming his command. See Jacques Dalloz, *La guerre d'Indochine, 1945–1954* (Paris: Le Seuil, 1987), esp. pp. 188–95.
15. Charles de Gaulle, *La France et son armée* (Paris: Plon, 1938), pp. 81f.

Now it was France's turn to contest America's drive for power. As his orders to de Lattre indicated, de Gaulle had little to enable him to defend France's interests "in a standing position."[16] "How short France's sword is," he lamented,[17] blaming France's predicament on the quarrelsome character of his compatriots, on prewar republican institutions that had reflected disunity instead of overcoming it, and on mediocre leadership. The France of the war years, "betrayed by her leaders and people of privilege,"[18] could afford neither American brashness nor British flexibility. "'Don't go head-on,'" Churchill advised de Gaulle, early in the latter's contentious relationship with Franklin Roosevelt:

> 'Watch how, by turns, I bend and then straighten up.' 'You can do that,' I observed, 'because you are based on a solid state, a united Nation, an undivided Empire, a great army. But I: where are my resources? And yet, as you know, I am responsible for the interests and destiny of France. The burden is too heavy and my weakness too great for me to bend.'[19]

De Gaulle resisted American ambitions, but found them normal. He saved his resentment for the form in which American ambitions were typically expressed. If the Americans had spoken as had the Athenians at Melos, de Gaulle might not have responded with an attitude of suspicion that sometimes seemed to border on paranoia. De Gaulle's impatience with America's style is visible in the different response Britain's contrasting style elicited. De Gaulle might have been expected to treat the British with the same suspicion he reserved for Americans. Like the United States but closer to home, Great Britain had great ambitions. France's traditional rival also had resources superior to those at France's disposal. British and French interests often clashed, as the wartime and immediate postwar competition for influence in the Middle East amply demonstrated. But Britain and France were openly playing the same game, and their competition was therefore unencumbered by distrust. Such frank competition was impossible with a country that constantly wrapped itself in its own virtue. Americans were by habit and temperament ideological crusaders: "the crusading urge which

16. *MG*, vol. 1, p . 182.
17. *MG*, vol. 2, p. 245.
18. *MG*, vol. 1, p. 216.
19. *MG*, vol. 1, p. 209.

its instinctive idealism inspired in the American people"[20] blinded most Americans to the "dominating instinct"[21] de Gaulle so clearly discerned in them.

De Gaulle traced the development of American behavior through two wartime administrations. American ambitions were equally visible during each, but Roosevelt gave full play to American views of power and international order, whereas Truman illustrated American assumptions about democratic stability.

De Gaulle's complex portrait of Franklin Roosevelt reflects both de Gaulle's understanding of America's style of international behavior and his appreciation of Roosevelt's skill as a political leader. De Gaulle describes Roosevelt – "cet artiste, ce séducteur"[22] – marshaling the resources and energy of his people to achieve international power, and exploiting his nation's restlessness, pride, and generosity to overcome America's isolationist tradition:

> Franklin Roosevelt was possessed by the highest ambitions. His intelligence, his knowledge, his audacity gave him the capacity for them. The powerful state he headed gave him the means. The war gave him the opportunity. If the great people he led had long been inclined to remain aloof from distant enterprises and distrust Europe, endlessly torn by wars and revolutions, a sort of messianism now raised the American spirit and turned it to vast designs. The United States, proud of its own resources, sensing that its internal affairs no longer offered sufficient scope for its dynamism, wanting to help the miserable and the enslaved of all the world, gave in to their urge to intervene, within which the dominating instinct lay concealed. That was the attitude to which President Roosevelt was so well attuned. So he had done everything to have his country take part in the world conflict.[23]

The "vast designs" made possible by Roosevelt's leadership and America's material resources would be realized at the expense of independent states:

> Now that America was waging war, Roosevelt intended that the peace be American, that the countries swept aside by the tempest be submitted to his judgment, that France, in particular, have him for savior and for arbiter. And so, the fact that in the midst of the struggle France revived, not in the convenient form of a fragmentary resis-

20. *MG*, vol. 1, p. 192.
21. *MG*, vol. 2, p. 80.
22. *MG*, vol. 2, p. 238.
23. *MG*, vol. 2, pp. 70ff.

> tance, but as a sovereign and independent nation, conflicted with his intentions. Politically, he felt no inclination for me.[24]

In de Gaulle's view, Roosevelt often understood the state interests America's democratic ideology served, but the American leader was not immune to the "elementary sentiments" that de Gaulle ascribed to Americans in general. If American ambitions explained official Washington's hostility to the Free French, American "elementary sentiments" explained the critical miscalculations that led to Soviet domination in Eastern Europe. Yalta symbolized these miscalculations, but they were visible in other areas of American policy, and when death removed Roosevelt from the scene, the miscalculations continued. De Gaulle spoke skeptically of Roosevelt's conception of the United Nations, again noting the combination of misplaced idealism and concealed ambition:

> For someone of his way of thinking, international democracy was a kind of panacea. According to him, the nations . . . would examine their conflicts and would take in each case the measures needed to prevent anyone from going to war. They would also cooperate for human progress. . . . Although he didn't talk about it, he expected that the mass of small countries would undermine the position of the 'colonialist' powers and would assure a vast political and economic clientele to the United States.[25]

Truman lacked Roosevelt's patrician polish, and as tension between the Western Allies and the Soviet Union mounted, the new president retreated from Roosevelt's idealistic notions of international security and cooperation. In his quest for international stability, Truman nonetheless subscribed to views that left France little room to maneuver and that de Gaulle considered dangerously unrealistic. America's simple ideas extended to the realm of democratic state development:

> As for the complicated problems of our old world, they did not intimidate Truman at all. He saw them through a simplifying lens. In order for a people to be satisfied, they needed only to practice democracy, New World style. To end the antagonisms that set neighboring nations against each other, for example, France and Germany, one needed only to set up a federation of the rivals, as the states of North America had been able to do. For under-developed countries to lean toward the West, there was an infallible recipe: independence. The

24. *MG*, vol. 2, p. 80.
25. *MG*, vol. 3, p. 199.

proof was America itself, which, once freed of its former possessors, became a pillar of civilization. Finally, faced with a threat, the free world had nothing better to do than to adopt the 'leadership' of Washington.[26]

Since Americans were the most likely victims of their own propaganda, the United States was likely to behave ill-advisedly in the international arena. American blunders at Yalta (4–12 February 1945) soon became irreversible, and Truman added others. Since the Soviets would never risk an armed confrontation, Communism, Truman believed, could only win if economic hardship pushed desperate European populations into the Soviets' waiting arms.

In sum, he [Truman] thought the problem of peace was only an economic one. The nations of Western Europe, whether they had won or lost the war, had to resume normal life as soon as possible. In Asia and Africa, the under-developed peoples needed to receive the means to raise their standard of living. That's what the issue was, and not frontiers, grievances, guarantees.[27]

France, de Gaulle informed Truman, envisioned international affairs "in a less simplified manner."[28] De Gaulle argued that a stable balance of power in central Europe would make it possible for East European peoples to assert their independence from Moscow, and he warned of the dangers of destabilization in the Third World.[29]

His advice went unheeded. The damage had, in any case, already been done. De Gaulle had been excluded against his will from the Allied summits at Teheran (28 November to 1 December 1943), Yalta, and Potsdam (17 July to 2 August 1945), but because he had been excluded and because his views had been disregarded, de Gaulle could lay responsibility for the postwar "loss" of Eastern Europe at the door of American diplomacy.

Resources determined ambitions; "elementary sentiments"

26. *MG*, vol. 3, pp. 209ff.
27. *MG*, vol. 3, pp. 210ff.
28. *MG*, vol. 3, p. 211.
29. *MG*, vol. 3, pp. 212ff. For a later short but comprehensive statement of de Gaulle's assumptions about the international system, see his speech of 31 May 1960 (following the U-2 incident and the subsequent failure of the Paris summit), *DM*, vol. 3, pp. 232–38. In the speech, de Gaulle affirms that "international life, like all life, is a combat" (p. 238), pleads for superpower détente, monitored disarmament and interstate cooperation based on respect for national autonomy, and affirms that "definitively and as always, it is only in equilibrium that the world will find peace." (p. 237).

disguised those ambitions and misled the men who held them, compromising their ability to use power either effectively or responsibly. De Gaulle publicly expressed his admiration for the British political system, contrasting Britain's parliamentary regime to France's imperfect parliamentary republics: in Britain, political cohesion meant that party competition and parliamentary politics did not preclude strong executive leadership.[30] De Gaulle's interest in the domestic institutional and political determinants of American foreign policy, however, rarely extended beyond the identification of the "elementary sentiments" that American leaders as different as Franklin Roosevelt and Harry Truman shared: Responding later to America's involvement in Vietnam, de Gaulle would never argue that the system "worked," or probe the domestic political imperatives that prevented the withdrawal of American forces.[31] Those arguments followed the events they sought to explain. De Gaulle's argument was ready before the events occurred.

THE GAULLIST CRITIQUE OF AMERICAN POLICY IN INDOCHINA, 1961–69

De Gaulle refrained from sustained public commentary on the final months of the French Indochina War. As leader of the Provisional Government that assumed power after the Liberation, he had been unable to secure the constitutional arrangement he thought necessary to the preservation of national unity and the reassertion of French power. On 20 January 1946, he presented his resignation to a stunned Cabinet. In April 1947, he launched the Rassemblement du peuple français (RPF), and the movement's popularity seemed briefly to threaten the life of the Republic. But the RPF's strength crested in early 1948, well before events in Indochina reached a critical juncture.[32] The Fourth Republic weathered the storm stirred up by the RPF and compounded by the renewed opposition of the Communist

30. For de Gaulle's view of the British political system, see for example his speech of 7 April 1960, delivered at Westminster, *DM*, vol. 3 (Paris: Plon, 1970), pp. 193–97.

31. See Leslie Gelb, "Vietnam: The System Worked," *Foreign Policy*, No. 3, Summer 1971, pp. 140–67, and Daniel Ellsberg, "The Quagmire Myth and the Stalemate Machine," in Ellsberg, *Papers on the War* (New York: Simon and Schuster, 1972), pp. 42–135.

32. On the RPF, see Jean Touchard, *Le gaullisme, 1940–1969* (Paris: Le seuil, 1978), ch. 4, and Jean Charlot, *Le gaullisme d'opposition, 1946–1958* (Paris: Fayard, 1983).

Party. The storm subsided, the Gaullist movement lost support, and de Gaulle withdrew from public life.

De Gaulle's relative silence in 1953 may have been conditioned by the prior failure of the RPF and by de Gaulle's enduring respect for Pierre Mendès's France, as well as by his perceptions of French options in Indochina. But whatever the explanation of his stance in 1953–54, he was less discreet in commenting on American policies in the early 1960s. "'I predict to you," de Gaulle told President Kennedy in June 1961, "'that you will bog down ever deeper into a military and political quagmire, no matter how many men you lose and how much money you spend.'"[33]

De Gaulle's "prediction" came at a time when the American military presence in Indochina was still numerically limited and advisory in nature. De Gaulle was probably unaware of the recommendations forwarded to President Kennedy by an interdepartmental task force in May 1961. On the basis of that report, President Kennedy would authorize the deployment of five hundred additional American military personnel to Vietnam, in violation of the Geneva Accords' 685-man limit on military missions.[34]

As the accumulating facts lent substance to de Gaulle's prediction, the French president continued and amplified his warnings. During the first half of 1964 (before the Tonkin Gulf incident), de Gaulle used state visits by the leaders of Laos and Cambodia to condemn the "incessant foreign interventions" in Southeast Asia.[35] In his press conference of 24 July 1964,[36] he criticized American policy in terms that he would repeat as American involvement in Vietnam escalated. American intervention, de Gaulle asserted, reflected an inability to recognize neutrality as a respectable political posture in the international arena, and represented a misapplication of force. It was, in other words, part of a familiar pattern of American behavior.

De Gaulle developed the most complete statement of his position in his famous speech in Phnom Penh, delivered on 1 September 1966. By then, American aircraft were pounding targets in North Vietnam, while casualties mounted in the widening

33. Charles de Gaulle, *Mémoires d'espoir*, vol. 1 (Paris: Plon, 1970), p. 269.

34. See Neil Sheehan et al., *The Pentagon Papers* (New York: Bantam/The New York Times, 1971), ch. 3, esp. Document 18 ("A Program for Action for South Vietnam," 8 May 1961), pp. 119–25. The United States had not signed the Geneva agreements, but had agreed to abide by the stipulated guidelines.

35. Texts of toasts in Charles de Gaulle, *Discours et messages* (hereafter *DM*), vol. 4 (Paris: Plon, 1970), pp. 136ff, 224–26; quote at p. 137.

36. *DM*, vol. 4, pp. 242–45.

ground war being fought in the South. The speech coincided with the first signs of serious dissent within the Johnson administration.[37] In January 1966, Assistant Secretary of Defense John T. McNaughton had warned in a memorandum, "We . . . have in Vietnam the ingredients of an enormous miscalculation."[38] Just days before de Gaulle's speech, the Institute for Defense Analyses gave the administration its assessment of the impact of Operation Rolling Thunder. The report began:

> As of July 1966 the U.S. bombing of North Vietnam (NVN) had had no measurable direct effect on Hanoi's ability to mount and support military operation in the South at the current level.[39]

Evidence of increased Communist strength in the South prompted General William Westmoreland to cable escalating troop requests to Washington. As de Gaulle journeyed to Cambodia, an anguished and now skeptical Secretary of Defense Robert McNamara weighed Westmoreland's request for 542,588 American troops in 1967.[40] American commentary on these events has focused on the institutional and political reasons why high-placed critics of American policy were unable to impose their views.[41] De Gaulle adopted a different approach.

De Gaulle's Phnom Penh speech began with a comparison between France and Cambodia ("how many points of kinship . . . !"[42]) and rapidly developed into a stinging critique of American policy. Twice, de Gaulle acknowledged the improbability that Washington would heed his advice, even though American interests would have been better served by the negotiated settlement he advocated than by the continued escalation in which the United States was engaged.

De Gaulle's effort to equate France – an economically and politi-

37. See George C. Herring, *America's Longest War: The United States and Vietnam, 1950–1975* (New York: John Wiley & Sons, 1979), pp. 174–79 and Sheehan et al., *The Pentagon Papers*.

38. See excerpts in Neil Sheehan et al., *The Pentagon Papers*, Document 109, pp. 491–93, quote at P. 491.

39. Text in Neil Sheehan et al., *The Pentagon Papers*, Document 117, pp. 502–9.

40. See Neil Sheehan et al., *The Pentagon Papers*, ch. 8. McNamara recommended against filling Westmoreland's request and in a memorandum of 14 October 1966, began to urge a reconsideration of American policy in Vietnam. See text in Neil Sheehan et al., *The Pentagon Papers*, Document 118, pp. 542–51.

41. See references in n. 31. In *Exit, Voice, and Loyalty* (Cambridge, Mass.: Harvard University Press, 1972, 1970), Albert O. Hirschman considers why high-ranking American officials in the Vietnam era were so reluctant to resign over policy differences.

42. *Dm*, vol. 5 (Paris: Plon, 1970), p. 80.

cally developed Western country – with Cambodia might seem implausible, but it served his argument. De Gaulle stressed the common situation in which the two peoples found themselves:

> For one as for the other, a history laden with glory and pain, an exemplary culture and art, a fertile soil surrounded with vulnerable borders and foreign cupidity, and, over it all, ever-hovering danger.[43]

De Gaulle alluded briefly and euphemistically to past French domination in Indochina, acknowledging that imperial France had found in Cambodia "a very useful association" and claiming that Franco-Cambodian relations had enabled Cambodia "to maintain its integrity," until the two countries had, "by common accord separated their sovereign ties."[44] After this preliminary lesson in proper great power conduct, de Gaulle returned to his analogy. Like France, Cambodia was putting its independence to constructive use in the international arena:

> We see the Kingdom [of Cambodia], despite grave difficulties, acting in favor of balance and peace in its part of the world, all the while maintaining its personality, its dignity, and its independence.[45]

But elsewhere in Indochina, peace had given way to a "chain-effect of massacres and ruins."[46] De Gaulle assigned responsibility for the developments in Vietnam to the United States. Little Cambodia had indicated the correct path; the US had opted for a different one. After the Geneva Accords, Cambodia had chosen "with courage and lucidity, the policy of neutrality."[47] The Cambodian strategy would have preserved the peace and kept rival superpowers at bay. But the United States, quickly captive to her customary "illusions concerning the use of force,"[48] had imposed her presence in Vietnam, provoking a nationalist response, destroying the peace, destabilizing the region, and dissipating her own credit throughout the world.[49]

De Gaulle insisted on both the futility of American efforts and on the likelihood that the Americans would persist in their mistakes. American efforts would be futile because "at this time," there was "no possibility that the peoples of Asia would submit

43. *Dm*, vol. 5, p. 80.
44. *Dm*, vol. 5, pp. 80ff.
45. *Dm*, vol. 5, p. 81.
46. *Dm*, vol. 5, p. 81.
47. *Dm*, vol. 5, p. 81.
48. *Dm*, vol. 5, p. 82.
49. *Dm*, vol. 5, p. 82.

to a foreign will coming from the other side of the Pacific, whatever its intentions and however powerful its weapons."[50] Genuine neutrality, reflecting the right of every nation to self-determination, was the only stable solution to the conflict precipitated by America's intervention. De Gaulle noted that self-determination was also a goal consistent with stated American political values.

If Washington refused to recognize the rights of Indochinese peoples to self-determination by setting a schedule for the withdrawal of American troops, the war would continue indefinitely, for the military defeat of a superpower seemed as unlikely to de Gaulle as did the permanent victory of a power opposed by nationalist forces. Given America's record, de Gaulle had no reason to believe that the United States would suddenly recognize the legitimacy of political neutrality: "such an outcome," de Gaulle said of a negotiated settlement made possible by a prior American commitment to withdraw its troops, "is not at all ripe today, supposing that it will ever become so."[51] In the face of American obstinacy, France could only voice her disapproval:

> France has taken her stand. She does so by her condemnation of present events. She does so by her resolution never to be drawn automatically into some future extension of the crisis, wherever it may be or whatever happens, and to keep its hands free in any case. She does so, finally, by the example she gave in North Africa, by deliberately ending a sterile combat on a terrain which her forces controlled without contest.[52]

De Gaulle returned to the subject of Vietnam two months later, in his press conference of 28 October 1966. Significantly, he chose to group questions about Vietnam, Europe, and the alliance together, and he began his response with the affirmation that "there is nothing more consistent that the policy of France."

> This policy, in fact, in face of the very diverse challenges that our time and this world present to us, aims essentially to keep France an independent nation.[53]

Independence did not mean isolation, and it in no way implied hostility.

> Independence means that we decide ourselves what we have to do and with whom, without that being imposed on us by any other state or institution.[54]

50. *Dm*, vol. 5, pp. 82ff.
51. *Dm*, vol. 5, p. 83.
52. *Dm*, vol. 5, p. 82.
53. *Dm*, vol. 5, p. 105.
54. *Dm*, vol. 5, p. 105.

The French stance would, de Gaulle admitted, annoy all the diverse "champions of our effacement."[55] It would foil the ambitions of those who favored Moscow's designs, but it would have other adversaries as well, "apostles" of Western unity or European integration who wanted France to surrender her identity to "those organizations dominated – everyone knows it – by the political protection, the military force, the economic power, and the multifarious assistance of the United States."[56] The result of such submission in the mid-1960s would have been the same result narrowly avoided in the early 1940s: "France would disappear, carried away by the Fates."[57]

DE GAULLE ON THE USE OF FORCE IN INTERNATIONAL POLITICS

Americans remember their Revolution – accurately – as an ideological struggle, not as a war of national liberation. Perhaps as a consequence, they tend to assume the primacy of ideological factors over nationalist aspirations in both interstate and intrastate conflicts in the contemporary world.

De Gaulle was unlikely to share that assumption. In a famous passage of the *Mémoires de guerre*, de Gaulle asserted the primacy of nationalist sentiments over all other forms of solidarity:

> In the world's incessant movement, all doctrines, all schools, all rebellions last only for a while. Communism will pass away. But France will not pass away.[58]

In urging an end to American intervention in Vietnam, de Gaulle frequently cited the example of France's withdrawal from Algeria. De Gaulle had not come back to power in 1958 with the intention of granting French independence; whatever he "understood" when he faced the cheering crowd in Algiers on 4 June 1958, neither the desirability nor the inevitability of independence was included.[59] Over the next three years, de Gaulle did nonetheless negotiate the withdrawal of French troops and the granting of independence. Scholars still debate when de Gaulle reached the conclusion that no solution to the Algerian conflict

55. *Dm*, vol. 5, p. 105.
56. *Dm*, vol. 5, p. 106.
57. *Dm*, vol. 5, p. 106.
58. *MG*, vol. 1, p. 232.
59. De Gaulle began his speech by exclaiming, "I have understood you." For text, see *Dm*, vol. 3, pp. 17ff.

short of independence was within reach.[60] Since de Gaulle, as a skillful political leader, took care to cover his tracks, we will probably never know when the fundamental shift in his thinking took place. But it would be a mistake to view de Gaulle's evolving Algerian policy as an improvised response in which de Gaulle began with his maximum goal and then, as he encountered insurmountable obstacles, revised his sights downward and finally settled for the least undesirable outcome possible. Writing in the *Mémoires de guerre* of Russian domination in Eastern Europe, de Gaulle affirmed a position from which he never retreated: "in the long run, no regime can hold on against national wills."[61]

De Gaulle placed so much emphasis on France's need to have and control its own military force that one might easily conclude that he thought force could be used to achieve offensive goals in the inevitable and unending competition among states. In fact, force played a complex but largely defensive role in his view of political development and interstate relations. De Gaulle clearly believed that only military strength (or geographic good fortune, of the sort that the United States enjoyed) could stake out and preserve a secure zone within which a community of individuals could develop a common form of cultural and political expression, thereby becoming a "people" in the political sense. This was the role – "a great role at a great moment" – Free French troops had played at Bir Hakeim: "The cannons of Bir-Hakeim announced to the whole world the beginning of France's revival."[62]

But if "France was made by sabre thrusts,"[63] force was only useful if effectively commanded by political will: "if it takes force to build a state, it is equally true that warlike effort prevails only by virtue of a policy."[64] In early modern Europe, national communities had been the byproducts of royal state-building and

60. See the discussion in Jean Lacouture, *De Gaulle*, vol. 3, *Le Souverain* (Paris: Le Seuil, 1986), Part I.

61. *MG*, vol. 3, p. 47.

62. *MG*, vol. 1, p. 257.

63. This is the first line of de Gaulle, *La France et son armée*.

64. De Gaulle, *La France et son armée*, p. 5. This is a constant theme of de Gaulle's political thought. See the discussion of civil-military relations in the concluding chapter of *Le Fil de l'épée*, and the following exchange with General Eisenhower during the controversy over the defense of Strasbourg: "'To get me to change my military orders,' this excellent soldier told me, 'You are invoking political reasons.' I replied to him, 'Armies are made to serve the policies of the state.'" (*MG*, vol. 3, p. 148.).

war.[65] Before national identities crystallized, boundaries could be lastingly changed by conquest. That was no longer the case, anywhere in the world; the mere idea of self-determination would subvert external rule in lands where independent nation-states had never existed. "The future will last a long time," de Gaulle reminded his audience,[66] and taking the long view, he argued against the stability of both imperial domination and domestic dictatorships. Imperial relations would be disrupted by the resurgence of nationalist aspirations, and dictatorships, in which one section of the community ruled in its own interest and by force, were simply the domestic equivalent of colonial relations. Thus de Gaulle, sensing in 1945 the impending rejection of his political project, dismissed the option of ruling without the explicit consent of the population:

> Outside a period of public danger, no dictatorship can hold unless one fraction [of the population], determined to crush the others, supports it through thick and thin.[67]

De Gaulle saw himself as the "the standard-bearer of France, not of any one class or party,"[68] and so he rejected the alternative of military rule once national survival was no longer at stake:

> The momentary dictatorship that I exercised during the storm and that I wouldn't hesitate to prolong or restore if the country were in danger – I don't want to hold on to it now that public safety has been reestablished.[69]

If the army's external role was chiefly defensive, it did have important domestic functions to fulfill. Once again, effective political leadership would be the condition of success. In de Gaulle's conception, the army builds and maintains the spirit of the nation, not by external conquest, but by the human and collective qualities it displays. Individuals lead privatized, routinized, self-interested lives; military courage, comaraderie, and

65. See de Gaulle, *La France et son armée.*

66. *MG*, vol. 3, p. 73.

67. *MG*, vol. 3, p. 238.

68. *MG*, vol. 3, p. 238.

69. *MG*, vol. 3, p. 238. Cf. pp. 237ff: "Apparently, it would be easy for me to prolong the kind of monarchy that I once assumed and that general consent later ratified. But the French people is what it is, and not another. No one can get it to do what it doesn't want. I would condemn it to terrible conflicts if I tried to impose my absolute authority on it arbitrarily and for an unlimited time, when the peril which had called that authority forth no longer existed." These lines were penned a decade after the events, but they are consistent with what de Gaulle did in the immediate postwar period. They also explain his attitude in May 1958.

self-sacrifice – "that agnegation of individuals in favor of the community, that hallowed suffering"[70] – remind us of what we share and of what we can accomplish together. In ways de Gaulle never fully explained, military heroism produced civilian cohesion. The Resistance had brought the Communist working class back into the national community:

> The tragedy where the country's survival was at stake offered a historic opportunity to those French people, who had been separated from the nation by the injustice that aroused them and by the error that misled them, to return to the national fold, even if only for the duration of the fighting. . . . I am sure that it will finally matter a great deal for the destiny of France that, in spite of everything, at a brief but decisive moment of her history, at her liberation, [France] was but one united people.[71]

Watching the reaction of the Consultative Assembly to the news of the liberation of Strasbourg, de Gaulle remarked: "The military has the virtue, sometimes, of summoning forth French unity."[72]

In the absence of unanimity, a national military force could be used by a recognized national leader to dissuade fractious domestic minorities from bidding for political control. In the weeks and months following the Liberation, de Gaulle had used his prestige with Resistance forces and the reassembled units of the regular army to insure the reestablishment of republican institutions free of Communist control.[73] There is, in de Gaulle's thought, a complex interaction between nation-building, state-building, and military prowess. Leaders – "specialists in the art of calling forth effort, yeast in the dough"[74] – build states, states build armies to pursue political goals, and armies make nationhood possible:

> Warrior values, military virtue, soldiers' service and suffering, without these no nation holds together or revives. In all times, our race has known how to produce these riches abundantly. But there also needs to be a national soul, will, and action – that is, a policy. If France had had an effective state between the two [world] wars, if she had been governed, if her army, facing the enemy, had been equipped and led, what a destiny could have been ours![75]

70. De Gaulle, *Le Fil de l'épée*, p. 15.
71. *MG*, vol. 1, p. 232.
72. *MG*, vol. 3, p. 137.
73. See *MG*, vol. 3, ch. 1.
74. De Gaulle, *Le Fil de L'épée*, p. 202.
75. *MG*, vol. 2, p. 272f.

By the time de Gaulle finished the *Mémoires de guerre*, he had concluded that one country's advisors can't build another's nation, or state. It was a lesson that moderated his role during the RPF years, informed his action in Algeria, and supported his critique of American policy in Indochina.

Comment

Pierre Mélandri

FIRST, ON MR. GARDNER'S PAPER, I would say that the problem with respect to the MLF is that *for the Europeans*, it was neither like a *safety-catch* nor like a finger on a trigger, so that French skepticism on its value was to some extent justified. Although I was very much in agreement with the analysis, I would question the suggestion that the U.S. and Great Britain never had a special relationship. This is not a French fantasy. The problem has been very well examined in the contribution by Geoffrey Warner in the book edited by Lawrence S. Kaplan, *NATO after Forty Years* (Scholarly Resources Inc., 1990) in which, among other things, Warner points out that in 1947 a still-classified UK-USA agreement on the exchange of intelligence was concluded, an agreement that seems to have been briefly interrupted only in 1956 (at the height of the Suez crisis) and in 1973 (during the October War). This is not to deny that there have been, as Warner shows, ups and downs in this special relationship. What happened was that when de Gaulle returned to power, this relationship was at a high point, owing to the return of Macmillan and the British interpretation of Suez, namely, that Britain could no longer do anything without the prior agreement of the United States. The Conference of Bermuda (March 1957) and the October 1957 meeting between the British and the Americans in Washington, where all sorts of new projects for collaboration were devised, were very important in that respect.

There is, by the way, in the Dulles papers a document entitled "Remarks to U.S. Ambassadors to Europe" dated May 9, 1958, in which the Secretary of State underlined the extremely close relationship that United States henceforth entertained with the United Kingdom, adding that probably never before in peacetime had two nations worked as closely together. He emphasized, however, that the U.S. did not want to advertise it because it involved jealousy; the French, then the Italians, and so on, would also want to be in on it. On the other side, it seems to me true that during the Kennedy period, this special relationship was much less obvious than it was at the end of the 50's.

Now, regarding Mr. Pierre's comments, I have two things to say. I have the impression that de Gaulle's three-power directorate proposal was intended to provide a kind of veto on the use of American arms and that this matter seems to have been vaguely discussed in June 1961. Mr. Couve de Murville states in his memoirs that Kennedy then said he was ready to extend the French something he had promised the British: to consult with them whether to use the bomb or not, except, of course, in the case where the U.S. was under an imminent threat that would imperil its existence. That prospect, however, quickly went awry. As for American nuclear assistance to the French, negotiations were undertaken during the years 1958–59 regarding American aid for French atomic submarines. However, the project largely failed, due to the adamant opposition of Admiral Rickover who persuaded the Joint Committee on Atomic Energy to reject it. What was left of it was only an agreement for American deliveries of highly enriched Uranium for a prototype built ashore. There was also in 1962 another mission, led by General Lavaud, and mentioned in Mr. Costigliola's paper, which the French were not able to carry through. Interestingly, from a French point of view, it was the United States that had been asking for something in that case. The Americans asked the French to buy their military equipment to compensate for the costs of the American presence in Europe. When the French presented their list, which didn't correspond with what the MacMahon Amendments had prohibited, but often dealt with nuclear equipment, it was refused.

Otherwise, concerning this session, I would simply like to say that it covers a period (1963–1969) which is obviously marked by much harsher relations, something Mr. Gardner rightly emphasized. At that point, the confrontations are clearer, and I think that, in light of the change in the international context (particularly in the East from 1964 on), General de Gaulle tried to explore the possibilities that seemed to be available on the other side of the iron curtain, to go beyond the blocs. In his desire to call into question the status quo, he would inevitably collide with American might.

Georges Pompidou, perhaps better than any one else, summed up French policy toward the U.S. during this period when he said in 1965: "The old division of the world into two monolithic blocs is outdated. Out of this emerges France's role. She is condemned by her geographic situation and her history to represent Europe." Was that an offensive design? I think that we must take into account the fact that the French leaders were worried about the stunning integrating capacity which America seemed to display at that time. Here again, Pompidou confided to Sulzberger, at the beginning of 1968, that General de Gaulle was working on the principle that Russia was everywhere on the defensive, and hence the greatest power was by far the United States. We, in Europe, and particularly in France, and here I quote Pompidou, "had to be careful not to be absorbed by the United States."

I would also say that this very tense period doesn't cover our whole time span since there probably was an inflexion in French policy towards the end of 1968 and the beginning of 1969. I have always had the impression that the "coup de Prague" had a stronger bearing on General de Gaulle's policy than was admitted and that the Soames proposition was in some way a sign on his part that he wanted to return to the pre-1964 strategy that we mentioned yesterday, namely building an independent Western European entity.

Finally, I would like to conclude by saying that, in fact, during this whole period, the General laid the groundwork for things that didn't bear fruit immediately, but which nonetheless demonstrated a certain logic in the face of what would become future problems. It is clear that from the second half of the sixties, because the United States could no longer give full priority to its imperial policy, but had to take into account very strong domestic pressures (the Great Society was launched in 1965), the problems of the Dollar and the imbalance of the world monetary system became much more acute. We had the first very serious crisis of the Dollar in March 1968: this indicated de Gaulle's warnings were well-founded. Yet 1968 reminded us too that French external ambitions may too have been overambitious and ironically ended with de Gaulle refusing (with Johnson's assistance, by the way) to devalue the Franc.

In essence, we should remember from this period that General de Gaulle didn't pursue a fundamentally anti-American policy, even though this policy was often in opposition to American interests. Charles Bohlen remarked one day that in fact, what Charles de Gaulle was trying to do was to continue the development of what the United States had envisaged at the time of the Marshall Plan, namely a Europe which would have independence and autonomy from the U.S. But, added Bohlen, the world wasn't ready yet. In view of what has happened recently in Eastern Europe, I conclude that General de Gaulle's policy at least partly seems to confirm what he said to Nixon in 1969: "I make policy for the newspapers for the day after tomorrow."

Witness

Jean-Marcel Jeanneney

I AM ENTIRELY IN AGREEMENT with what Mr. Calleo said earlier, so I will limit myself to mentioning and accentuating certain points. It is clear that General de Gaulle's position shows that American policy during his time was to reject the right of exchange. Contrary to what is sometimes thought, the American balance of payments at that time (the current account) was even, and even slightly positive. As a consequence, the issuing of dollars in excessive quantities resulted simply in financing investments. Here we come back to the problem that was posed yesterday of American investments abroad, in which de Gaulle saw a process of domination. His riposte was very simple: to demand the conversion of dollars into gold, hoping thus to force the Americans to modify this policy.

A second important point: General de Gaulle was always – in France as well as abroad – very conscious of the risk that inflation constitutes. It guided him during his whole presidency and as late as November 1969, when he refused to devalue the franc. Not without reason, inflation appeared like a kind of a drug to him, a kind of drug that threatened the whole system. It was clear – and he was aware of it – that the issuing of dollars of this kind was an inflationary policy. This also explains the hostility of the French government, through Michel Debré, to the creation of special drawing rights, which seemed to de Gaulle like a form of world inflation and which fed upon, and took the place of, the inflation caused by the dollar itself. In this respect he was right, because this was precisely the moment, in 1965–66, when Eurodollars and special drawing rights were developed, that world inflation began. In this there is a perfect coincidence for both economists and quantitavists alike.

De Gaulle thought that this would lead to a catastrophe. Here again, he showed himself to be a prophet. In the end it led to floating exchange rates, which make things easy for governments, but which are also immensely risky. Where General de Gaulle was wrong, in my opinion, was in thinking that we could correct that situation by returning to the gold standard system. That is when he was influenced by Jacques Rueff. What attracted him to the gold standard was that it was a value which, in a way, escaped governments. It was a non-national value. Only what he didn't know is that, in fact, the gold standard had never really properly functioned, except at the time when gold coins were in circulation – and it was out of the question to put them in circulation again. A return to the gold standard was unthinkable. No one defends it anymore, except, I've been told, a few American senators.

Witness

Jean Lacouture

I AM GOING TO RETURN TO THE QUESTION of Vietnam and Indochina that I spoke about yesterday as a commentator, but today I am going to do so as a witness. My presentation will be from a different angle. Yesterday, I was concerned more or less with the criticism coming from the United States of French policy in Indochina, and particularly that of General de Gaulle. Today I will talk about the criticisms de Gaulle made about American policy in Indochina and Vietnam.

I alluded yesterday to certain errors committed, at least from my point of view, by de Gaulle during the period 1945–1946 in Indochina. But as we all know, one can sing off key and still be a good music critic. So I am going to strive to show that a certain number (if not all) of the positions taken by de Gaulle were justified concerning American policy in Vietnam in the 1960s. First, if we are trying to find the reasons for which de Gaulle intervened rather vigorously in this domain, I believe we can eliminate the idea of vindictiveness, which also was firmly rejected yesterday by several of de Gaulle's close collaborators whose testimonies we can believe. Let's eliminate, then, this idea that it was a revenge for certain difficulties experienced in the 1940s. But all the same, let's remember that de Gaulle – I alluded to it yesterday – was rather hostile to the idea of substituting the United States for France in Indochina. Thus, there is no revenge, but only suspicion regarding a historical process that would have led to the replacement of one Western power by another. After all, for de Gaulle, Indochina was a French-speaking country. There was this historical legacy, whatever good or bad had been done, and the idea then of this substitution was very badly perceived by him.

So there was here this idea of blocking a historical process, which he could not tolerate. But there is another, perhaps more important element, which is the refusal of de Gaulle to accept the U.S. as policeman of the world – an idea more or less implied in the steps taken by President Roosevelt in the 1940s. The idea was propounded many times that Dakar and Saigon be transformed into bases, from which a kind of multilateral force – well, let's try to find another formulation – would be able to maintain and control peace in the world. De Gaulle disliked this idea – not only in the 1940s but also in the 1960s, that the U.S. be the policeman of the world. It was obviously quite imaginable that he oppose it.

And then there was something that seems to me even stronger in Charles de Gaulle's position, and which was contained in his famous conversation, mentioned yesterday, with Mr. John Foster Dulles on 5 July 1958. There Dulles and de Gaulle disagreed because Dulles said that there are good guys and bad guys and that France must help the good guys to prevail over the bad ones. To which de Gaulle answered: "No, I do not believe that in politics there are good guys and bad guys. There are only nations in the midst of circumstances." Yesterday, Olivier Guichard reminded us to what extent the idea of circumstance was important to de Gaulle. And in Vietnam there were circumstances and there were nations. There was above all a Vietnamese nation that wasn't willing to accept any foreign rule – only, alas, a foreign ideology. . . .

From 1958 on, de Gaulle was not a partisan of the reunification of Vietnam at any cost, no more than for the reunification of Germany at any cost – of course. But all the same, this notion of nationhood prevailing over a supposed good or evil was evidently very dear to him. Then, there is another thing that must be said. Despite the difficulties he suffered in the 1940s in Indochina, de Gaulle never stopped being interested in that country. Naturally, because French history and Vietnamese history were linked, but also because he thought that it was a country with an interesting strategic situation.

General de Gaulle continued to be interested in Vietnam later, and in a way unusual for him, for when in 1954 a government of the Fourth Republic (which was not the human institution he respected the most) negotiated the Geneva Agreements, he welcomed this diplomatic move. The author of this diplomatic initiative was a premier of the Fourth Republic, M. Mendès France, and backing him was also unusual for the general. From then on, General de Gaulle became a discreet advocate of the semi, partial, or temporary solution of Geneva and supported the very imperfect solution that had been found there. But we can observe that, just as he supported Mendès France's pacification of 1954, he later sent to Hanoi one of his trusted men, Mr. Edmond Michelet. And we can notice the emergence of an attitude more or less in favor of North Vietnam, although he was, as we all know, a very determined anti-Communist and had a constant antagonism for South Vietnam.

I will mention, with respect to his well-known antipathy toward the South and Mr. Diem, that in 1959 he allowed his finance minister, Mr. Antoine Pinay, to make a visit to South Vietnam. Don't misunderstand me. I said that he let him go to South Vietnam, meaning that he didn't prevent Mr. Pinay from going. Mr. Pinay wanted to go and France had diplomatic representation there. The trip took place, and I happened to accompany Mr. Pinay, (which was the first and last time I did that) [i.e., accompany M. Pinay]. I saw how happy Mr. Pinay was to be in South Vietnam and meet Mr. Diem. I would say, if I wanted to be even naughtier, that Mr. Pinay enjoyed meeting Mr. Diem because he had – I'm going a little too far here – found someone more dull than himself, which made him comfortable. But the fact is that upon returning, Mr. Pinay tried – to use an American translation – to sell South Vietnam and Mr. Diem to General de Gaulle. It didn't work. This is one of the reasons for the disagreement that later led to Mr. Pinay's resignation.

And so we can follow the constant interest of the general for Vietnam, which manifested itself in a striking way during John Kennedy's visit to Paris in 1961. This was mentioned earlier, that is, de Gaulle's appeal and public warning to John Kennedy not to get mired in the quick sand and rice paddies of Indochina. A little later, the French policy in favor of the neutralization of Indochina was proclaimed. This was a rather important move that would have consequences and was examined with some interest by the United States.

There is also another very important event: the recognition of the People's Republic of China in 1964. This recognition by France and de Gaulle was not intended entirely as a diplomatic service to Indochina, even though that was clearly one of the elements and it was recognized as such. The following days, when the editorials of the *Observer* spoke of this gesture as a diplomatic ice-breaker, it was mostly because the introduction of the People's Republic of China into the international club made China more apt to negotiate about Vietnam, which was their greatest diplomatic problem in Asia at that time.

At that time, a series of events took place in which I was rash enough to become somewhat involved – something I usually refuse to do, for a journalist is a journalist and should stick to his journalistic work: transmitting facts, commentaries, and news. As it happened, one time, during a trip to the U.S., I became more involved in things than usual. I will quote a statement I made, of which I am not proud, but I believe it is necessary to be honest. During a visit to the United States, in the mid-1960s, where I met a lot of people and talked a lot about Vietnam, I was introduced by my dear friend Joseph Kraft, whom many of us miss, to Senator Robert Kennedy, who himself was asking a lot of questions, not only because of what he and his brother had done in Vietnam, but also to figure out how to get out. I remember a conversation with Senator Kennedy, who asked me: "Do you think de Gaulle can help us, in our present situation, to get disentangled from the Vietnam affair?" I answered, I must admit, "Personally, I don't believe that de Gaulle will help you, because I believe he is not really upset to see you get bogged down in this affair, for that could make it easier for his policies in Europe." Well, in general, I am not by nature a Machiavellian. I made this incursion into Machiavellianism once in my life, and, in fact, it was unfortunate because it was a stupid prediction.

On the contrary, although there were ups and downs, Charles de Gaulle contributed to America's disentanglement from Vietnam. I can affirm that, in the end, he did put a certain number of techniques and meeting possibilities at the U.S.'s disposal. He offered the U.S. the services of his eminent collaborator Manac'h, who was director of Asian Affairs in the French Foreign Office. It would be an exaggeration to say that he made any gifts to the United states, but he did give carte blanche, so to speak, to Mr. Manac'h to devote himself largely to Vietnamese affairs, to provide all kinds of services, and to meet on many occasions with, most notably, Senator Kennedy and many others, including

Henry Kissinger. These were, I think, quite useful elements. Similarly, de Gaulle authorized a man to whom he was very close because of his role during the war, Mr. Raymond Aubrac, to play a role. Mr. Aubrac, who had been a heroic leader of the resistance, later became a friend of Ho Chi-Minh and a member of the Pugwash group. Within that group, with the consent of de Gaulle, or more precisely of Mr. Manac'h, Mr. Aubrac organized contacts between Mr. Kissinger and Vietnam. and later, another prominent Gaullist, Jean Sainteny, veteran of "Ho Chi-Minism," helped organize meetings between Kissinger and representatives of Hanoi.

Therefore, we can consider that there were a whole series of boosts given, or services rendered, to find a solution to the Vietnamese problem. I would say that in contrast to the overall gist of his actions, the Phnom Penh speech seemed rather dissonant. I happened to be present in Pnom Penh during General de Gaulle's speech, and I remember being surprised by the largely anti-American tone of it, knowing what I knew about what was in the works. (This speech had been prepared with Mr. Manac'h, who was present, and I was sitting next to him in the stadium at Phnom Penh.) It was a sort of challenge or warning to the U.S., which, after all, hadn't taken into account General de Gaulle's errors in either Indochina or Algeria. This speech had a weakness, it seems to me, in that it proposed nothing in exchange. The criticism was harsh, it was justified, but I remember discussing it that night with some of my American colleagues. An American diplomat, whose name I no longer remember, told me: "This speech isn't very pleasant for us, but we would willingly take it into consideration if France (meaning de Gaulle) proposed, if not a form of mediation, at least to get involved in the debate." It's rather surprising to think, when one knows de Gaulle, that in effect he was content to criticize or give warnings without proposing, to complete his speech, any positive moves. In the end, the initiatives that Mr. Manac'h was taking in Paris, plus other more important ones in the U.S. and Vietnam, culminated in the conference of 1968. This conference was held in Paris, to General de Gaulle's satisfaction, even though other events taking place in Paris at the time did not set a very good atmosphere for the conference. Anyway, Paris was chosen as the site for this conference. Was it a great diplomatic success? One could consider that it represented a lot of maneuvers and speeches, only to end up replacing Geneva with Paris as the diplomatic capital of Indochina.

Witness

Bernard Tricot

MR. LACOUTURE JUST GAVE ME A TRANSITION between Vietnam and the policy of grandeur. I remember that in 1967 or 1968, I once had to present to de Gaulle, for his signature, a telegram sending formal congratulations to Mr. Diem for some anniversary (I cannot recall exactly which one). I saw the general frown, put on a stone face, push aside the telegram, and say to me: "I will not sign it. I will not telegraph Mr. Diem because he offended the dignity of the French people." This unusual language, even emanating from him, struck me. I once again admired his classical education, because all that was Latin translated into French. Seeing my incomprehension, he commented: "Don't you remember that some years ago Diem had the French uniforms of the Vietnamese army replaced with American uniforms, and on this occasion he let the officers and the non-commissioned officers burn their French stripes. Therefore, I will not sign this telegram."

I would like to make a few brief comments on the policy of grandeur, even though I am in no way a specialist on foreign policy. Considering General de Gaulle's policies as a whole, and as leader of France, a few comments need to be made to react, not against certain asperities this policy might have had in relation to foreign countries, but to oppose the notion that the policy was chimerical. In that the policy was excessive, that there was a great gap between the ambitions of the French and the means at their disposal, even in Charles de Gaulle's France, so there was an element of unreasonableness in this policy. De Gaulle did make some rare confidences that can give credence to this notion that his policy was chimerical. One day he told me in passing: "Well, you see, since 1940 I have always acted as if . . . as if France had not been beaten, as if most of the French in 1940 had been on the side of the resistance, as if. . . ." etc. But in fact, there was nothing chimerical about that because the "as if" did not indicate ignorance, or a refusal to face the facts. He knew very well what had existed, and that France was no longer the great country it had been in the past. But he wanted to change this, to reverse the decline. He thought, as he often said, that France needed grandeur to be herself. But grandeur did not necessarily mean the domination of others, or the exploitation of power, or exaggerated enterprises.

I think there is one aspect of de Gaulle's personality, of his psychology, of which I have been particularly aware, perhaps because I had been dealing with the Algerian affair for a long time: his sense of moderation and his desire for equilibrium. All in all, there was a kind of moderation – a surprising word when used to describe de Gaulle, but which I believe to be justified. He hated what was excessive and exaggerated. It is well known, for example, that in the area of political institutions and regimes, when he spoke of dictatorships or of Napoleon, he always said: "These enterprises were exaggerated, and in the end, that sort of thing leads to disaster and leaves a country weaker than before."

One also finds this concern in political institutions. He wanted to reestablish in France a separation of powers, which had been compromised for a long time by parliamentary domination, accompanied, as a matter of fact, by the weakness of the parliamentary institution. Separation of powers is real only if there is a certain balance, even when one power is stronger than the others, takes the initiatives, has the deciding power, or most notably, in certain cases, calls on popular opinion to express itself directly by referendum. But all the same, there is a desire for balance.

The desire for equilibrium also applies in a domain that is close to foreign affairs: the field of armament. How many times, in Defense Council meetings or in the Council of Ministers, did we hear him, in response to this or that armament project, especially nuclear armaments, say: "It is agreed, in principle, it's decided. But as for its realization, we shall see. We will see when we know the cost." He was often heard to say: "Evaluate the cost, we will make a definitive decision later." Therefore, contrary to the idea that financial worries were secondary for him, even for projects very important for him like the creation of an independent French nuclear force, it had to be done without financial exaggeration, conciliating France's financial and technical capacities.

One again can find the notion of equilibrium in neighboring areas – for example, in the budgetary balance and obviously in the balance of the country's economic development. Concerning foreign policy, one could say that although he was hostile to the Eastern bloc, if he wanted to see the return of a kind of "concert of nations" (a 19th century expression he sometimes used, which one can admit was a bit archaic), it is because he thought that nations were a reality, beyond the blocs, which would later regain all their strength, but also because he thought that European equilibrium ought to be reestablished.

So this policy that may sometimes have seemed a bit extreme was, in the end, a measured one. He had a strong will, but one wrapped in moderation. And it seems to me that this has now been recognized by most everyone. Already, concerning the last years of General de Gaulle's government, there are images which now return to my mind that give me the feeling that, at the summit of nations, there was already a kind of recognition of Charles de Gaulle's moral authority, an authority largely based on his wisdom. I recall Eisenhower's funeral at the beginning of 1969. I can still see those heads of states and governments who, in a vast lounge in the White House, were hovering around General de Gaulle. They all wanted to welcome him, leaving in a corner poor Mr. Trudeau, who didn't join us and who was almost a bit isolated. We almost felt sorry for him. But there was a global move towards de Gaulle that was very impressive.

I also recall a gesture by President Nixon when de Gaulle received him in the beginning of 1969, first in Paris and then at the Trianon. There was a rather long private conversation between Nixon and General de Gaulle, and then the two heads of state went to join the American and French delegations. (Mr. Kissinger, the American Secretary of State, was there.) I can still see Nixon. I can still hear him telling his colleagues as he approached the conference table, and then asking Charles de Gaulle to repeat in front of the two delegations, what de Gaulle had told him about the politics and policies of the East/West confrontation, about the fact that these policies couldn't last forever, about the importance of nations throughout the world, and about the fact that individual nationhood would return with all its vigor. I can still hear Nixon saying: "Listen to the old man, he has interesting things to say."

Part III
Opinions, Perceptions, and Misperceptions

CHAPTER FIVE

SOME EYE-WITNESS VIEWS

14

Dealing with De Gaulle

Henry Kissinger

This is the sort of occasion to which one agrees a year ahead of time, then suddenly it's upon you, and, being in the presence of so many experts on the subject, one doesn't quite know how to proceed. My topic deals with de Gaulle. I suppose what the organizers had in mind is that I should describe my dealings with de Gaulle. Unfortunately, they were extremely skimpy and confined to two occasions. One was when President Nixon visited Paris in February 1969, and the second was when President de Gaulle came to Eisenhower's funeral in late March 1969, just before he retired from office. So I will speak briefly about those occasions and then talk about the fundamental problem of the dialogue between Americans and de Gaulle, which concerns approaches to international relations, philosophical conceptions of how nations cooperate, analogies with the role of the Soviet Union – as well as some differences – and the role of France in de Gaulle's day.

My initial experience with de Gaulle was limited rather humbly to a reception on the occasion of President Nixon's visit to Paris. We were all in the Elysée when an aide came over and said, "The president would like to talk to you." I went over and, without further introduction or in fact discretion, de Gaulle said to me, "Why don't you get out of Indochina?" These were the very first words I heard from General de Gaulle. I told him it would produce a credibility problem. President de Gaulle said, "Where, for example, would it produce a credibility problem?" So I said, "For example, in the Middle East." President de Gaulle said, "How very odd. I thought it was your opponents who had the credibility problem in the Middle East." That, I suppose, took care of me for the evening.

The next day, President Nixon took me around to a conversation with President de Gaulle, which I cannot say filled de Gaulle with unrelieved joy, since he did not believe that heads of state should be accompanied by aides during their conversations. So he did the best he could by completely ignoring me. But President Nixon, who had many great qualities, also had a certain suicidal impulse; at the end of the meeting he turned to me and said, "Why don't you tell President de Gaulle what you thought of his presentation?" (which concerned the organization of Europe). My suicidal impulse, being even more highly developed than President Nixon's, propelled me to say, "How does President de Gaulle propose to prevent Germany from dominating the Europe he has just described?" President de Gaulle looked down at me – as I have described in my own memoirs – as from some high alpine height to a little foothill, and said, "Par la guerre." By war. Next question.

Then, as we were all having drinks, I again got involved in a conversation with de Gaulle. We were discussing various historical figures and somehow the subject got around to Bismarck. We were discussing Franco-German relations, and I made the comment that one of the sources of the difficulties prior to World War I was that Germany had made excessive demands on France after the war of 1870, which I believe is historically true. De Gaulle said, "I'm glad they did because it gave us an opportunity to take back by force what they took from us by force." One thing I cannot say is that I contributed to the education of President de Gaulle.

The only other time I met him was when he came to the funeral of President Eisenhower. I won't repeat all the conversations we had then because some of them were somewhat melancholy and personal, not that they were personal to me, but I had the sense that he would not stay in office very long. The point I want to mention is that there was a reception at the White House with some 60 heads of state, plus a heavy sprinkling of Liberal senators who had expressed disagreement with generals, megalomaniac presidents of France, among many other things, until General de Gaulle appeared in the uniform of a Brigadier General. Whereupon they left the Shah of Iran, and whoever else was there, and dashed for de Gaulle, forming a circle around him. I remember thinking that if by chance de Gaulle moved to a window of that room, it would tip and everyone would slip out. It was a remarkable demonstration of the power of a single personality, because he wore the uniform of a Brigadier General and said nothing. He did not call attention to himself in any way. As he walked into the room, Senator Fulbright was the first to charge for him, followed by most of the Liberal members of the Senate Foreign Relations Committee. He attracted the majority of the people in that room. Anyway, these are the personal observations I can offer you.

I always had extraordinary respect for President de Gaulle. I think he was a truly astonishingly great man. If one looks at the years 1962 to 1965, at the height of the debate between America and France, when de Gaulle was being accused of "folies de grandeur," of megalomania, of arrogance, of an excessively assertive France, they were the days of perhaps his greatest triumph. People had forgotten the fact that France had had an internal revolution in 1958, that it was engaged in a bitter war in Algeria during that period, and that there had been several coups against de Gaulle (in 1959, in 1960, and again in 1961). For France to have emerged at the end of all this as excessively assertive, or to be regarded as threatening to dominate Europe, was in itself a huge achievement because it showed that de Gaulle had succeeded in restoring France's self-confidence. His basic problem was how to restore a sense of identity and a sense of purpose, and this was at the heart of the philosophical dispute between de Gaulle and the United States, as it still is between the United States and other countries.

In the United States, we are now in a period in which international events have fulfilled almost every objective we set for ourselves in the 1940s and 1950s. These were objectives which coincided precisely with America's philosophy that international affairs is a hard struggle to achieve moral values. The United States prevailed in this struggle not by concentrating on the operation of the balance of power, but on building an international consensus in which we could achieve our aims through the purity of our motives, the excellence of our prescriptions, and the ability to create cooperative structures. And more or less, we achieved many of these objectives. Whether it was as a result of our policy or of the disintegration of the Communist world need not now be discussed. Throughout this period America was frequently assailed by a temptation to isolationism, which was based on two contradictory impulses. One was the proposition that we were too good for this world, and the other was the proposition that we are not yet good enough for this world, and should therefore strenuously work on our moral improvement. Now we are in 1990; the Communist ideology has disintegrated substantially and its satellite orbit is collapsing. What does America stand for now, and what does it want to achieve? What philosophical guides do we have? How do we visualize how international relations operate? I am not even talking about our policies. I am talking about criteria, and I have a great longing for an American version of de Gaulle – somebody to appear who would do for us what de Gaulle did for Europe in the late 1950s and the early 1960s.

If we look at the debate that occurred then, the American view was cooperation – that Europe should unify and become supranational, the same way the United States was formed in 1789. Indeed, this is what President Kennedy specifically invoked when he put forward his declaration of interdependence. We looked at the alliance as if it were a technical problem of assembling a certain number of boards in which burdens were assigned on the basis of a kind of quota. Overall efficiency would be the motive of all the participants of the Atlantic relationship. There would be an appropriate division of labor, in which case the United States would take care of the nuclear problem, the Europeans would emphasize conventional weapons, and all the forces would be integrated under a single command. The Americans' view was quite well known and was fundamentally challenged by de Gaulle, but on the philosophical and not on the practical level.

Above all, on that philosophical level, because they had totally different problems. The United States emerged from World War II hugely successful. We had nearly 60 percent of the world's gross national product and had totally defeated two enemies. For the United States, World War II was a culmination of history, but for France, the end of World War II and the period that followed was a culmination of an extended period of frustration. France understood clearly that its world had ended in 1918 and that it could never withstand Germany alone. Yet now it was being treated by Great Britain as if it were the dominant country on the continent and all its fears of Germany were imaginary; America simply withdrew across the Atlantic. Nothing is more poignant than the French effort of the 1920s and 1930s to construct the Maginot line, which was done at a moment when the German army was limited to 100,000 men, when the Rhineland was demilitarized, and when the French army was the largest in Europe. So what did France do? It built a defensive line against a German attack that was only possible if the Germans broke the demilitarization provision of the Treaty of Versailles – i.e., the demilitarization provisions of the Rhineland. Still, France thought that would not be enough to restrain Germany. It was also totally inconsistent with French political strategy, which had guaranteed the small countries in Eastern Europe and which could be implemented only by an offensive military strategy. So the interwar period in which France was technically the victor was a period of tremendous frustration for it. Then came the collapse of 1940, followed by the postwar period in which France had to fight for its seat at the table, suffered enormous domestic divisions, was caught in a series of colonial wars in Vietnam, frustrated at Suez, and caught in a colonial war in Algeria. The problem for de Gaulle was not how to relate France to a division of labor, but his conviction that before France could relate itself to anybody, it had to relate itself to itself, that it had to have some sense of its purpose. He once said in a speech, and I'll just read a few lines of it: "Once upon a time, there was an old country all hemmed in by habits and circumspection. At one time they were the richest and mightiest people among those on this end of the world stage. After great misfortunes, it came to withdraw within itself. While other peoples were growing around it, it remained immobile. In an epoque when the power of the state depended on industrial might, the great sources of power were stingily meted out to it. It had little coal, it had no petroleum," and it goes on, "and finally after two World Wars had decimated, ruined and tormented it, many in the world wondered if it would succeed in getting back on its feet." That was the problem de Gaulle was addressing. Therefore, he could never accept the proposition that the division of labor and burden sharing were of themselves a motivation. For him, the philosophical problem was to define the burden as a French burden.

It came down to a philosophical debate about how nations cooperate. The United States stresses the concept of partnership, consensus, and cooperation. De Gaulle always tended to emphasize the idea of the political. Americans had a very optimistic conception of the nature of man. De Gaulle had a less positive one. Man, he said, limited by his nature, is infinite in his desires. Thus the world is full of opposing forces. Of course, human wisdom has often succeeded in preventing these rivalries from degenerating into murderous conflicts. But the competition of efforts is the condition of life. Our country finds itself confronted today, as it has for two thousand years, with this law of the species. Therefore, the duty of a leader is to understand the balance of these forces, and to help to contribute to equilibrium.

American leaders protested their good faith and became personally angry when de Gaulle wanted physical reassurances. For his part, he treated them as if they simply did not understand the nature of history. De Gaulle was not concerned with the good faith of any one American president that he dealt with, but with the forces that a future president would have to evaluate. It was his view that, in the end, the calculations of any president depend sooner or later on his assessment of the balance of forces. And this is what de Gaulle addressed.

When Dean Acheson came to France during the Cuban missile crisis, having ridiculed de Gaulle in many public statements, he was astonished to find after briefing the various European leaders that the European leader who was most cooperative and most helpful was in fact President de Gaulle. He often told the story about how he had a briefing team present, but first explained to de Gaulle what he was going to do (not what we were planning to do). My understanding is that de Gaulle asked, "Are you planning to do it, or have you decided to do it?" Acheson said, "We are going to do it, but I have a briefing team outside that will explain to you why we're doing it." De Gaulle's response was: "When a great ally acts out of need, I will not act like a police reporter." He refused to see the briefing team. He supported us because he understood that if Soviet Russia was permitted to put short or medium range missiles into Cuba, it would change the balance of power in the world. And if it changed the balance of power in the world, France could not be unaffected. To make that calculation, he did not have to be part of an integrated command.

On the other hand, if he had not agreed with that calculation, it would have been a somber occasion to be part of an integrated command in which you go to the edge of nuclear war simply because you have no other option. Now there was all along a fundamental difference between de Gaulle and the United States about the nature of the alliance. For a man like de Gaulle, defense had to be the essential attribute of something. For American leaders, defense was measured as a total calculation of what was needed, in which France had no greater status than any other component. In fact, the American approach was to make foreign countries consultants in the American decision-making process. De Gaulle was of the view that consultation is meaningful only if all partners proceed to have another choice, and he therefore always insisted that he have another choice. He explained this by saying that France had been materially and morally destroyed by the collapse of 1940. That is why, with regard to the United States, it found itself in a position of dependence, constantly needing our assistance in order to avoid collapse. In regard to international undertakings in which French leaders were taking part, it was often with the view of dissolving France in them, as if self-renouncement were henceforth its sole possibility and indeed its only ambition, while these undertakings in the guise of integration were automatically taking American authority as a possibility.

This is why de Gaulle withdrew his forces from the integrated major command. Of course, the integrated command was in any event a rather strange phenomenon because all the integrated command does is to plan joint action; the forces are always under national command. It was therefore more a symbolic gesture. All the NATO command did was to make joint plans for the contingency that the forces are released to it. And all de Gaulle did was to say, "I do not promise automatically to release our forces to it," and he theoretically stopped integrated planning in which successive NATO commanders had managed to coordinate their planning with French planning in quite an effective way. Any of you who have felt this strategic tension will probably agree with me, whether you share the French views on strategy or not. I think the most consistent, the most creative, the most systematic thinking on strategy in Europe today takes place in France. And I believe that it is closely related to the fact that the French, at least in their minds, feel the ultimate responsibility for their own defense. All of this led predictably to great debates between the United States and France about their own nuclear weapons with which, again, we are quite permanently faced as a guarantee of France's survival. And de Gaulle replied, as I think everybody would agree with today, that the credibility of the use of nuclear weapons had to decline and that therefore France had to have the possibility of posing its own threat.

Strangely enough, there was always a consistent philosophical dispute about the Soviet Union. The United States in the postwar period oscillated between periods of intransigence and periods of conciliation. We now read constantly that Gorbachev is on the road to Damascus, that he had an inspiration that turned him into a pluralistic democrat and an adherent to market economics. For all I know, this may be true. I am not going to debate this issue now. But the fact is that we have been saying something like this in every decade since the 1940s. In 1943, Senator Connally, not known for his radical sympathies when Stalin announced the abandonment of the Comintern or when the Germans were at the gates of Moscow, remarked that the huge concessions of the Russians proclaimed that for years they had been approaching the abandonment of communism, and that the whole world would be gratified by this happy culmination. The same was more or less said in the 1950s. In 1964, Dean Rusk said that Brezhnev had learned the incompatibility between Communism and meeting the desires of his people. The point I am making is that America has never abandoned these two propositions: one, that communism is evil and must be destroyed, and two, that conversion is possible, and that some day some group of leaders will emerge to solve all our foreign policy problems.

De Gaulle never had such views. De Gaulle looked at Russia as an historic phenomenon, and as an historic phenomenon the Russian empire had expanded from the Duchy of Moscovy to the center of Europe, to the shores of the Pacific, to the gates of India – nor did it get there by plebiscite. In 1961, during the Berlin crisis, de Gaulle said the following: "There is in this uproar of imprecations and demands organized by the Soviets something so arbitrary and so artificial that one is led to attribute it either to the premeditated unleashing of grand confrontations or the desire of leading attention away from great difficulties." This second hypothesis – of drawing away from great difficulties – seems all the more plausible to me since, despite the coercions, isolations, and acts of force in which a government insistently encloses the country that bears its yoke, and despite certain collective successes it has achieved by drawing on the endurance of its subjects, its internal failures and its character of inhuman oppression are felt more and more by both the elite and the masses, whom it becomes more and more difficult to deceive and to subjugate. One can go on with quotations from de Gaulle about the character of the Communist system, which is one of the reasons that during the Berlin crisis America was much more eager to negotiate than France. In sum, de Gaulle was concerned with defining a French national interest.

He believed the properly understood French national interest required, for the foreseeable future, alignment with the United States. He was not prepared to put this into the service of abstract concepts of integration. Now his view of how to implement this went through several phases. When he thought that there was a global threat to peace, as in 1958, he proposed the Directorate, later ridiculed as the directory – joint action by France, Britain, and the United States. It was, in fact, rejected by the United States. In the 1960s he decided to organize Europe, but his primary objective was to create an equilibrium that had to be taken seriously by the other countries. What does this mean for the present day? And, above all, what did it mean for that period?

I believed then, as I believe now, that de Gaulle was extremely helpful to the Western world. For the United States, it was not so important whether France followed every one of the frequently changing prescriptions of the United States' strategic doctrine, but whether France took itself seriously in assessments of the international situation and was compatible with our fundamental objectives. This has, on the whole, been the situation in the entire post-de Gaulle period. Second, I do not think the historic American attitude toward foreign policy is indefinitely sustainable. I do not believe that we can continue to operate foreign policy on the principle that every problem can be settled into constituent parts, that these constituent parts can be given a terminal date, or that this terminal date can be achieved by organizing forces that operate on the basis of abstract, moral, or legal principles.

My first experience in government was in 1961, during the Berlin crisis. At that time, the Kennedy White House was dedicated to the proposition that we could find some negotiating position which would get the support not of France, but of India, the leader of the moral force in the world as it was then perceived. We struggled very hard to develop some position that would get the support of the non-committed nations led by Nehru. I was the skunk at the garden party, saying that there was no conceivable position that India could support on the subject of Berlin. Why should India run any risks for a city three thousand miles away with which it had no historical connection, and which involved no Indian national interest, even the most broadly conceived?

It is, in fact, very difficult to develop the concept of the national interest in the United States. In 1936, when the Germans reoccupied the Rhineland, President Roosevelt asked the State

Department what that meant. What it meant was that, if it was not opposed, the French system of alliances was in a shambles and that the overturning of the Versailles agreement became a largely German decision from then on. However, the State Department listed only the legal engagements that Germany had broken in entering the Rhineland, and pointed out that the United States had not been a part of any of it and the matter, therefore, involved no American interest whatsoever. Now this is something that British or French statesmen would not have understood, and it would have been totally foreign to de Gaulle's approach to foreign policy. We also see it in the contemporary approach to foreign policy, which is that America is still not clear whether the first persons we turn to when something happens are our lawyers – to determine the legal framework – or whether we dare to define a national interest. One of the ironies of the present situation in the world, to me, is that neither of the two most influential countries in the West, the United States nor Germany, has a vision of the national interest. We, for reasons I have given, and Germany because it was unified so late that it spent all its energies on unifying rather than on defining what it would do with its unity.

In all of this, I ask myself, "What would de Gaulle say in present circumstances?" And I've asked that of my French friends here. I think his vision of Europe was one in which France would lead the way politically, and Germany might play a major economic role. I do think he would have attempted to vindicate some such position. How he would have done this, whether it is still possible to do so, whether it was ever possible to do so, I do not know. Would he accelerate the construction of Europe in order to contain Germany, or would he move to the British position of trying to get a veto over the voice of an integrated Europe? I tend to think he might have moved to accelerate the construction of Europe and tried to include the East European countries in order to have a counterweight. Would he have tried to implement the idea of a Europe from the Atlantic to the Urals? I don't think so. I believe he accepted that as a phrase being used while America was overwhelmingly dominant; but creating a balance between the two sides of the Atlantic on largely European resources seemed improbable. My instinct is that his sense of history would be such that he would know that the Urals are not a dividing line, that either Russia is part of Europe up to Vladivostok or it is not a part of Europe at all. But his attitude would have depended very much on his assessment of the trends in the Soviet Union. If his assessment was that the Soviet Union would sooner or later return to the policy of the Czars and repress the nationalities, he would surely have treated it as a potential threat to Europe, and have tried to organize Europe along the Polish-Soviet frontier. If he judged that the Soviet Union was disintegrating, and that at the end of the day all that would be left would be the Duchy of Moscow and Siberia, then he might have tried to add the various pieces falling off to some European construction as a counterbalance to Germany.

Now this looks like a very relativistic approach. On the other hand, I believe that the approach of de Gaulle provided more objective criteria than the changing mood of American politics. Wherever you are in that debate, you need only to review the last 40 years to see how many different strategic dispensations have been put forward as sealed in truth, how many shifts in the assessment of the importance of certain countries have occurred, and the criteria to which these were attached.

I believe that sooner or later the United States will have to develop some operational concept of the national interest. And when that happens, we will have to be, whether we like it or not, students of de Gaulle. Winston Churchill, writing about the balance of power in the 1930s, reviewed all the various peoples with whom Britain had been allied and whom it had opposed. At the end, he said the key point to remember was that it was not a question of sentiment or personal preference, but that England was pursuing a law of public policy to preserve the liberties of Europe. I believe that de Gaulle's approach to international politics was of the same school. He was a man who detested Communism, but he was also not a man given to crusades. He was the leader of a country that had suffered centuries of upheaval and decades of unfulfilled aspirations. He had to restore its sense of identity in order to make it meaningful to others. I believe he will go down as one of the great men of this century.

❖15❖

The State, De Gaulle, and the United States

Olivier Guichard

Michel Debré should have spoken here tonight. Something tied him very strongly to General de Gaulle, and this was the obsession with what the French call "the State," the obsession with good institutions – that is, the institutions of sovereignty. I share this obsession; this is even the clearest and most durable thing I learned from the general.

It might seem strange to you that, within the context of our discussion devoted to trans-Atlantic exchanges under de Gaulle, I begin with this subject: the State. In reality, it is the same subject, and this is why I gladly accepted this invitation. Although I am not a diplomat and was only a very distant witness to the diplomatic preoccupations of the general, I think I understand the deeper origins of his preoccupations regarding this matter.

Henry Kissinger once said in one word everything I would like to develop here tonight. According to him, the fundamental question that de Gaulle constantly wrestled with was: "How must nations cooperate?" And this was a concern that he had trouble communicating to the Americans, of course, but also to his other partners.

The Man of Nations in the Age of Empires

The tragedy for the general was that he lived his political life in a period that wasn't suited for him. He believed in, and had a deep feeling for, the idea of "the Nation." He had to live and act in an age of "Empires." The tragedy was even more poignant for him personally. Indeed, until 1940, as long as the French nation kept its appearance of power and autonomy and belonged to a system of power for which de Gaulle was made, he himself was nothing, or almost nothing. He was projected onto the scene at a time when the collapse of France opened the period of empires, of colonial confrontations. And of course, he threw himself into it only to argue, from the first instant, in favor of the rights of nations inside empires. The rights of nations against empires. The rights of the French nation, but also of any nation. He saw himself as the champion of a cause that didn't correspond completely with the cause of freedom. Freedom was sufficient for millions of men to define their camp, but it wasn't enough for him.

In this "Gaullist" anniversary year, history has paid the general the greatest possible tribute. History closed this half-century in which he lived and suffered, and against which he fought. I wouldn't say the power of empires has disappeared, but the time of nations is returning. Our reflection tonight, these days of academic debates, thus take on a special flavor.

When the son of General de Lattre, a young officer, was killed in Indochina, de Gaulle cheered up the father by writing to him: "Your son is now serving France in heaven." Surprising formulation! I am not sure if the general is serving France in heaven. In any case, he never stopped being attentive to it, and we could imagine his joy at our opportunities today, and his worries about what we are going to do with these opportunities that we deserve so little. The general died shortly after the Soviet tanks crushed the Spring of Prague. Twenty years later, the Europe which he had heartily wished for has become possible. Twenty years too late, if we think of the fears the new era has aroused: it may be more complicated than the routine of Yalta. But the general wouldn't have been scared. We are not always intellectually prepared to live in this less structured world. He had been preparing for it in advance; he knew how to prepare himself for the unthinkable. 1940 had found him ready. 1958 had found him ready. And in some ways, 1968 had found him ready. And of course, 1969 for his departure, as in 1970, for his death.

But the problem was that the general had known only the age of empires, during which he necessarily encountered the United States.

AMERICAN LEADERSHIP

For thirty years, the United States was at the heart of Gaullist difficulties. As soon as it entered the war, it placed itself at the head of an empire that fought for freedom. As the postwar period transformed itself very rapidly into a kind of pre-World War situation, a new composition of the empire succeeded the old one. The allies and the adversaries changed, but the leadership remained in Washington.

This posed a problem that can be divided into two parts.

The first part concerns the language of the psychology, or meta-psychology, of people and their leaders. It is a rather common observation that the United States lived and interpreted its position of leadership in a somewhat exalted manner, a manner which, from General de Gaulle's point of view, complicated things. It did not offend him that the United States should hold, in a coalition or alliance, a large place in accordance with its large means. But he had trouble accepting that the United States considered itself invested with a sort of divine or simply historical mission, or which gave it a sort of pre-eminence of divine right or of historical right. This is what Stanley Hoffmann understood: "The French interpretation of American policy put into question American values."

One needs a better understanding of America than I have to explain the reasons for this state of mind, but I believe that it was this aspect of the problem that counted the most for the general. He knew from experience that one doesn't lead people without giving them a high opinion of themselves, without even giving them the sentiment that they are accomplishing a unique mission, of universal interest. If this language had been essentially for domestic use, and made to speak to Americans in their language, which tends to moral universalism, I don't think that General de Gaulle would have had any criticism of it.

The principal difficulty came from the second aspect of the problem: that which links psychology to diplomacy, and the language of motivation to the language of realization.

For the general, as much during the war against the Axis powers as during the Cold War against the Communist empire, the coalition had, if I may say so, an essentially circumstantial character. It was the affair of one enemy and one moment. Even if the moment was long, and it was particularly clear that the Cold War would be very long, de Gaulle always saw beyond that moment. And beyond it, America was one continent and Europe was another. America had no place in Europe. It was as simple as that.

However, de Gaulle could legitimately have the impression that for the United States everything had to take place as if the union of circumstance was a unity of destiny, as if the circumstances had drawn a new political continent made to last indefinitely, a trans-atlantic continent. In a letter to Paul Claudel in 1950, he said the following: "Immediately after the first steps toward direct American action in Europe (1941), I had, within the limits of my terribly reduced means, tried to make the American policy makers understand that it was of World interest that they explain themselves to the Europeans." And he added that three reasons were combined to make this explanation impossible: "The passionate refusal of Roosevelt, British intrigues, and the ambiguity of Vichy." The interesting phrase here is this "explanation to the Europeans." Europe emerged from the war without having explained itself to the United States. And in what condition! Naturally, when the general wrote this in 1950, he said that France, having regained its sovereignty and freedom, could again demand explanation, made necessary by the new circumstances of the Cold War. But if France was legally sovereign, she was not led on her own. And he added: "Today, there are still intrigues from London. Roosevelt is no longer here. But there is an official France more inconsistent than ever."[1]

A young man of thirty at the time, I traveled the cities and towns of Aquitaine and Burgundy to help the general elect his candidates in the legislative elections of 1951. Even for one of his militants, there was something poignant at the sight of this national hero campaigning inside a system he justifiably disdained. Why was he doing it? So the "Official France" could become "consistent" again. To obtain an "explanation" between the United States and Europe. So that the logic of Empires didn't prevail definitively over that logic of nationhood and of the European community, this continent of nations. Take, for instance, his great electoral speech at Nantes, where he said everything he had to say in four pages and in one paragraph: "What I believe to be necessary for the salvation of our country." Well, this paragraph ended, culminating with the two following statements: "I want to act by guiding Europe towards its unity, by combining our defense with the Atlantic states serving as allies, but not as masters." End of paragraph.

The more one studies the general, the more one is struck by the extraordinary unity and continuity of his thought. This is notably

1. Letter to Paul Claudel, 18 December 1950 in Charles de Gaulle, *Lettres, Notes et Carnets*, vol. 6, May 1945–June 1951 (Paris: Plon, 1984), p. 461.

the case regarding institutions. The constitution of 1958, with its final or aborted transformations between 1962 and 1969, was entirely included in the speech of Bayeux, in 1946. But this is equally true in the area that concerns us here.

It is natural that the academic magnifying glass focuses on differences, but they also result from circumstances. De Gaulle was very respectful of circumstances and he never ceased to adapt his policies to them. I am so conscious of this that, using one of his expressions, I even wrote one day that he had no doctrine other than the "doctrine of circumstances." But this tortuous path imposed by circumstances had a meaning only if it respected the higher orientation of principles.

What are the principles here? French sovereignty, Franco-German entente, and European union. France, France-Germany, Europe. Everything revolved around these poles. And the question of the United States acted reactively, always revealing the good way to approach a problem. He wrote, for example, in 1955 to Coudenhove-Kalergi: "Europe cannot be built without a direct agreement (direct is the important word here) between France and Germany. But this entente cannot pass through Washington, which, in Bonn and Paris, unfortunately, hasn't been taken into consideration."

None other than Europeans can build Europe. I think that American pressure had some positive effects because it forced the general to be more European than he would have been spontaneously. Confronted with the United States, he knew that he couldn't oppose it alone. Instead of "France!", he had to answer "Europe!" But naturally, he knew more about what it shouldn't be than what it was supposed to be: "The failure of the EDC – which was nothing but a theory – seems to me a simple and rather vulgar incident in an enterprise which is beginning and therefore, a quarrel which has only just begun. But a certain unity of Europe is inscribed in the future. What kind of unity? How will it be accomplished? What steps should we go through? This is a 'political' problem." Politics. Circumstances.

THE ANTI-AMERICANISM OF THE GENERAL

I cannot give, at this point in my speech, my sentiment on the classic subject: the anti-Americanism of de Gaulle. "Il y a des reproches qui louent" (La Rochefoucauld). [Some reproaches are praise.]

When one has had, like myself, the opportunity to hear the general express himself in private and without constraints, one could have the impression that he was against a lot of things. He knew the words that exalted people in their own eyes, as well as the words that demolished and disdained them. But, almost always, he kept the latter for personal use. He supposedly called the French people by the pejorative term "veaux," meaning calves. Does this mean that the general was anti-French? Some have said it, I admit it, but they were often the same ones who accused the general of anti-Americanism. But if the general was as anti-French as he was anti-American, I don't very well see what the problem is!

Let's be serious. The man who sought a certain quality of personal relations with American presidents as different as Eisenhower, Kennedy, and Nixon, was not anti-American. "I don't think he is anti-American at all" (Chip Bohlen, 1967). One should not forget either the importance that de Gaulle attributed, naively perhaps, to the reactions of the masses. I saw how much they warmed his heart during the 1950s when he visited the countries of Black Africa. He believed in this appreciation because he was sure he wasn't a demagogue. If throngs cheered him, it wasn't because he flattered their egos. Also, I am sure he never forgot the welcome he received in New York in 1945, and in all of America in 1960. He had done nothing to deserve the applause other than to say the truth about France, and sometimes rudely. Precisely because of the quality of this applause, he never stopped saying it.

De Gaulle's trip to Mexico and the way he defied President Monroe at his doorstep is often mentioned in connection with de Gaulle's anti-Americanism. In a famous speech, in Spanish, the general offered to the Mexicans: "Marcheremos la mano en la mano!" He had used this expression itself twenty years before, but for the American people. On 6 November 1945, addressing a "salute of recognition" to the G.I.s leaving the country, he said: "You are leaving European soil. . . . It is hand in hand that our two countries must march towards the future." There was much more in this idea than simple rhetoric. One could say that de Gaulle made his proposition to the Mexicans spitefully because the United States had not accepted to march "hand in hand," and on the same level, with him. I simply believe that this affectionate image corresponded to his way of understanding relations between nations. He loved them all. He thought them all equally indispensable, because he knew that only they could anchor our fragile and storm-tossed humanity. He would have liked to march hand in hand with all of them, particularly yours.

This was not always the case, and many experienced – in France, as in the United States – these "trans-Atlantic misunderstandings," these disagreements, these confrontations, as a tragedy. A tragedy that tore apart a friendship like Greek tragedies tore families apart because of fate. But the general didn't live these ups and downs – that would most probably be his term – at all on that level. He lived them with the greatest serenity. For him they proved something. "Rise, desired storms," said our poet. Without being romantic, like Lamartine, de Gaulle had wanted these storms.

Naturally, one might ponder the balance-sheet of the Franco-American storm.

Each prevented the other from accomplishing his goal. De Gaulle prevented the EDC, the multi-lateral force, Kennedy's "Atlantic association," and the European political union under American command from happening. In brief, he succeeded in blocking the logic of imperialism at the moment when it had the most strength. Conversely, de Gaulle never obtained his "explanation." He didn't obtain, in 1945, the polarization of the Germanies around France nor, in the 1960s, the creation of a non-ambiguous association partnership between the Federal Republic and France. He wasn't able to convince the Europeans that a political union under French impetus was worth trying.

Thus, nothing saw the light of day, neither the Atlantic Europe nor the European Europe. We could ask ourselves: Aren't we still at that point today?

But everything is not negative. First of all, these reciprocal impediments did not destroy the effectiveness of the alliance when it faced the Eastern blocs. At each juncture, the general was able to show that the two superpowers were not morally equivalent, that he would always be on the side of the United States.

Next, if one places one's self in the perspective of the general, one notices that the impediments weren't balanced. The Atlantic Europe is no longer possible. Its hour has passed. The European Europe remains possible. But in what form? Since the collapse of Communism and the liberation of the Eastern bloc, it has become necessary in everyone's eyes.

We owe something to de Gaulle for having obliged Europe to

take its destiny into its own hands, to the United States for having understood that we had to draw on our common histories to keep hope alive.

Both seem to have meditated upon this Jesuit rule: "No constraint is tolerable except on the basis of a liberty exercised."

❖16❖

De Gaulle's Defense Policy and the United States from 1958–69

Pierre Messmer

It was the Algerian crisis that brought General de Gaulle back to power in 1958, and he wanted to solve this crisis. For almost four years, despite the protests, the acts of terrorism, and an attempt at "pronunciamiento," he unwaveringly followed the path that led to the Evian agreements, signed on 18 March 1962, giving Algeria her independence. General de Gaulle thought the colonial era was over. "Colonialism has no future anywhere, even in the USSR," he stated once. Who would argue otherwise today?

He knew that the modernization of the French army, a necessary condition for the grandeur of France, was subordinated to the needs of the ending colonial campaigns. In 1958, out of a military of over one million men, more than half were kept overseas (the proportion was the highest for the ground troops and the lowest for the Navy). The French forces outside of Algeria were, for the most part, assigned to NATO and thus under American command. Their heavy equipment – ships, airplanes, tanks – were, for the most part, American or built with essential American aid.

General de Gaulle didn't accept this position of dependence. His hands freed, he was able to pursue the defense policy that he had articulated several times before. For the record, I will cite two excerpts from his speech on 3 November 1959 at the Institut des Hautes Etudes de la Défense Nationale:

> "France's military defense must be French . . . her effort must be her own effort . . . it is indispensable that France defend herself on her own, for herself, and in her own way. . . . "

> "Obviously, we have to be able to acquire, during the next few years, a force capable of acting on our behalf . . . it is evident that a nuclear

> arsenal will be at the base of our force . . . which must belong to us. Since France can be destroyed from any point on Earth, our force must be able to strike any where. . . . "

Everything to be decided and accomplished in the next ten years was announced at that point.

This defense policy, which was in evident contradiction with that of the United States, caused tensions that had repercussions on all of Franco-American relations. The two most serious crises occurred over the issues of nuclear armament and the organization of NATO command.

My purpose is to trace briefly the causes, the developments, and the consequences of these two conflicts.

Under the Fourth Republic, research had been done on nuclear explosives and, after 1955, their manufacture had been actively prepared. The decision to proceed to a first nuclear explosion in the Sahara during the first trimester of 1960 was taken on 11 April 1958, one month before the return of General de Gaulle to power.

On these beginnings, historians already have a lot of material, and more will be available with the work currently underway under the supervision of Prof. Duroselle. But the governments of the Fourth Republic, whose precariousness led them to prudence, were discreet about their actions and even more about their intentions, which were deliberately kept vague. The United States, in principle hostile to any kind of nuclear proliferation, could therefore regard our projects, which some specialists thought wouldn't be completed for a long time, with courteous indifference.

Everything changed with General de Gaulle. On 1 February 1960, he saluted the Reggane explosion with a "Hurrah for France." Most importantly, the government presented the parliament with the first "program law relative to certain military equipment" (proposed on 18 July 1960, promulgated on December 8, published in the *Journal officiel* on December 10), which allocated 3,983 million francs to "special research whose objective is the realization of a powerful thermo-nuclear arsenal, while a medium-strength stock of nuclear bombs is rapidly constituted" (report of the presentation of the law). The same program allocated more than one billion francs for the production of Mirage IV bombers, 770 million for "research on special equipment" (missiles), and 250 million to start building the first nuclear-propelled submarine.

The French program of nuclear armament emerged from clandestinity because of a long-term financial investment. It became irreversible. In France, no one was fooled and the opposition expressed itself passionately on this issue in parliament.

The Senate rejected the project twice with a large majority of the vote. Prime Minister Michel Debré had to engage the responsibility of the government three successive times on this same project, using Article 49, paragraph 3, of our constitution, in order to obtain its adoption in the National Parliament.

While the parliamentary opposition parties – Communist, socialist, centrist, and far-right created a storm in France, the first American reactions, while no doubt hostile, stayed moderate. The United States was applying the prohibitions of the McMahon law of 1946 (amended in 1954 and 1958) to France. The application was rigorous with regard to arms since the Congress never recognized that we had made significant progress in this area. The enforcement was more flexible concerning submarines: the transfer of technology to the British was allowed, but it was denied to us. But the delivery of a small quantity of very enriched Uranium for the land-prototype of our reactor was allowed without much control, which helped us very much.

The less nuclear the arms we wanted were, the easier the dialogue was. The purchase of twelve KC 135 planes was authorized without any problem, even though it was known they would be used to re-supply our strategic bombers.

American diplomacy followed the same line. At the United Nations, it joined forces with those who asked us to halt our nuclear experiments; in Europe, it showed its approbation of our neighbors who criticized, by principle or by jealousy, our new policy of defense, but it avoided over-dramatizing. This relative moderation could be explained by the sentiment that the French would not be able to finish their projects, lacking scientific knowledge, technical capabilities, and financial resources.

When the senators questioned Admiral Rickover and asked him if French engineers would be capable of doing anything with the enriched Uranium that the French had asked for, he answered categorically: "Absolutely not." When Robert McNamara, whom I used to meet periodically at meetings of the NATO defense ministers, told me that the funds allotted in our program law for the construction of a Uranium enrichment factory at Pierrelatte, or to make strategic missiles, had to be multiplied by the number Pi (3.14159), he was right, but he hardly hid the fact that he wanted to discourage me.

Little by little, the climate became heavier. We launched more and more test missiles (28 from 1960 to 1969) and a new center was opened in 1966 in Mururoa, Polynesia. After the end of the Algerian war, the money saved by the reduction by almost half of the military personnel was used to increase the credits allocated to nuclear arms systems, which attained their highest level in 1967 – more than ten times in real-value those of 1960.

At the same time, the United States revised its strategy. On 16 June 1962, in a speech at the University of Michigan, Robert McNamara, the Secretary of Defense, defined the new American strategy of "flexible response," which we called the doctrine of gradual response. The French, like many Europeans, saw in it a veiled way of confining nuclear risks to Europe. De Gaulle opposed it, bluntly. His strategy consisted of reprisals on cities – the only dissuasive strategy, in his view.

A little bit later, it was President Kennedy's personal intervention that prevented British Prime Minister Macmillan from beginning an already planned cooperation on rockets with us. This resulted in a notable cooling of Franco-British relations.

A few days before the signing of the Moscow agreement of 5 August 1963 "on the prohibition of nuclear experimentation in the atmosphere, in space, and under water," President Kennedy wrote to General de Gaulle, asking him to remain open and reserve judgment. In exchange, he proposed to explore together "the paths which could render the three prohibited areas useless." General de Gaulle responded politely, but he refused to give up the experiments that were absolutely necessary. In reprisal, Washington began applying rigorously article 1, paragraph 2, of the Moscow treaty, which forbade the encouragement, in any way whatsoever, of all nuclear testing. He therefore did not allow the delivery of a big main-frame computer that was asked for in 1964 by the Commissariat for nuclear energy and that some thought might be used for military ends. The French government replied by deciding to manufacture it in France. In the end, the American administration canceled the embargo and the computer was delivered on the condition that it be used only for civilian purposes.

Throughout these deliberations, the construction and organization of French nuclear forces were continuing imperturbably. A second military program law covering the years 1965 to 1970 was voted by the parliament without too much difficulty. At the same time as the nuclear and later thermonuclear launchings, the tests and the manufacture of ballistic missiles were carried through. The rise of French power became tangible:

– in 1967, the 62 Mirage IV bombers carrying the A bomb became operational;

– in 1967, the "Redoutable," the first nuclear submarine missile launcher, and in 1969, "le Terrible" were completed; and

– in 1971, the first unit of surface-to-surface strategic ballistic missiles, implanted in the Alps, on the plateau d'Albion, was delivered.

Sooner or later, the United States would have to confront a de-facto situation that it hadn't wanted, but that it had to take into account.

The first step towards this recognition was taken by President Richard Nixon on his visit to Paris, on 28 February 1969. He made it known to General de Gaulle that he accepted the de-facto reality of the new French nuclear capacity. Henry Kissinger, who was accompanying him, simultaneously gave this information to the Minister of the Armies.

But meanwhile, another storm had shaken the relations between the two countries: the withdrawal of French forces from NATO command.

I will recall the facts only briefly because they are well known. Calling a press conference on 21 February 1966, for the first time since his reelection to the presidency of the Republic, General de Gaulle declared: "Our effort aims at reestablishing a normal situation of sovereignty in which what is French on the ground, in the air, under water, in forces, and all foreign elements in France, would be under the sole command of the French authorities."

This was perfectly clear and it meant the following: the withdrawal of French forces from NATO command, and the departure from French territory of the staffs, combat units, and foreign lines of communication, even if they were allied. Within the next year, these new policies were implemented.

What reasons did General de Gaulle have for such a grave decision? He had been cogitating the idea for a long time, as we know since he had withdrawn the French Navy in the Mediterranean from NATO on 7 March 1959. He gave the reasons himself: "Nothing can make an alliance remain the same when the conditions under which it was concluded have changed."[1] A

1. Press Conference on 21 February 1966.

statement more valid than ever today. What had changed for France in 1966? De Gaulle said it:

> "The perspective of a World War because of Europe is dissipating."[2]

> "Our country having become . . . by her own means a nuclear power, has reached the point of exercising herself the vast political and strategic responsibilities that are attached to this capacity."[3]

> "As for the military command which must bear the incomparable responsibility of commanding on the battle-field, if it ceased to hold this honor and this duty, if it was only an element in a hierarchy which wasn't ours, it would be the end of its authority, of its dignity, of its prestige in the eyes of the nation and therefore, in the eyes of the armies."[4]

For General Norstad and his successor General Lemnitzer, Supreme Allied Commanders, the third argument was the only one that seemed irrefutable. The former informed me of this during a meeting that our respective functions required we attend. In order to answer the problem, he suggested – most certainly with the agreement of his government – that a French officer be named Commander in Chief. But there was nothing in this proposal that could satisfy General de Gaulle.

In any event, the withdrawal of French forces from NATO, and the departure from France of the American and Canadian forces that were stationed there, stirred up real emotions in the United States and some concern from our European allies. In his memoirs, President Lyndon Johnson wrote: "What bothered me the most in De Gaulle's decision, was that it threatened the unity of NATO."

Soon, it became clear that the Atlantic Alliance in which France remained was in no way threatened and that the unity of NATO could be preserved. Some arrangements were concluded between the Chiefs of Staff – these were the Ailleret-Lemnitzer agreements, still in place today – to prepare the intervention of the French forces alongside their allies in case of conflict.

The crisis subsided.

Thirty years have passed since General de Gaulle defined the principles and the means of his defense policy for France. For the most part, this policy was maintained by his successors; France is

2. Ibid.
3. Ibid.
4. Speech at the Institut des Hautes Etudes de la Défense Nationale, on 3 November 1959.

a nuclear power and she didn't enter the integrated NATO command. Much better, today nobody seriously contests this policy, in neither Europe nor the United States. Thus, General de Gaulle won the battle, durably, over those who criticized him, inside and outside of France, especially the Americans.

Why, almost alone against all, did he succeed? Foremost, because he had the conviction that his policy of defense was a vital necessity for his country. Thus, he would yield to no pressure. On the contrary, for the United States, the Gaullist policy, as bothersome as it was, threatened in no way its national security. The American administration could then, with regrets but without any danger, wisely accept it, which eventually it did.

There is another reason, perhaps an even more important one. Contrary to many heads of state who, even in international relations, give priority to the short term, to the next election, to popularity polls, and to the moods of the media – in brief, to the tactical instead of the strategic – General de Gaulle made his decisions according to his idea of Frances's position in the world.

We know the tools he used to interpret events and, often, to predict them: respect for the human being and the rights of peoples to dispose of their own destinies, the strength of national sentiment compared to the fragility of empires. His decisive acts and his great speeches can be set in a historical perspective, in the long term, as it is easy to observe today in Eastern Europe. De Gaulle's foreign and defense policies were built on the bedrock of realities and certainties. Even though his policies may sometimes seem ambiguous, they make it possible to respond usefully to changing situations – and thus they are still solid today.

CHAPTER SIX

PUBLIC OPINION AND MUTUAL MISPERCEPTIONS

17

The Mischief-Maker: The American Media and De Gaulle, 1964–68

James Chace and Elizabeth Malkin

"In regard to de Gaulle," Roosevelt told Churchill on the eve of the American landing in North Africa in 1942, "I have hitherto enjoyed a quiet satisfaction leaving him in your hands."[1] That sense of satisfaction was soon to change. FDR was determined that the French government in metropolitan France would choose its leader after an American military occupation, and that leader would not necessarily be de Gaulle. To accomplish this, Roosevelt believed that "the United States has the whip hand."[2]

But Roosevelt was wrong. Not only did de Gaulle succeed in establishing himself as the incarnation of French republican legitimacy, but in so doing he managed to alienate Roosevelt and the other wartime leaders of the United States, Secretary of State Cordell Hull, and General George Marshall. Nor did de Gaulle intend to accept the secondary role Roosevelt had assigned France after the war, a France stripped of its colonies and dependent on the United States.

By the time of the Normandy landing in June 1944, de Gaulle was effectively in control of the French Committee of National Liberation that would soon become the provisional government

1. Cited in Robert Dallek, *Franklin Roosevelt and American Foreign Policy*, New York: Oxford University Press, 1979, p. 396.
2. Dallek, *op. cit.*, p. 377.

of liberated France. Yet FDR "would not now permit that 'jackenape' to seize the government," as he told Secretary of War Henry Stimson ten days after the allies had landed in France. Hull, according to Stimson, "hated de Gaulle so fiercely that he was almost incoherent on the subject." And when de Gaulle, not having been informed in advance of D-Day, refused to broadcast support of the invasion as it began, this put General Marshall into a "white fury."[3] FDR, during four days of talks with de Gaulle in Washington in June 1944, made it clear that France would have a reduced role in the postwar world and would lose some of her colonies; de Gaulle concluded, not surprisingly, that to regain her place, "France must count only on herself." Inevitably, de Gaulle's conception of France's postwar role clashed with Washington's view of France's national interest, and the institutional memories of de Gaulle's wartime dealings with the White House, the State Department, and the military were never wholly forgotten.

Always in the background was de Gaulle's suspicion of the cabalistic design of the Anglo-Saxons. Coupled with Great Britain's desire to maintain its "special relationship" with the United States, the stage was set for further conflict during the Eisenhower and Kennedy administrations, though both presidents came into office with the expectation that they could get along with the general.

While the American view of de Gaulle was by no means always negative – the romanticizing of the Free French during World War II reached new heights in two of Humphrey Bogart's most famous films, *Casablanca* and *To Have and Have Not* – the press later came to echo official opinion. In this respect, de Gaulle's fortunes waxed and waned as his leadership of the political movement, the RPF, which he headed in the 1940s and 50s, gave way to his role as the savior of France during the civil breakdown in May 1958, followed by his taming of the rebellious generals in 1961, and the settlement of the Algerian war in 1962.

With his domestic quarrels settled, the general then turned to his grand design of freeing France from military and political dependence on the United States, which, first of all, required France to withdraw from the NATO military command structure in Europe. (France remained within the Atlantic Alliance and relied on the U.S. security guarantee to Western Europe embod-

3. See also Dallek, *op. cit.*, p. 459.

ied in the 1949 North Atlantic treaty.) This also entailed moving forward with France's own nuclear capability and the establishment, under French leadership, of a continental system of military, political, and economic cooperation that necessarily excluded Great Britain, so long as the "special relationship" remained a British priority. By the mid-1960s, when General de Gaulle's aims collided with a whole host of American political, economic, and military policies, relations between the United States and France had grown so bitter that one American congressman proposed disinterring the thousands of American war-dead in France, transporting the bodies across the Atlantic Ocean, and burying them at home. According to Representative L. Mendel Rivers, a South Carolina Democrat, there was surely one cause of the acrimony between the traditional allies: Charles de Gaulle, "the most ungrateful man since Judas Iscariot betrayed his Christ."[4] Rivers and his colleagues on Capitol Hill, however, were merely reflecting a national mood, one which prompted women to return French-made handbags to New York department stores and Chicago restaurant owners to stop serving French wines.

The tensions had developed sharply after de Gaulle's first veto of Britain's entry into the Common Market in January 1963, and culminated with his 27 November 1967 press conference. That semi-annual lecture (as U.S. newspapers often called the splendidly stage-managed event) irritated even the more even-handed newspaper commentators. As columnist C. L. Sulzberger observed in *The New York Times* after the worst of the furor had died down, "This overinsistence on U.S. power and on the need for French 'independence' of it is having angry trans-Atlantic echoes."[5] Those echoes resounded off the portrayal of de Gaulle and his actions that Americans received through the U.S. media.

Beginning in 1966, when de Gaulle withdrew France from the integrated military command of the North Atlantic Treaty Organization, he appeared to be increasingly hostile towards the United States. His criticism of U.S. involvement in Vietnam, his call for a return to the gold standard and an end to the dominance of the dollar, his stance on the Middle East, his two vetoes against British entry into the European Economic Community, his seemingly inexplicable support for Quebec's liberation, and his singularly

4. *The New York Times*, 8 December 1967.
5. *The New York Times*, 11 February 1968.

imperial style all contributed to ill-feeling in the United States. The uproar prompted one American journalist in Paris to produce a short book making "the case for de Gaulle," in which he argued "if the citizens of our democracy adopt en masse a paranoic delusion, it can only be because they have been poorly informed."[6]

A study of how several publications interpreted a number of flashpoints in Franco-American relations between 1964 and 1968 suggests the way many Americans understood the disputes over NATO, Vietnam, the international monetary system, and the Middle East. Much of the commentary surrounding the issues did little to challenge vague prejudices against a politician who was somehow "not on our side." The views in *The New York Times*, *Time* magazine, the *St. Louis Post-Dispatch*, and *The Chicago Tribune* do not present a monolithic image of de Gaulle, but they all demonstrate a growing exasperation in attempting to understand French foreign policy.

NATO

It should have come as no surprise to American reporters who followed European affairs when de Gaulle announced, at a 21 February 1966 news conference, that France intended to claim sovereignty over troops on its soil and French troops abroad. Since his 1958 proposal to establish a three-power directorate with the United States and Britain had been rejected, de Gaulle had been disengaging France from NATO's integrated military command, beginning with the French Mediterranean fleet and the refusal to permit nuclear weapons in France unless under French control. It was not a policy designed to win sympathy with American editorialists. After de Gaulle withdrew French officers from NATO's naval staff in April 1964, *The Chicago Tribune* weighed in with isolationist irritation:

> De Gaulle could be doing the United States a favor. If his doctrines are adopted, the defense of Europe would revert to the Europeans and there would then be no reason to retain large American forces on the continent.[7]

When de Gaulle carried out his plans to leave the alliance command, notifying allied leaders by letter in the second week of

6. John L. Hess, *The Case for De Gaulle: An American Viewpoint* (New York: William Morrow and Company, Inc., 1968) p. 1.
7. *The Chicago Tribune*, 4 May 1964.

March 1966, the *Tribune* struck an aggressive editorial note that characterized much of the press opinion surrounding the French decision:

> He may calculate that even if American forces are removed from France they will still have to defend it. And with French security thus presumably assured, he feels free to take time off for another exercise in French sovereignty and personal vanity. He thinks he can eat his cake and have it, too. [. . . H]e had better be prepared to defend France himself.[8]

Time concluded that de Gaulle's move would not ultimately affect the defense of Europe, and argued that in waiting to remain part of the alliance, he would be able to "have NATO's defense for France and kick it, too."[9] C. L. Sulzberger, who generally sought to explain de Gaulle's policies in some detail, maintained that the withdrawal

> doesn't sacrifice French claims to U.S. protection in any ultimate crunch. [. . .]De Gaulle's alliance policy, is, as I have said earlier, to have and eat his cake, and so far it works.[10]

The reasoning behind de Gaulle's policy, according to much of the U.S. media commentary, was a narrow and potentially destructive nineteenth-century nationalism, an ideology Americans unhesitatingly associated with Europe's wars. French nationalism, as Americans knew of it, contrasted with what was seen as the benevolent U.S. attempt to promote "internationalism." *The Washington Post* said:

> It is an odd kind of greatness that must assert itself through an effort to pull down the structure that 15 nations, acting in concert, have so arduously built for their common defense.[11]

The implication here was that de Gaulle was a "maverick" (in the words of *The New Orleans Times-Picayune*)[12] and would find little support for his views elsewhere in Europe. Those views were seen as disruptive and potentially dangerous. *The Chicago Tribune*, characteristically, reminded readers of the Communist threat de Gaulle could be provoking. A military analysis by Wayne Thomas warned:

8. Ibid., 10 March 1966.
9. *Time*, 18 March 1966.
10. *The New York Times*, 17 June 1966.
11. Quoted in *The New York Times*, 13 March 1966.

> In the view of [the] Frenchmen [who believe in NATO] and of the people of the other European nations in NATO, communist encroachments would follow any breakdown in the common front, despite de Gaulle's apparent belief that no longer is there a Russian threat to western Europe.[13]

Thomas was certainly abusing his poetic license in summing up the fears of millions of Europeans, steeling themselves against the Communist menace. But he was writing for a readership that saw global politics in an exclusively Cold War context. De Gaulle's own context – his aspirations for France and his vision of a world that was not dominated by the superpowers' ideological crusades – did not fit that framework.

There was a slightly different tack to some editorializing, one which might have been reflecting the Johnson administration's attempt to put the best face on the affair by describing the French withdrawal from NATO as an opportunity to reform the alliance. Tempering the criticism of de Gaulle's obstructionism came a recognition that NATO had not, perhaps, been flexible enough to changing conditions, particularly the loosening of ties between the Soviet Union and Eastern Europe seen at the time. An editorial in the *St. Louis Post-Dispatch* argued:

> Much as American leaders may hate to admit it, de Gaulle is right when he says the alliance needs revision to meet present-day needs. The *extreme nationalism* he stands for does not offer the best basis for adjustment, but neither does a desperate American commitment to things as they used to be.[14]

In *The New York Times*, news analyses and editorials portrayed de Gaulle's move as a harmful and expensive annoyance that would only isolate France, but writers also found blame for the United States. Hanson Baldwin wrote in a Sunday news analysis:

> President de Gaulle, as a jealous guardian of French greatness, has been the catalyzer. [. . .]But many other factors have contributed. The erosion of time has been one of them; the alliance has been too static, tending to meet the problems of today with policies evolved to meet the far different policies of yesterday. The United States has contributed in the past, by major mistakes and clumsy diplomacy, to what many Americans regard as General de Gaulle's dogmatism.[15]

12. Ibid., 13 March 1966.
13. *The Chicago Tribune*, 20 March 1966.
14. The *St. Louis Post-Dispatch*, 26 February 1966.
15. *The New York Times*, 13 March 1966.

And an editorial questioned whether de Gaulle was completely alone in his view of NATO, noting that the "French President strikes a responsive chord in Europe when he says NATO's machinery was erected to meet a Soviet threat different from the present one."[16]

Two strands emerge from this varied commentary. The first is a portrayal of de Gaulle's move as capricious and ultimately damaging to the U.S. effort to maintain a strong alliance against the Eastern bloc. The French president's anachronistic nationalism, according to this view, had cut France off from the Atlantic community even though he was still depending on NATO's protection. At its most visceral level, this approach frames the issue as one of "How dare he?", not "Why does he dare?" The other line of analysis makes a pass at the second question, although it does not take up de Gaulle's challenge to the whole structure of existing collective security arrangements. *The New York Times* editorials, for example, chipped away at the belief that all the NATO allies were in harmony over the organization's structure. The basic assumption that the world was divided into two competing blocs was not questioned, but the concerns de Gaulle's move had raised over Washington's policies within the Western bloc were at least noted.

GOLD

While de Gaulle's withdrawal from NATO's integrated military command involved a series of dramatic events, his challenge to what he perceived as U.S. economic hegemony, played out in the arcane world of international finance, received sporadic coverage. His attack began in 1965 when he called for a return to the gold standard and the government began converting dollars into gold. The commentary was quick to ridicule the general's apparent devotion to the archaic notion of the gold standard – *Times* columnist Russell Baker joked about de Gaullefinger – but was wary of the damage the gold-buying policy could do to the international monetary system. *The New York Times* acknowledged weaknesses in the system, which used the dollar (and the pound, to some extent) as reserve currencies, but called de Gaulle's franc diplomacy "disconcerting."[17] Marquis Childs, a Washington cor-

16. Ibid., 13 March 1966.
17. *The New York Times*, 5 February 1965.

respondent for the *St. Louis Post-Dispatch*, warned de Gaulle could make the dollar drain intolerable and admonished:

> One way to bring about disaster is to set nation against nation in the tangled world of money and finance. [. . . D]e Gaulle boasted that the European Common Market now has more gold than the United States. [. . . This] is calculated to stir all our nationalism and our resentment that an ally in two wars should be so disdainful.[18]

After de Gaulle rejected a U.S. proposal for a world conference to consider reforms in the system in July 1965 and continued buying gold [i.e., selling dollars] throughout most of 1966, the commentary became harsher. He was seen as rigidly committed to an impossible policy, and one description – "mischief-making" – stuck. Edwin Dale explained in *The New York Times* Sunday Week in Review section:

> As in other areas, General de Gaulle has been fairly successful as a nay-sayer in economic matters, but he has not been particularly successful in imposing France's will on other countries. There is not the slightest chance, for example, that the world will return to settlements only in gold for international transactions.[19]

But the purpose behind de Gaulle's policy, destabilizing as it might have been, was not entirely dismissed as unreasonable. C. L. Sulzberger described the French gold hoard as a monetary "force de frappe," akin to France's independent nuclear force. By stockpiling gold, de Gaulle was creating insurance for France against a depression, or revaluation, and enhancing France's status as an international financial power against U.S. dominance. That dominance was symbolized by the dollar's role as a reserve currency and American investments in European industries. Sulzberger concluded, "The mere fact that his monetary or his nuclear policies embarrass Washington while giving Paris more maneuverability simply makes them more piquant for the general."[20]

It was after Britain devalued the pound in November 1967 that de Gaulle's policy took on a more ominous and underhanded significance. An editorial in the *St. Louis Post-Dispatch* stated, "The French piously disclaim attacks on either the pound or the dollar, but their activities belie them."[21] A news analysis in *The*

18. *St. Louis Post-Dispatch*, 7 February 1965.
19. *The New York Times*, 25 July 1965.
20. Ibid., 28 August 1966, 26 January 1967.
21. *St. Louis Post-Dispatch*, 27 November 1967.

New York Times business section by reporter Richard Mooney presented de Gaulle's motives as deliberately destructive:

> It may not be within General de Gaulle's power to whittle 'the Anglo-Saxons' and their money down. It would be painful for the world if he succeeded, because the strength of Western Europe and the rest of the Western world are inextricably related to the strength of the United States. But neither the impracticality nor the inadvisability of the general's objective has kept him from harrassing.[22]

New York Times Paris correspondent Henry Tanner noted

> a wide consensus that the French Government, on instructions from President de Gaulle, has gone out of its way to make things difficult for Britain and through Britain, for the United States.[23]

Overwhelmed by this sort of commentary was any clear discussion of weaknesses in a system that enabled Britain and the United States to maintain persistent balance-of-payments deficits. Richard Mooney's analysis did note that "Parisians and some other Europeans think that there are mischief-makers and worse in Washington." And a *Times* editorial pointed out that de Gaulle had exposed the

> weaknesses in what he considers to be 'Anglo-Saxon' hegemony in international financial arrangements. [. . .] So long as (Britain and the United States) are in balance of payments difficulties they cannot hope to regain the political leverage that goes with strength. The only way to curb de Gaulle's undeniable capacity for making mischief is by eliminating the problems that have fostered it.[24]

But as in the case of France's withdrawal from NATO's command structure, de Gaulle had succeeded only very modestly in forcing discussion in the U.S. media of the status quo as it related to France. His seeming intransigence submerged any debate over his purposes and larger issues. Ultimately, the "nuisance value" of de Gaulle's tactics served to obscure his aims.[25]

VIETNAM

De Gaulle's criticism of U.S. involvement in Vietnam, delivered in increasingly self-righteous terms, produced perhaps the most

22. *The New York Times*, 22 November 1967.
23. Ibid., 25 November 1967.
24. Ibid., 28 November 1967.
25. Stanley Hoffmann, *Decline or Renewal? France Since the 1930s* (New York: The Viking Press, 1974), p. 301, for discussion of "nuisance value."

diversity in opinions on any of the issues troubling Franco-American relations. The range of response in the U.S. media reflected the deep divisions within the United States itself over the war. Beginning with his call for the neutralization of the Indochinese states in early 1964, through to his June 1967 speech blaming the Arab-Israeli War on the war in Vietnam, de Gaulle irked the U.S. government and prompted reactions from praise to condemnation in the U.S. media. A *The New York Times* editorial of 1 February 1964 said, "it would be wise for the United States now to welcome rather than to resent General de Gaulle's renewed interest in the Vietnamese problem." On the same page, in contrast, C. L. Sulzberger remarked that "it is infinitely regrettable that de Gaulle chose to apply his views unilaterally at our expense." One theme that ran through much of the more critical commentary on de Gaulle's position was irritation that the French, given their colonial history, would have the nerve to tell the United States what to do. *Time* wrote:

> De Gaulle made it sound as if Americans had wanted to move into the Indo-Chinese mess – and not, as was really the case, that the United States entered the scene with great reluctance to salvage something from the mess left behind by the disastrously defeated French.[26]

The conflict over Vietnam flared again in September 1966 after de Gaulle's speech in Pnom Penh, in which he called for a U.S. commitment to withdrawing its troops. If Americans had ever doubted de Gaulle's intentions, this editorial in *The Philadelphia Inquirer* belligerently aimed to set the record straight:

> Charles de Gaulle has shown himself, in every way possible and on every possible occasion, the implacable enemy of this country. He has been viciously hostile on the Vietnam situation; has sided openly with the North Vietnamese and the Chinese Communist regime at Peking; and has called for U.S. withdrawal from South Vietnam. [. . .] Heeding his advice on what to do about the enemy in Vietnam would be the height of folly.[27]

If, instead, Americans were looking for a standard-bearer to confront their own government's policy, they could find one in the *St. Louis Post-Dispatch* portrayal of de Gaulle in Cambodia:

> The United States does not enjoy particularly cordial relations with the French President, partly because General de Gaulle has had the courage to pursue policies the United States opposes. But in the con-

26. *Time*, 31 July 1964.
27. Quoted in *The New York Times*, 4 September 1966.

> text of Indochina the General's independence, as well as his intimate knowledge of the former French possession and has sane views as to its future, could be of great value to the United States.[28]

Three days later, the *Post-Dispatch* expressed its hope that Washington was listening to de Gaulle's advice, which "stemmed from a realistic view of the facts."

Where the commentary was rather less favorable, de Gaulle was treated with suspicion. *The New York Times* worried that he might follow up with a diplomatic initiative and advised the Johnson administration to "accent the positive in its response" to a Prince Sihanouk-de Gaulle communique.[29] *Time* found the message "characteristically unhelpful" and resented de Gaulle's comparison with the French withdrawal from Algeria. The Algerian comparison seemed particularly unjust to American defenders of the war in Vietnam, who saw no connection between a colonial situation and what they considered the struggle against Communist aggression.[30]

De Gaulle increased the pressure at an October news conference, where *New York Times* correspondent Henry Tanner noted a much harsher tone and remarked that de Gaulle "seized not one" opportunity "to say nice things or to sound reassuring."[31] That was hardly de Gaulle's style. *The Chicago Tribune* editorial board had no patience at all for the French president, who was fully prepared to let all Vietnam fall to Communism, according to an editorial titled "Cracked Record." De Gaulle's observations were "so predictable" that they hardly merited comment, the newspaper said.[32] This Cold War accusation demonstrated most clearly how easily de Gaulle was first labeled anti-American and therefore barely distinguishable from a Communist sympathizer. Such reasoning categorically rejected any consideration of de Gaulle's foreign policy on its own terms, ignoring even the simplest exposition of his views.

THE MIDDLE EAST

The end of 1966 appeared to mark the beginning of the final and most intractable phase of disintegrating Franco-American rela-

28. *St. Louis Post-Dispatch*, 1 September 1966.
29. *The New York Times*, 3 September 1966.
30. Hoffmann, op. cit., p. 345.
31. *The New York Times*, 29 October 1966.
32. *The Chicago Tribune*, 29 October 1966.

tions; de Gaulle's stance in the Six-Day War and towards Israel highlighted all that separated French and American foreign policy. He condemned Israel as the aggressor, linked the hostilities in the Middle East to the war in Vietnam, and courted the Arab nations. In U.S. newspapers, he was now portrayed as dangerously irrational, obsessed with American power, and increasingly irrelevant. A *New York Times* editorial found "elements of perception" in the Vietnam-Middle East connection, noting that the war in Southeast Asia undermined international cooperation and heightened tensions. But that acknowledgment did not temper the criticism:

> The extreme and accusatory position taken by President de Gaulle on the Middle East situation did nothing to enhance the grandeur of France or to advance the cause of peace. [. . .] It is too bad President de Gaulle has allowed his personal antagonism against the United States thus to pervert his innate good manners, logic and sense of justice.[33]

The Chicago Tribune, titling its editorial "De Gaulle Ceases To Be Funny," remarked that de Gaulle's trick of

> taking two unrelated wars and making them one, and then saying that the resulting product is all the fault of the United States is not an achievement of which French logic may be proud.

The editorial described the Middle East as a "prime target" for Communist expansionary moves and concluded that "as reality has no place in [de Gaulle's] gallery of prejudices, he simply gives it a lordly command to vanish."[34] *Time* accused "le grand Charles" of sulking and then taking out his pique in public, calling it "the ludicrous sight of a disappointed politician trying to talk himself into a position of prominence."[35]

The New York Times did advance one interpretation of de Gaulle's Middle East policy, arguing that he had "been acting as if to try to correct the balance," but warned that his moves had "exacerbated rather than helped a dangerous situation."[36] Indeed, according to one scholar's analysis, balance was exactly what de Gaulle was seeking: fearing a perpetuation of the superpower confrontation in the Middle East, de Gaulle tried to return to the equilibrium that he considered to have been broken. Since the Israeli victory had given the advantage to the United States, he chose to realign with Egypt before the Soviet Union stepped in.[37]

33. *The New York Times*, 24 June 1967.
35. *Time*, 30 June 1967.
36. *The New York Times*, 2 July 1967.
37. Hoffmann, op. cit., pp. 346–48.

Whatever the aims of de Gaulle's policy, the effect of it, as far as U.S. media commentary was concerned, was to eliminate any influence he may still have had in international affairs; if de Gaulle scorned the facts of the bipolar world order as it was being played out in the Middle East, then his opinions, based as they were upon illusion, carried no weight. *Time* said de Gaulle had been "exposed as an emperor without clothes" during the crisis. "Suddenly it turned out to be unimportant for anybody to take his advice or even listen politely."[38] *New York Times* correspondent Henry Tanner perceived that French officials were losing confidence in the president's ability to "influence and perhaps change" events:

> General de Gaulle, one close observer of the Elysée says, has come to prefer being right to being influential, and his statements now are philosophical and moral judgments more than practical political advice.[39]

Americans, however, do not take kindly to moral judgments that affect their interests and values.

The hostility to de Gaulle reached its most intense with his press conference of 27 November 1967, when he described Jews as "an elite people, self-confident and domineering" during a discussion of the Middle East. Although he also vetoed British entry into the Common Market for a second time and outlined his plans for an independent Quebec at that news conference, it was the comment on the Jews that generated the strongest response, both in France and in the United States. De Gaulle, according to one editorial in *The New York Times*, appeared to have lost any claim at all to understanding reality: "President de Gaulle's press conference this week suggests once again that as his years increase, so do his ambitions, his illusions, and also his cynicism." The editorial accused him of using blatant anti-Canadian and anti-Semitic propaganda, found a "kind of anachronistic nationalistic imperialism" in his approaches to the Québecois that was "strongly reminiscent of the Hitlerian approaches to Austrians and German-speaking Czechs," and warned a "stern test may be ahead for the forces of French democracy and decency" in their opposition to anti-Semitism.[40] This was language calculated to demolish whatever standing de Gaulle may still have

38. *Time*, 21 July 1967.
39. *The New York Times*, 2 July 1967.
40. *The New York Times*, 3 December 1967.

had as a statesman in American eyes. Even the reporting of the news conference itself in *The New York Times* left no doubt about de Gaulle's perceived prejudices; he was described as "more combative and defiantly nationalistic than ever before," and correspondent Henry Tanner found that "the sharp edge of President de Gaulle's anti-Americanism showed when he declared that Europe could not afford to be weakened by discussions with Britain."[41]

Time did not hesitate to call de Gaulle's comment on the Jews anti-Semitic and noted that "the general's skeins of rationality grew considerably tangled in spots."[42] Four months earlier, *Time* had conceded that de Gaulle's policies "usually contain a degree of rationality," and found a "Machiavellian kind of sense" in de Gaulle's efforts to improve relations with the Arab countries, although the magazine wondered at his Quebec escapade.[43] By the end of the year, however, de Gaulle had lost all sense of reason for the writers at *Time*.

It is worth noting that even at this point in the Franco-American relationship, where the image of de Gaulle was at its most insulting, the commentary in the U.S. media varied. The *St. Louis Post-Dispatch*, for example, did not pick up on de Gaulle's discussion of the Middle East or Canada, but focused instead on the longstanding concerns raised by the veto of Britain and continued attacks on American power. As a result, the shift in tone from earlier stories was not quite as marked as it was in *The New York Times* or *Time*. The newspaper did not have a correspondent in Paris, where de Gaulle's description of the Jews and its aftermath received close coverage. Instead, correspondent Thomas Ottenad wrote in a news analysis from Washington:

> With ruthless realism, the French President saw an opportunity to hit the British when they were down and at the same time aim a glancing blow at the United States. [. . . He] restated two favorite themes – forestall any challenge from Britain within Europe and weaken America's pre-eminent position in the Western world. These are his constant weapons in his unchanging if futile effort to restore the ancient grandeur that was France.[44]

41. *The New York Times*, 28 November 1967.
42. *Time*, 8 December 1967.
43. *Time*, 4 August 1967
44. *St. Louis Post-Dispatch*, 4 December 1967.

The U.S. Media and De Gaulle

We began by stating that the views of de Gaulle presented by the U.S. media were not monolithic; the shifts of opinion between 1964 and 1968 are not easily delineated. And, as the commentary on Vietnam particularly showed, de Gaulle's policies and statements were analyzed in terms of quite different assumptions surrounding each issue. The *St. Louis Post-Dispatch* and *The Chicago Tribune*, although both newspapers of that nebulous realm known as the American heartland, took very distinct approaches to de Gaulle and his policies. Within the same newspaper, different interpretations from editorial boards, columnists, and correspondents in Washington and Paris jostled for prominence. The complexity of some of the issues, such as the international monetary system, made for facile explanations. The historical and ideological baggage weighing on others, such as Vietnam and the special relationship with Britain, defy cold analysis. Despite the variegated treatment de Gaulle received in the press, however, the U.S. media's reactions to Gaullist policy and rhetoric did reveal some basic tendencies.

Before the NATO crisis, much of the discussion surrounding de Gaulle's foreign policy was focused on de Gaulle's motivations. *Time* wrote after de Gaulle recognized the Peking government in January 1964:

> Where de Gaulle may be doing a service to the United States is in forcing it to make clearer just what its internationalism means. At any rate, it is certain that de Gaulle does not recognize Red China or do anything else merely to stick his thumb in Washington's eye. His moves may be foolish or dangerous, but they are never so infantile.[45]

Here, de Gaulle's purposes and his actions were separated. The French president may have been wrong in endangering a collective policy, the article implied, but he had reasons that were perhaps rather more sophisticated than simple vindictiveness. In the same article, *Time* noted that

> the French base their international relations on mutual interests, and when that is not convenient, on French interests alone. [. . .] There is a clear and explicit blueprint in de Gaulle's own writings.

Time was hinting at something here which was perhaps the most overlooked element in much of the discussion of de Gaulle – the

45. *Time*, 7 February 1964.

nature of French society and the political culture that had given rise to such a personality. The "great man" notion of history serves journalists well, limited as they are by the immediacy of their profession. But the great men cannot be seen apart from the people they claim to lead. De Gaulle often was.

Other explanations of de Gaulle's foreign policy dispensed even more simplistically with the reasons for his actions and moved directly to their results – namely, the dangers they posed to Franco-American relations and to the smooth operating of the alliance. *St. Louis Post-Dispatch* Washington correspondent Thomas Ottenad summed up de Gaulle's basic objective as "the recapture of some of the glory and grandeur once held by his proud nation and giving France a greater voice in world affairs." But he warned:

> If de Gaulle continues what many Americans regard as deliberate slights aimed at this country, a bitter, anti-French sentiment could easily emerge.[46]

In another approach, a news analysis in *The New York Times* by Max Frankel, written from Washington and titled "The Riddle of De Gaulle," broke down the problem of understanding the French president into knowing his ends and observing his means:

> It is easy [. . .] to conclude that the Gaullist purpose is to pursue status for France and to make her a first-rate power that will be consulted on major world questions and whose primacy in Europe is beyond question. But the means by which the general pursues that ambition are not inevitable and not even always predictable.[47]

As relations worsened, the study of de Gaulle's purposes were overwhelmed by a series of actions that so inflamed Franco-American relations that the U.S. media concentrated completely on his tactics and their effects. This was an analysis that reflected the American preoccupation with the matter at hand, rather than de Gaulle's designs, his long-range vision, and his indifference to immediate success.[48] American journalists may have perceived the Gaullist attempt to disengage regional conflicts from the superpower grip, but de Gaulle's sharp attacks on the United

46. *St. Louis Post-Dispatch*, 8 March 1964.
47. *The New York Times*, 16 March 1964.
48. Stanley Hoffmann, *Decline or Renewal? France Since the 1930s* (New York: The Viking Press, 1974), pp. 318, 328.

States came increasingly to be described on their own. They created their own context, divorced from the policy principles editorialists and columnists had once tentatively sought to outline. De Gaulle's stance provoked an overreaction in U.S. public opinion, one that defined French foreign policy as simply anti-American.[49] Ultimately, the question of whether de Gaulle was satisfied merely with promoting French power or whether he needed also to chip away at U.S. power came to serve as the U.S. media's basic exposition of French foreign policy.

By 1966, the emphasis on the tactics of de Gaulle's foreign policy meant that whatever coherence was to be found in his overall design was completely obscured by his conflicting strategies. C. L. Sulzberger, who had carefully analyzed de Gaulle's foreign policy throughout the 1960s, was reduced to this simplification:

> This fear that France and Europe might be dominated by the USA has become obsessive. [. . .] For de Gaulle is firmly committed to prune American influence wherever, whenever and however he can, even joining our adversaries to do so, because for him, we have become too powerful, and that, in his eyes, is dangerous for France. In the Gaullist lexicon our sin is being strong, not hostile.[50]

A *St. Louis Post-Dispatch* editorial pointed out that "others certainly are weary of a frustrating accommodation to an aging autocrat's idiosyncrasies."[51] He was now seen as so remote from the realities of global politics that *New York Times* humor columnist Russell Baker joked after the November 1967 press conference, "President de Gaulle's announcement that France would withdraw from earth was hardly unexpected."[52] One analyst even argued that de Gaulle was organizing a campaign to bring down the United States, which was already weakened by the war in Vietnam, and "divide the spoils of the American empire." That view, outlined in an article by Harold Kaplan in *The New Leader*, was summarized and disseminated in a *Time* article at the beginning of 1968.[53] By this point, de Gaulle's foreign policy had been distilled and distorted to one basic element – the destruction of U.S. power – and carried to its logical extreme.

49. Edward A. Kolodziej, *French International Policy under De Gaulle and Pompidou* (Ithaca, N.Y.: Cornell University Press, 1974), p. 574.
50. *The New York Times*, 23 July 1967.
51. *St. Louis Post-Dispatch*, 24 June 1967.
52. *The New York Times*, 30 November 1967.
53. *Time*, 12 January 1968.

By the end of 1967, before internal disruptions in France and the United States distracted attention from the animosity between them, de Gaulle's vision for France had been all but lost in the commentary. In de Gaulle's approach to international politics, style was policy, rhetoric a form of action, and style, which, however, was not the sum of policy, overwhelmed everything else. If de Gaulle was to use foreign policy as the stage from which to project French grandeur, then he needed an audience.[54] His audience across the Atlantic, however, may have missed the message for the maneuverings, the end-game for the brilliant moves de Gaulle made across the international chessboard.

54. Hoffmann, *op. cit.*, p. 287; see also chapter 8 for the discussion of de Gaulle as a political artist.

18

Walter Lippmann and Charles De Gaulle

Ronald Steel

"I cannot pretend to write dispassionately about General de Gaulle," wrote Walter Lippmann in 1960 in frank acknowledgment of the intense admiration he felt and so vividly expressed in his syndicated newspaper column.[1] Among all of Europe's leaders, de Gaulle was probably the least understood and the least respected by Washington officials. Lippmann, the most influential journalist of his day, was one of the few in his profession to take de Gaulle seriously, to understand his historical role, and to explain his intentions without prejudice or partisanship. He did this in the face of considerable disapproval, and even hostility, from U.S. government officials not only because he admired de Gaulle's global vision, but also because he saw the general as the incarnation of a restored France and a revitalized Europe. For Lippmann, the French leader was not a *poseur*, as he was for Franklin Roosevelt, or a troublemaker, as he was for FDR's successors, but a man of vision and integrity whose views merited attention because they were based on a profound understanding of history and civilizations. Through his prestigious column, which was a kind of Bible for American opinion-makers, Lippmann played a crucial role in explaining, and even justifying, Gaullist policies that were often opposed by the American government. No one else in American public life so admired de Gaulle; no one else was nearly so influential in presenting the Gaullist view to the American public.

1. "Today and Tomorrow," Lippmann's syndicated newspaper column, 21 April 1960 (hereafter referred to as T&T).

LIPPMANN'S FRANCE

Lippmann's appreciation of de Gaulle as political leader and statesman was rooted in Lippmann's view of France both within Europe and in the larger world. For Lippmann, France was always and indisputably one of the great powers. The political construction of Europe was impossible without the participation of a democratic and unified France. Similarly, France had a determinant role to play upon the world stage. To his mind, no important question of European politics or security could be answered without French involvement. "Let us not imagine," he wrote during World War II, "that the rest of Europe, which has always looked to France, is not watching how we treat France. Let us not imagine that Europe can be resettled without the full participation of France, and without the influence which France alone can exert."[2]

Lippmann considered France not only a dominant player in Europe, but of key importance to America's global interests. Both as a colonial power during World War II and the early years that followed, and as a post-colonial power with worldwide interests, France was a vital partner. "France," Lippmann reminded his readers in 1943, "is a member of the great defensive system in which the American republics live. . . . The security of France is an American interest, and the security of the American position is a French interest."[3]

Lippmann was a Gaullist not only because he admired the general's vision and character, but also because the general incarnated the view of France in which Lippmann so firmly believed. The importance that Lippmann attached to France is evident in his earliest comments after the fall of France in June 1940. In the terrible moment of defeat and cowardice, it was de Gaulle who stepped forward to claim what remained of the French ideal, and Lippmann who hailed him. Events had shown, he wrote in 1940, "how thoroughly right were the Frenchmen who wished to retire to northern Africa and continue the war, how grossly mistaken were those Frenchmen who brought about the capitulation of France."[4]

Lippmann was first drawn to de Gaulle because the general stood in such striking contrast to those French officials who

2. T&T, 26 June 1943.

3. Lippmann: *US Foreign Policy: Shield of the Republic* (Boston, Little Brown & Co.), 1943, pp. 131–32.

4. T&T, 14 December 1940.

"made the terrible mistake of thinking they could ingratiate themselves with the victors by rendering themselves completely helpless." They surrendered not only France, which was overrun, but the empire and the fleet as well. "They surrendered," he continued,

> also their moral position by the unprecedented folly of hastening to fasten upon themselves the guilt for war and to exonerate their conquerors. They were misled into believing that the more impotent they were, the better terms they would receive. No greater error was ever committed by an intelligent people. Had they followed the advice of General de Gaulle, continued their resistance from Africa and Asia Minor and on the seas, they would at the very least have had some power with which to negotiate. . . . [5]

Despite resistance to de Gaulle in Washington, Lippmann stressed his importance as an alternative to the collaborationist Vichy regime. The capitulation of France meant not only the consolidation of Nazi rule on the continent, but the possibility of German control of French economic and military assets around the world. This also had serious repercussions for the postwar world, for it would compromise the role that France could play. The participation of the Gaullist-led Fighting French forces meant, Lippmann wrote in late 1940, that "instead of a French government at Vichy which is the prisoner of Germany, there would be an independent French government on free French territory to which the French people would look for their liberation."[6] Further, a compromised France would be unable to help rebuild postwar Europe. For this reason, the U.S. and Britain needed Frenchmen unsullied by collaboration and were "compelled for their own survival to liberate France and to foster the restoration of the power of France."[7]

For the Roosevelt administration, de Gaulle was a nuisance and was treated with a disdain bordering on contempt. Lippmann was so distressed by this treatment that he complained directly to FDR's roving ambassador. There was "no reason in the world" why the Gaullists should be dealt with "so rudely and inhumanely," he wrote Norman Davis.[8] Having threatened to go public unless the situation was remedied, Lippmann followed

5. T&T, 17 September 1940.

6. Ibid.

7. *US Foreign Policy, op cit.*, p. 132.

8. Lippmann to Norman Davis, 31 January 1942, Lippmann Collection, Yale University library.

through a few months later, in July 1942, when he publicly called on Washington to recognize de Gaulle's organization as a "necessary and critical move in the development of a Western front in Europe" once Allied troops were landed.[9] In October, he went even further by publicly calling for a provisional government in North Africa "under the leadership of that man of proven faith, General Charles de Gaulle."[10]

The view of France that led Lippmann to champion the liberation movement during World War II also caused him to defend French independence of action – even when deemed hostile to prevalent conceptions of American interest – during the Fifth Republic. De Gaulle as president stood apart and aloof, seeking to play the role of independent power broker within Europe, between Europe and America. Though this angered Atlanticist policymakers, and while Lippmann did not always support de Gaulle's actions, he understood and explained to Americans the Gaullist drive for independence. "France stands apart because France is able to stand apart," he wrote in 1964.

> No European really likes to be dependent on Washington. But for the time being at least, France alone has solved the problems which preoccupy and divert the other [European powers]. France has liquidated its empire. France has strengthened and stabilized its financial position. France has induced a high level of economic growth. . . . The main preoccupation of Gaullist France has not been her territorial unity, as in Germany. It has not been, since Algerian independence, what to do with the remnants of an imperial past, as in Britain. The main preoccupation [. . .] has been the restoration of French self-respect and self-confidence.[11]

THE "SOUL OF FRANCE"

It was in August 1942 on a trip to London that Lippmann, already halfway into de Gaulle's camp, fell all the way. The general, alerted to the columnist's sympathetic position by his Washington emissary, René Pleven, and well aware of his importance, treated Lippmann to an hour of dazzling monologue, displaying the grasp for history and language that later impressed so many. Lippmann emerged from the meeting convinced that France had found a leader worthy of its nobler qualities.

9. T&T, 16 July 1942.
10. T&T, 28 October 1942.
11. "What Preoccupies Europeans," *Newsweek*, 21 December 1964.

On his return to New York, Lippmann spoke at the Foch memorial dinner of the French-American Club. Describing de Gaulle and his French National Committee as the "true leaders of the French nation," he compared de Gaulle to George Washington and declared that the administration would be "guilty of an inconceivable folly if we failed to use the military genius of this extraordinary man." If American officials found de Gaulle intractable, he suggested, it was because "they have lacked the historical imagination to appreciate his position." "In his own eyes and in the eyes of the bravest and the truest of the French, he is charged with the exalted mission of restoring the liberty, the greatness and the honor of France," Lippmann explained. "He cannot fulfill his mission if he does not insist at all times upon being treated as the representative of a great power with the most scrupulous and, if you like, tiresome respect for all the rights and interests of France. Can we not understand that in this way only, by being wholly and completely French in the face of all his allies, can he carry the complete conviction of his good faith to the people of France."[12] So pleased were the Gaullists that they distributed thousands of copies of Lippmann's speech as promotional leaflets.

Word soon got back to the general of this remarkable tribute from his influential American admirer. A cable arrived at Lippmann's home from the general's London headquarters: "In explaining the reality of French resistance and in stressing its unity, you have rendered a service to France that she will never forget."[13] While France may have forgotten, de Gaulle never did. On becoming premier after the liberation, he anointed Lippmann as commander of the Legion of Honor. Lippmann was one of the few journalists to whom the general regularly granted interviews, both in power and in exile, and one of the handful invited to the sanctuary of his home.

Because Lippmann believed that only a France purged of Vichy collaborationism could assume its rightful role as a great power in the postwar world, he bitterly opposed the U.S. decision to work with Vichy officials in North Africa following the Allied invasion. When General Eisenhower, on the advice of diplomat Robert Murphy, appointed the Nazi-sympathizer, Admiral François Darlan, as supreme political authority over

12. Lippmann address to French-American Club, 28 October 1942, Yale Lippmann Collection.

13. Yale Lippmann Collection.

North Africa, Lippmann wrote a stinging note to Secretary of State Cordell Hull and Chief of Staff George Marshall. Recognizing that such a deal might be useful for military purposes, Lippmann warned against letting Darlan run the provisional government. Taking his case to his readers, he declared that the greatest obstacle to a union of the resistance groups was "an unreasoning prejudice against General de Gaulle on the part of certain of our officials" – by which he clearly meant Murphy, Hull, and even Roosevelt. "For while General de Gaulle has made mistakes, as indeed who has not," he explained, "he is one of the historical figures of our generation whom it is as stupid as it is mean not to welcome to our cause."[14]

After Darlan's timely assassination, U.S. officials tried to circumvent de Gaulle by appointing the ineffectual General Henri Giraud as political head in North Africa and secretly promising him that no "outside elements" (meaning Gaullist) would be allowed in the government without his permission. Denouncing Washington's "manipulation of public opinion" and its "official propaganda campaign for Giraud against de Gaulle," Lippmann demanded recognition of the French Committee of National Liberation as the sole trustee of French interests.[15] Although de Gaulle, he declared, had become "ever more intensely the acknowledged leader of the overwhelming mass of the French nation," the British and Americans had tried to impose their own will on those charged with the French national liberation movement. Defending the man he called "the greatest living soldier of France," he warned against a prejudice that was "rapidly making this man, already the symbol of French national resistance, the symbol also of French, and not only of French but of European, independence."[16] These words, written in the summer of 1943, seem like an eerie preview of the themes that de Gaulle himself would sound after his return to power more than 15 years later.

In November 1944, a few months after the liberation of Paris, Lippmann dined with de Gaulle and his family. The general complained to his guest that the recently reopened American embassy had been staffed with the same people who had followed Pétain to Vichy in 1940 – career diplomats who had no sympathy for the Gaullist movement or its efforts to purge

14. Lippmann to Hull and Marshall, 17 November 1942, Yale; T&T, 19 November 1942.

15. T&T, 10 July 1943.

16. T&T, 26 June 1943.

France of defeatism and collaboration. On his return to Washington, Lippmann wrote a sharp column declaring that it would be a "capital error not to staff the embassy with men who have no prejudices from the bad past" and against whom Frenchmen had no prejudices. Lippmann also spoke to Secretary of War Henry Stimson about the matter, but neither intervention had much effect upon the State Department.[17]

Unlike virtually anyone else in official Washington, Lippmann saw de Gaulle in the way that the general saw himself: as someone who had assumed, in a time of great duress, the obligation of making fallible Frenchmen true to their cultural and historic potential. If this required de Gaulle to mythologize himself, so be it. Neither Roosevelt nor later presidents understood or appreciated this. For them, the general's comparisons of himself with Jeanne D'Arc were ridiculous; for Lippmann, they expressed a symbolic truth. "His historic role in the French disaster, like hers in the days before, was to rally the nation and to compel the government to resist the invading enemy," Lippmann explained to his readers. It was no more conceited for de Gaulle to evoke the Maid of Orleans than for American presidents to think of themselves in terms of Washington or Lincoln. De Gaulle could unite the French people, Lippmann wrote at the time of the general's return to power in 1958, because "his mystery, which communicates itself to the French when they are in trouble, is that, being authentic and not time-serving, he touches those chords of memory which bind a nation together."[18] In Lippmann's view, de Gaulle's historic role as one who restored the greatness of France put him far above the petty cavils of his detractors. De Gaulle would always be remembered, Lippmann wrote in the tumultuous days of 1968, as "the man who preserved the soul of France."[19]

EUROPE AND THE ALLIANCE

In Lippmann's view, de Gaulle's historic role extended beyond the restoration of France to the rebuilding and independence of Europe itself. Unlike most officials of the American government, Lippmann both understood and approved the need for Europeans to defend interests different from, though not necessarily

17. T&T, 2 December 1944; Stimson diary, Yale, 28 November 1944.
18. T&T, 5 June 1958.
19. "The Gaullist Question," *Newsweek*, 17 June 1968.

in conflict with, the United States. While he did not always share de Gaulle's vision of what a reconstituted Europe should look like, he was neither mystified nor offended by it. Just as Lippmann had made it his task to explain and justify the Gaullist position during World War II, when de Gaulle's obduracy was the method for asserting French interests, so following the general's return to power in 1958 Lippmann once again served as a kind of intermediary between Washington and Paris.

Rather than resenting de Gaulle's assertive acts of independence, Lippmann tried to put them into context. As he had stated during the war: "Can we not understand that in this way only, by being wholly and completely French in the face of all his allies, can he carry the complete conviction of his good faith to the people of France."[20] So in 1963, when de Gaulle infuriated American officials by vetoing British admission to the Common Market – thereby scuttling the Kennedy administration's view of how Europe should be united – Lippmann again explained that while de Gaulle might be irritating, he "never has been a fool, and though his roots are deep in the past, again and again it has been shown that he is endowed with second sight about the future." The problem de Gaulle was addressing, he insisted, was that the postwar era was over, and that Europe had recovered from the demoralization and weakness that had made it so abjectly dependent on the United States. "We are not dealing with a wicked man who can be or should be slapped down," he argued. "We are dealing, I believe, with a prophetic man."[21]

While Lippmann sympathized with de Gaulle's conviction that the cold war was but a brief moment in the history of Western civilization and Communism a passing phenomenon, he confessed that he found the general's opposition to the Atlantic community "a little hard to take." France, he pointed out, had been twice saved because she belongs to a community that Americans crossed the oceans to defend, and his challenge to the United States was based more on French ambitions than French power. De Gaulle's problem for Lippmann was that his long-term vision was better than his short-term perception, that he tended to "watch the horizon without paying sufficient attention to the foreground." Maintaining that detente had not yet arrived, no matter how inevitable it might eventually be, Lippmann believed

20. Address at French-American Club, 28 October 1942.
21. T&T, 31 January 1963.

that Americans were right in opposing de Gaulle's rejection of a wider Atlantic community.[22]

Were Lippmann a Frenchman instead of an American, he probably would have approved even de Gaulle's anti-Atlanticism. In column after column during the early 1960s, he cited approvingly de Gaulle's conviction that the postwar world had come to an end. This meant unavoidably the decline of American political influence on the continent. "General de Gaulle did not himself cause this change," he observed, "but he is the first to be acting upon it." De Gaulle's position was particularly strong because he did not want anything from the United States.[23] De Gaulle's European policy, "no longer post-second world war but post-cold war," rested on the belief that military alliances, in the nuclear age, were precarious and thus obsolete. The French could not rely on any alliance unless they led it. To many, this was Gaullist nationalism. But Lippmann asked: "Is that not the way Americans feel about our alliances?" Gaullism, he warned, was spreading in Europe – not because Europeans applauded French nationalism, but because de Gaulle was basing his policies on post-cold war realities.[24]

But of course Lippmann was an American and one with particularly close ties to the Kennedy administration. He was persuaded by Pentagon strategists that the U.S. must resist de Gaulle's demand for a European, i.e., French, voice in American nuclear strategy. There could be only one finger on the nuclear trigger. Lippmann argued this position forcibly both in his columns and lectures, and even in Paris, where in November 1962 he hailed Kennedy's handling of the Cuban missile crisis, and explained that the demands of centralized control prevented consultation with the European allies.[25]

Thus while understanding, and even sympathizing with Gaullist objectives, including France's *force de frappe* and the creation of a more independent Europe, Lippmann could nonetheless criticize some of de Gaulle's policies as being premature or short-sighted. He was disturbed by the exclusionary nature of the Franco-German entente that was a centerpiece of Gaullist diplomacy, by the notion of a Europe "from the Atlantic to the

22. "The Gaullist Explosion," *Newsweek*, 4 February 1963.
23. "Europe Without America," *Newsweek*, 18 February 1963.
24. "Gaullism Today," *Newsweek*, 24 June 1963.
25. Ronald Steel: *Walter Lippmann and the American Century* (Atlantic Little Brown, Boston), 1980, pp. 534 and 537.

Urals" that would exclude the United States, and by the general's decision to "proceed relentlessly with the notion of creating a so-called Europe which excludes Great Britain, which ignores the smaller countries now in the Common Market, which freezes out the neutrals, and which disdains a partnership with the United States."[26] Yet Lippmann's criticisms were continually muted by his admiration for de Gaulle's vision and for the self-respect and strength he had brought to his country. "France stands apart because France is able to stand apart," he told his readers in late 1964.

> No European really likes to be dependent on Washington. But for the time being at least, France alone has solved the problems which preoccupy and divert the others. [. . .] And, though France is a free country and in no sense a totalitarian police state, she has subdued the political and factional struggle which for so much of the postwar period made France almost ungovernable.

De Gaulle's mission and great accomplishment, he explained, was the "restoration of French self-respect and self-confidence after the defeat and the disgrace of 1940. The renascence of the French spirit has been General de Gaulle's mission, and only those who understand what this means will not be puzzled by the pride and the pomp of French Gaullism."[27]

It was not only de Gaulle's restoration of French pride that won Lippmann's admiration, but also his vision of world politics and of France's role in the world. From the earliest days of the French resistance, Lippmann hailed de Gaulle's global vision and his efforts to rally France's empire in defense of the defeated and occupied French homeland. De Gaulle's insistence in the 1960s on exerting French influence on world problems irritated American officials, who insisted that the United States alone was a global power, but elicited Lippmann's approval. De Gaulle, he wrote, had habitually "viewed European affairs in a world context": in 1940, when he insisted that the war would be won because it had become worldwide, and after his return to power, when he urged London and Washington to join Paris in a NATO directorate to deal with problems outside the alliance. The offer was disdainfully rejected, but Lippmann supported de Gaulle's criticism of American unilateralism and insisted that it is "unrea-

26. Lippmann: *Western Unity and the Common Market* (Atlantic Monthly Press, Boston), 1962, p. 51.

27. "What Preoccupies Europeans," *Newsweek*, 21 December 1964.

sonable not to recognize that the French complaints and criticism of our military relations with Europe have substance and that they cannot be dismissed as the nonsense of a querulous old man."[28]

In 1964, de Gaulle once again incurred the wrath of U.S. administration officials by urging that Vietnam and all Southeast Asia be neutralized as the only way of preserving any degree of Western influence in the area. Lippmann, who already was beginning to turn against the war, tried to persuade the White House that de Gaulle's plan had merit and was not merely a formula for a disguised Communist takeover. But at that point the Americans had no doubt that they could succeed where the French had failed a decade earlier. After a frustrating meeting with Johnson administration officials in May 1964, Lippmann wrote a spirited column praising de Gaulle's neutralization proposal as the best hope for escape from the Vietnam quicksands. "We are missing the main point and we are stultifying our influence when we dismiss the French policies as not really serious, as expressions of personal pique or personal vanity on the part of General de Gaulle, as inspired by 'anti-Americanism' and a wish to embarrass us," he insisted. The French believed that Russia and China were on a collision course, and that Peking, in order to stabilize its southern frontier, would accept Southeast Asia's neutrality.[29] After the article appeared, Lippmann went to the White House and argued with President Johnson for two and a half hours about the merits of de Gaulle's plan.

Following Johnson's election that November, Lippmann flew to Paris where he conferred with de Gaulle; Edgar Faure; Couve de Murville; the new head of the Communist party, Waldeck Rochet; and the American ambassador, Charles Bohlen. Lippmann was particularly distressed by Bohlen's hostility to de Gaulle, and later told Johnson that he should replace the ambassador with someone less antipathetic to the French president. Lippmann also tried to explain that de Gaulle, despite his vision of a Europe "from the Atlantic to the Urals," did not want American troops to leave the continent until the Europeans had organized their own defense. De Gaulle, he told Johnson, would never agree to the Multi-Lateral Force (MLF), a plan hatched in the State Department which offered the Germans access to nuclear weapons through participation in a NATO fleet. This

28. "The Other Trouble," *Newsweek*, 9 May 1966.
29. T&T, 21 May 1964.

half-baked plan, Lippmann argued, was poisoning relations with France, creating a German appetite for nuclear weapons, and persuading de Gaulle that Washington sought to break up the new entente between Paris and Bonn. Johnson took the point and a few weeks later shelved the MLF.

The main topic at the White House that day, however, was not Europe but Vietnam. Johnson pressed Lippmann for details of de Gaulle's neutralization plan, and wanted to know how it could prevent Communists from taking over the entire country. Lippmann could only repeat what de Gaulle had told him: that it would take a million Americans to pacify Vietnam, and that a lasting military victory was impossible. Unless the West pressed for neutralization now, de Gaulle had warned, all of Southeast Asia would eventually fall into China's orbit. Lippmann sensed that Johnson was looking for a way out of the morass of Vietnam, but believed that he could not walk away from a commitment he had inherited from Kennedy, and that, despite de Gaulle's warnings, a military victory was possible.[30]

Johnson continued to sink into Vietnam, and by 1965, Lippmann became an outspoken, and increasingly impassioned, critic. His disenchantment with Johnson, the contrast between de Gaulle's recognition that the days of empire had passed, and the U.S. insistence on maintaining imperial outposts merely intensified his admiration for the general. On his twice yearly trips to Europe, he made it a point to meet with de Gaulle and to present the Gaullist view to his readers. In a column written in June 1968, when it was not yet certain whether de Gaulle would retire, Lippmann wrote that "whatever becomes of him now, his place in history is secure" – secure because he was the first statesman in the West to move to liquidate the cold war, the first one to begin "the critical experiment of remaking modern society without a totalitarian organization of power," the man who made party democracy work in France after the collapse of the parliamentary republic, the man "who preserved the soul of France."[31]

LEADERSHIP

Lippmann, who was an early follower of Theodore Roosevelt, was drawn to strong leaders with a sense of vision. It is not surprising that he admired de Gaulle. What is surprising, to those

30. *Walter Lippmann and the American Century, op cit.*, pp. 555–56.
31. "The Gaullist Question," *Newsweek*, 17 June 1968.

who have followed Lippmann's career, is that he never became seriously disillusioned with de Gaulle, as he did with virtually every other leader he had once admired. Perhaps this was due to de Gaulle's superior virtues; more likely to the fact that Lippmann, living in another country, did not have to deal with him on a daily basis, and focused only on the general's foreign, rather than domestic, policy. In this case, distance may have lent a certain enchantment.

But enchanted Lippmann was. The "capacity to act upon the hidden realities of a situation in spite of appearances is the essence of statesmanship," Lippmann wrote decades before he ever heard of de Gaulle. "It consists in giving the people not what they want but what they will learn to want. It requires the courage that is possible only in a mind that is detached from the agitations of the moment."[32] In de Gaulle, Lippmann found someone who defined his conception of statesmanship.

For this reason, Lippmann welcomed the return of de Gaulle to power in 1958, describing him as a "man of extraordinary historical insight and imagination" who came to power because the governing apparatus of France had collapsed. Rather than a usurper, Lippmann viewed him as a savior "with no trace of the modern vulgar dictator."[33] Recalling the unfortunate history of Roosevelt's wartime relations with de Gaulle, Lippmann called on Americans to try to understand the vision of the man who had resurrected and saved the soul of France. For Lippmann, one of de Gaulle's greatest qualities was the ability to touch the "chords of memory" that hold nations together. When the general visited Washington in April 1960, Lippmann published the most glowing tribute he had ever made to a public figure. "The secret is that he is more than a great man," but truly a "genius," he wrote of de Gaulle. He was gifted with the "capacity to see beneath the surface of events, to see through the obvious and conventional and stereotyped appearance of events to the significant realities, to the obscured facts and forces which will prevail."

As one of the first Americans to recognize de Gaulle's special genius, Lippmann was among the most persistent in trying to explain de Gaulle's vision of a revitalized France and a restored Europe, and among the few who defended him at a time when the White House considered him an enemy. More than any other journalist, Lippmann saw, and made others see, the historical

32. Lippmann, *A Preface to Morals*, Macmillan, New York, 1929, ch. 13.
33. T&T, 5 June 1958.

greatness of de Gaulle. "I find that almost three weeks after the fall of France," he wrote in his 1960 tribute, "I had learned enough to be able to write that 'in the misfortune of France it should be our fierce pride to be the last to forget the greatness of France. We must wish to be the first to remember . . . that France is indispensable, as indispensable to the maturity of Western civilization as Hellas was to its birth – and as imperishable.' I learned to say that only from General de Gaulle."[34]

34. T&T, 21 April 1960.

❖19❖

Conditional Surrender: De Gaulle and American Opinion

Theodore J. Lowi and Martin A. Schain

It is an enduring myth that heads of state and other international leaders are often more admired abroad than at home. The prophet is not without honor, save in his own country. It has been argued, for example, that Richard Nixon's popularity in other countries continued to grow during the Watergate crisis almost in inverse proportion to its decline in the United States. In fact, there has been no systematic study of the popularity of political leaders outside of their own countries.[1] The little evidence that exists suggests that, although important leaders are often admired by foreign political elites when they are unpopular at home, the reaction of mass publics is less clear. Thus, European political leaders were often sympathetic to the plight of Richard Nixon as the Watergate affair evolved between 1973 and 1975, but mass public opinion was far more negative.[2]

Our thanks to Barbara Hinkley, Philip Converse, and George Ross for their help in developing this survey. We would also like to thank Jane Maestro-Sherer and Leslie Schultz of CISER, the Survey Research Facility of Cornell University, and the staff of the American Political Science Association, without whose help the national survey would not have been possible. Finally, we are grateful to the Institut Charles de Gaulle, which sponsored this research.This article was first published in *PS: Political Science and Politics*, volume XXV, no. 3, September, 1992.

1. The literature on American attitudes toward their own leaders is rich and abundant. There are, however, relatively few systematic studies of attitudes toward foreign leaders. American perceptions of Soviet leaders and the Soviet Union have been analyzed extensively, but more general analyses have been limited to studies of the perceptions of American policy-makers of foreign leaders. See Ralph K. White, ed., *Psychology and the Prevention of Nuclear War* (New York: New York University Press, 1986), section II (esp. Ch. 3), pp. 34–97 and section VI, pp. 253–301, for an extensive bibliography on these subjects.

2. German opinion of Nixon, for example, tumbled from 41 percent "good" in January 1969, to 19 percent in November 1973. See Elisabeth Noelle-Neumann, editor, *The Germans: Public Opinion Polls, 1967–1980* (Westport: Greenwood Press, 1981), p. 423.

Charles de Gaulle did not fit the pattern, at least not in the United States. His 30 years of world prominence, from 1940 to 1970, may have produced a roller-coaster pattern of popularity in France, but the limited data we have indicates that in the U.S., he became increasingly unpopular as he consolidated his power during the Fifth Republic, and, in the process, challenged the hegemony of the United States.[3] Among American political elites, he seems to have been consistently unpopular, and revisions in that assessment were not to come before his second retreat to Colombey in 1969.

On the centenary of de Gaulle's birth (and the twentieth anniversary of his death), we undertook a reevaluation of the current public status of de Gaulle in America through a survey of a select group of opinion leaders whose preoccupations would enable them to form considered judgments about him as a political leader, and whose judgments would be transmitted to succeeding generations of university students. The first of our two samples was drawn from members of the American Political Science Association (277 respondents), and the second from the members of the Conference Groups on French Politics and Society (53 respondents). Political scientists and specialists on the study of France compose a mid-elite of great relevance to the evaluation of leadership. Although far from a decision-making elite and also far from being a representative sample of the American public, 20,000 political scientists and 300 specialists on France from a variety of academic disciplines reach hundreds of thousands of students and, through them, have more influence than perhaps any other source on the rating of all leaders,

3. In France, General de Gaulle was more popular when he was in power than when he was out of power. During his first period of "retirement" in Colombey, his popularity grew slowly, but at a low level. Thus, in December 1955, only 1 percent of Frenchmen surveyed wanted him to head a government. This percentage increased during the following two years, as the Fourth Republic became deeply involved in the Algerian War. By January 1958, it had grown to 13 percent. While this was hardly a massive mandate on which to base a bid for power, de Gaulle's percentage was as high or higher than that of any other Fourth Republic leader. While he was president, "satisfaction" was highest when the regime was most severely challenged from without (the two revolts in Algeria), and lowest when challenged from within (the miners' strike in 1963 and the 1968 events). It is also important to note that de Gaulle's personal popularity declined in the 1960s as Frenchmen indicated a greater willingness to vote for "a party" rather than "a man." Moreover, as the general's personal popularity waned, support for the institutions of the Fifth Republic that were identified with him (especially the popularly elected presidency) increased. See Jean Charlot, *The Gaullist Phenomenon* (New York: Praeger, 1971), ch. 2. .

particularly foreign leaders, in American public opinion. Our survey is able to capture the attitudes of influential teachers toward Charles de Gaulle and also the amount and type of information about de Gaulle that is passed along to American university students. In this sense, by learning more about our attitudes towards de Gaulle, we also learn more about ourselves. It has the additional advantage, for comparative purposes, of being a replication of the French national survey sponsored by the Charles de Gaulle Institute of Paris.[4]

DE GAULLE AND AMERICAN ELITES

De Gaulle's introduction to America was, to say the least, inauspicious. He was intensely disliked by President Roosevelt, and that view was shared by Roosevelt's Secretary of State, Cordell Hull, and important military advisors. Part of their problem was that they were trying valiantly to maintain diplomatic relations with the Vichy Government, but the dislike and the distrust went well beyond de Gaulle's steadfast opposition to any cooperation, indeed collaboration, with Vichy. Simply put, the American leaders did not believe that de Gaulle had the support of the French people or that he could rally the French against the Germans. And de Gaulle's standing as a leader was not at all helped by the fiasco of 1940, when, under Churchill's direction, there had been a plan to use General de Gaulle in an attack on the collaborationist government in Dakar as a means of rallying all of French West Africa against the Nazis. As a consequence, the entire French Army and French Fleet remained faithful to Marshal Pétain. This explains the decision by Roosevelt later on to organize the invasion of North Africa without the involvement of the Free French.

Undaunted by the well-known negative attitudes of the Americans toward him, de Gaulle's conduct continued to convey the impression that he was as much at war with his French and British allies as he was with the Germans. His rivalry with Admiral François Darlan and General Henri Giraud led General Eisenhower to refer to all of them as "those damn Frogs." Even as the North Africa campaign was being planned, and Eisenhower was in a position to make demands on these French generals for their cooperation in using the railways, docks, and other facilities, de

4. SOFRES, *De Gaulle en son siecle* (Montrouge: SOFRES, 1990).

Gaulle insisted on being dealt with "in my capacity as president of the French Government," and therefore refused to respond to Eisenhower's demands unless they were put in writing and forwarded to the French Committee for National Liberation (FCNL), in essence the French Government in exile. Eating his words about "the necessity of dictatorial action," General Eisenhower wrote such a memorandum and waited three days for the FCNL, 14 members, to approve his requests unanimously.[5] It remained for President Roosevelt, using all of the skills at his command, to get the two bickering French generals, Giraud and de Gaulle, to shake hands. To Roosevelt, this was a momentous event:

> We had so much trouble getting those two French generals together that I thought to myself that this was as difficult as arranging the meeting of Grant and Lee – and then suddenly the press conference was on, and Winston [Churchill] and I had no time to prepare for it, and the thought popped into my mind that they had called Grant 'Old Unconditional Surrender' and the next thing I knew, I had said it.

Thus, according to Roosevelt himself, the concept of "unconditional surrender," which became central to the policy of the allies against the Axis powers, got its name, if not its substance, from a summit agreement between the two French generals.[6] But whose surrender? In Eisenhower's opinion, the compromise worked out represented "a definite victory" over de Gaulle. He cabled his own supreme commander, General George Marshall: "de Gaulle has definitely lost ground and is not . . . in a position to control anything here. . . . Within a matter of weeks de Gaulle will, in the opinion of all our people and of the conservative French, have declined to a position of practical impotency."[7] De Gaulle, of course, steadily gained ground, extended his influence over French wartime affairs, and with the same pride and persistence that put him above all other French military officers, eventually captivated the French people.

The most illuminating story about his wartime role is probably his "liberation" of St.-Pierre and Miquelon, two small islands near the coast of Eastern Canada. The U.S. had promised the Vichy Government that it would do nothing to modify the status of the French-American territories in the Western hemisphere

5. This account is taken from Peter Lyon, *Eisenhower: Portrait of The Hero* (Boston: Little Brown, 1974), pp. 212–18.

6. Robert Ferrell, *American Diplomacy in the Twentieth Century* (New York: WW Norton, 1988), p. 212.

7. Ibid., p. 218.

(not only the two Canadian islands, but the much larger islands of the Caribbean, including Guadeloupe and Martinique). In spite of those assurances, de Gaulle gave the order to the Free French naval forces to liberate the two French-Canadian islands, and that was accomplished on the 24th of December 1941, to the great joy of the inhabitants. The American Secretary of State, Cordell Hull, was so furious over this action that he actually threatened to send an American warship up to the islands to fire on the new government. He satisfied himself instead with a non-published diplomatic note protesting the invasion with unusual intensity.[8] What was so typical about de Gaulle's invasion of those two little islands was that he consistently chose the route of French grandeur at whatever cost, including the alienation of France's most important ally.

Nothing had changed 17 years later when de Gaulle returned to power, first as premier. De Gaulle's return to power in 1958 was almost as jolting to Americans as his wartime role had been. Although Europeans in general had already begun to express some discomfort with American dominance of Europe through NATO, de Gaulle almost immediately took the European lead, styling the American role, as, among other things, imperialistic. Whatever satisfaction this gave European egos, de Gaulle was perhaps as much an irritant to them as to Americans, particularly in his steadfast commitment to an independent as well as a leadership role for France. As Paul Kennedy points out in his important 1989 book *The Rise and Fall of the Great Powers*, "France has always had an impact upon affairs far larger than might be expected from a country with a mere 4% of world GNP. . . . " Kennedy goes on to observe that "sheer national assertiveness" and "a driving sense of mission and cultural uniqueness" had made the French the natural candidates to lead postwar Europe.[9] What Kennedy was really describing was not the French but de Gaulle personally; or, he was confirming de Gaulle's own sense that he was in fact the personification of France. This exalted attitude of oneself is far more remote and troublesome to Americans than simply the conduct of a foreigner. It has all the qualities of "the man on the white horse" against which the entire American political character is historically mobilized.

8. Raoul Aglion, "Les ennemis du général de Gaulle aux Etats-Unis," a paper presented at the conference on "De Gaulle et son siècle," Paris, 19–24 November 1990.

9. Paul Kennedy, *The Rise and Fall of the Great Powers* (New York: Vintage, 1987), p. 428.

Although some of the more sophisticated American leaders conceded that there was a certain logic to de Gaulle's commitment to an independent nuclear capacity for France, most viewed his demand of independence for France as destructive of NATO unity against the USSR in the Cold War. The acceleration of the Fourth Republic development of atomic weapons in what became the *force de frappe* was troubling enough, but the de Gaulle plan to aim his retaliatory capacity "in every direction" was an ultimate sort of irritant.

Nevertheless, it is probably fair to say that de Gaulle did not become a front-page sensation in the United States until his 1966 military withdrawal of France from NATO and the expulsion of NATO forces from France. This, coupled with his consistent criticism of America's Vietnam policy, obviously contributed to the sense among American political leaders that Charles de Gaulle was no friend of the United States.

Yet, during a period that should have been the nadir of de Gaulle's relationship with the American people, this relationship actually began to warm up. The first indication of a warm-up can be noted in the attitudes of a few U.S. policy-makers, especially among the top foreign policy elite. A few liberal journalists and senators wrote and spoke positively about de Gaulle's declaration of independence against NATO, in face of the large majority prepared to condemn de Gaulle for that independence. Some of the favorable comments he received were probably inspired by the belief that de Gaulle was secretly favorable to the American presence in Vietnam despite his consistent public harping against our conduct there. In any case, the shift of American elite references to de Gaulle was clear after 1969.

Up to that point, virtually all references by American elites had been negative. Hardly a reference could be made to de Gaulle without some weighty negative adjective attached to it. Eisenhower made no secret of his fear and dislike of the general — which, by the way, was mutual on the side of de Gaulle. Ike stressed de Gaulle's anti-Americanism; de Gaulle referred to Ike as "con." Former Secretary of State Dean Acheson had carried the wartime animosity to de Gaulle through the 1950s and into the 1960s. In his memoirs, he refers to de Gaulle as that "controversial mystery" out to destroy European unity.[10]

Among masses of Americans in the 1960s, President de Gaulle

10. Dean Acheson, *Present at the Creation* (New York: WW Norton, 1969), pp. 77 and 329.

was one of the least admired world leaders. Asked to rank de Gaulle on a thermometer scale (from highly favorable to highly unfavorable), Americans in 1965 tended to follow the example of their leaders: only 31 percent of those surveyed ranked him favorably (5 percent highly favorably).[11]

With Nixon's election, the shift was clear. Nixon not only admired de Gaulle's role as an international leader, he also admired and carefully studied de Gaulle's role as a head of state and head of government in another major democracy. Arthur Schlesinger, drawing from his own informants in the Nixon administration, observed that Nixon "admired no contemporary statesmen so much as de Gaulle . . . [and] after his reelection he began what can be profitably seen as an attempt to establish a quasi-gaullist regime in the United States."[12]

Without necessarily intending the trip to be a gesture of special admiration for de Gaulle, Nixon reports that the primary purpose of his first trip abroad as president was to meet with de Gaulle and to secure his cooperation as vital to the ending of the Vietnam War and to the establishment of a new relationship with the People's Republic of China.[13] Kissinger's biographers, Marvin and Bernard Kalb, refer to de Gaulle as Nixon's "political model in many ways." And de Gaulle was just as much a model for Kissinger himself. Kissinger had carefully studied de Gaulle's conduct toward Algeria as the model for the U.S. withdrawal from Vietnam.[14] In his memoirs, Nixon refers to the alienation of de Gaulle from America as though it was a product of the 1960s, disregarding the long history of mutual alienation extending back to 1940.[15] This only emphasizes the extent of the change in American elite attitudes toward de Gaulle, and is the basis for our opinion that this is the beginning of the upward revision of de Gaulle in the hearts and minds of Americans.

11. Rankings were even lower in Germany and Britain, when this question was asked in a somewhat different way. Only Brezhnev was ranked lower among world leaders. See *The Gallup Poll*, 1965, pp. 1963-64. The (successful) French initiative to promote and develop ties with Germany in the 1960s did little to cement de Gaulle's popularity among the masses of (West) German citizens. By September 1968, after the chaotic "events" the previous spring that were capped by the Gaullist electoral victory in June, only 22 percent of German respondents had strong faith in de Gaulle as a world leader, and only 17 percent saw him as a friend of Germany. See Noelle-Neumann, *The Germans . . .*, p. 456.

12. Arthus Schlesinger, Jr., *The Imperial Presidency* (New York: Popular Library, 1974), pp. 247–48.

13. Richard Nixon, *The Memoirs of Richard Nixon* (New York: Grosset and Dunlap, 1978), pp. 370–71.

14. Marvin and Bernard Kalb, *Kissinger* (Boston: Little Brown, 1974), p. 352.

15. *The Memoirs of Richard Nixon*, p. 370.

DE GAULLE AS HISTORY

By 1990, de Gaulle had been dead for 20 years, and we felt that the time was appropriate to examine the evaluation of his historical standing among those in America who were interpreting his legacy for scholars and students. We generally presumed that the shift in elite opinion during the 1970s, as well as the passage of time, has had some impact on mid-elite opinion.

In our analysis, we focused on those variables that the literature indicates should most affect orientations towards de Gaulle. Thus we first examined knowledge (awareness and information) of Charles de Gaulle as a political leader. The literature suggests that knowledge should vary with age and involvement, and that evaluation changes with knowledge.[16] We then looked at the image of de Gaulle as a leader, and related this to evaluations of his policies. Finally, we attempted to understand these evaluations by analyzing their relationship to the ideological commitments of our respondents.

1. Knowledge and Awareness

Very few political scientists claimed to know too little to respond to most questions. On almost two-thirds of the questions asked, the response rate approached 100 percent. For the remaining third, the "don't know" responses averaged about 10 percent of the sample. However, the mean tends to exaggerate the lack of response, since "don't know" responses rarely exceeded 5 percent, and was above the mean in only a few very specific kinds of questions (see below). Not surprisingly, "don't know" responses among political scientists were twice as high as those among specialists on France (11 percent vs. 5.2 percent), but lack of response tended to be highest for both groups on the same questions:

16. There has been an important scholarly debate on how Americans form attitudes toward foreign policy issues (rather than leaders), and from this discussion we can gain some insights about opinion formation about foreign leaders. For example, Jon Hurwitz and Mark Peffley argue that, as individuals attempt to deal with information on foreign policy, they try to relate it to their more general and abstract beliefs, and that those policies that are most constrained are related to areas in which people have interests and commitments. For a good summary of the discussion of formation of foreign policy attitudes, see the article by these authors, "How are Foreign Policy Attitudes Structured? A Hierachical Model," in the *American Political Science Review*, vol. 81, no. 4, December 1987. We should also point out that there is almost no literature on the attitudes of middle-level elites, such as university professors, who are key molders of mass attitudes but not decision-makers, even though it is widely presumed that their influence on generations of students is important if not crucial.

those that asked for evaluations of specific policies during the Gaullist period, and questions that asked respondents to compare Mitterrand's defense policies and policy towards the third world with those of de Gaulle.

We had thought that the age of respondents would vary directly with their response rate, especially on questions that appeared to presume information, but this was not the case. For example, the largest "don't know" response on the national survey was to the question asking respondents if they "agreed or disagreed" with the extension of the vote to women when de Gaulle was in power the first time. Almost 36 percent did not respond to this question, but there was no consistent relationship to the age of the respondent.

Nevertheless, with the exception of questions cited above, the level of information respondents brought to the questions, and their willingness and ability to evaluate de Gaulle as president, as well as Gaullist policies, were far in excess of what a random sample of the public would present, and was also far in excess of what we had expected.

2. *Image as a Leader*

We were particularly interested in how American academics characterize de Gaulle as a leader. In general, they tend to view him as a strong national leader, but not one who is particularly sympathetic in terms of American democratic values. Their image of de Gaulle is strongly linked to his qualities as the leader of a nation-state, rather than his qualities as a person. Thus, 43.6 percent of the full sample reported that "grandeur" was the first quality brought to mind by the mention of de Gaulle's name, while another 21 chose "authority" and 8 percent chose "long-range vision." No one chose "respect for others" or "open-mindedness," which did not surprise us, but very few chose "excessive patriotism," "sticks to his ideas," "realism," "decisiveness," or "too stubborn," and that did surprise us.

The association between de Gaulle and grandeur, authority, and long-range vision varies somewhat with the involvement of our respondents with the study of French politics. The sub-sample from the Conference Group on French Politics and Society were more likely to choose these descriptions than our sub-sample of APSA members, as were those whose information about de Gaulle comes from their own scholarship. Among those less involved with the study of French politics, the youngest and oldest age cohorts are less likely than those who matured intellectually "under" de Gaulle (i.e., those now between the ages of 40 and 60) to see him in this way. Among those who have been less involved, there is very little difference among age cohorts. In this sense, to have "known" de Gaulle means to see his leadership image in a certain coherent way: 84 percent of the sub-sample from the Conference Group, and 75 percent of those whose information comes from their own scholarship see the former French President in terms of grandeur, authority, and long-range vision (in that order).

In fact, the image of our respondents of de Gaulle corresponds to their image of the democratic process under the Fifth Republic (see Table 1).

On the other hand, when asked to place de Gaulle in the context of French history, American academics rank him relatively low. When asked "Among those *historical figures* listed below [all important figures in French history], which ones do you feel are the most important in the history of France," de Gaulle only received 3 percent first choice mentions, as compared to 52 percent for Napoleon I, 13.8 percent for Louis XIV, and 15.7 percent for Charlemagne. Among specialists on France, only 4 percent chose de Gaulle, but 65 percent chose Louis XIV and Napoleon I (about the same percentage for each). De Gaulle ranked higher on the second and third choices, especially among French specialists.

The French view of French history is quite different. Respondents to the same question in the French mass survey gave far greater historical importance to de Gaulle. Eighteen percent

TABLE 1

Which two words do you feel best describes the political process under the Fifth Republic in France?

	% of Academic Sample
Democracy	13.8
Effectiveness	10.5
Stability	43.1
Authority	30.2
Discussion	2.2

ranked him first (2 percent less than for Charlemagne), while 51 percent ranked him among their top three choices (no one exceeded that percentage).

When respondents were asked to choose the most important leaders of the *twentieth century*, no one placed General de Gaulle among their first choices (a majority chose Lenin, Hitler and Franklin Roosevelt – in that order), and less than 3 percent ranked him among their second and third choices. We should compare these responses to those given the French and German mass surveys to the same question: 74 percent of the French and 20 percent of the German respondents chose de Gaulle as one of three of the most important leaders of the twentieth century.[17] The American responses probably say more about the respondents' evaluation of the importance of France in the twentieth century, compared with the Soviet Union and Nazi Germany, than about the leaders themselves, however.

Nor do they feel special warmth for the memory of Charles de Gaulle. Using a method that has been used to evaluate affect towards political leaders, the respondents were presented with a thermometer of values ranging from 0 to 100, a low value expressing a feeling that "you do not care very much for him," a middle value of 50 expressing a neutral feeling, and 51-100 expressing a warm, positive attitude (See Table 2). American academics note "warmer" feelings for Mitterrand than for de Gaulle, and, by far, the warmest feelings for John F. Kennedy; so do students, although fewer students than academics feel "warmly" towards de Gaulle (51-100). Here there is a difference between political scientists and the specialists on France. As we might expect, among the French specialists the warmest affect is reserved for the two French leaders, but, above all for Mitterrand.

As a group, American respondents may feel more warmly about Kennedy and Eisenhower, but for them, the continuing *consequences* and *impact* of Charles de Gaulle are far more important than those for either American president (see Table 3). This is consistent with their evaluation of the importance of Eisenhower and Kennedy in the twentieth century: both American presidents rank well below President de Gaulle.

This response may be related to the way that American academics evaluate "consequences." It is probable that de Gaulle gets a high rating because of his role in founding a new Republic,

17. See SOFRES, "Image du général de Gaulle auprès des allemands de l'ouest," May 1990, p. 2.

TABLE 2

Giving a number from 0-100, please rate your reaction to the following leaders according to the following "thermometer":
1. 51-100 indicates you feel warmly and positively towards him.
2. 0-49 indicates that you do not care very much for him.
3. 50 means that you feel neutral.

(percentage 51+)

	Rating	Pol. Scientists	Fr. Specialists
De Gaulle	51–75	37.1%	43.4%
	76–100	8.1	18.9
	Total	45.2	62.3
Mitterrand	51–75	46.9	47.2
	76–100	8.1	26.4
	Total	55	73.6
Eisenhower	51–75	38.6	28.3
	76–100	12.9	1.9
	Total	51.5	30.2
Kennedy	51–75	48.5	57.7
	76–100	16.5	11.5
	Total	65	69.2

whereas the "consequences" political scientists have in mind for other leaders would have more to do with the influence of the policies associated with them. No other leaders except Lenin and Mao can be looked at as "founding fathers."

3. POLICY EVALUATION

On the more specific aspects of de Gaulle's behavior, the attitudes of American academics varied considerably. For example, 74.2 percent approved of his criticisms of U.S. intervention in Vietnam, 88.2 percent approved of his recognition of the People's Republic of China, and nearly 67 percent judge that de Gaulle's policies and commitments were beneficial to the entire French people rather than to the rich or to the poor. On the other hand, 80.3 percent disapproved of his support for "Québec libre," 86.4

TABLE 3

De Gaulle died in 1970, Eisenhower in 1969 and J.F.K. in 1963. Now in 1990, do you think that what they did while in office still has consequences that are (percentage):

	Very Important	Quite Important	Of little Importance	Not at all Important
De Gaulle	55.5	40.8	3.7	0
Eisenhower	14.5	50.8	33.8	0.9
Kennedy	15.1	51.4	30.8	2.8

percent disapproved of his veto of British entry into the Common Market, and 49.4 percent disapproved of the postwar nationalizations under de Gaulle. In general, Americans evaluate the impact on France of Gaullist foreign policy positively (51.8 percent are positive, 20.5 neutral), defense policy quite positively (39.1 percent positive, 21.5 neutral), and policy on the construction of Europe with significant reservations (27.2 percent positive, 21.5 neutral). But American academics were least enthusiastic about de Gaulle's social and economic policy (25.7 percent positive, 37.6 percent neutral).

Here, too, we found that those most involved with the study of French politics tended to judge Gaullist policies more favorably than scholars who have not worked in this area (see Table 4). For the less popular policies (social policy and the construction of Europe), the judgments of younger (24–30 years old) scholars who have worked on France tend to be far more positive than those of their older colleagues. In this sense, de Gaulle's reputation has been enhanced by time. This conclusion is confirmed by an analysis of the thermometer scale, which shows the highest degree of "warmth" for de Gaulle among the youngest age cohort of those most involved with the study of French politics.

We found that some judgments about Gaullist policy are related to our previous discussion about the de Gaulle's image as a leader. We had presumed, for example, that whether de Gaulle's criticism of the United States was seen positively or negatively would have an important impact on how respondents gauged their own "warmth" towards him, as well as their judgments about how well the institutions of the Fifth Republic worked under de Gaulle, and their judgment of the consequence of what he did. By and large, this did not prove to be true. Indeed, there is no significant relationship between approval or disapproval of his criticism of the United States, and the evaluations requested in any of these questions (see Table 4).

TABLE 4

Percentage of academics who approve/disapprove of de Gaulle's criticism of U.S. Vietnam policy who:

	Approve	*Disapprove*
Feel Warmly about de Gaulle (rate him 51-100)	47.7	43.6
Feel 5th Republic Worked well under de Gaulle	88.9	92.7
Judge consequences of what de Gaulle did to be still "very/quite important"	97.5	90.9

Those who disapprove of de Gaulle's criticism of the United States tend to feel less warmly towards the general, and judge the consequences of what he did to be less important, but the differences are marginal, and far less than what we expected to find.

On the other hand, evaluations of domestic policy, especially social and economic policies, turned out to be a far better indicator of differences in judgment of Gaullist leadership (see Table 5).

TABLE 5

Percentages of academics who Evaluate Social and Economic Policy Under de Gaulle as positive/neutral/negative who:

	Positive	Neutral	Negative
Feel Warmly about de Gaulle	53.0	47.2	32.4
Feel 5th Republic Worked well under de Gaulle	96.2	93.4	77.8
Judge consequences of what de Gaulle did are still "very/quite important"	56.6	56.4	51.4

Americans with negative judgments about Gaullist social and economic policies (almost 22 percent – almost as many who have positive judgments – 26 percent) are far less sanguine both about de Gaulle as well as the way the Fifth Republic functioned under his leadership.

4. DE GAULLE AND IDEOLOGY

The more critical attitude that Americans demonstrate with regard to de Gaulle's social and economic policies may be related to their judgment about his ideological position. Although during his lifetime there was an attempt to portray de Gaulle as a political figure who could not be easily defined in ideological terms (and, indeed, he attracted a socially and ideologically diverse electorate), American academics overwhelmingly now see de Gaulle as a man of the right; far more a man of the right than Eisenhower, who was also portrayed in the United States as not easily definable. If we look at Table 6, it is interesting to note that, from the perspective of well-informed and well-educated

TABLE 6

Do you think of the following as "right," "left" or "not definable in ideological terms?

	Right	Left	Not Definable	
De Gaulle				
Political Scientists	79%	1%	20%	100%
French Specialists	68	0	32	100
Students	76	4	20	100
Mitterrand				
Political Scientists	4.8	80.4	14.1	100
French Specialists	0	88.7	11.3	100
Students	8	84	8	100
Kennedy				
Political Scientists	10	41.7	48.3	100
French Specialists	13.5	36.5	50.0	100
Students	16.1	51.6	32.3	100
Eisenhower				
Political Scientists	63.7	0	35.9	100
French Specialists	73.6	0	26.4	100
Students	51.6	6.5	35.5	100

Americans, it is John F. Kennedy above all who emerges as the least well-defined in ideological terms, although students seem particularly unsure about Eisenhower. Specialists on France, who are familiar with the less ideological Gaullist image, are those most inclined to see him in non-ideological terms.

Given this perception of de Gaulle as a man of the right and Mitterrand as a man of the left, it is interesting to note that our sample of academics tends to see the political orientations of both presidents as close in ways of governing and in those aspects of policy that were closest to de Gaulle's heart. Not surprisingly, French specialists, who are less likely to see de Gaulle as a man of the right (but more likely to see Mitterrand as a man of the left), are most likely to see the similarities in the political orientations of both men. For our sample, the differences in the overall political orientation of de Gaulle and Mitterrand seems to be based on their evaluations of domestic policy, particularly of social and economic policy and policy on building Europe (see Table 7).

TABLE 7

Would you say that Mitterrand has remained close to the important orientations of Gaullist policy in the following areas:

(% Very close/Quite close)

	Pol. Scientists	Fr. Specialists
Way of governing	55.9	82.4
Defense	58	65.4
Foreign Policy	43.5	69.2
Third World Policy	42.7	59.6
Const. of Europe	29	30.8
Economic Policy	19.8	23.1
Social Policy	13.2	17.6

However, the differences perceived by our respondents are important, because the policy areas for which differences are perceived between the two presidents are the same areas which we have found are important as a determinant of both feeling about de Gaulle, and evaluations about how well the Fifth Republic worked during his presidency.

5. Ideology and de Gaulle

Until now, we have found that judgments about Gaullist leadership vary with whether our respondents are specialists on France, and their judgments of social and economic policy under de Gaulle. However, we also presumed that their own political orientation would color both their judgments of Gaullist policy and their perceptions of de Gaulle as a political leader. In fact, this proved to be true, but in ways that are consistent with our more general analysis.

Sixty-three percent of our national sample defines itself as "left" or "liberal," (6 percent higher than among our student sample) and 71 percent voted for Dukakis in 1988 (8 percent more than the students). Ideological orientation however, had virtually no impact of the judgments of American academics about the importance of the consequences de Gaulle's presidency: between 90 and 99 percent of our academic and student samples felt that the consequences were "very" or "quite" important, regardless of political orientation. There was some variation by ideological orientation on the functioning of the Fifth Republic under de Gaulle (conservatives felt that it functioned better than liberals), but the variation was between 87 and 97 percent. When comparing Presidents de Gaulle and Mitterrand, a majority of all respondents, regardless of ideological orientation, saw their "way of governing" as close; but those respondents furthest to the left and those furthest to the right were significantly more inclined to see it as close, while those who were ideologically more moderate tended to see differences.

However, ideological differences were more important when respondents were asked to give their feelings about de Gaulle, and when they were asked to make judgments about specific policies. These differences are most evident on the "thermometer" scale (see Table 8). Conservatives were almost twice as likely to express warm feeling for de Gaulle than were those on the left. They were also twice as likely to see de Gaulle as not definable in ideological terms, and considerably less likely to see him as a man of the right (see Table 9). In other words, American academics who define themselves as further to the right, feel warmly about de Gaulle even though they find it more difficult to define him politically, while those who define themselves further to the left feel more negatively about de Gaulle *as* a man of the right.

TABLE 8

Giving a number from 0–100, please rate your reaction to the following leaders according to the following "thermometer":
1. 51-100 indicates you feel warmly and positively towards him.
2. 0-49 indicates that you do not care very much for him.
3. 50 means that you feel neutral.

	Percentage of each ideological group (academics) indicating positive or negative feelings:				
Ideological orientation:	0–49	50	51–75	76–100	
Left	50	10	33.3	6.7	=100
Liberal	41.1	12.1	39.7	7.1	=100
Center	44.4	9.9	34.6	11.1	=100
Conservative	23.5	2.9	50	23.5	=100

TABLE 9

Do you think of the following as "right," "left" or "not definable in ideological terms?

	Percentage of each ideological group's judgment of de Gaulle's ideological orientation (academics):			
Ideological Orientation:	*Right*	*Left*	*Not Definable*	
Left	83.1	0	16.9	=100
Liberal	78.2	0.7	21.1	=100
Center	75	1.3	28.8	=100
Conservative	65.7	0	34.3	=100

The ideological orientation of our respondents is also a key to understanding their judgment of domestic policy under de Gaulle, particularly social and economic policy. The further to the left our respondent, the more critical he or she is of these policies under de Gaulle (see Table 10).

TABLE 10

Percentage of each ideological group evaluating the impact on France of social and economic policies under de Gaulle as:

Ideological Orientation:	*Positive*	*Neutral*	*Negative*	
Left	15.0	42.5	42.5	=100
Liberal	30.9	39.0	30.1	=100
Center	32.9	53.4	13.7	=100
Conservative	49.9	43.7	6.4	=100

In judgments on similarities between de Gaulle and Mitterrand, the patterns that we noted above appear to remain when we control for ideological orientation. However, on those policies where American academics perceive differences, there is a greater tendency for those on the left to see those differences. Thus, perceptions of similarities and differences on defense and foreign policy do not vary as much by ideological orientation as perceptions of social and economic policies, policy on Europe, and policy with regard to the third world (see Table 11). Howev-

TABLE 11

Would you say that Mitterrand has remained close to the important orientations of Gaullist policy in the following areas:

Percentage of each ideological group judging de Gaulle and Mitterrand "very" or "quite close" in the following policy areas:

	Left	*Lib.*	*Cent.*	*Cons.*
Defense	66.1	48.1	64.3	73.6
Foreign Policy	55.2	44.5	53.9	61.7
Third World Policy	48.3	39.8	56.3	61.8
Const. of Europe	27.6	24.6	36.7	35.3
Economic Policy	19.3	18.5	20	32.4
Social Policy	8.8	14.8	13.8	20.6

er, in general, conservatives are much more likely to see similarities consistently than those of the left.

What is most striking about our findings, then, is how, and the degree to which, the ideological orientation of American academics determines their judgment about de Gaulle and his presidency. On reflection, it is not entirely surprising that American academics judge the Gaullist past through their ideological perspective of the present. It is important to emphasize, however, that our sample judged the institutional and (in many cases) the policy impact of President de Gaulle in very positive terms, although they perceived themselves on the other side of the political spectrum from the president. Thus, a higher percentage of academics on the left than on the right judged the consequences of de Gaulle as "very important" (58 percent vs. 51 percent); a higher percentage on the left also saw de Gaulle and Mitterrand as similar in the way that they govern (69 percent vs 65 percent). Ninety percent of the academics on the left (7 percent fewer than those on the right) agreed that the Fifth Republic functioned "well" or "very well" under de Gaulle.

CONCLUSION: THE CONTRADICTIONS OF CHARISMA

The image of and judgments about Charles de Gaulle seem to have changed considerably since the early 1970s. In many ways, the Nixon/Kissinger view has been sustained in the academic community. Though very few of the academics or students in our survey hold Richard Nixon in high esteem, they obviously share in Nixon's very high esteem for de Gaulle's manner and role as leader of the French people and head of the French state. They would almost certainly agree with the observation made by Henry Kissinger at Columbia University in April 1990 that de Gaulle was capable of commanding the respect of world leaders by his very presence, without uttering a word.[18] If charismatic leadership is based on the "belief in the extraordinary quality of the specific *person*," then de Gaulle was certainly charismatic.[19] These evaluations are not influenced by judgments about de

18. Kissinger's remarks were made on 6 April 1990, at the conference on "De Gaulle and the United States: A Conference Marking the Centennial Year of Charles de Gaulle," at Columbia University and New York University. (See Chapter 14, page 329.)

19. This definition of charismatic leadership is taken from Max Weber, "The Social Psychology of the World Religions," in H. H. Gerth and C. Wright Mills, *From Max Weber* (New York: Oxford University Press, 1958), p. 295.

Gaulle's opposition to U.S. policy in Vietnam. In contrast to the American departure from Vietnam, they would agree with Kissinger's remark that de Gaulle managed to leave Algeria "in such a way that the departures seemed an act of policy so that France could keep some of its dignity. . . . That was his great achievement, not the precise outcome of the war."[20]

If, on the other hand, evaluations of de Gaulle's leadership are also based on feelings of warmth, judgments of domestic policy during his presidency, and seeing him as a man not captured by the traditional left-right division of French politics, then the evaluation of the "charisma" of his leadership is far more qualified, and depends on the ideological orientation of the respondent.[21] Even from the distant gaze of 21 years, American intellectuals who classify themselves on the left and their students (more than two-thirds of our sample) remember de Gaulle with little warmth, his social and economic policies with less than enthusiasm, and his political orientation as distinctly partisan. Thus, these Americans seem to agree that de Gaulle was a leader of consequence and authority, a leader who built institutions that have endured, but not one who is "loved" according to the evaluations of his policies and the political orientations of the respondents.

However, in those areas in which de Gaulle is perceived most positively – the governmental system of the Fifth Republic, defense policy, and foreign policy – Mitterrand is seen by most respondents as quite close to his predecessor's orientations. If charismatic leadership involves the routinization of new patterns of governing, then to American academics and their students President de Gaulle was, in this sense as well, such a leader.[22] For our American respondents, there is little relationship between their judgments of de Gaulle on the basis of the institutions he built and routinization of key policy areas, on one hand, and their feelings of warmth and judgments on domestic policy, on the other.

20. Kalb and Kalb, *Kissinger*, p. 352.

21. These are all related to Weber's concept of charismatic leadership. See Gerth and Mills, *op. cit.*, pp. 248–49.

22. See Gerth and Mills, *op. cit.*, pp. 262–63.

Comment

Stanley Hoffmann

I STARTED WITH THE NOTION of diplomatic styles, and rather quickly came to the conclusion that this was not enough. For what went on during World War II – after the liberation, during the RPF period, and of course in the Fifth Republic – amounted to a triple conflict: a clash of interests, a clash of styles, and a clash of perceptions. Let me begin with the clash of interests. Here I am referring to what Hans Morgenthau would have called interests defined as power and largely determined by geo-political considerations, so that these interests really go way beyond the question of personalities of leaders. It seems to me that the differences between de Gaulle and the Fourth Republic should not be exaggerated. De Gaulle often did what the Fourth Republic politicians could not, or did not, dare to do but would have liked to do, and there has been a remarkable American continuity (French beliefs about American incoherence not withstanding). In this clash of interests, the polarities, if one can use this word, are the following: first, the United States was a great power facing a country with a leader who had practically no power to begin with in World War II, and limited power later. This contrast colored the policies of both, because of the impatience of the United States with de Gaulle's constant resistance and the desire of de Gaulle not to be crushed by the American elephant. A second clash of interests pits America as the leader of a coalition, during both World War II and the Cold War, against a country with a very string national desire for what might be called self-control, controlling its own destiny. In the Fourth as well as the Fifth Republic, if you combine these two oppositions, you find a contrast between one country, the United States, which likes to be at the head of what theorists of international relations (a dreadful breed) call "bandwagoning," i.e., it wants to lead a coalition, and a country with a traditional quest for a balance of power, which it prefers to simply being a part of a whole. And there is a contrast between the United States, with a strong desire for military control of its allies, and France, with an ardent desire for military independence.

The final polarity in the realm of clashes of interests is perhaps the most interesting: the United States as a status quo power, for which a bipolar word is just fine, facing France, which had a strong interest in an "escape from Yalta," and escape from either the collisions or the collusions of bipolarity, and which practices a double revisionism: against the division of Europe, even if the end of that division should mean the reunification of Germany, but also against the domination of the United States in the Western half of Europe. A country, in other words, with a clear preference for multipolarity.

Second, there was a clash of styles. I have a slightly peculiar definition of style, which I have used before. It is really a bundle of beliefs, on the one hand, and methods, on the other. You can't leave out the beliefs. This bundle comes out of historical experiences, basic ideology, and institutional constraints. What are the key polarities here? Some have to do with substance, or national philosophies, if you like. The United States is not just any leader of a coalition; it is very much concerned with "the unity of the free world." There is an American notion of democratic universalism, whereas the French resistance to this American leadership is not just any kind of resistance. What de Gaulle stands for is the dogma of national independence not just for France, but for everybody all over the world. As a consequence, there are very different threat perceptions: American policy is dominated by the Soviet threat, as it had been earlier by the Nazi threat. De Gaulle, of course, does believe that there is a Soviet threat that requires alliance with the United States. But it is not the only nor necessarily always the dominant threat. The really dominant threats are the threats to French independence, wherever they come from. This is the touchstone. This is why, for example, in World War II, de Gaulle's main concern was not to receive independence from anybody else, but to take it, to grab it. And in the Fifth Republic, this explains why his concern was for finding the maximum possible space within the alliance, and with transcending it. We heard very elegantly from M. Messmer about another difference of substance, a collision of two globalisms. American globalism relegated France to being only a regional power; the French very Gaullist view was that France had to have a policy of global activism, from Phnom-Penh to Montreal, and from Latin America to Turkey, if you like.

Then come all of the polarities having to do with method. On one side, we find American pragmatism. Because the United States believes that the ends are given and accepted by all, the ends go without saying, and therefore it makes possible a policy of piecemeal adjustments. On the other side, we find de Gaulle's very strategic view. Never does he accept any scheme without a prior, very clear agreement on the ends, because otherwise one gets trapped in an "engrenage." Then, there is a second opposition between the American consensual method, this rather enveloping way of trying to get everybody to agree on the details of the grand design as set by the United States, and de Gaulle's method of shock and obstruction, which is perfectly natural, if one has been a theorist and practitioner of tank warfare.

The American pragmatic tendency of problem solving, which is very largely concerned with dealing with difficulties so as to get things done, clashed with the general's very French concern with "dire le droit," saying what is right rather that reaching solutions or agreements at all costs. To him, it seems to me, saying what is right, even if it's not going to come to pass until twenty or thirty years later, is much more important than making an insignificant small contribution to somebody else's design. On this set of polarities, what I would call American sentimentality or sentimentalism, i.e., the combination of the notion of democracy as the cement of the coalition and celebration of the virtues and habits of cooperation (accompanied by a fair amount of self-congratulation), collided with de Gaulle's rather unsentimental view, that nations have only interests but no affections, that it is reciprocity that matters and should serve as the temporary cement of relations. It isn't going to be what I would call the glue of good, or of good will.

Third, there is a clash of perceptions. It's not only a clash that results from the combination of different interests and different styles. When it comes to perceptions, I think that there was a fundamental asymmetry. For the de Gaulle of before 1940, there are no prejudices about the United States. One can go through all of his writings: the United States is a tabula rasa, and indeed, at first he is rather well disposed towards the U.S., especially when he had his first clashes with England in 1940 and 41. Whereas, from the beginning, official Washington does not like General de Gaulle. Who is this upstart, who is this man who acts "comme si" (the great pedagogic method of de Gaulle, to act "comme si," so that things happen): Who is this man who acts as if France had not fallen in 1940? Here the polarities are the following: on the one hand, the United States perceives de Gaulle as archaic (what is more archaic than 19th century multipolarity, national independence, the stress on the nation state? Don't we all know this wonderful passage from Sorensen, who wrote that there is something absurd in trying to restore the grandeur of a nation the size of Texas). The United States perceives de Gaulle as domineering because of his tactics, of his rude interventions in places like Quebec. They interpret him as a spoiler, selfish, petty. And finally they look at him as dictatorial, both abroad and at home. They were never entirely sure that he was really supported at home – deep down, the French could not have really gone for this! As for de Gaulle, he perceived the United States not so much as hypocritical (I don't think that is the problem), but as not self aware of the degree to which American ideology is really a figleaf of American interests. This is something that was very well put by Anne Sa'adah in her paper. It explains the difference between his reactions to the United Kingdom and his reactions to the United States. France and the U.K. play the same game, and know they play the same game. Now, America plays the same game, too, but denies it, and denies it at it's own peril. It is this denial that makes the United States believe that they can accomplish in Vietnam what the French could not in Indochina. Furthermore de Gaulle perceives the United States as simplistic. A few simple ideas, democracy, international organization, the free world, anti-communism – that is not enough to create order in this complicated world. He certainly does perceive the United States as imperialistic, in World War II with its designs all over former French colonies, and later in it's global actions. Finally, I think he perceived the American policy as really dangerous, dangerous for peace if it should lead to a collision with the Soviet Union, dangerous if it should lead to too much of an embrace with the Soviet Union, because in that case there is a danger for all the other nations. This is the skeleton of what I would have said, had I been given more that ten minutes!

Comment

Robert O. Paxton

THE FIRST MAJOR CONCLUSION to draw from these papers as a whole is that American opinion of de Gaulle was far from uniform. To cover this subject really thoroughly, one would have to distinguish among the different levels: government, media, general public. But even if you look at one particular case, such as the very influential political commentator Walter Lippmann, Americans' judgments of General de Gaulle varied massively across time.

There were two periods when public opinion, setting aside government opinion for a moment, was highly favorable to de Gaulle. The first one, at least after the Dakar fiasco, runs from early 1941 to the liberation, culminating in de Gaulle's triumphant ticker-tape parade up Wall Street.

Mr. Aglion, I thought, made a very important contribution in delineating some of the ways in which French exiles contributed to government circles' disapproval of de Gaulle during that period. The general run of American opinion, deprived of these specialized judgments, responded very warmly to de Gaulle as leader of the Free French. In fact, this seems to me the point during the war on which the Roosevelt administration had its greatest difficulty with domestic opinion, particularly the "provisional expedient" of working with Admiral Darlan after the American landing in French North Africa. I don't think of another case where a book had to be commissioned, like William L. Langer's *Vichy Gamble*, to try to counter the generally hostile view of Americans about what had gone on in U.S. policy toward France.

The second period is 1958–62. Not only did Americans admire the way in which de Gaulle extricated France from the Algerian morass, in a manner that allowed it to retain its pride and its unity despite the threat of civil war, but also they admired de Gaulle's achievement of stability in the Fifth Republic. Looking at these two periods together, the three most courageous and far-seeing accomplishments of de Gaulle met with general approval by the American public.

Now we come to the period of hostile American public opinion in the mid-1960s, when de Gaulle set out aggressively to challenge the system of defense, the monetary system, and world international relations, in the West at least. This is the period for which James Chace and Elizabeth Malkin have studied the press. And here, of course, American opinion was violently negative. The press is only part of the story. General opinion doesn't always get excited about foreign policy matters. You can tell something is up when artifacts begin to appear. I have a dart board of General de Gaulle, a representation of his face that you are supposed to throw darts at. My students gave it to me in 1966. I remember there was a series of these; there was Khrushchev, too. It's eloquent that entrepreneurs were producing this kind of thing for mass consumption. Kay Lawson told me that she has a de Gaulle voodoo doll that you stick pins in. This shows the excessive, passionate, and naive quality of American exasperation with de Gaulle from 1963 until 1969 when Nixon and de Gaulle, each eager for his own reasons to bring the quarrel to a public end, fell into each others arms.

Now, why was this response so very passionate and electric? You'll say that it was because there were real differences of policy between the United States and France. Everybody has said so in this conference: there were basic, fundamental disagreements of aim and intention, not just differences of language or style. I certainly agree with that, but it doesn't seem to be enough, because equally serious disagreements with other countries did not reach the same passionate proportions. When Great Britain recognized Communist China, for example, no one paid much attention; when de Gaulle did, there was a tremendous furor. And then consider the Vietnam War. Sweden, for example, countered American policies toward Vietnam more actively than de Gaulle. De Gaulle made statements, but he did not actually harbor American draft resisters as the Canadians and the Swedes did. In practice, de Gaulle was relatively cautious on this matter. It was all language. The Swedes, who did much more, have never been unpopular for their stance on Vietnam. So I don't think that policy differences are the explanation. There must be other reasons for the peculiar electricity of this anger.

So perceptions come back in. It suddenly occurs to me that my three categories are the same as Stanley Hoffmann's. We have real differences, we have perceptions, and we have style. Perceptions are indeed extremely important, because it was clearly impossible for the average American to perceive General de Gaulle's acts between 1963–66 as anything other than anti-Americanism. Because Americans see foreign policy, as has been said over and over again, in terms of friends and foes. If de Gaulle is not with us in this polarized world, he is therefore on the other side. James Chace's point is that the American press failed almost unanimously, with the possible exception of Walter Lipmann, to try to explain to Americans the complex political strategies of de Gaulle. At times of Russian expansionism, he acted upon basic assumptions of American support, as he showed in 1961 and again in 1968. At other calmer times, he sought to explore the alliance's limits and assert French independence. De Gaulle pursued several options at once to enhance French independence and self-confidence, which were in the American interest. Americans were not prepared to understand that, and could only interpret it personally. That's part of the reason.

Another reason it seems to me, is that de Gaulle reinforced by his manner (and now we are getting into style) some of the points of friction that have always irritated the Americans about the French: American convictions that old-style balance-of-power diplomacy leads to war, their rejection of European social hierarchy, their sensitivity to real or perceived disdain by sophisticated Europeans. De Gaulle managed to touch all those traditional raw nerves.

Finally, I have a question to ask about style. We do not have a French witness on this panel, but I ask anyone here to tell me whether or not the abrasive manner of de Gaulle's assault upon United States preferences in the mid-1960s was politically functional or not. Did he sharpen his tone in order to increase his domestic support after his poor showing in the 1965 presidential elections? Or did he do it because it felt good, or because his words ran away with him? Wonderful phrases like his denunciation of Volapuk must have been enormously satisfying. Did it also help de Gaulle's domestic popularity to pull the eagle's tail? Stanley Hoffmann said a while ago that many people in France disapproved of this. It seems to me that, as time passed, the Atlanticists diminished and people in France disapproved less of it, as they tried desperately to recover confidence and unity after the Algerian war. It couldn't have hurt de Gaulle particularly to provoke a little American anger, which never really mattered that much. It has been said repeatedly here that American leaders tried hard not to respond angrily. De Gaulle understood perfectly well that for reasons of national interest the two countries were going to continue to work together in all major issues. He was perhaps enjoying himself without much real cost; perhaps his country enjoyed the spectacle; perhaps politically it even helped him a little. I'd like to be enlightened on this point.

Comment

Tony Smith

MUTUAL SUSPICION: A SOURCE OF FRANCO-AMERICAN MISPERCEPTION

Our panel is on mutual misperceptions between the French and the Americans, a subject that has been abundantly treated throughout this conference. The issue appears simple enough: to misperceive the message of another party presupposes an inability to understand the meaning of the communication being transmitted. The problems arise in trying to understand why these blockages occur.

On occasion, misunderstandings occur because of ambiguities inherent in communication, which each side then resolves in favor of interpretations that mesh with its own way of viewing the world. Those who concern themselves with such mistakes frequently go on to insist that had each side only correctly understood what the other intended, then surely the relationship between the two countries would have been all the happier.

Frequently, misperceptions cannot be dealt with so easily, however. The forces abetting the misunderstandings are too deep, too powerful to admit of such a happy resolution along the lines of "I'm okay, you're okay, we just have to learn how to communicate better."

Consider, for example, a case in which each party makes a statement that the other should in fact understand for the sake of its own self-interest . . . but does not. Here is a kind of misperception worthy of close analysis, for it invites us to study the perverse nature of our thinking and emotions: instances when we would be helped if we but listened to another. Yet we refuse. Why?

Our own conference offers an example. In his luncheon address of the first day, Henry Kissinger made himself out to be a Gaullist, pur sang. Where were his Gaullist sentiments in 1969, however, when the general was warning Kissinger of the mistakes he could make in Vietnam? True, President Nixon borrowed the notion of "peace with honor" in Vietnam in part from what de Gaulle had managed to accomplish in Algeria. Yet the fact that today the United States still does not have diplomatic relations with Hanoi serves to illustrate the point that the lesson was not well learned. Should we not see this as an example of the way in which Washington habitually viewed French advice as being suspect, as "poisoned," that is, as recommending actions to Washington that were not designed to further American interests so much as to reduce American influence in the world? Thus, when a good piece of advice came along from de Gaulle, one that might have indeed served American interests, Washington reacted suspiciously – on occasion perversely doing the opposite of the advice because of what was believed, even if unconsciously, to be its tainted source.

The shoe has also been on the other foot: there have been times when the United States has given France good advice, but in some degree because of its source, de Gaulle pursued an opposed policy. Surely the most important instance of such a misperception occurred (once again) over Vietnam, though this time in the late 1940s, not the late 1960s. Not only did the United States oppose the French return to Indochina in 1945 – a central concern of de Gaulle's – but it also criticized the general's talk in 1949 (when though out of office he was often in the press) that France should back its puppet emperor Bao Dai there, and that any negotiations with Ho Chi Minh amounted to "capitulation." Indeed, the United States opposed the entire postwar imperial restoration of France in terms it now appears that de Gaulle would have been well-advised to respect. Why was the general so obstinate? One may assume that a part of the reason the French were so unwilling to see the reality of the strength of colonial nationalism after 1945 was that the Americans were telling them to pay attention to it. Here, then, is another example of misperception based on suspicion of the good faith of the party offering the advice.

A final example of some importance has to do with the French position on the construction of Europe after 1945. It seems undeniable that part of the French resistance to this idea stemmed from the suspicion that it was in good measure an elaborate plan to use Europe as a junior partner of the United States, an enterprise wherein a French bid for preeminence would be permanently denied. Thus, while the general doubtless respected his gifted compatriot Jean Monnet and his vision for Europe, he betrayed more than a hint of a suspicion that the man got along too well with the Americans.

Since de Gaulle's departure from power more than two decades ago, this legacy of mutual suspicion has endured. At times, the sentiment has been well deserved. But on more than one occasion its consequence has been misperceptions of a sort that has led each side to damage its own self-interest in its mistaken conviction that the other was trying to maneuver it onto terrain that would curtail its power in world affairs.

The moral in world affairs, as in personal relations: always give your antagonists good advice on the grounds that they will then deliberately fail to heed it to their own detriment.

Witness

Etienne Burin Des Roziers

IT IS OFTEN ARGUED IN FRANCE that the foreign policy of the Fifth Republic, apart from its new style, was not fundamentally different from that of the Fourth Republic. This view has been expressed by Alfred Grosser, among others. I am not of that opinion. As I noted under both Republics as a diplomat abroad, I can testify that the instructions I received changed completely as soon as de Gaulle came back to power.

I remember a meeting that I attended in Rome in 1956. The entire diplomatic staff of our embassy was there to listen to a high official at the Quai d'Orsay. His opening remark was of a blunt frankness: "I take it that we all agree that, in the present circumstances, it belongs to the United Sates to lead the western world and that, consequently, the appropriate international role of France is to try to influence in the right direction the external policy of the American government. . . . "

De Gaulle's attitude was almost the reverse. Of course, he attached the greatest importance to the relations between France and the United States. But "independence" was the key word of his policy. "Il ne faut jamais se confondre" ("Never let yourself be absorbed"), he would often repeat, meaning that France would carefully avoid any involvement that might implicate her in decisions that were not entirely her own. That was the "clean hands" policy, the counterpart of which was that of "free speech."

Could such a rigid understanding of independence be reconciled with the American leadership or even the "partnership" advocated by President Kennedy? I frankly doubt it.

Notes on Contributors

RAOUL AGLION was one of the first Free French officials in New York 1940–41. He is the author of *De Gaulle et Roosevelt: La France libre aux Etats-unis* (Paris: Plon, 1984) among other works.

DAVID CALLEO is the Dean Acheson Professor and Director of European Studies at the Paul Nitze School of Advanced International Studies at Johns Hopkins University. He is the author of *The Bankrupting of America* (New York: William Morrow, 1992).

JAMES CHACE is Henry Luce Professor in Freedom of Inquiry and Expression at Bard College. The editor of the *World Policy Journal*, he is also the author of *Consequences of the Peace: American Foreign Policy after the Cold War* (New York: Oxford University Press, 1992).

RICHARD CHALLENER is Professor of History Emeritus at Princeton University. He is the author of *Admirals, Generals and American Foreign Policy 1898–1914* (Princeton: Princeton University Press, 1973).

FRANK COSTIGLIOLA is Professor of History at the Univerity of Rhode Island. He is the author of *France and the United States: the Cold Alliance since World War Two* (New York: MacMillan, 1992).

ROBERT DALLEK is Professor of History at the University of California at Los Angeles. He received the Bancroft Prize for his book *Franklin D. Roosevelt and American Foreign Policy 1932–1945* (New York: Oxford University Press, 1979).

LLOYD GARDNER is the Charles and Mary Beard Professor of History at Rutgers University. His most recent book is entitled *Spheres of Influence: the Great Powers Partition Europe from Munich to Yalta* (Chicago: I.R. Dee, 1993).

OLIVIER GUICHARD, principal staff aide to General and President De Gaulle, 1947–60.

JOHN S. HILL is Assistant Professor of History at Ohio State University. He has recently published an article in the *Journal of Modern History*, September 1992, entitled "American Aid to French Reconstruction: From Lend-lease to the Marshall Plan: 1944–1947."

HENRY KISSINGER was the National Security Advisor to President Richard M. Nixon, 1969–1975 and Secretary of State from 1973.

RICHARD F. KUISEL is Professor of History at the State University of New York at Stony Brook. His most recent book is entitled *Seducing the French: the Dilemma of Americanization* (Berkeley: University of California Press, 1993).

THEODORE J. LOWI is the John L. Senior Professor of American Institutions at Cornell University. He is the author of *The End of Liberalism: Ideology, Policy and the Crisis of Public Authority* (New York: Norton, 1969).

PIERRE MESSMER, Officer in the Free French army 1940–45, President De Gaulle's Minister of Defense 1960–69.

KIM MUNHOLLAND is Professor of History at the University of Minnesota. He is the author of *Origins of Contemporary Europe 1890–1914* (New York: Harcourt Brace, 1970), among other books.

ROBERT O. PAXTON, Mellon Professor of Social Sciences, Columbia University and Director, Institute on Western Europe, author of *Vichy France* (New York: Columbia University Press, 1982) among other works.

ANDREW J. PIERRE is Senior Associate of the Carnegie Endowment for International Peace. His books include: *The Conventional Defense of Europe* (New York: New York University Press, 1986).

ANNE SA'ADAH is Associate Professor of Government at Dartmouth College. She is the author of *The Shaping of Liberal Politics in Revolutionary France* (Princeton: Princeton University Press, 1990).

MARTIN A. SCHAIN, Professor of Politics at New York University, co-author of *Politics in France* (New York: Little Brown, 1992) with Henry W. Ehrmann.

RONALD STEEL is Professor of International Relations at the University of Southern California. His books include *Pax Americana* (New York: Viking Press, 1967).

CHRISTOPHER THOMPSON is a doctoral candidate, Institute of French Studies, New York University.

NICHOLAS WAHL, Milton Petrie Professor of European Studies, New York University and Director, Institute of French Studies. Author of *The Fifth Republic* (New York: Random House, 1959).

IRWIN M. WALL is Professor of History at the University of California at Riverside. He is the author of *The United States and the Making of Postwar France 1945–1954* (Cambridge: Cambridge University Press, 1991).

Contributing Commentators and Witnesses

WILLIAM JAMES ADAMS, Arthur F. Thurnau Professor of Economics, University of Michigan.

ROBERT R. BOWIE, Counselor, U.S. Department of State 1966–68, Dillon Professor of International Affairs Emeritus, Harvard University

ETIENNE BURIN DES ROZIERS, General de Gaulle's *aide de camp*, Algiers, 1943–44, Paris, 1945–46; chief of staff to President De Gaulle 1962–67,

STANLEY HOFFMANN, C. Douglas Dillon Professor of the Civilization of France, Harvard University.

JEAN-MARCEL JEANNENEY, President de Gaulle's minister of industry, 1959–62 and minister of social affairs, 1966–68.

JEAN LACOUTURE, journalist, biographer of de Gaulle.

MELVYN LEFFLER, Department of History, University of Virginia.

ERNEST MAY, Charles Warren Professor of History, Harvard University.

PIERRE MÉLANDRI, History, University of Paris-X, Nanterre.

TONY SMITH, Jackson Professor of Political Science, Tufts University.

BERNARD TRICOT, chief of staff to President de Gaulle, 1967–69.

Index